REVISED EDITION

Michigan

Gardener's Guide

REVISED EDITION

Michigan

Gardener's Guide

Tim Boland   Laura Coit   Marty Hair

COOL SPRINGS PRESS

Nashville, Tennessee
A Division of Thomas Nelson, Inc.
www.ThomasNelson.com

Published by Cool Springs Press, a Division of Thomas Nelson, Inc., P. O. Box 141000, Nashville, Tennessee, 37214.

Boland, Timothy.
    Michigan gardener's guide / by Tim Boland, Laura Coit, and Marty Hair.-- Rev. ed.
        p. cm.
    Includes bibliographical references (p.   ).
    ISBN: 1-930604-20-3 (pbk. : alk. paper)
    1. Landscape plants--Michigan. 2. Landscape gardening--Michigan.
    I. Coit, Laura. II. Hair, Marty. III. Title.
SB407 .B58 2002
635.9'09774--dc21

                                           2001006791

First printing 2002
Printed in the United States of America
10 9 8 7 6 5 4 3 2

Managing Editor: Billie Brownell
Horticulture Editor: Ann Hancock
Production Artist: S.E. Anderson

On the cover: New England Aster, photographed by Dency Kane

Visit the Thomas Nelson website at www.ThomasNelson.com

Acknowledgments

We are grateful to the many people who generously shared their horticultural knowledge during the preparation of this book, both for its initial publication and for this revision.

For their technical assistance and support, we especially thank Jim Adams, Doug Badgero, Bob Bricault, Andrew Bunting, William Carlson, Frederick Case, Carolyn Coit, Lowell Ewart, Tim Flint, Bruce Fox, Erica Glasener, Nancy Goulette, Susan Gruber, Ann Hancock, and George Hartley.

We also thank Judy Hollingworth, Don Juchartz, Dean Krauskopf, Scott Kunst, Greg Lyman, Cheryl Lyon-Jenness, Nancy McDonald, Mary McLellan, David Michener, Stuart Ouwinga, Paul Rieke, Miriam Rutz, Donna Schumann, Patty Shea, Jane Taylor, Lee Taylor, and Frank Telewski.

Ann Hancock of Michigan State University is the horticulture editor for this edition.

We appreciate the attention of the staff at Cool Springs Press for suggesting and supporting this revised edition with its expanded text, new graphics, bigger photos and improved design.

Thanks, too, to the many generous and kind readers who have told us that they enjoyed *The Michigan Gardener's Guide*.

We hope this revised edition is useful to them, as well as to others who are just now discovering the pleasures of gardening in Michigan.

Table of Contents

The Pleasures of Michigan Gardening 11

How to Use This Book 20

USDA Cold Hardiness Zone Map 21

Annuals 22

Groundcovers 49

Hardy Bulbs 63

Lawns 83

Ornamental Grasses 90

Perennials 102

Shrubs 153

Trees 190

Woodland Flowers and Ferns 220

Plant Sources 234

Public Gardens 236

Words About Roses 240

Integrated Pest Management 245

Toxic Plants: Caution 248

Gardening with Native Plants 250

Gardeners on the Web 254

Glossary 255

Bibliography 261

Photography Credits 263

Plant Index 264

Meet the Authors 272

The Pleasures of Michigan Gardening

Gardening in Michigan is a pleasure. The landscape stages its own theater, a natural drama in four acts. The plot unfolds with new life in spring that turns lush and green in summer, transforms to brilliant golds and reds in autumn, and lies serenely dormant in winter. Gardening heightens our awareness of the seasons and cycles of nature, bringing it right into our own backyards.

Michigan's motto—"If you seek a pleasant peninsula, look about you"—is as true of its gardens as of its sandy lakeshores, fields, and woods. The state's unique climate, geography, and natural features make it a special place to tend a plot of land.

This book is for people wondering which of the thousands of plants available will do best in Michigan gardens. We include profiles of 184 trees, shrubs, and flowering and foliage plants, selected because they will thrive here, and we explain how to plant and care for each of them.

We selected plants for this book based on our own experiences of growing them in Michigan. As a group these plants are relatively easygoing when given an appropriate site. They have minimal problems with pests and diseases. They are rewarding to grow, offering a range of beauty, color, winter interest, and wildlife habitat. For this revised edition, we have expanded our coverage of native plants, reflecting the growing recognition among Michigan gardeners of the valuable attributes this group of plants can bring to areas ranging from formal gardens to more naturalistic landscapes.

Gardening is America's most popular hobby, and it is immensely popular in Michigan. The opportunity to spend time outside is certainly a good reason to garden, and studies suggest that tending plants or even just looking at them from a window offers rewards in improved physical and mental well-being.

Michigan gardeners are fortunate, because our climate offers enough warmth, sunlight, and natural moisture to support a richly diverse group of both native and cultivated plants. Snow cover, prevalent in most parts of the state, insulates plants in winter. Our soils range from sandy to loamy to clay, but, for the most part, they are fertile enough to grow beautiful gardens.

Our climate may be a concern to newcomers, especially those moving to Michigan from warmer climates. It's true that for several months of the year the weather here can be gray or snowy and cold, but that doesn't mean that gardens have to be boring in winter. Selecting woody plants with interesting bark and colorful fruits, incorporating ornamental grasses, and planning for good landscape design make for an attractive garden in every season. While gardening in Michigan is full of challenges, it's just as full of rewards.

Michigan's Gardening Traditions

Michigan is a vast state—more than 400 miles from the Upper Peninsula's Copper Harbor on Lake Superior to Monroe near the state's southeastern border—and its climate is varied. There is such a range of climates, soils, and native plants that there is no single style of gardening in Michigan or even a trademark plant that characterizes the gardens in the state. Yet Michigan has a rich tradition of people who care about gardening and horticulture. Native Americans who lived in this region used plants for food, medicine, and many other purposes. According to legend, they showed French explorers how to make a vitamin-rich tea from white cedar, and the grateful French nicknamed the plant "tree of life" or arborvitae.

According to Miriam Rutz, a landscape historian at Michigan State University, the French explorer Cadillac brought a gardener to Detroit in the early 1700s to design gardens and orchards, and southeastern Michigan was famous for its gardens for the next 150 years.

The earliest scientific explorer to visit the region was Thomas Nuttall, a botanist who visited the Great Lakes in 1810 to survey what was growing here. Nuttall found nearly two dozen plants that had never before been described, including, at Mackinac Island, the dwarf lake iris, *Iris lacustris*. The only place in the world this plant exists is along the northern Great Lakes shoreline, mainly in Michigan. It is on the state and federal lists of threatened plants, and in 1998 the dwarf lake iris became Michigan's official state wildflower.

Michigan was the first state west of the Alleghenies to form agricultural and horticultural societies, which were organized in the 1840s and 1850s, according to Miriam Rutz's research. What is now Michigan State University was founded in 1855 as the Agricultural College of the State of Michigan, and it has had a continuing impact on research and teaching about horticulture, gardening, and agriculture. An early professor was William J. Beal, a native of the Adrian area, who taught botany, horticulture, and forestry from 1870 to 1910.

One of Beal's experiments is ongoing. In 1888 he buried some bottles containing weed seeds, with the idea of digging up a bottle every five years and planting the seeds to see how long they would remain viable, or able to grow. Since Beal's death, others have continued this germination project, and the time between unearthing the bottles is now twenty years. The fifteenth bottle was dug up at dawn one day in

April 2000. The moth mullein seeds were planted and they germinated. Five buried bottles remain, with the next scheduled to be unearthed in 2020. This is the world's longest continuous botanical experiment. Beal was also instrumental in the establishment in 1873 of the W. J. Beal Botanic Garden, one of the oldest continuously operating botanical gardens in the country.

Among Beal's students was South Haven native Liberty Hyde Bailey, who became a horticulture professor in 1885 and chaired the first horticulture department in the nation at what is now Michigan State University. Bailey is recognized as the dean of American horticulture. He wrote nearly two hundred books on horticulture and agriculture, and he led a national commission on country life, which resulted in the formation of the Cooperative Extension Service and its youth component, 4-H, around the country. Bailey, who later moved to Cornell University, raised the study of agriculture to a science.

Outside the universities, the mid- to late 19th Century was a time of tremendous interest in gardening and horticulture as well as agricultural expansion. Nurseries and seed merchants were opening, among them Dexter Ferry's in Detroit. At one time his company, later Ferry-Morse, was the world's largest producer and distributor of garden seeds.

Gardening and plant study were popular activities, and some residents scoured their regions collecting plants. Some collections are preserved at the University of Michigan, founded in 1817, and at Michigan State University.

As new residents arrived in Michigan from other countries, they brought with them their own traditions of gardening. German, Italian, Irish, Polish, and Scandinavian people, as well as others, located here. People from Holland settled in western Michigan, and their strong interest in gardening is reflected in the area's commercial horticulture industry, private and public gardens, and the annual Holland Tulip Festival, which now draws a million visitors and features more than $2^1/2$ million tulips in flower.

In the later 1800s, people indulged in the Victorian gardening craze of carpet bedding, in which annuals are arranged in colorful patterns. Today, some of the state's public gardens plant annuals every season for a similar effect.

As the 1800s ended and the 1900s began, women's clubs across Michigan were working on civic improvements, creating and landscaping parks and school yards, and planting trees. When Michigan's farm population peaked in 1912, membership in the Grange was 52,836. The Grange supported development of 4-H and sponsored fairs, as well as many other activities.

In 1920, Genevieve Gillette became the first woman to graduate from the landscape architecture curriculum at what is now Michigan State University. She worked on many projects, including a low-cost housing development in which she incorporated "thrift gardens" so that each family could raise its own vegetables. Gillette also led campaigns for the formation of state and national parks in Michigan.

Louisa Yeomans King gardened in Michigan, but her work and insights were recognized throughout the whole country in her day. King, who described gardening as "this art, this adorable occupation," moved to Alma with her husband, Francis King, in 1907. She created gardens around their home, Orchard House, and became a garden writer whose work was published in many national magazines and books. In 1912, King founded the Garden Club of Michigan, and she became one of the first vice-presidents of the Garden Club of America the following year. She was the inaugural president of the Woman's National Farm and Garden Association in 1914.

In the first decades of the 20th Century, Michigan's wealthy industrialists were intrigued by formal French and Italian landscapes, and their properties reflected that design influence. Meanwhile, both Henry Ford and Edsel Ford hired Chicago landscape architect Jens Jensen to map out more naturalistic landscapes using many native plants. The era of the estate gardens lasted until the Depression.

With progressive landscapes in public parks as well as private residences, Michigan had an active gardening culture through the 1920s. The southwestern part of the state was especially influenced by the prairie style of landscape design popular in Chicago.

Gardening and horticulture, both as hobbies and as businesses, got a boost as greenhouses became more common and provided a way to overwinter plant material.

Commercial vegetable production thrived in Michigan in the 1920s and 1930s. After World War II, some of that work shifted to California, and the smaller growers who remained in Michigan turned to selling flats of annuals at local markets to supplement their incomes. The bedding plant industry has continued to grow, and Michigan is among the top producers in the nation.

In both World Wars I and II, Michigan gardeners put their patriotism in the soil when their government asked them to plant first Liberty Gardens and then Victory Gardens. There were 800,000 Victory Gardens statewide in 1943.

Growing Smarter

Interest in gardening continues to grow as gardeners become more knowledgeable. Magazines, books, the Internet, and cable TV channels make it possible to learn about gardening at any hour, day or night.

People can chose to join many specialty plant groups, among them organizations devoted to native plants, hostas, bonsai, cacti and succulents, and roses. Active garden clubs include chapters of the Federated Garden Clubs of Michigan, the National Woman's Farm and Garden Club, and the Garden Club of Michigan. They hold meetings, set up educational programs, and organize civic improvements;

many also sponsor summer garden tours that are open to the public. Thousands of Michigan residents have graduated from the Michigan Master Garden program, which is offered in many counties statewide through the MSU Extension.

Know Your Zone

During the summer, people often discuss the heat and its effects on plants, but the degree of cold in the winter is also important in determining which plants will survive. The United States Department of Agriculture (USDA) has divided a map of the country into regions called hardiness zones based on their average minimum winter temperatures. Michigan's coldest areas, in the interior northern Lower as well as the central and western Upper Peninsula, are classified as Zone 3, with average winter lows from -30 to -40 degrees Fahrenheit. A few spots of southern Michigan are in the relatively balmy Zone 6, with an average minimum expected temperature of zero to -10 degrees Fahrenheit.

This book includes a map of Michigan showing the USDA Hardiness Zones (see page 21), and each plant profile lists the zones for which the plant is recommended. If no zone information is given, the plant is suitable for all parts of the state. Being aware of zones is especially important when ordering plants from mail-order catalogs.

Even within a zone, there are often significant variations. Soil, rainfall, exposure, and humidity can all affect plant hardiness. Valleys and low-lying areas often have later frosts. Areas near the large lakes will have longer growing seasons than places that are inland. City dwellers find their average temperatures warmer than those in surrounding rural areas because the concentrated buildings, cement, asphalt, and pollution retain heat.

Michigan's growing season, measured from the last frost in the spring to the first frost in the fall, varies from about 70 to 170 days in different parts of the state. The last frost date in spring is especially important in determining when it is safe to plant annuals and vegetables outdoors. If you don't know your local frost dates, call the county office of the MSU Extension.

The Great Lakes that nearly surround Michigan act as a cushion, keeping the temperature lower in summer and warmer in winter than in surrounding states. The lake effect brings moisture—and, yes, more clouds—but Michigan gardeners are most interested in the resulting moderate temperatures and abundant water. This moderating effect is one reason for the state's commercial success in growing fruit.

Location, Location, Location

Just as in choosing real estate, the three most important things to consider when selecting a plant are location, location, and location. Analyze the site and the amount of sun it gets, the kind of soil, and its hardiness zone. Matching the plant to the site gives plants a good chance to thrive and stay healthy, which is the best way for them to resist pests and disease.

Soil has several components. There are tiny fragments of rock and minerals, and the decomposing bits of plants and animals make up the soil's organic material. Soil also contains air, water, and small organisms.

The soil's texture depends on how much sand, silt, or clay it contains. Sand is grainy and has the largest-sized particles; a handful of sand will fall apart when released. Silt has a texture often described as floury or smooth. Wet clay feels slippery and remains in a ball when squeezed.

The ideal garden soil in general is sandy loam, which contains sand, clay, and silt and has a porous structure. But if that's not what is in your garden, don't despair. You can improve your soil by adding organic material such as well-rotted compost, shredded leaves, or aged manure. This improves the drainage and porosity of heavy clay soils, and it helps sandy soils by making them better able to retain moisture. Worms, bacteria, and other microorganisms in the soil feed on the organic material and break it down, making more nutrients available for the plants.

For a source of free organic material, start a compost pile. Add leaves, healthy plant material, soil, and vegetable scraps from the kitchen, and moisten the pile regularly. The material will break down into what gardeners call "black gold." For more information on how to start a compost pile, consult your local extension office or a book on the subject.

Plants need a number of nutrients for growth—including nitrogen, phosphorus, potassium, and others that may be found in the soil—in addition to hydrogen, oxygen, and carbon. To determine if necessary nutrients are lacking in your soil, call your county office of the MSU Extension and get instructions on how to take a soil test for analysis at Michigan State University. The soil test results will

also tell you the soil pH, or whether the soil is acidic or on the alkaline side. This is important because the soil's pH determines which nutrients are available to plants.

A soil that is rich in organic material will provide adequate nutrients for many garden plants. The plants selected for this book do not require much—or, sometimes, any—additional fertilization. See specific chapters and entries for recommendations.

Deer are a major challenge for gardeners in many parts of Michigan. Some gardeners use electric fences to exclude these foragers. Your county extension office may offer other solutions.

Light Requirements

For best growing results, plants need to be placed where they will receive the proper amount of light. The light requirements are indicated in each plant profile.

Plants and Names

This book uses both common and botanical names for plants. If you rely on common names when purchasing plants, you may be disappointed, especially if you're ordering from a catalog and the plant you receive turns out to be different from the one you wanted. The botanical name is unique to each plant and identifies the very one you have in mind.

Botanical names follow a system called binomial nomenclature. The first Latin word identifies the genus, while the second word is the species. For instance, *Stachys byzantina* 'Silver Carpet' is an especially desirable lamb's ear that rarely flowers. *Stachys* is the genus name, *byzantina* is the species, and 'Silver Carpet' is the name of the cultivar (cultivated variety).

Don't be intimidated by botanical names. The more you use them, the easier they become. A wise gardener, discussing the pronunciation of Latin names, once said, "Say it with authority and no one will doubt you."

The Trouble-Free Criteria

The plants in this book are found in chapters—annuals, groundcovers, hardy bulbs, lawns, ornamental grasses, perennials, shrubs, trees, and woodland flowers and ferns. Each plant profile includes specific information as well as suggestions on how to incorporate the plant into your landscape. The plants we include are generally easy to grow and relatively free of pests and diseases. We had to make choices, and in some cases we excluded favorite garden plants because they didn't meet the easy-to-grow, trouble-free criteria. Sorry, all you hollyhock lovers out there!

We also omitted plants that can outcompete native plants. Both ivy and vinca, two of the most popular and widely used groundcovers, will choke out native plants if they escape from gardens and grow into natural areas; so will most types of the popular perennial purple loosestrife (*Lythrum* spp.). This concern is particularly relevant for people whose property borders wetlands, water, or woods because seeds can be carried a distance by wind, water, and birds. Other plants to avoid because of their invasive tendencies are autumn olive (*Elaeagnus umbellata*), common and tallhedge buckthorn (*Rhamnus catharticus* and *R. frangula*), crown vetch (*Coronilla varia*), several species of honeysuckle (*Lonicera*), Norway maple (*Acer platanoides*), and Oriental or round-leaved bittersweet (*Celastrus orbiculatus*).

The MSU Extension offers many publications about home horticulture, most either free or very inexpensive. For a free copy of the publications catalog, write to the Michigan State University Bulletin Office, 10-B Agriculture Hall, Michigan State University, East Lansing, MI 48824-1039.

Enjoy Gardening in Michigan

Michigan offers a unique gardening experience. Capitalize on it by creating a distinctly Michigan garden. Use native plants to their best advantage. Play up the changing seasons. Strive to choose the right plant for the site, and allow plenty of time to enjoy what you create.

Have fun, and know that there are no hard-and-fast rules in gardening. Don't be a slave to advice! Instead, experiment to learn what works best for you. Take time to teach youngsters about the pleasures of gardening, and let them experiment, too. You'll be enjoying high-quality family time and making sure that a new generation will continue Michigan's long gardening tradition.

"Resolved: to have a garden. If this wish is sincere, the garden will materialize. If ground is unpromising, it can be made good. If the size of lot is small, then ingenuity and imagination must be specially brought to bear upon it. With these, and taste, the smallest garden will be far more lovely than the largest without them."

—Louisa Yeomans King, *The Flower Garden Day by Day*, 1927

How to Use This Book

Each entry in this guide provides information about a plant's characteristics, habits and requirements for growth, as well as our personal experience and knowledge of the plant. Use this information to realize each plant's potential. You will find such pertinent information as mature height and spread, bloom period and seasonal colors, sun and soil preferences, water requirements, fertilizing needs, pruning and care tips, and pest information. Each section is clearly marked for easy reference.

Sun Preferences

Symbols represent the range of sunlight suitable for each plant. The symbol representing "Full Sun" means the plant needs 6 or more hours of sun daily. A ranking of "Part Sun" means the plant can thrive in 4 to 6 hours of sun a day. "Part Shade" designates plants for sites with fewer than 4 hours of sun a day, including dappled or high shade. "Full Shade" means the plant needs protection from direct sunlight. Some plants can be grown successfully in more than one exposure, so you will sometimes see more than one light symbol with an entry.

Full Sun   **Part Sun**   **Part Shade**   **Full Shade**

Additional Benefits

Many plants offer benefits that further enhance their appeal. These symbols indicate some of these benefits:

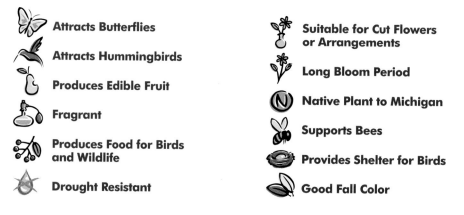

Attracts Butterflies

Attracts Hummingbirds

Produces Edible Fruit

Fragrant

Produces Food for Birds and Wildlife

Drought Resistant

Suitable for Cut Flowers or Arrangements

Long Bloom Period

Native Plant to Michigan

Supports Bees

Provides Shelter for Birds

Good Fall Color

Companion Planting and Design

For most of the entries, we provide landscape design ideas as well as suggestions for companion plants to help you achieve striking and personal results from your garden.

We Recommend

This section describes cultivars or varieties we have found particularly noteworthy, as well as interesting related plants and other relevant information.

USDA Cold Hardiness Zone Map

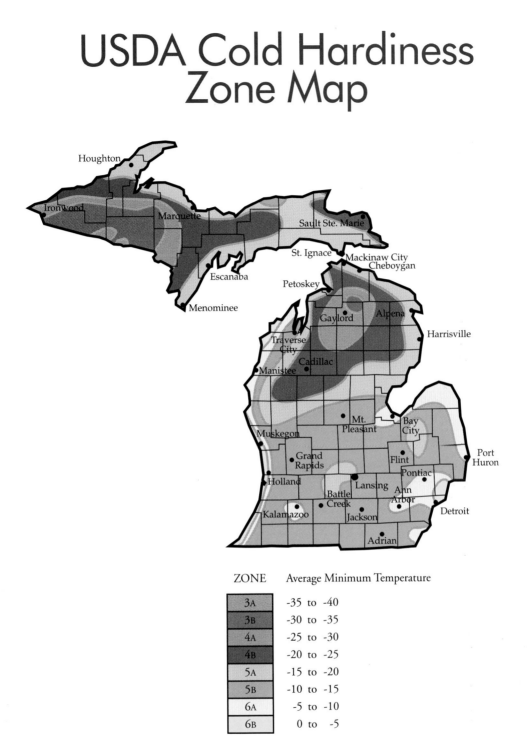

ZONE	Average Minimum Temperature
3A	-35 to -40
3B	-30 to -35
4A	-25 to -30
4B	-20 to -25
5A	-15 to -20
5B	-10 to -15
6A	-5 to -10
6B	0 to -5

Hardiness Zones

Cold-hardiness zone designations were developed by the United States Department of Agriculture (USDA) to indicate the minimum average temperature for that region. A zone assigned to a plant indicates the lowest temperature at which the plant can be expected to survive. Michigan has zones ranging from 3a (the coldest) to 6b. Though a plant may grow in zones outside its recommended zone range, the zone ratings are a good indication of which plants to consider for your landscape. Check this map to see which zone your Michigan garden is in.

Annuals
for Michigan

Planting annuals is a rite of spring for many Michigan gardeners. Annuals grow from seed, bloom, and set seed in one growing season, then die by the time winter arrives. They make it possible to fill a bed, border, container, or hanging basket with color that lasts from late spring until frost, all at a relatively low cost.

Annuals offer a long season of bloom. They begin to flower soon after they are planted, taking the garden from plain to drop-dead gorgeous in a relatively short time. Because they generally grow in the upper eight inches of soil, annuals require less elaborate soil preparation than do longer-lived plants. While our grandparents grew many of the same annuals we grow today, hybridizers are developing new varieties, many with disease resistance and other important characteristics that were not available a generation ago. At the same time, many heirloom varieties are being rediscovered for their quaint charm and more natural habits.

Getting Started with Annuals

Many annuals are available as seed to start indoors under lights well before the last expected frost in spring, and as young plants in multiple containers called cell-packs that can be purchased at garden centers and nurseries in spring. Some annual seed may be sown directly in the garden in late spring. Some annuals will self-sow, which means they leave seeds that will grow into new plants the following year.

When to plant annuals outdoors depends on the date of the last expected frost in your area. If you are not sure of that date, call your county's MSU Extension office to find out.

Look for healthy transplants that are green and have sturdy stems but few if any flowers at time of purchase. Plants without flowers are more likely to have better root systems and to establish faster after planting.

Plants started inside or in a commercial greenhouse should be hardened off (gradually acclimated to outdoor conditions) for several days. Move the pots or trays outside to a place sheltered from direct sun and wind for a few hours, and take them back inside at night. Every day, give the plants a bit more time outside, returning them to the house at night. After five to seven days, the plants should be tough enough to plant outdoors—but before you do that, examine the soil where they will be planted. The soil should be of at least average fertility and well drained. Adding well-rotted compost, decomposed leaves or leaf mold, or aged manure will improve both heavy clay and sandy soils.

Planting and Care Basics

Loosen the soil in the bed to a depth of at least eight to twelve inches, and remove weeds and debris. For a mass planting, you can use a bulb planter to make planting holes quickly.

Pop the young plants from their cell-packs by squeezing the bottoms and pushing up; avoid yanking them by the stems or leaves. If the roots are intertwined into a tight ball, loosen them slightly with your fingers so they will spread readily once they make contact with the soil.

Annuals are generally planted at the same depth in the soil that they were growing in the containers. Pinch off any flowers or buds at planting time to focus the plant's energy on getting established.

After planting, firm the soil around the plant and water well, then give the transplants a boost of starter fertilizer such as 3-10-3. Some gardeners prefer to mix a slow-release fertilizer with the soil at planting time. Water the annuals and they'll soon start performing.

If you didn't use slow-release fertilizer, feed annuals every few weeks or every month, depending on the plant and your garden's soil fertility. The annuals selected for this book are generally resistant to serious pests and diseases.

As the season progresses, provide water during dry periods and keep the soil around the annuals weed-free. Mulching with a two- to three-inch layer of finely shredded bark, cocoa hulls, or other organic material helps keep moisture in the soil and discourages weeds. Maintain a mulch-free zone right around the base of the plant so air can circulate.

Many annuals will continue blooming most of the season if they are deadheaded regularly. To deadhead, pinch off the faded flowers before they go to seed.

Brazilian Verbena

Verbena bonariensis

In cultivation since Victorian times, Brazilian verbena has recently become trendy. Often reaching four feet tall, it adds height and color to the garden, eventually becoming an airy cloud of luminous purple. Each erect, virtually naked stem is topped with clustered heads of lavender-violet flowers that attract butterflies like crazy. No other annual has the combination of height and grace that makes Brazilian verbena a perfect accent for perennial beds. It is particularly useful for adding interest to newly established areas where tall perennials have not yet reached their mature size. Its stiff, straight stems make Brazilian verbena a favorite with flower arrangers. It is a self-sower, and volunteer plants will often surprise the gardener by finding their own best location.

Bloom Period and Seasonal Color
Early summer until frost with red-violet flowers.

Mature Height × Spread
3 to 4 ft. × 2 ft.

When, Where, and How to Plant
Plant in spring after the danger of frost is past. Brazilian verbena is tolerant of a wide range of soils. Full sun is necessary for best growth, but a few hours of shade is okay. Plants are increasingly available in cell-packs or 4-in. pots, but they often look like lanky stalks with few leaves. Pinch back to three sets of leaves to create well-branched plants. Seeds can also be direct-sown in the garden. Follow the directions on the packet. Direct-sown and self-sown plants bloom later than transplants. Spacing closely (8 to 10 in.) will produce an airy mass of tangled stems.

Growing Tips
Brazilian verbena needs little special care. Water during extended dry spells. Mulch will help conserve moisture and discourage self-sowing. Extra fertilizer is unnecessary.

Care
Brazilian verbena is rarely troubled by insects or disease. Unless the flowers are deadheaded, scads of seedlings appear the following year. Mulch to discourage volunteers if you are concerned about self-sown seedlings—or remove spent flowers before the seed scatters.

Companion Planting and Design
Add Brazilian verbena to annual borders, perennial beds, mixed plantings, and cut-flower gardens. In the fall, it combines attractively with the white aster-like flowers of boltonia and the early orange-red autumn color of flame grass. Fill an informal large annual bed with Brazilian verbena, orange zinnias, and the yellow flowers and feathery foliage of dill. In full flower, this combination will attract a crowd of butterflies. Consider using this verbena as a tall accent in a large planter.

We Recommend
Most gardeners are familiar with the common garden verbena, *Verbena × hybrida*, an excellent trailing annual for heat tolerance and summer flowers. Another verbena, *V. tenuisecta* 'Imagination', is similar in habit, but the foliage is lacy and the smaller flowers are purple. 'Imagination' can tumble out of a container, edge a walk, or fill in the front of a well-drained perennial bed.

Cleome

Cleome hassleriana

When, Where, and How to Plant

Sow seed indoors three to four weeks before last frost and harden off young plants before setting them into the garden. Cleome may also be sown directly outdoors in late spring, or purchased as young plants to set out in late spring. It may be difficult to find at garden centers, since cleome won't be in bloom in cell-packs. Plant in a sunny, well-drained spot—the more sun, the better. Space plants 18 in. to 2 ft. apart. Follow the instructions for planting annual transplants on page 23. After planting, feed with a transplant fertilizer such as 3-10-3 to get the plants off to a good start.

Growing Tips

Cleome, which is native to South America, excels in hot weather. It also tolerates dry soil. In poor soils, the application of a balanced fertilizer such as 10-10-10 a few times during the growing season may be beneficial.

Care

Cleome is usually free of serious pests or diseases. It can get top-heavy and somewhat floppy as the season progresses. Some gardeners stake plants early in the summer to help cleome stand up to wind and rainstorms. To reduce self-sowing, consider removing the seedpods, or be prepared to remove the volunteer cleome plants in the spring.

Companion Planting and Design

Cleome is perfect for planting behind other plants in a border or in a bed all its own, although it is more attractive with shorter plants in front to mask its somewhat rangy stems. It makes a fine display behind perennials or in a mixed cottage garden. Use cleome as an annual screen, or grow it against a wall or fence. It was a favorite of Victorian gardeners, who often featured cleome as the tall central component of a circular bedding scheme.

We Recommend

Cleomes in the 'Queen' series are widely available in shades of pink, violet, and white. 'Rose Queen' with its deep-pink buds and lighter-pink flowers is a favorite.

Gardeners who desire a tough yet airy, colorful, and freely flowering annual will appreciate cleome. Whether grown from seed or transplants, cleome quickly leaps to four feet or even taller. Its colorful globe-shaped blooms that begin in midsummer are downright interesting. The flowers have protruding curving stamens that give the flowers a wispy look and have led to the common name spider flower. They are followed by intriguing seedpods. Like most good things, cleome has a downside. Its leaves are sticky, the stems are thorny, and the plant self-seeds freely. Some people find cleome unpleasantly fragrant, although others don't notice much of a scent. All in all, cleome's advantages outweigh its drawbacks; it is a strong performer with a lofty colorful presence.

Other Name
Spider Flower

Bloom Period and Seasonal Color
Midsummer until frost in shades of pink, lavender, purple, rose, and white.

Mature Height × Spread
3 to 5 ft. × 18 to 24 in.

Coleus
Coleus × hybridus

There's nothing shy about coleus. This is a shade plant with a cutting-edge attitude. Its bright, improbable, even gaudy colors—neon green, pink, bronze, white, maroon, chartreuse—add irreverent zip to a shady spot. The result is an exuberant and almost tropical mood. Coleus has flowering spikes, but they're quite forgettable when compared with its spectacular leaves. In fact, there are scores of color combinations to choose from, some with frilled leaf edges. Coleus is easy to root from cuttings in water, making it a favorite plant for student observation in plant science and botany classes. It grows in leafy, erect mounds about one to two feet high and wide and thrives in a location where there is plenty of moisture. This plant is eager to please.

Bloom Period and Seasonal Color
Grown for its multicolored foliage from spring to fall.

Mature Height × Spread
1 to 2 ft. × 8 to 12 in.

When, Where, and How to Plant
Purchase young plants to set outdoors after the weather warms. Coleus is sensitive to frost, so it's better to wait than to rush to plant outside. After planting, feed with a transplant fertilizer such as 3-10-3. Coleus grows best in rich, well-drained soil and light filtered shade to full shade. In areas with more light, it may wilt without enough moisture. Consult page 23 for tips on planting annuals. Space plants 8 to 12 in. apart.

Growing Tips
Do not allow coleus to dry out. A mulch is recommended. For lush growth, feed with a dilute liquid fertilizer every three weeks.

Care
Coleus is generally free of pests and diseases. If it gets too tall or spindly, simply pinch it back to encourage bushier growth. It's best to pinch off the flower spikes as they appear to encourage foliar growth. Coleus stems may be cut in late summer to bring indoors. Root in water or sand and then pot. Keep the plants where they will receive bright light and cool room temperatures. Take more cuttings in spring to plant outdoors.

Companion Planting and Design
Coleus is appropriate for beds, borders, window-boxes, or containers. The festive foliage adds to the usual cast of shady characters, including impatiens, begonias, hostas, and astilbes. With so many colors available, it's best to limit a planting to one or two main colors to make a strong, clear statement. Use several coleus plants alone in a container for a stunning effect, or combine them with other plants.

We Recommend
With the advent of the tropicalismo style of gardening, the popularity of coleus is on the rise. Old forms dating back to the Victorian bedding craze are returning to cultivation. Type "coleus" into an Internet search engine and you won't believe your eyes! Look for these forms with extraordinarily colored foliage in the section of your garden center that sells specialty container plants.

When, Where, and How to Plant

Plant cosmos in late spring. Cosmos establishes quickly once the soil warms. Or sow directly in the garden in late spring. Give cosmos a location in full sun. Well-drained soil is a must. Cosmos tolerates soils of poor to average fertility. Too rich a soil or too much fertilizer makes for lush leaves and few flowers. Consult page 23 for planting tips. Allow cosmos plenty of space between plants—at least 1 to 2 ft. Pinch back young plants at planting to encourage branching.

Growing Tips

These plants almost thrive on neglect, requiring little in the way of care when grown in full sun. Give them an occasional drink of water during dry periods. Cosmos grows better without fertilization.

Care

Cosmos is usually free of serious pests and diseases, although plants may be plagued by mildew late in the season. Space the plants so there is good air circulation between them and avoid wetting the foliage when watering. Sometimes cankers will girdle the stems of cosmos. Remove and destroy affected plants. Taller varieties may be staked or supported by inserting twigs in the soil at the time seeds are planted. As the cosmos grows, it will obscure the twigs and benefit from the support. Cosmos may self-sow.

Companion Planting and Design

Cosmos is especially valuable in hot, sunny locations that might stress more heat-sensitive annuals. Plant cosmos in mixed beds behind shorter annuals and perennials. Dwarf varieties are a good choice for containers. Cosmos is lovely in available spots in perennial beds or an informal meadow-type planting. It is particularly charming behind a white picket fence or against a dark stone wall.

We Recommend

'Sonata' is a favorite because it has 3-in. flowers on relatively small plants, about 24 to 30 in. 'White Sonata' has satiny white petals that glow in the evening garden.

The tall, waving stems and daisylike flowers of cosmos are perfect for cottage gardens or anywhere the goal is a loose, relaxed effect. The plant's ferny leaves, branching form, and substantial height create a painterly, romantic vision. Cosmos is easy to start from seed sown directly in the garden in late spring, making it a wonderful annual for children to grow. It is reliable and grows quickly to several feet tall, sometimes even taller than the young gardeners who cultivate it. Flower petals, which are actually separate ray flowers, are available in several colors as well as singles and doubles. The bright-yellow centers of cosmos are really disk flowers. Excellent for cutting and use in arrangements, cosmos is native from Mexico to Brazil.

Bloom Period and Seasonal Color
Midsummer to frost in shades of pink, white, and magenta.

Mature Height × Spread
1 to 5 ft. × 18 in.

Miller

ecio cineraria

When color in the garden gets a little too hot and heavy, bring on dusty miller. Its silvery foliage offers a visual cooling for the reds, oranges, and yellows of many annuals and perennials. A close look at this plant's stems and leaves reveals that they are covered with a thick mat of whitish hairs. Keep dusty miller compact and within bounds with one or two prunings during the summer. Plants that are growing in windowboxes are more attractive when kept to a smaller size, perhaps eight to nine inches tall. Many plants grown for foliage prefer the shade, but dusty miller loves the sunny garden, where its cool green-gray leaves provide relief among the annuals and perennials that are revved up in summer's heat.

Bloom Period and Seasonal Color
Grown for its silvery foliage from spring to fall.

Mature Height × Spread
8 to 15 in. × 12 in.

When, Where, and How to Plant
Buy young plants in late spring to set into the garden. Dusty miller may be used in full sun, part sun, or filtered sun, but it performs better in more sunlight. It prefers well-drained soil of average fertility. Follow the general planting directions on page 23. Space plants 8 to 10 in. apart. Plants in containers may be set closer together. After planting, feed with a transplant fertilizer such as 3-10-3.

Growing Tips
Plants may be fed occasionally with a balanced fertilizer such as 10-10-10. Water during extended dry periods, or when the soil is dry.

Care
Dusty miller is rarely troubled by pests or disease if located in well-drained soil. To encourage leaf growth, pinch back flowers if they appear. Prune back once or twice a summer to maintain a rounded, compact form. Plants will continue to be attractive into fall, often even after a frost. Dusty miller, actually a tender perennial, may overwinter in milder zones. These hardy souls may not be as neat and compact their second year in the garden.

Companion Planting and Design
Use dusty miller with red or pink geraniums in a box or containers for a dreamy combination. It is excellent for edging, formal bedding, and for creating patterns. Dusty miller—like artemisias and other plants with silvery green leaves—is invaluable for adding contrast and an almost icy element to the garden palette. Its leaves cool down the bright reds and oranges of hot-colored marigolds and zinnias. It is also lovely among the pinks, purples, and blues of cooler-colored geraniums and impatiens.

We Recommend
'Cirrus' has rounded foliage, good weather resistance, and grows about 10 to 12 in. tall. 'Silverdust' is shorter and its leaves are more finely cut. The foliage of 'New Look' is close to white. A different plant with ferny gray foliage, *Tanacetum ptarmiciflorum* 'Silver Lace', is also sold under the common name of dusty miller.

Flowering Tobacco
Nicotiana alata

When, Where, and How to Plant

Flowering tobacco is cold-tolerant and may be planted in the garden earlier than more tender annuals. But cautious gardeners wait until the danger of frost is past. When choosing plants, look for healthy rosettes of foliage. Flowering tobacco seldom comes into flower in the cell-pack, which could explain why it's not more common in garden centers. Nicotiana likes moderately rich, well-drained garden soil. Plant in full sun or in locations that receive partial sun. Afternoon shade is particularly beneficial. Follow the general instructions for annual planting on page 23. Plant-starter fertilizer, such as 3-10-3, can be applied at this time to encourage root growth. Space plants about 8 in. apart.

Growing Tips

Water during hot, dry weather. Mulching to conserve moisture is beneficial. If sited correctly, additional fertilizer is unnecessary.

Care

Nicotiana is rarely trouble by pest and disease problems. After the first flush of flowers, deadhead plants. Rebloom will occur in a few weeks. Flowering tobacco can and probably will self-sow. These seedlings will not be the same as the original plants. You can experiment and let them grow, but if you want to retain the original color, weed them out and replant every year.

Companion Planting and Design

The white, light pink, and green flowers brighten lightly shaded locations and are attractive with coleus. Flowering tobacco combines well with perennials and can mask the yellowing foliage of bulbs or add color to newly planted perennial beds. Drifts of a single hue allow you to create planned combinations, while the mixes offer a cheerful abundance of color. Green-flowered tobaccos can be planted in perennial beds without any worry of a color clash.

We Recommend

The 'Merlin', 'Domino', 'Havana', and 'Nicki' series all have excellent flower production and extended blooming periods, and have performed well in Michigan. Try *Nicotiana langsdorffi* (3 ft.), a charming self-sower with fresh green flowers that dangle like small tubular bells.

Charming flowers on graceful stems, light fragrance, ease of cultivation—finally, a tobacco you can feel good about! A popular annual for nighttime fragrance, the original plant, called jasmine tobacco, opened its white flowers on lanky stems in the evening and closed in the morning sun. Plant breeders have produced a range of selections with flowers that stay open all day. Unfortunately, only a trace of the original fragrance remains in the newer plants. These shorter, more floriferous flowering tobaccos—each plant resembling a bouquet of bloom—are available in a range of colors from white, crimson-red, and shades of pink to a surprisingly refreshing green. This easygoing chartreuse mixes well with almost any other flower color, including orange, purple, or magenta. Watch for hummingbirds!

Other Name

Nicotiana

Bloom Period and Seasonal Color

Early summer to frost in shades of white, crimson, pink, and green.

Mature Height × Spread

10 to 24 in. × 12 in.

Geranium

Pelargonium × hortorum

Though native to South Africa, red geraniums are now as American as apple pie. Their bright globes of clustered flowers start blooming in early summer and stage a continuous show until frost. Versatile geraniums are equally appropriate in an informal cottage garden and in formal urns outside a stately mansion. Their habit is controlled but relentlessly cheerful. They are sometimes called zonal geraniums because the foliage is marked with distinct bands. Both seed-grown and cutting-grown geraniums are available. Seed-grown geraniums tend to be sold in flats for bedding. They usually have single flowers and are economical for mass plantings. Robust cutting-grown geraniums, sold in pots, are more expensive and have longer-lasting semidouble or double flowers. For a specimen plant, it is worth the few extra cents.

Bloom Period and Seasonal Color
Early summer to frost in shades of red, pink, lavender, orange, and white.

Mature Height × Spread
1 to 2 ft. × 12 to 18 in.

When, Where, and How to Plant
Purchase plants of blooming size in late spring. Geraniums prefer a mostly to completely sunny area with well-drained and fertile soil. Set into the garden at the same depth they were growing in containers. Remove flower buds at the time of transplanting to direct the plant's energy into root establishment. Plant about 12 in. apart. Water plants in well. After planting, feed with a transplant fertilizer such as 3-10-3.

Growing Tips
Water when the soil is dry. Avoid watering late in the day or evening. Flower clusters that stay wet are more susceptible to fungus problems. In average soil, fertilize plants with a liquid fertilizer at the rate specified on the label once or twice during the growing season. Container-grown plants benefit from a weak fertilizer (half-strength) every ten to fourteen days. Remember to apply fertilizer to damp, not dry, soil to avoid burning the plants. A 2-in. layer of organic mulch will help conserve moisture.

Care
Regularly deadhead to encourage more blooms. Pinch back stems to encourage bushier growth. With proper growing conditions, geraniums are usually trouble-free. If the plant is getting leggy or is not blooming, it probably needs more sun. Pick off and destroy any leaves that develop brown, sunken spots.

Companion Planting and Design
A classic bedding plant, geraniums are at their best in mass displays. They also work well as additions to mixed beds and borders. Keep in mind that the intense colors that catch your eye in the greenhouse can be difficult to use in the garden. Geraniums are wonderful in containers and windowboxes. Choose cutting-grown varieties for containers; you'll get a better show.

We Recommend
New varieties of geraniums continue to be introduced each year. 'Sincerely Yours' is one of the best traditional reds. For something different try 'Sassy Dark Red', a very dark crimson, or 'Melody Blue', the closest yet to a true lavender-blue.

When, Where, and How to Plant

Plant bedding plants in the spring after the danger of frost is past. Seed can be sown in the garden following the directions on the packet. A sunny location with well-drained soil is best. Globe amaranth tolerates poor and sandy soils. Gently remove plants from containers or cell-packs and plant in the garden 8 to 12 in. apart. Position so the plants are growing at the same soil level that they were in the container. Firm the soil and water. Plant-starter fertilizer, such as 3-10-3, will encourage root growth.

Growing Tips

Tolerant of heat and dry conditions, globe amaranth resents being overwatered but will need irrigation during prolonged dry spells. In soils of normal fertility, no additional fertilizing is necessary.

Care

Globe amaranth is easy to grow and pest- and disease-free. Deadhead any flower that begins to deteriorate. To dry flowers, pick throughout the growing season or wait and harvest the entire plant before heavy frost. Strip the leaves and hang the plants upside down in a well-ventilated location to dry.

Companion Planting and Design

Use globe amaranth in annual beds, cutting gardens, or mixed plantings. Try it in hot spots and for color in low-maintenance areas. Take advantage of globe amaranth's heat and drought tolerance by combining it with other sun-loving plants. The white- and pink-flowered forms have a silvery sheen and flatter other plants that have silver foliage, like dusty miller. For plenty of color, combine 'Woodcreek Red' or 'Strawberry Fields' globe amaranth with bright gold gloriosa daisies, rich purple heliotrope, and tall lavender-purple Brazilian verbena for a flamboyant color combination that will provide plenty of cut flowers.

We Recommend

'Buddy' and 'Gnome' are dwarf varieties, tidy and compact, suitable for potting, massing in beds, or edging. 'Strawberry Fields' has longer stems and larger, scarlet-red flowers that hold the vibrant color as they dry. A similar selection, 'Woodcreek Red', has performed well in Michigan gardens.

Large bunches of globe amaranth are often seen for sale in Michigan farmers' markets, but it's easy to grow your own. The cloverlike flowers (actually papery bracts that hold the tiny true flowers) seem to last forever—all summer in the garden and all winter in a vase. These sturdy ball-shaped flowers, resembling little pompons, are fun for children to grow and harvest. Several compact selections have been bred for landscape use, but the taller ones are best for producing cut and dried flowers. Mixed-color plantings of annuals can be jarring, but the standard globe amaranth mix of magenta, pink, and white flowers (sold as 'Mix' or 'Mixed Colors') is an exception. The paler colors temper the magenta and the whole group mingles pleasantly.

Bloom Period and Seasonal Color

Midsummer to frost in shades of red-violet, magenta, pink, orange, red, and white.

Mature Height × Spread

8 to 24 in. × 8 to 12 in.

Gloriosa Daisy

Rudbeckia hirta

The hot, dry locations that intimidate other garden plants don't bother gloriosa daisy for a minute. This improvement on the familiar roadside native black-eyed Susan is a tough, resilient plant that's perfect for spots with full sun. Like other members of the daisy or composite family, the gloriosa daisy really has two types of flowers: the outer ones are ray flowers in yellow, orange, or bronze, and the center is a cluster of brown disk flowers. These flowers are eye-catching to say the least, and gloriosa daisy makes a bold statement in the garden. In size and overall feel, it blends well into the perennial border. Gloriosa daisies are short-lived perennials grown as annuals; they flower the first year they are planted. They make spectacular cut flowers.

Bloom Period and Seasonal Color
Early summer to frost in golden yellow, mahogany, and orange; some are bicolors.

Mature Height × Spread
12 to 36 in. × 12 to 18 in.

When, Where, and How to Plant
Gloriosa daisies are fairly easy to transplant and establish outdoors in May, before planting more-tender annuals. Sow seed outside in the garden after the last frost date, or buy gloriosa daisies as transplants in the spring. Select a site in full sun and ordinary to fertile, well-drained soil. Plant nursery-grown transplants 14 to 24 in. apart in a prepared garden bed. Make sure the plant remains at the same level it was growing in the container or cell-pack. Firm the soil around the transplant and then water. A water-soluble plant-starter fertilizer, such as 3-10-3, could be applied at this time to encourage root growth.

Growing Tips
Gloriosa daisy is tough and easy-to-grow. Although it is somewhat drought-tolerant, water plants during extended dry periods. In average soils fertilization is unnecessary.

Care
Gloriosa daisy is usually problem-free, and it thrives in hot weather. Give plants adequate space to avoid foliar diseases like powdery mildew. Deadheading as well as cutting to use the flowers in arrangements will encourage more flowers. Taller varieties may profit from staking. Gloriosa daisies may self-sow.

Companion Planting and Design
The dwarf types are great plants for containers because they are not fussy about heat or dry soil. All varieties are good for beds, low-maintenance meadows, and cutting gardens. Use the smaller types for containers and windowboxes. Gloriosas make a brash and brilliant statement, but since plants may be bare of leaves toward the bottom, surround them with low-growing annuals such as French or signet marigolds. In a mixed bed, try them with Russian sage, purple coneflower, 'Autumn Joy' sedum, and orange or yellow zinnias. Use it in naturalistic meadow-style plantings with switch grass, blazing star, and butterfly weed.

We Recommend
One of the nicest gloriosa daisies is the cultivar 'Indian Summer', which was an All-America Selections winner in 1995. It has performed well in Michigan, providing much color on sturdy stems well into the fall.

Heliotrope
Heliotropium arborescens

When, Where, and How to Plant

Plant transplants from cell-packs in the spring, one week or so after the frost-free date. You can grow heliotrope from seed, but this is not a plant likely to germinate and grow well on a windowsill. It takes almost three months to grow plants large enough to set outside. Heliotrope likes warmth, sun, and moist but well-drained soil. Follow the general directions for planting annuals on page 23. Apply plant-starter fertilizer, such as 3-10-3, to encourage root growth. Space heliotrope at least 1 ft. apart to allow plants room to grow stocky and strong instead of tall and spindly.

Growing Tips

Keep heliotrope well watered during dry spells. Apply a 2-in. layer of organic mulch to conserve moisture. In a soil of average fertility, fertilize several times during the summer with liquid feed, such as 10-10-10, at the rate recommended on the package.

Care

Plants are generally pest- and disease-free. Deadhead (remove faded flowers) as the blooms turn from purple to brown. Bring heliotrope inside to enjoy over the winter if you can provide a cool sunny location. Heliotrope roots from cuttings.

Companion Planting and Design

Use heliotrope in annual displays, cottage gardens, perennial beds, and containers. Plant heliotrope with tangerine pot marigold, and bright-yellow melampodium; a small clump of variegated silver grass (*Miscanthus sinensis* 'Variegatus') would be the perfect vertical accent. Heliotrope will also work well in a mixed planting of annuals, perennials, and roses, cottage-garden style. Combine it with candy pink multiflora petunias, lime-green flowering tobacco, hazy lavender-blue Russian sage, and the pink-flowered hybrid rugosa rose 'Frau Dagmar Hastrup' for an unforgettable fragrant garden picture.

We Recommend

Heliotropium 'Marine' (to 18 in.) has consistently grown well in mid-Michigan. 'Marine' has large deep-purple flowers, a pleasing fragrance, and attractive foliage. A new cultivar, 'Mini Marine' (to 10 in.), is shorter and more compact. Try it in a sunny windowbox or patio container.

Cherry-pie, an alternative common name for heliotrope, refers to the sweet, fruity fragrance of this charming old-fashioned annual. The original fragrance that inspired the name has been bred out of the modern seed-grown selections, although a delightfully sweet scent remains. Heliotrope performs well year after year in the annual trials at Michigan State University, offering velvety purple flowers, sweet fragrance, and dark-green, deeply veined leaves. The handsome foliage, almost as big an asset as the flowers, flatters a wide range of other garden plants. Heliotrope was popular in Victorian times for bedding, cut-flower, and conservatory use. There are no longer scores of cultivars of heliotrope, but this plant's rich color, interesting foliage, and pleasing fragrance merit rediscovery. Cherry pie, anyone?

Other Name

Cherry-pie

Bloom Period and Seasonal Color

Early summer to frost in deep purple or lavender.

Mature Height × Spread

14 to 18 in. × 1 to 2 ft.

Zones

To Zone 4

Hyacinth Bean
Lablab purpureus

If you want a show-stopping vine, send hyacinth beans scampering up a fence or post. Soon you'll see slightly furry leaflets, purple stems, and, later, clusters of purplish flowers. The blooms are followed by shiny mahogany seedpods that hang as curious ornaments among the dark-green purple-tinged leaves. When it comes to foliage, flower, and seedpod, hyacinth bean is one of the most attractive annual vines around. In hot sunny weather, this tropical vine practically erupts with rapid growth. It requires a long growing season to reach flowering size, so starting seed indoors gives the plants an advantage over those sown outside. Dramatic and unusual, these handsome annual vines will attract curious stares from those unfamiliar with their charms. They are definitely fun to grow.

Bloom Period and Seasonal Color
Midsummer to frost in pinkish-purple or white.

Mature Length
10 to 20 ft.

Zones
To Zone 5 (it may not flower in colder zones)

When, Where, and How to Plant
Plants are seldom offered at nurseries, but they can be easily grown from seed. Hyacinth bean loves heat, so there's no point in starting the seeds too early. Indoors, begin about four weeks before the last frost. Sow the seed in 3-in. peat pots. Later, when weather has warmed up to summery conditions, plant the peat pots directly in the garden. This will lessen transplant shock. Hyacinth bean may also be sown outdoors after all danger of frost, but may not begin flowering until late summer, putting the plant in peril if there is an early frost. It does best in full sun and well-drained soil. Space the seeds or plants about 12 in. apart and make sure the vine has something to climb on. After planting, feed with a transplant fertilizer such as 3-10-3.

Growing Tips
Keep plants well watered until established, and then water when the soil is dry. In poor soil, use a balanced liquid feed every three weeks. In colder zones, the growing season may not be long enough for hyacinth bean to reach blooming stage.

Care
Once established, hyacinth bean isn't prone to attack by pests or disease. Provide support for climbing. Save the seedpods for next year for your own garden and to share with admiring neighbors.

Companion Planting and Design
Plant hyacinth beans for an annual screen or a cover on a fence, trellis, or post, or let it scramble over the ground. It is one of the finest annual vines for quickly screening a view, covering a fence, and offering interest and color with its leaves, blossoms, and seedpods. For twice the show, plant it together with morning glories. Its ultimate height depends on the size of the structure; one year, Tim and Laura let it grow high into a defunct television antenna.

We Recommend
A cultivar called 'Ruby Moon' has bicolored flowers in light and darker pink.

When, Where, and How to Plant

Buy transplants to set into the garden in late May or early June. Impatiens grow best after the soil has warmed. Plants set out in cool, wet spring weather won't start to take off until conditions improve. Impatiens thrive in rich, well-drained soil. In heavy clay or sandy soils, dig in compost or other soil amendments before planting for best results. Use impatiens in part sun to shade. They flower more effectively where they receive at least some sun, and many varieties can tolerate considerable amounts of sun if they receive adequate moisture. Space impatiens about 8 to 12 in. apart. Plant them so they are growing in the garden at the same depth that they were in their containers. After planting, feed with a transplant fertilizer such as 3-10-3.

Growing Tips

The more sun they get, the more water impatiens need. Wilting foliage is a sign that the plants are desperate for moisture. Mulch to conserve water. Feed impatiens with a general fertilizer such as 10-10-10 every three to four weeks if desired. Too much nitrogen may result in lush foliage but scarce flowers.

Care

Impatiens are usually free of serious pest and disease problems. Impatiens are easy to overwinter indoors. Take cuttings from the stems in late August, root them in water, and place them in potting soil or a soilless mix. Plants may be cut back in spring and those trimmings rooted as well.

Companion Planting and Design

Impatiens are ideal in beds, in the shade of trees, and in containers and windowboxes. They make a lovely display on their own or combined with other shade-loving plants. Use paler-colored impatiens in shady areas and brighter colors where there is more sun.

We Recommend

It's hard to beat the 'Super Elfin' series for abundant blooms and compact habit. It's now available in over twenty different designer colors including 'Lipstick' and 'Melon'.

Drive around shady residential areas in the summer and you'll see impatiens in nearly every yard. These brightly colored annuals dress up the front of foundation plantings, beautify the base of lofty shade trees, and spill charmingly over the sides of baskets, windowboxes, and containers. In the last few decades, impatiens have outsold petunias, becoming the nation's most popular bedding plant. The plants are easy to grow in shade, and newer varieties also tolerate sun. A single plant, with proper water and fertilizer, can grow into a flower-covered mound up to eighteen inches high and wide. It will bloom all summer and into September and October or until hit by frost, when it will quickly wilt and die. Double impatiens have flowers resembling fluffy miniature roses.

Other Name

Busy Lizzie

Bloom Period and Seasonal Color

Early summer until frost in shades of pink, coral, red, purple, and white.

Mature Height × Spread

6 to 18 in. × 6 to 24 in.

Love-in-a-Mist

Nigella damascena

The exquisite flowers of love-in-a-mist are worthy of unhurried examination, but the culture is a quick study: good drainage, sun, soil, and a seed packet are all you need! The romantic common name, love-in-a-mist, describes the delicate flowers enveloped by a ferny web of soft threadlike foliage. The horned, inflated seedpods, striped with maroon, are useful in arrangements and in herbal wreaths. The most beautiful forms of this easily grown but short-lived annual are those with sky blue blossoms. Nigella is a delicate plant in appearance and stature. A determined self-sower, its small ferny seedlings are a welcome sight in the spring garden. It often finds the best place to grow and flower, that very place you hoped to remember to plant.

Bloom Period and Seasonal Color
Summer in blue, rose, and white.

Mature Height × Spread
12 to 18 in. × 6 to 8 in.

When, Where, and How to Plant

Nigella has a taproot and doesn't like to be transplanted; sow directly in the garden for best results. Plant seed early to obtain the greatest show before the hot temperatures of summer arrive. Sow seed 1/4 in. deep in spring as soon as soil is workable. Germination generally takes about two weeks. Plant in normal garden soil with good drainage in full sun or partial shade. Thin seedlings to 6 to 8 in. apart. When transplanting from cell-packs, use extreme care and disturb the roots as little as possible. Water to settle the soil.

Growing Tips

When love-in-a-mist reaches maturity (in about six weeks), blooming ceases; successive sowings from early spring through early summer can be made to ensure a long period of bloom. Water during extended dry spells. In average garden soil, extra fertilization isn't necessary.

Care

Love-in-a-mist is typically free of pests and disease. In the spring, hoe out unwanted seedlings. Remove plants when they become unattractive. To harvest the pods for their ornamental value, pick them after the maroon coloration has begun to develop. If you wait too long, they will become brown. Each *Nigella* pod contains many black seeds, which can be saved, shared or left to scatter on their own.

Companion Planting and Design

Love-in-a-mist is best used as a filler in perennial beds, cottage gardens, and herb gardens, and in the cut-flower garden, where it is grown both for its flowers and its seedpods. Let love-in-a-mist find a home in unusual places; for example, sow seed in a rose bed. The delicate plants set off the sturdy roses and don't compete significantly for water or nutrients.

We Recommend

Mixed colors are widely available in garden centers. The single color selections may need to be ordered from seed catalogs. 'Oxford Blue' (to 30 in.), a tall double-flowered form, brings a unique deep blue color and delicate grace to perennial borders. The shorter 'Miss Jekyll' is also blue.

Marigold

Tagetes patula

When, Where, and How to Plant

Sow seed indoors four to six weeks before the last frost date or outdoors in late May to early June. Marigolds grow best in warmer weather. Transplants will bloom sooner than seed sown directly in the garden. Choose a location in full to part sun and well-drained soil of poor to average fertility. Flowering is reduced in partial shade. Space marigolds 6 to 9 in. apart, depending on type. Plant them slightly deeper than they were growing in containers. After planting, feed with a transplant fertilizer such as 3-10-3. Plant seed of marigolds in the garden according to directions on the seed packet. The seed germinates quickly, usually in five to seven days.

Growing Tips

Soil that is rich may stimulate lush foliage but few flowers. The same is true of frequent fertilizer applications. Water when soil is dry. Marigolds will tolerate drought but prefer more regular moisture. A 2-in. layer of organic mulch will conserve moisture.

Care

Deadhead or remove faded flowers often to prevent plant from setting seed and to improve appearance. Marigolds are sometimes troubled by a disease called aster yellows that turns their tips greenish yellow. Plants with this problem should be removed and destroyed.

Companion Planting and Design

Showcase marigolds in a mass, or mix them with other sun-loving annuals such as ageratum, cosmos, zinnias, gloriosa daisies, and spider flowers. French marigold's compact form makes the plants superb for edging or massing in areas with poor soil such as under a fence, and they do well as container plants.

We Recommend

The single French types, which have a more natural appearance than the doubles, are becoming very popular again, with some heirloom selections available. One favorite single is the 'Disco' series. Signet marigold, *Tagetes tenuifolia*, has mounds of delicate ferny foliage and loads of tiny flowers. Its more natural habit makes signet marigold easier to combine with perennials.

The pungent, distinctive aroma of marigolds is the essence of summer. These nearly carefree annuals offer a riot of yellow, orange, and mahogany in rounded full flowers that resemble small carnations. The hues are especially vibrant in fall when the plants end the season with a burst of vigor. French marigolds have fernlike leaves, and their flowers can be single or double or crested. Marigolds appeal to both beginning and experienced gardeners who seek reliable color beginning in early summer. Their large seeds are easy to handle, and the plants grow readily from seed planted indoors in spring or outside in late May. Many Michigan children are introduced to gardening in school when they start marigold seeds in paper cups, often as gifts for Mother's Day.

Other Name

French Marigold

Bloom Period and Seasonal Color

Early summer to frost in shades of yellow, orange, and mahogany or bicolors.

Mature Height × Spread

6 to 18 in. × 6 to 12 in.

Mealy-cup Sage
Salvia farinacea

The mealy-cup sage, in contrast to the bright-red flowers of its flashier cousin the scarlet sage (Salvia splendens), offers a subtle combination of violet-blue flowers on bluish stems and somewhat grayish green foliage. White selections, subtle and refined, have pure-white flowers emerging from woolly silver stems. Sometimes called blue sage, mealy-cup sage is a tireless performer, providing fresh foliage and violet-blue spikes with little effort. The unenticing common name refers to the whitish powder or meal that coats the stems and buds. Mealy-cup sage blooms from late June until frost on upright, bushy plants. It is not a scene-stealer; it sets off other plants in borders and is a cool blue presence in annual bedding combinations.

Bloom Period and Seasonal Color
Early summer to frost in blue and white.

Mature Height × Spread
16 to 20 in. × 1 ft.

When, Where, and How to Plant
Plant blue sage in spring after the frost-free date for your area, in full sun in well-drained soil. It will tolerate partial shade. Follow the general directions for planting annuals on page 23. Apply a plant-starter fertilizer, such as 3-10-3, to encourage root growth.

Growing Tips
Water plants during extended dry spells. Apply a 2-in. layer of organic mulch to conserve moisture. In average soils, additional fertilizer is unnecessary.

Care
There are no serious pest and disease problems. Deadhead flowering spikes to encourage more bloom. The flowers are excellent for cutting and for use as an everlasting. The stems and flowers dry to a deep blue, unusual among dried flowers. To dry mealy-cup sage, harvest the flower spikes when they are almost but not quite fully open. Fasten small bunches with rubber bands, and hang them upside down in a well-ventilated location out of direct sun.

Companion Planting and Design
Use mealy-cup sage in drifts in annual displays, cutting gardens, and containers. Try deep blue 'Victoria' with 'Rose Queen' spider flower and magenta or pink geraniums. Or, for an elegant look, plant the 'Silver White' mealy-cup sage with white 'Sonata' cosmos, pale-pink petunias, and dusty miller. Mealy-cup sage also works well in drifts in perennial beds, where it can be planted over the yellowing foliage of bulbs. The violet-blue color complements the primrose yellow of 'Moonbeam' coreopsis or 'Moonshine' yarrow.

We Recommend
Violet-blue 'Victoria' has performed well in Michigan, as has 'Rhea Blue', a slightly more compact selection. 'Strata', a 1995 All-America Selections winner, has a unusual combination of blue flowers on silver spikes. If you like red salvia, try *Salvia coccinea*, the Texas sage. This adaptable and long-blooming annual has a graceful growing habit and loose spikes of beautiful red flowers attractive to hummingbirds. 'Lady in Red' is an All-America Selections winner and has done well in Michigan.

When, Where, and How to Plant

Plant melampodium from cell-packs or containers after the danger of frost is past. Seed may also be directly sown in the garden after the frost-free date. It grows well in the heat of summer and with full sun and well-drained soil. Plant nursery-grown transplants 7 to 10 in. apart in a prepared garden bed. Make sure the plant remains at the same level it was growing in the container or cell-pack. Firm the soil around the transplant and then water. A water-soluble plant-starter fertilizer, such as 3-10-3, could be applied at this time to encourage root growth. To direct-sow outside, follow the directions on the seed packet. Flowering will be later than for purchased transplants.

Growing Tips

Water until established. It is fairly tolerant of dry conditions, but water during severe drought or if plants look water stressed. A 2-in. layer of organic mulch will help conserve moisture. Generally, mclampodium will not require fertilizer.

Care

Melampodium doesn't need any special care and has no insect and disease problems.

Companion Planting and Design

Use melampodium in sunny beds, borders, pots, planters, and windowboxes. The cheerful yellow flowers of melampodium mix well with other hot colors. Try melampodium with the bright scarlet red of 'Lucifer' crocosmia, the similar but larger yellow-orange daisies of sunflower heliopsis, clear yellow of 'Golden Showers' coreopsis, and the orange of butterfly weed. To create a similar color scheme with annuals, plant golden marigolds, orange zinnias, and gloriosa daisies with melampodium. The tall stems and purple flowers of Brazilian verbena would be a sensational accent. For another look, combine with the deep blue spikes of mealy-cup sage for that favorite Michigan color combination, maize and blue.

We Recommend

There are only a few cultivars. 'Medallion' (20 to 22 in.) is a compact and floriferous selection. 'Showstar' (24 in.) is another. 'Million Gold' (16 to 18 in.) is probably the shortest.

A little known but easy annual, melampodium flowers all summer long, producing hundreds of inch-wide yellow daisies on bushy plants with medium-green foliage. Melampodium has no easy common name or wide range of colors, but its beauty and toughness make it an excellent annual for Michigan gardens. Its tiny sunflowers, abundance of fresh green foliage, and open habit give melampodium a natural appearance, more like a perennial than many of the flashy annuals that produce large, colorful flowers at the expense of a genuine appearance. Melampodium needs no special coddling, deadheading, or fertilizing. Relatively new to cultivation, melampodium may not always be available at local garden centers. Ask for it and create a demand. Seed is easily obtained from mail-order catalogs.

Bloom Period and Seasonal Color
Early summer to frost in golden yellow.

Mature Height × Spread
15 to 25 in. × 18 to 24 in.

Zones
To Zone 4

Moss Rose
Portulaca grandiflora

Portulaca or moss rose is an annual for difficult places, but there is nothing difficult about its character. Moss rose tolerates hot, dry areas and infertile soils, and it produces satiny flowers in bright, glowing colors that cover low-growing mats of succulent pointed foliage. Blooming from early summer to fall, the one- to two-inch frilly blooms, available as singles or doubles, have bright yellow-orange centers. In the past, moss rose flowers closed by midafternoon or when the sun went behind a cloud. Modern selections remain open most of the day, even when it is overcast. Moss roses are valuable for problem spots in the garden, and they are attractive additions to windowboxes, hanging baskets, and pots.

Other Name
Portulaca

Bloom Period and Seasonal Color
Early summer to frost in white, pink, magenta, orange, yellow, and red.

Mature Height × Spread
6 to 9 in. × 6 to 8 in.

When, Where, and How to Plant
Plant moss rose in the garden after danger of frost has passed and soil has warmed. Locate moss roses in full sun. They tolerate infertile soil—in fact, they prefer it—but the site must be well drained. They will not tolerate sites that remain wet. Follow the general planting directions on page 23. Plant them 6 to 8 in. apart. After planting, feed with a transplant fertilizer such as 3-10-3. Water the plants in well at planting.

Growing Tips
Moss rose is an easy-to-grow plant. After it starts showing new growth, little additional water is needed. Portulaca can withstand drought and thrives with almost no care. Fertilizer is unnecessary.

Care
Pest and disease problems are negligible. Moss roses are apt to self-sow. Though still attractive, the second year's flowers may not be quite as lovely or the same flower color as the parents. If the area gets close scrutiny, pull out the volunteers and replant with new ones. But if the self-sown crop is in a more casual bed, a crop of volunteer moss roses can put on a free, enjoyable display.

Companion Planting and Design
Moss rose is useful for edging paths or beds, growing in exposed locations such as between paving stones, or surrounding bricks in full-sun conditions that would bake other plants. They are excellent grouped in the front of a perennial bed or in containers. Moss roses are wonderful for rock gardens. The fleshy leaves help the plant retain water even in dry exposed locations.

We Recommend
The 'Sundial' series has performed well in trials in Michigan. It has double flowers and is available in ten colors. 'Sundial Mango', a beautiful peachy orange, is one of our favorites. Think pale orange is too hard to use? Plant a hanging basket with 'Sundial Mango', add something trailing and lavender-blue like fanflower (*Scaevola*), and finish with 'Blackie' sweet potato vine for contrast. Wow!

Pansy
Viola × *wittrockiana*

When, Where, and How to Plant

Set plants out in the garden or in containers about two to three weeks before the last frost. Gardeners in Zones 5 and 6 may purchase plants in September for flowers in the fall and the following spring. Place pansies in sun to light shade. Pansies need excellent drainage and rich soil; amend with compost or shredded leaves if necessary. When planting pansies in the fall, avoid areas that stay wet all winter. Follow the general directions for planting on page 23. Space plants about 4 to 6 in. apart. After planting, feed with a transplant fertilizer such as 3-10-3.

Growing Tips

Mulch to keep the soil cool. Pansies need moist conditions to thrive and do not tolerate drought. Water when necessary. For lush growth and flowering or in poor soils, feed pansies with a general fertilizer such as 10-10-10 about every three weeks while they are growing actively. Mulch fall-planted pansies with evergreen boughs after the ground freezes.

Care

If you have the time, pinching off faded flowers encourages more bloom. In early summer, warmer weather will cause some pansies to stall, and they may be replaced with more heat-tolerant annuals or cut back in July to encourage reblooming in fall. Pansies are generally disease-free. If slugs are a problem, surround the plants with a ring of diatomaceous earth.

Companion Planting and Design

Use in beds and containers. In fall, use pansies over newly planted bulb beds. The pansies will bloom into early winter and return in the spring to flower at the base of daffodils, tulips, and other bulbs.

We Recommend

The most cold-tolerant pansies have small to mid-sized blooms. Among the hardiest are the series named 'Crystal Bowl', 'Universal', and 'Maxim'. They make darling cut flowers. Violas are similar to pansies but a little shorter, with smaller blooms; those in the 'Jewel' series are especially hardy. *Viola tricolor* is the familiar Johnny-jump-up.

It's easy to be sentimental about pansies. With their cheery colors and markings like tiny faces, pansies are an old-fashioned favorite with continued appeal for gardeners today. Their bright yellow and purple flowers are often the first annuals seen at garden centers, and they shine during the cooler spring and early summer weather. Pansies thrive in rich soil with plenty of moisture and cool weather, typical conditions of spring and fall. Newer types better tolerate warmth. Fall planting, common in the Southern states, is becoming popular among Northerners, including Michigan residents. These plants are sown in greenhouses in July for sale in September. The fall-planted pansies flower on warmer days into November and December—well beyond the early frosts—and they revive, if mulched, at the first hint of spring.

Bloom Period and Seasonal Color

Spring and fall in blue, violet, white, orange, yellow, bronze; sometimes multicolored.

Mature Height × Spread

6 to 9 in. × 8 to 12 in.

Petunia
Petunia × hybrida

Petunias are prized in the annual world for their long season of bloom and colorful funnel-shaped flowers. Newer hybrids offer advantages over older varieties of petunias, which for years were the country's most popular bedding plant (impatiens now hold that title). Petunias come in a wide range of colors, some veined or striped, ruffled, single, or double. Multiflora petunias are covered all season with smaller (about two inches), more delicately sized blooms that are better able to withstand rainstorms without permanent damage. Less weather-resistant, grandiflora petunias have larger (about four inches), showier flowers, but not as many flowers at any one time. A natural for garden beds as well as hanging baskets and containers, petunias quickly become a cascade of color.

Bloom Period and Seasonal Color
Early summer to frost in shades of pink, red, purple, blue, rose, and yellow; may be zoned or striped.

Mature Height × Spread
8 to 12 in. × 12 to 18 in.

When, Where, and How to Plant
Buy transplants to set into the garden after chance of frost. Pinch back young plants to encourage more compact growth. Petunias are more cold-tolerant than many annuals so may be set out a few weeks earlier. Petunias prefer sunny to mostly sunny locations. Well-drained soil is a must; those grown in heavy clay will not thrive. Space petunias 6 to 12 in. apart depending on the cultivar. After planting, feed with a transplant fertilizer such as 3-10-3.

Growing Tips
In poor or average soils, fertilize about once a month with a general fertilizer such as 10-10-10 at the rate recommended on the product. In dry periods, provide water. Avoid watering late in the day. Plants that stay wet overnight are more prone to disease.

Care
Remove faded blooms to encourage new growth. Both the flower and the seedpod must be removed to redirect the plant's energy into more flowers. Any petunia that's getting scraggly may be sheared in early July. Cut the plants back in half and then fertilize. Some people do this chore just before they leave for summer vacation. By the time they return, the petunias will be blooming again. Petunias are resistant to most pests and diseases.

Companion Planting and Design
Multiflora petunias are excellent for many uses in the garden, including bedding, edging, and additions to perennial beds. Use grandiflora petunias in protected locations and in containers. The petunia's naturally cascading habit and showy flowers make it ideal for pots and hanging baskets.

We Recommend
Multiflora petunias are the most resistant to disease, heat, and drought. 'Primetime', 'Carpet', 'Celebrity', and 'Madness' are a few of these multiflora types. Petunias in the 'Wave' series are veritable miracle plants. Heat- and drought-tolerant, they cover the ground quickly and produce an explosion of flowers. Try petunia 'Purple Wave' or 'Cherry Wave' in mixed containers and hanging baskets for brilliant color.

Pot Marigold
Calendula officinalis

When, Where, and How to Plant

Plant small transplants in spring after the danger of hard frost. *Calendula* tolerates cool temperatures and can be direct-sown in spring before the frost-free date. Pot marigold prefers sun—it will tolerate a bit of shade—and moist, well-drained soil. Follow the general directions for planting annuals on page 23. It's easy to sow seed directly in the garden, and germination will take one to two weeks. Thin plants to 8 to 12 in. apart.

Growing Tips

Water transplants until established. Pot marigold is not particularly drought-tolerant and should be watered during dry spells. Apply a 2-in. layer of organic mulch to conserve moisture. Pot marigold does not have high fertility requirements and will not need special fertilization.

Care

Pot marigold is generally free of pest and disease problems. Deadhead plants to encourage rebloom. In Michigan's relatively cool summers, pot marigold blooms throughout the summer. If plants begin to languish in a heat wave, cut back the flowering stems and wait for cooler temperatures to restore vigor. Pot marigold is quite cold-tolerant. It flowers late into the fall and does not go black at the first touch of frost. It does self-sow, producing volunteers. If you originally planted a named selection, the flowers on these volunteer plants may not be as attractive as those of their parents.

Companion Planting and Design

Plant in annual beds, cottage gardens, cutting gardens, herb gardens, and containers. The bright yellow and tangerine flowers blend easily with other hot colors but are particularly brilliant when combined with blue or purple flowers. In the cottage or herb garden, combine pot marigold with the blue starry flowers of borage, another edible flower, and 'Dark Opal' basil.

We Recommend

Recently, many new types have been selected. Since they are so easy to grow from seed, try some of these: 'Pacific Beauty' for long-stemmed double flowers and heat tolerance; 'Bon Bon', a dwarf for bedding and pot culture; and 'Touch of Red', with petals edged in dark red.

Pot marigold, that orange-flowered stalwart of British cottage gardens, now comes in a range of colors—apricot, tangerine, lemon, cream—so luscious they will make your mouth water. Fortunately, you can indulge. The flowers have been used since medieval times for culinary, cosmetic, and medicinal purposes. A contemporary reason to grow pot marigold is for its beautiful large, silky-petaled flowers, which bloom from early summer to late fall. And the petals still make a colorful garnish for a salad! Flower types include single and semidouble to fully double, some with a contrasting maroon-brown center. The petals have a silky sheen and are soft to the touch. This plant is easy to grow, and its blossoms make wonderful cut flowers, lasting up to two weeks in a vase.

Bloom Period and Seasonal Color
Early summer to frost in orange, yellow, and cream.

Mature Height × Spread
1 to 2 ft. × 8 to 12 in.

Zones
To Zone 4

Purple Fennel
Foeniculum vulgare 'Purpurascens'

Fennel, *often grown in the herb or vegetable garden, deserves to escape its culinary confines and mingle with the garden flowers. The purple-foliaged form called bronze, copper, or purple fennel commands the ornamental gardener's attention. The soft ferny threadlike foliage forms a shimmering smoky purple-bronze cloud that dramatically sets off annuals, perennials, and summer-flowering bulbs. Young plants have the deepest purple coloration, which later changes to a purplish bronze. Both the seeds and the foliage of fennel can be used in cooking for a distinctive anise flavor, but the beautiful lacy contrast that purple fennel provides in the garden is its greatest asset. Purple fennel's delicate purple-smoke color combines well with almost any hue, setting off bright orange and yellow and equally flattering to pastel colors.*

Other Name
Bronze Fennel

Bloom Period and Seasonal Color
Yellow flowers in late summer; grown for its purplish foliage.

Mature Height × Spread
3 to 6 ft. × 8 to 12 in.

Zones
To Zone 4

When, Where, and How to Plant
Purple fennel is best grown from seed in average, well-drained garden soil and full sun. Seed can be planted directly in prepared beds as soon as the soil is workable. It will germinate in approximately two weeks. Plant nursery-grown seedlings after the danger of hard frost. Transplants can also be purchased in cell-packs; these won't grow as well as plants directly sown in the spring garden. Look for healthy plants without exposed roots, and try to disturb the roots as little as possible when planting. Follow the general planting directions on page 23. Space fennel at 8 to 12 in. apart.

Growing Tips
No special care is needed. Purple fennel is drought-tolerant and will need water only during extended dry spells. Fertilization is unnecessary.

Care
Fennel's yellow Queen Anne's lace-type flowers appear in late summer. To preserve the foliage effect for a while, remove the flowers as they appear. A prolific self-sower if allowed to form seed, fennel will produce plenty of seedlings for next year's garden. Self-sowing can be a nuisance. Generally free of pests and disease, its foliage may be munched on by the striped caterpillar of the swallowtail butterfly. The arrival of the beautiful butterflies later in the season more than makes up for any lost foliage. Purple fennel is actually a perennial that is grown as an annual. It may occasionally overwinter in Zone 5.

Companion Planting and Design
Plant in herb gardens, cut-flower gardens, perennial beds, and annual displays. Purple fennel provides a sublime backdrop for large showy flowers such as the orange-red daylilies or salmon-peach lilies. Experiment with purple fennel's ability to calm bright combinations. In an annual bed, mix purple fennel with red zinnias, 'Lady in Red' Texas sage, lavender-purple Brazilian verbena, and tall 'Blue Horizon' ageratum.

We Recommend
The named selections 'Smokey' and 'Giant Bronze' are available. The larger selections can be very dramatic.

Snapdragon
Antirrhinum majus

When, Where, and How to Plant

Plant snapdragons in spring. They tolerate cool conditions, so they may be planted a few weeks before the last frost date. Choose selections that resist rust, and plant them in full sun. Soil should be light, rich (amend if necessary with compost), and well drained. Avoid planting in heavy clay. Consult page 23 for planting tips. Space plants 8 to 15 in., depending on the plant's ultimate size. They should be pinched back for a more compact, bushier form. After planting, water well and feed with a transplant fertilizer such as 3-10-3.

Growing Tips

Apply a 2-in. layer of organic mulch to conserve moisture. Generally, snapdragons have a flush of bloom during the summer and then reflower later. They can be tricky to grow. They dislike conditions that are too wet or too dry. To stimulate flowering, fertilize the plants with a balanced food such as 10-10-10 as they near their expected size. After that, do not feed again until the snapdragons finish blooming. At that time, they may be cut back and fed again.

Care

Rust, the bane of older types of snapdragons, appears as small brown powder-filled dots on the underside of leaves. It is a fungus. Plant only snapdragons that are resistant to rust. Improve air circulation around plants through adequate spacing. This will help the plants stay healthy. Taller types may be staked at planting. Deadhead regularly to improve appearance and redirect the plant's energy to new growth.

Companion Planting and Design

They are especially suited to cottage gardens, old-fashioned gardens, and perennial beds, but not for mass bedding. Position smaller snapdragons at the front of beds, and use the taller ones toward the middle to the back of the border.

We Recommend

The 'Liberty' series (18 to 28 in.) has done well in trials in Michigan. These are quick to reflower on long, sturdy stems and are available in a wide range of colors.

Plants that do tricks fascinate youngsters—and grown-ups as well when they think no one is looking. Snapdragon's "trick" is an all-time favorite: Pinch the sides of the bloom together to see the dragon's mouth snap open and closed. In addition to tricks, snapdragons offer many treats. This old-fashioned garden staple presents spikes loaded with flowers in pastel pinks, peaches, and purples. A cluster of pure white snapdragons adds formal grace to a perennial border. Snapdragons are useful for edging and bedding and, of course, in the cutting garden. Heights range from under twelve inches to several feet tall, and some cultivars have ruffled flowers. Popular in the 1800s, snapdragons remain in vogue with gardeners over a century later because they perform well in sunny locations.

Bloom Period and Seasonal Color
Early summer to frost in pink, yellow, peach, purple, mahogany; some are bi- or tricolored.

Mature Height × Spread
6 to 36 in. × 8 to 15 in.

Sunflower

Helianthus annuus

A trip to the lake, red ripe tomatoes, and big bouquets of sunflowers are all part of late summer in Michigan. Sunflowers are currently riding a tide of popularity, appearing on posters, fabric, and breakfast cereal boxes and in advertisements. And it's no wonder. Their cheerful countenance and sunny flowers are irresistible. The huge seed-producing types like 'Mammoth', which are used for sunflower seed and oil, are too ungainly for most gardens, but dozens of smaller, more ornamental types are now available, including plants for cut flowers and dwarf selections suitable for bedding. Sunflowers, if given sun and average soil, are easy to grow from seed and trouble-free. The seeds of sunflowers are attractive to birds, especially goldfinches, and to squirrels and chipmunks as well.

Bloom Period and Seasonal Color
Late summer to frost in yellow, gold, bronze, creamy white, brown.

Mature Height × Spread
2 to 12 ft. × 1 to 2 ft.

When, Where, and How to Plant
Sow seed in the spring after the danger of frost is past. Seed germinates quickly, often within a week. Easy to grow, sunflowers will prosper in full sun and soil of average fertility. Plant seed at the depth recommended on the seed packet. For the easiest and quickest method of spacing plants, sow three seeds together at the desired spacing, usually 1 to 3 ft. When the seedlings reach about 6 in., leave one and cut down the extra seedlings at soil level. Don't pull or the roots may be disturbed. If planting transplants, follow the general directions on page 23. Water plants to settle the soil.

Growing Tips
Although these plants are somewhat drought-tolerant, regular watering when rain is scarce will promote good health. Sunflowers generally do not require fertilization.

Care
Sunflowers are rarely troubled by pests and disease. However, rabbits may be troublesome until the plants are established; place a cage around the seedlings. Large plants may need to be tied to a stout stake to keep them upright, particularly in windy locations. A double row can be self-supporting. Cut flowers regularly to promote flower production.

Companion Planting and Design
It can be difficult to find the perfect place to plant sunflowers. Most are large, and coarsely textured. Plant them in large borders or cut-flower beds, or consider the vegetable garden. The recent smaller selections are suitable for beds, borders, or even large containers. The giant seed-producing types are best confined to vegetable gardens or country fence lines. In a residential landscape, just one row at the edge of a small vegetable plot will provide armfuls of flowers and plenty of seed for birds.

We Recommend
The vast array of sunflower seeds available in any garden center attests to their current popularity. Check the ultimate size and spacing to be sure you have enough space to accommodate your selection. Our favorite for cut flowers is 'Autumn Beauty' (5 to 6 ft.), a blend of yellow, bronze, red, and mahogany including bicolors.

Begonia × semperflorens

When, Where, and How to Plant

Buy young plants in late spring to set out when the soil warms and nighttime temperatures stay above 50 degrees Fahrenheit. If the weather is cool and wet after transplanting, wax begonias may be slow to establish. Wax begonias are best in partial shade but will tolerate sun with adequate moisture. They prefer well-drained soil of average or better fertility. Follow the general directions for planting on page 23. Space wax begonias 6 to 10 in. apart, depending on the height of the variety selected. The transplant tag will have specific spacing instructions. After planting, feed with a transplant fertilizer such as 3-10-3.

Growing Tips

Wax begonias are easy to maintain. They require regular water, especially plants growing in sun. Those in sunny locations should be mulched to conserve moisture and help keep the soil and roots cool. Use a slow-release fertilizer, or feed with a balanced fertilizer such as 10-10-10 every three weeks or as desired.

Care

Wax begonias are usually not troubled by pests or disease. Begonias may be dug up and potted in late summer, then brought indoors for the winter as houseplants. Start cuttings from those plants in early spring, then plant outside when the weather warms. Begonias are "clean" plants; that means they need no deadheading to look their best.

Companion Planting and Design

These low-maintenance annuals are often used for landscaping and commercial bedding. Play up their neat, compact shapes by using them as miniature hedges along a path or as bedding plants for color and interest from both the blooms and the foliage. They make a stunning contrast when grown with dusty miller. A more vibrant companion is coleus. The brightly colored begonia flowers will echo the shades in the coleus leaves. Begonias also perform well in containers and baskets.

We Recommend

For containers or hanging baskets, try begonia 'Dragon Wings', an angelwing begonia. It has abundant clusters of deep-coral flowers.

Wax begonias bring a festive look to the garden. These dependable minimal-care annuals are deservedly popular for their crisp effect and vibrant colors. Silky yellow-centered flowers of white, pink, or red dot mounds of green or bronze leaves. Wax begonias are tidy long-flowering plants that do not require deadheading, and they bloom continuously from early summer until frost. Once considered a plant for shady spots, newer wax begonias tolerate and even thrive in sun as long as temperatures stay below 90 degrees Fahrenheit and the roots are kept cool with mulch. Since there are many choices among annuals for full sun, however, play up the wax begonia's strengths by displaying it in filtered light, part shade, or shade.

Other Name

Fibrous-rooted Begonia

Bloom Period and Seasonal Color

Early summer to frost in shades of red, white, rose, pink, and coral; foliage may be green, bronze, or variegated.

Mature Height × Spread

6 to 24 in. × 6 to 10 in.

nia

...innia spp.

The Aztecs grew classic zinnia, Zinnia angustifolia, centuries ago as an ornamental plant, but today this
eager-to-please annual is unknown to many gardeners.
'Crystal White' won the All-America Selections award for
bedding plants, and it deserves the celebrity. These free-
flowering zinnias have been getting top marks in the
Michigan State University annual trial garden for years.
Narrow dark-green foliage supports a multitude of small
white, orange, or yellow daisies. Classic zinnia flowers
like crazy until frost. It would be impossible to discuss
classic zinnia without mentioning the common zinnia,
Zinnia elegans, a well-loved and easy-to-grow but sometimes disease-prone summer beauty. This is the definitive
cut-and-come-again annual; the more flowers you pick,
the more flowers are produced. A bouquet of zinnias is
one of summer's delights.

Bloom Period and Seasonal Color
Early summer to frost in white, yellow, pink, red,
and orange.

Mature Height × Spread
8 to 24 in. × 1 to 2 ft.

Zones
To Zone 4

When, Where, and How to Plant
Zinnias are not frost-tolerant, and seed won't germinate—it may even rot—in cold soil. Wait until a
week or so after the frost-free date to sow seed or set
out transplants. Full sun is best for zinnias. Zinnias
prefer fertile, well-drained soil. Classic zinnia is
more tolerant of poor, dry soils than is common
zinnia. Follow the directions for planting annuals
on page 23. Zinnias are simple to grow from seed,
which can be directly sown in the garden after the
ground has warmed. Germination will take five to
seven days. Space plants of classic zinnia 6 to 10 in.
apart and common zinnia 8 to 18 in. apart.

Growing Tips
Zinnias flourish in hot, dry summers, but water
regularly during dry spells. Classic zinnia is more
drought-tolerant than common zinnia. A liquid
fertilizer applied every three to four weeks at the
rate recommended on the package will promote
healthy, strong growth.

Care
Classic zinnia is pest- and disease-free and never
needs deadheading or support. Plants of the common zinnia, especially the tall cutting types,
should be pinched to promote bushy, well-
branched forms. Taller types may need staking.
Remove flowers as they fade. All zinnias are
susceptible to foliar diseases. Avoid sprinklers, and
water at ground level to keep the leaves dry.

Companion Planting and Design
Both types work well in garden beds and borders.
Use classic zinnia for edging, sunny patios, and
annual and perennial beds. White selections are
easy to use in the garden, mixing effortlessly with
other colors. Try them with bright-pink portulaca
and purple verbena in a hot site. Common zinnia
can also be planted in vegetable gardens for
cut flowers.

We Recommend
Several selections of classic zinnia are available,
and, except for flower color, they are quite similar.
'Crystal White' has larger flowers. Choose disease-
resistant selections of common zinnia. 'Scarlet
Splendor', another All-America Selections winner,
boasts 4- to 5-in. red flowers. It has performed well
in Michigan.

Groundcovers *for Michigan*

Groundcovers are often described as being carpetlike because they spread over a large area, forming a dense mat. And just as there are many kinds of carpets, there are many different groundcovers for the garden.

Bringing Life to the Garden

Grass is by far the most popular way to cover the soil "wall to wall," but there are also scores of attractive groundcover options. These can bring life to the garden in much the same way a well-placed Oriental rug can bring interest to a living room.

Some groundcovers are just a few inches tall but will run quickly over the soil surface. Ajuga, for example, grows low, with its leaves so tightly packed together that it creates the effect of a rippling sea of bronze and green. Other plants used as groundcovers may be taller and form spreading clumps. The dwarf Chinese astilbe is twelve inches tall and has a fernlike texture and an overall delicate effect.

Some groundcovers stay a deep-green color all year; others are variegated, purple or maroon, and

deciduous or semievergreen. Some have tiny insignificant flowers, while others have beautiful blooms. Many plants beyond the Big Three—pachysandra, ivy, and vinca—can be used as groundcovers if planted in a mass.

Use groundcovers to unify and tie together various garden elements. Their rich colors and textures form a strong horizontal layer to contrast with trees, shrubs, and other plants. Groundcovers can border a lawn, spread under trees, and meander into woodland gardens. Although most widely used in full to partial shade, there are groundcovers for sunny areas, too.

The groundcovers selected for this book are easy to grow and, once established in a favorable site, require little care. Groundcovers sometimes thrive where lawns struggle or are hard to maintain, as in deep shade or on a hard-to-mow slope. They can be a viable low-maintenance and environmentally sound alternative to a lawn.

Groundcovers perform other tricks, too. Their leaves disguise the ripening foliage of daffodils and other spring bulbs. They often grow so densely that their planting areas stay weed-free, which is good news for gardeners who want to maintain an attractive area with minimum maintenance. Evergreen groundcovers give the pleasure of green, full-of-life color even in dreary January and February.

If the only groundcovers you've met so far are pachysandra, ivy, and vinca, read on. You're about to make the acquaintance of some new and useful plants.

Choosing the Right Groundcover

Look at private and public gardens for ways to use groundcovers in your area. Pay attention to heights, textures, and overall effects. Consider how much groundcover you'll need and where you can obtain it. Due to their spreading nature, most herbaceous groundcovers are easy to propagate by division in spring. They are also available at garden centers or through mail-order catalogs.

Find a groundcover that will be appropriate for your soil and exposure. Plants selected specifically for a site will have the best chance of being healthy, growing vigorously, and creating dense mats. Beware of certain fast-spreading groundcovers such as goutweed or others described as vigorous or aggressive. These can turn into invasive garden thugs. Even traditional groundcovers such as vinca and English ivy may spread into nearby natural areas, choking out the native plants.

Planting a Groundcover

Soil preparation for groundcovers is just as important as it is for a new lawn or perennial bed. Mark the outline of the area to be planted and remove turf and weeds. A soil test will determine if any nutrients are required.

Unless the area is immediately surrounding a mature shade tree, loosen the soil to a depth of six to twelve inches, depending on the type of groundcover being planted. Correct drainage problems and work in well-rotted compost, aged manure, leaf mold, or other organic material to improve heavy clay or sandy soils.

It's risky to plant a groundcover right around the base of a large shade tree. The tree's feeder roots are close to the soil surface and extensive digging can damage them. Rather than turning the soil over for the whole area, dig only small pockets, amend with organic material, and plant the groundcover into the holes.

For larger plantings that are not under mature trees, prepare the bed, cover it with a two- to three-inch layer of mulch, then set out the groundcover containers. Spacing depends on each groundcover's growth rate and how fast you want the plants to completely cover the soil. Closer spacing will result in rapid cover. Planting farther apart is more economical, but it will take several years to cover the area. See individual entries for more on spacing.

Start planting at the rear of the bed. Remove the groundcover gently from its container and plant, pulling the mulch away from the area surrounding the crown. The groundcovers should be positioned so they are at the same level they were in their containers.

Water after planting and during dry periods until the groundcover is well established. Weeding is crucial until the plants fill in. After that happens, maintenance chores are few. As long as the soil is average or better and groundcovers are planted in sites that match their light and drainage requirements, they should required little extra fertilizer. Those selected for this book are relatively free of insect and disease problems.

Creating a Tapestry

In addition to entries in this chapter, other plants in this book can be used for groundcovers. You'll find mention of these in the chapters on perennials, woodland plants and ferns, and shrubs.

Combine plants that cover the ground for a tapestry effect. Intermingle drifts of plants with similar cultural requirements. Add bulbs for spring interest, and the distinction between groundcover planting and the rest of the garden becomes delightfully blurred.

Bigroot Geranium

Geranium macrorrhizum

Geranium macrorrhizum *earns its place among the hardy geraniums. Hardy in every sense of the word, bigroot geranium truly stands up to adversity. Add beautiful and easy-to-grow to its list of attributes, and you've got a perennial groundcover with a place in almost any Michigan garden. The common name, bigroot geranium, describes its thick, fleshy roots, which give it the ability to overcome root competition and drought to form a dense groundcover. Its lobed leaves create a beautiful texture over the surface of the soil. The foliage has a unique feature—fragrance—that separates bigroot geranium from any other. The crushed leaves emit a distinctive "piney fresh" clean scent. In addition to the scalloped foliage, this tough geranium has attractive flowers and bronzy scarlet fall color.*

Bloom Period and Seasonal Color

Pink, rose, or white flowers in late spring.

Mature Height × Spread

12 to 15 in. × 18 to 24 in.

When, Where, and How to Plant

Plant container-grown bigroot geranium in spring or September. With adequate moisture, it may also be planted in summer. *Geranium macrorrhizum* prefers partial shade and well-drained soil. It will grow in full sun if provided with moisture-retentive soil and a layer of mulch. Bigroot geranium tolerates dry shade, but it isn't for hot, dry locations. Plant 12 to 15 in. apart. Dig holes and position the plant so that the soil level is the same that it was in the pot. Keep moist until established.

Growing Tips

Although tolerant of dry conditions, bigroot geranium should be watered during drought for best performance. Plants in full sun may need extra irrigation. In soils of low fertility, fertilize in the spring with a light application of balanced fertilizer such as 10-10-10.

Care

For propagation or rejuvenation, divide plants in the spring. Dig clumps and break apart, and replant pieces, each with a portion of thick stem and root. The rosettes of foliage on rhizome-like stems produce roots, and you can plant a section with few or no roots and still have success. Firm the soil around the new divisions, and keep moist until established. A layer of mulch is beneficial. There are no pests or diseases to bother bigroot geranium except voles.

Companion Planting and Design

Use this hardy geranium as a groundcover under woody plants, in shady beds by the house, as an overplanting for bulbs, or in a perennial border. It complements shrub roses and spring bulbs. Ideal with daffodils, the geranium's foliage expands to mask the dying foliage of the daffodils.

We Recommend

Several good cultivars are available. 'Album' is a notable selection with white flowers and pinkish-red calyces. 'Ingwersen's Variety' has pale-pink flowers and glossy foliage. We highly recommend *Geranium × cantabrigiense*, a hybrid between bigroot geranium and Dalmatian cranesbill. It has a ground-hugging habit and a multitude of flowers. Many other geraniums make superior groundcovers. (See the entry for hardy geranium in the chapter on perennials.)

Bugleweed

Ajuga reptans

When, Where, and How to Plant

Container-grown ajuga may be planted from spring to early fall. Keep new transplants watered during hot weather. Bugleweed prefers partial shade and moist, humus-rich soil. Plant it in a well-drained area to avoid disease such as crown rot. If the soil is heavy or infertile, amend before planting. Space plants 8 to 12 in. apart. Water after planting and during dry periods until the plants are established. Mulch to conserve moisture.

Growing Tips

Bugleweed requires no special care other than occasional watering during dry weather. Plants in sun, however, require additional water. A general fertilizer such as 10-10-10 may be applied in the spring.

Care

The plants may be sheared after flowering to encourage new foliage and improve the appearance. Variegated forms will occasionally revert back to green. Remove the green-leaved pieces to maintain the true coloration. Take divisions by separating the leaf rosettes that form at the end of the creeping aboveground stems called stolons, or lift clumps and split apart. Crown rot can wipe out whole patches of bugleweed. Destroy infected plants and contact your county extension agent for control measures. Bugleweed is susceptible to aphid infestations that cause the leaves to curl. Control is usually unnecessary.

Companion Planting and Design

Bugleweed is one of the fastest growing groundcovers and is useful for small- to medium-sized areas. Its foliage and low habit make it a useful contrast to landscape plants, particularly shrubs, hostas, and astilbes. Bugleweed makes a fine, if somewhat assertive, groundcover in a woodland garden with ferns, hostas, and other perennials in a lightly shaded corner. Use ajuga where you want a dense mat covering the soil surface. Use it to border a path or as a strip along the edge of a patio where it can be contained by hard surfaces.

We Recommend

Interesting cultivars include 'Bronze Beauty', which has metallic bronze foliage and deep-blue flowers, and 'Catlin's Giant', with purple-green foliage.

Ajuga or bugleweed really deserves the label "groundcover." Its glossy, deeply veined leaves spread quickly to form a rippled carpet of green, purple, bronze, or variegated colors over the soil surface. The spikes of flowers, usually blue, appear above the low-growing leaves in May and early June, creating drifts of color that complement spring-blooming shrubs. The leaves remain a selling point all season. Plant bugleweed in shady banks, under flowering shrubs, along driveways and patios, or beneath hedges. The best place is where the area will meet a hard surface such as pavement or brick. Ajuga is an aggressive spreader and will quickly invade a lawn, so select another groundcover if you need one to border grass.

Other Name
Ajuga

Bloom Period and Seasonal Color
Late spring in blue or sometimes pink.

Mature Height × Spread
3 to 10 in. × 12 to 14 in.

Canadian Wild Ginger

Asarum canadense

Mix Canadian wild ginger with woodland plantings of spring wildflowers, ferns, and other shade-loving plants. Wild ginger's bold low-growing leaves are heart- or kidney-shaped and about six inches wide with a surface that is slightly fuzzy yet satiny, like sueded silk. It's easy to miss the small maroon flowers, which are hidden under the leaves near the base of the plant in spring, but the urn-shaped blooms are so unusual that they're worth a close look. The strong scent of the rhizomes of this Michigan native accounts for its common name. In a suitable location, Canadian wild ginger spreads by rhizomes to form large stands. New varieties of wild ginger, many from Asia and the southeastern United States, are highly prized by collector gardeners.

Bloom Period and Seasonal Color
Maroon flowers in spring; grown for green foliage.

Mature Height × Spread
4 to 6 in. × 12 in.

When, Where, and How to Plant
Plant about 8 in. apart in spring or early fall in a woodland setting or cool, shady spot of the garden. If necessary, enrich the soil before planting by digging in shredded leaves or other organic matter. Dig a hole as deep as the container and twice as wide. Water the transplants regularly while they become established. Wild ginger will spread in organically rich soil with adequate moisture.

Growing Tips
In the fall, allow tree leaves to remain in place, or mulch beds with shredded leaves. The leaves break down gradually, releasing nutrients. No other fertilizer is required. Water wild ginger during dry spells.

Care
Remove any remaining leaves in early spring before new ones emerge. Plants may be divided in the spring. Dig up a clump and cut the rhizomes into sections. Replant at the same depth it was growing previously. Wild ginger has few pest or disease problems. Some people's skin is sensitive to compounds in its leaves.

Companion Planting and Design
Canadian wild ginger is an ideal groundcover under trees or evergreens in partial shade. Its handsome, persistent foliage makes it an ideal companion for woodland ephemerals like bloodroot and Virginia bluebells, which go dormant in the summer. Add Jack-in-the-pulpit and trillium to recreate a Michigan woodland association. The broad leaves of Canadian wild ginger are an appealing contrast with maidenhair and other finely textured ferns, and with sweet woodruff, *Galium odoratum*. Underplant Canadian wild ginger with snowdrops, squills or 'Tete-a-Tete' narcissi. These early-spring bulbs will be finished blooming by the time the Canadian wild ginger leaves reach their mature size.

We Recommend
European wild ginger, *Asarum europaeum*, has bright glossy leaves that may be evergreen in protected locations. The leaves have a more formal effect than those of Canadian wild ginger.

Creeping Juniper

Juniperus horizontalis

When, Where, and How to Plant

Plant in spring or early fall. Full sun is important for strong, dense growth. Plants in shade will become leggy and open with age and will not make effective groundcovers. Creeping junipers can be used in many difficult garden situations, from sandy, dry soils to heavy clay. They are adaptable to slightly acidic and alkaline soils. Space plants at least 3 to 4 ft. apart because they spread over time. Plant as a container-grown or balled-and-burlapped shrub. See the shrub chapter introduction for details on planting.

Growing Tips

Once established, creeping juniper won't require watering. It has low fertility requirements and won't require extra fertilization.

Care

Twig blight, *Phomopsis juniperovora*, is a common ailment of junipers that develops in the early spring, particularly in wet weather. The tips of the branches become a reddish brown, eventually turning an ash gray as needles die. Remove infected branches by pruning back to healthy growth. To avoid infection altogether, plant in open, dry areas and provide good drainage. Do not use overhead irrigation on your juniper plantings; this provides the moist conditions that favor disease development.

Companion Planting and Design

Use creeping juniper to cover a steep slope, to fill in a rough spot, or anywhere you need winter color. Its salt tolerance makes it useful along walks and driveways where deicing salts are commonly used. The evergreen foliage of creeping juniper sets off shrubs with attractive bark and stems. Creeping juniper complements perennial plantings and is superb in a rock garden or on top of a stone wall.

We Recommend

A wide range of cultivars exists with different heights, textures, foliage color, and winter color. 'Blue Chip' has excellent blue needle color, purplish winter color, and a low spreading habit. It may even reach 8 to 10 ft. wide. 'Wiltonii' or 'Blue Rug' is an extremely low-growing form, topping out at 4 to 6 in. The foliage is silvery blue, turning light purple in the winter months.

One doesn't have to travel far from the beaches of Lake Michigan to find incredible juniper plants spread low and wide in the hottest, driest sandy soils imaginable. Their performance in nature is a sure sign that these wild plants can be a valuable addition to our cultivated landscapes. Spreading to form an impenetrable weed barrier, creeping juniper offers steel blue or bluish-gray needles, attractive blue berries, and a striking purplish hue over the winter. Creeping juniper's toughness has led to extensive use in commercial landscapes, but its public persona shouldn't challenge its appeal. With a little imagination, the gardener can find a range of creative uses for this stalwart ground-covering shrub. For a spring surprise, grow Dutch crocus through its low horizontal branches.

Bloom Period and Seasonal Color
Grown for its bluish green or steel-blue foliage.

Mature Height × Spread
1 to 2 ft. × 4 to 6 ft.

Dwarf Chinese Astilbe

Astilbe chinensis var. *pumila*

Astilbes require dappled shade and rich, moist soil, but this dwarf form of Chinese astilbe bends the rules. It endures sun or dry shade and less-than-rich soil. Not a clump-former like most astilbes, this carpeting perennial spreads by underground stems to form a weedproof mat. An excellent groundcover, dwarf Chinese astilbe grows at a moderate pace and never becomes invasive. The medium-textured, ferny foliage, bronzy when new, hugs the ground. From late July through September, rose-purple flowers are borne on stiff spikes. They aren't as spectacular as the feathery plumes of the more familiar hybrid astilbe, but they add flowers to shade gardens when not much else is in bloom. Later, the flowering stalks provide interest in the winter garden.

Bloom Period and Seasonal Color
Rose-purple flowers in midsummer.

Mature Height × Spread
8 to 12 in. × 18 in.

When, Where, and How to Plant
Plant container-grown plants in the spring or September. Dwarf Chinese astilbe prefers partial shade and moist, rich, well-drained soil. It has proven to be tougher than other astilbes, tolerating sun in heavy, moist soil and dry soil in shade. Plant container-grown plants at the same depth they were growing in their pots. Space at approximately 12 to 18 in. depending on how large the plants are and how rapidly you want coverage. Keep well watered until established. Mulch plants for best results.

Growing Tips
In sun, dwarf astilbe will need watering during dry spells. With sun and dry soil, the foliage cups, indicating water stress, or it may scorch. In soils of low fertility, fertilize plants in the spring with a light application of balanced fertilizer such as 10-10-10.

Care
Dwarf Chinese astilbe is pest- and disease-free. You can remove the flowering spikes if you don't like their appearance when they turn brown. If left on the plant, however, they will persist into winter, providing attractive contrast against snow. Dwarf Chinese astilbe can be spread to form large sweeps. To increase your planting, divide plants in the spring when the foliage is emerging. Dig sections to be divided, and separate into pieces with a knife or sharp spade. Replant at the same level, and keep well watered until new roots form. You can also use a spade to make divisions without lifting the entire planting.

Companion Planting and Design
Plant in partial shade as a groundcover under trees and shrubs, in a shade garden, or in moist, sunny perennial beds. For an interesting tapestry of ground-covering plants, use dwarf Chinese astilbe with the satiny leaves of Canadian wild ginger, big-root geranium, and hosta in partial shade.

We Recommend
Plants sold as *Astilbe chinensis* var. *pumila* may vary somewhat in height and color. Plants may also be given the cultivar name 'Pumila'. 'Veronica Klose' has flowers in a richer shade of pink. 'Finale' has light-pink flowers.

When, Where, and How to Plant

Container-grown plants can be planted in spring and September. Native to the moist woods of Asia, barrenwort prefers partial shade and rich, moist, well-drained soils. Many epimediums will tolerate dry, shady conditions. Plant in the garden 12 to 14 in. apart. Dig holes and position the plant so the soil level is the same as it was in the pot. Water thoroughly.

Growing Tips

Although remarkably drought-tolerant, epimedium should be watered during extended dry spells. In average soils, fertilization should be unnecessary.

Care

These plants are pest- and disease-free. If you leave the foliage for winter interest, cut it back in early spring to make way for the flowers. To increase your planting, divide clumps in the spring when new growth is just emerging. Lift plants to be divided, and pull apart the shallow fibrous roots into clumps. Replant in the garden at the same depth. Keep moist until established. Mulch to conserve moisture.

Companion Planting and Design

Plant in the shade garden, as a shady foundation planting, in a woodland garden, and as a under-planting for trees and flowering shrubs. Combine epimedium with the bigroot geranium and wild oats for an appealing contrast of color and texture and year-round interest in the shade.

We Recommend

A range of species and cultivars of barrenwort exists. All are excellent for partial shade and may be used as a groundcover or as a shade perennial. *Epimedium × versicolor* is a vigorous choice for use as a groundcover. The red barrenwort, *E. × rubrum*, hardy to Zone 4, forms spreading clumps. It has crimson and white flowers, foliage stained garnet red in the spring, and reddish fall color. Another great choice, the longspur barrenwort, *E. grandiflorum*, has showy flowers with delicate spurs. The best selections are 'Rose Queen' with purple-pink flowers and 'White Queen' with long-spurred white flowers. Both have bronzy leaves in early spring.

The glossy heart-shaped leaflets of epimedium, sometimes called barrenwort or bishop's hat, form a beautiful carpet under trees and shrubs. In mid-spring, delicate sprays of little spurred flowers arise from the ground on wiry stems. The foliage, often suffused with bronzy red as it emerges, provides a coppery hue to the fall garden. Although initially slow, once established, barrenwort forms a handsome weed-free carpet. Epimedium can take abuse and yet remain attractive all season. Some epimediums are very tough, tolerating difficult dry shade. In mid-Michigan, hybrid epimedium has prospered with the root competition under the dense shade of a Colorado blue spruce. Excellent as a groundcover, barrenwort also makes a delightful addition to a shade or woodland garden.

Other Name
Barrenwort

Bloom Period and Seasonal Color
Mid-spring in yellow, rose, orange, or white.

Mature Height × Spread
8 to 12 in. × 12 to 18 in.

Zones
To Zone 5

Japanese Sedge
Carex morrowii

Ornamental grasses have become popular garden plants over the last decade or so and are becoming more common in our landscapes. Japanese sedge is not technically a grass, but it acts like one in the garden. The habit of Japanese sedge is mounded, forming a grasslike hummock. Massed, it makes an elegant, fine-textured groundcover. Its clumps of highly ornamental leaf blades are often striped, offering bold or subtle variegation. 'Ice Dance', a recent introduction with a beautiful creamy white coloration, spreads slowly from underground shoots. Sedges are easy-care plants that demand little help from the gardener after planting but receive much admiration for the graceful beauty they add to the garden.

Bloom Period and Seasonal Color
Grown primarily for the striped foliage.

Mature Height × Spread
12 to18 in. × 12 to 18 in.

Zones
To Zone 5

When, Where, and How to Plant
Plant Japanese sedge in the spring for the best results. Choose locations in partial shade with moist, well-drained soils. Avoid dry situations. Plant according to the general directions for planting groundcovers on page 50.

Growing Tips
Keep newly planted sedges moist until established, and provide water during extended dry spells. For groundcover plantings, apply a 2-in. layer of organic mulch, like composted leaves, to conserve moisture and reduce weeds. The Japanese sedge and its cultivars will produce more luxuriant growth if you apply a balanced 10-10-10 fertilizer to the garden bed before new growth emerges in spring.

Care
Sedges are rarely bothered by insect or disease problems. Cut back old foliage in early spring before new growth emerges. Foliage from the previous growing season insulates the crown of the plant, so withhold cutting back until spring. Plants can be divided every three years or so if they lack vigor or to increase your stock.

Companion Planting and Design
Massed, this sedge creates a low-maintenance groundcover with a slowly spreading habit. The fine texture of sedges, unusual in the shade, provides interesting contrast with other woodland denizens such as hosta, Solomon's seal, and the many colorful selections of coralbells and foamflower that are available. Variegated selections bring light to shaded areas.

We Recommend
'Silk Tassels' is a beautiful selection with very fine variegation on the thread-thin foliage. It creates a graceful, low-growing 6-in. groundcover. The palm sedge, *Carex muskingumensis*, sounds exotic, but it is one of our most beautiful native sedges. The stems flare upwards off a central stalk and radiate in all directions with a drooping effect. Found in moist habitats in nature, it deserves a place in the garden where it can receive rich soil and a steady supply of moisture. Try it near ponds or other water features.

When, Where, and How to Plant

Plant container-grown spotted dead nettle in the spring and late September. With adequate watering, they may also be planted in summer. Lamium prefers moist, well-drained soil in partial shade. Plant 12 to 18 in apart. Dig holes and position the plant so that the soil level is the same as it was in the pot. In partial shade, plants will fill in quickly. Water well after planting.

Growing Tips

Lamium is not drought-tolerant. Water spotted dead nettle during dry spells, especially where there is competition from tree roots. In the average shady garden, lamium won't need extra fertilizer. Mulch to conserve moisture.

Care

Spotted dead nettle can get leggy and sparse if planted where there is too much root competition. Shear it back to keep it compact and force fresh new foliage. You may also want to shear lamium back after flowering to keep plants compact and create denser cover. Dead nettle is easy to divide. In spring or early summer, dig sections and pull apart. Replant and keep new divisions moist until established in their new location. If sited correctly, pests and disease shouldn't be a concern.

Companion Planting and Design

Use lamium in drifts with other shade-lovers for an attractive mix. The silver-streaked foliage of dead nettle is attractive with bulbs, particularly those with white flowers such as summer snowflake and 'Thalia' daffodil. The silver variegation also sets off the color of blue-foliaged hostas. Try the vase-shaped 'Krossa Regal' hosta underplanted with lamium 'White Nancy' for an elegant mix of silver, white, and green.

We Recommend

Cultivated selections of dead nettle have various amounts of variegation, different flower colors, and more compact, spreading growth. 'Beacon Silver' has rose-purple flowers and silver leaves with narrow green borders. 'White Nancy' is attractive and has wider green margins than 'Beacon Silver'. 'Beedham's White' has the novel combination of bright yellow-green leaves with a creamy stripe.

Lamium brings sparkle to the shade. Each green leaf is marked with a stroke, splash, or almost complete coat of silver, adding light to dim parts of the garden. Lamium grows quickly, rooting at the leaf joints to form an appealing groundcover. The short flower spikes, although not the main attraction, create quite a show. The spring blooms are typically deep rose-pink, but cultivars exist with pale pink and white flowers. Use spotted dead nettle as a groundcover under trees and shrubs, on a shaded slope, in shade gardens, and as a cover for bulbs. The prettiest and most useful types are those with a broad stripe of silver down the middle of the leaf. The variegation creates movement, mimicking the appearance of dappled light.

Other Name

Spotted Dead Nettle

Bloom Period and Seasonal Color

Late spring in rose-pink, pale pink, and white.

Mature Height × Spread

8 to 12 in. × 12 to 16 in.

Lily-of-the-Valley

Convallaria majalis

About the same time that daffodils are blooming, the sturdy green shoots of lily-of-the-valley are pushing up from the soil. By mid-May, dainty stalks arch over the leaves and bear the white ball-like buds. As they open, lily-of-the-valley releases its sweet fragrance, which for many gardeners is the essence of spring. Lily-of-the-valley spreads by rhizomes, or underground stems, and will quickly carpet an area with part sun, part shade, or even full shade. In fact, lily-of-the-valley is such a strong grower that it can be invasive. Keep it within bounds with barriers, or place it where the plant's spreading nature is a plus, such as a groundcover under shrubs. Note that lily-of-the-valley is toxic, including the red-orange fruits it sometimes bears in fall.

Bloom Period and Seasonal Color
White or pale-pink flowers in late spring.

Mature Height × Spread
6 to 8 in. × 12 to 18 in.

When, Where, and How to Plant
Container-grown plants may be planted from April through September. Sections of lily-of-the-valley rhizomes or underground stems with two or three pips, which are shoots or "eyes," should be planted in spring. Place in part to full shade. Lily-of-the-valley prefers moisture-retentive soil but will grow nearly anywhere that isn't under water. If the plants are grown in full sun and it is hot and dry, the leaves will become yellow and ratty as the summer progresses. Pot-grown plants should be spaced 8 to 12 in. apart. Sections of rhizomes can be set 6 in. apart and 1 to 2 in. deep.

Growing Tips
Once established, lily-of-the-valley needs little care. Water during hot, dry periods to extend the life of the foliage. Some gardeners topdress the plants with well-rotted compost or aged manure in late fall. Plants grown beneath trees will require additional water and fertilizer.

Care
Lily-of-the-valley is not prone to pest and disease problems. After leaves die in the fall, rake out the foliage. Plants that are producing fewer flowers than in previous seasons may be dug and divided in spring or fall.

Companion Planting and Design
The best use is as a groundcover in a defined shady area that will not receive foot traffic. Lily-of-the-valley is valuable for covering slopes to prevent erosion. Combine it with ferns, hostas, and astilbes. It can be a nuisance in perennial borders. Its value as a groundcover is in late spring and summer; by August, the leaves begin to look ratty, especially if the plants are grown in sun and there has been little rain. Still, lily-of-the-valley has strengths, including the ability to grow under shade trees where few other plants will survive.

We Recommend
'Fortin's Giant' (12 to 15 in.) has large leaves and flowers and is a vigorous grower. 'Flore Pleno' has double flowers. Also try var. *rosea*, which has flowers in pale pink and is not as invasive as the other two.

Mother-of-Thyme
Thymus praecox ssp. *arcticus*

When, Where, and How to Plant

Plant thyme in the spring to early summer. It prefers full sun and dry, free-draining soil of moderate to low fertility. It will grow in heavier soils and a bit of shade, but growth will be leggy in partial shade. It won't tolerate poor drainage. Space plants of creeping thyme about 12 in. apart. Smaller selections should be spaced closer together. Dig holes and position the plant so that the soil level is the same that it was in the pot. Don't plant too deep or plants may rot. Firm the soil and water well.

Growing Tips

Keep moist until established. Once established, thyme shouldn't need watering or fertilizer.

Care

If located in sun and dry soil, thyme will have few pest and disease problems. Rot can be a problem in wet sites. Thyme doesn't like to be heavily mulched. Some thymes develop a semi-woody habit. In the spring your plants may have some dieback. Cut back hard to live wood to promote compact growth. Thyme is easily divided in spring. Dig clumps and pull apart into sections for replanting.

Companion Planting and Design

This creeping groundcover is perfect for planting by sunny patios and in perennial beds. Use it to advantage by letting it spill over onto walks or over the top of rock walls. Mother-of-thyme is useful for filling in between pavers or the risers of sunny steps, but it can't withstand the pressures of heavy traffic. Use creeping thyme to weave together a range of perennials. For a sunny patio, combine a variety of thymes with lavender, sedums, lamb's ears, and star-of-Persia.

We Recommend

Mother-of-thyme suffers from a confusing array of botanical names. *Thymus praecox* ssp. *arcticus* is the current accepted name, but plants are often offered for sale as *Thymus serpyllum*. We like the cultivar 'Coccineus' for its reddish-purple flowers on dark stems and dark green leaves. It turns bronzy in the winter.

The fine-textured mats of mother-of-thyme blanket the ground. When the plant is crushed or trod upon, a fragrance both savory and invigorating fills the air. It's not surprising that thyme has been used for centuries as a healthful tonic. Mother-of-thyme, sometimes called creeping thyme, forms carpets of small glossy leaves topped in late spring and early summer with round clusters of tiny rose-lavender flowers. Although widely used as a groundcover and in perennial gardens, thyme is still considered first and foremost an herb. So when shopping for mother-of-thyme, look in the herb section of nursery catalogs and garden centers or you may miss out. In places where thyme is growing well—full sun and well-drained soil—underplant with species tulips for a spring treat.

Other Name
Creeping Thyme

Bloom Period and Seasonal Color
Late spring to early summer in rosy purple, pink, or white.

Mature Height × Spread
1 to 6 in. × 10 to 12 in.

Pachysandra
Pachysandra terminalis

Among the "Big Three" evergreen groundcovers, pachy-sandra is the most popular. Unlike ivy and vinca, pachysandra does not have the potential to be invasive, so it is a fine choice for gardeners throughout much of Michigan. Its glossy, notched leaves are pachysandra's trademark. Although the leaves droop a bit in extreme cold, they remain a welcome sight all year. The white flowers usually appear in late winter to early spring. Pachysandra is at home in the casual woodland garden as well as on a formal estate. It is often planted as an elegant groundcover to sweep around the bases of trees and shrubs. Even heavy shade, such as the kind found under maples, will not deter pachysandra from creating a lush swath of green.

Other Name
Japanese Spurge

Bloom Period and Seasonal Color
White flowers in spring.

Mature Height × Spread
6 to 10 in. × 8 to 12 in.

Zones
To Zone 4

When, Where, and How to Plant
Container-grown pachysandra may be set out in spring or summer. Plant pachysandra in part to full shade to ensure healthy, attractive growth. Although it will not be as vigorous where exposed to full afternoon sun, pachysandra will survive if it receives adequate moisture. Set 6 in. apart for good cover. Pachysandra is a slower grower than some other groundcovers. If spaced farther apart, it will take several years to fill in, increasing the need for weeding. Mulch new plants to conserve moisture and discourage weeds.

Growing Tips
Water plants during dry spells. Soaker hoses are useful to water large plantings. In late winter, pachysandra may be fertilized with 10-10-10 or a fertilizer for acid-loving plants and watered well.

Care
Once pachysandra is established, it is so dense that weeds are usually not a problem. Pinch off any browned leaves in late winter to improve the plant's appearance. The plants may be divided in spring to early summer. In full sun, leaf scorch may occur. Leaf blight can infect stressed pachysandra plantings and ruin them. Outbreaks are most frequent in warm, humid weather and on plants that were previously injured from winter damage, recent transplanting, or shearing, or stressed from placement in full sun. Healthy, vigorous plants resist leaf blight. To treat leaf blight, contact your county extension agent.

Companion Planting and Design
Pachysandra is a gorgeous evergreen groundcover for full to partial shade. Send it spreading under deciduous trees and shrubs or tall evergreens. Plant bulbs such as daffodils within beds of pachysandra to add seasonal interest.

We Recommend
'Green Carpet' pachysandra is a standard. Pachysandra 'Variegata' has green-and-white variegated leaves that shine in deep shade, although it is less vigorous. 'Green Sheen' pachysandra has remarkable glossy leaves. *Pachysandra procumbens* is the Allegheny spurge, native to woodlands of the southeastern United States. It is attractive with spring wildflowers and hardy to Zone 5.

Hardy Bulbs *for Michigan*

Gardeners bury hardy bulbs in the garden as colder weather hints at the approach of winter, leaves are falling from the trees, and garden flowers are turning brown and dying. Even as one season is ending, the gardener who plants hardy bulbs celebrates the certain renewal of life come spring.

A Welcome Sight

Nothing is more welcome in February or March than yellow winter aconites or a crisp white snowdrop nodding from a bright-green stem. Later in the growing season, when showier plants are in flower, these tiny blossoms might go unnoticed. But at the end of a grueling winter, they are a harbinger of spring and a cause for joy.

Spring bulbs add bloom to a season of little color. They create dramatic displays, offer surprises around the base of a tree, and make elegant combinations with shrubs and perennials.

Many hardy bulbs excel in woodland gardens, where their natural beauty is perfect under trees. The bulbs receive sun so they can bloom before the trees finish leafing out in spring and shade the area.

Plant hardy spring-blooming bulbs in perennial beds and where annuals will be planted in late May or early June. Naturalize bulbs in turf and lower-maintenance areas as well as under roses, in groundcovers, and under shrubs.

Planting Hardy Bulbs

Hardy bulbs, which also include certain corms, tubers, and rhizomes, are planted in September and October, spend the winter in the frozen ground, and generally flower from March to late May. Lilies, which bloom in summer, are planted in fall or spring.

In contrast, tender bulbs such as cannas and dahlias will not survive a Michigan winter outdoors. They must be dug up in the fall and stored inside or treated as annuals and replanted in late spring each year.

When buying bulbs, select the largest ones and avoid any that are shriveled, soft, or moldy. As with all garden plants, it is important

to prepare the bed before planting. Bulbs will rot if they stand in water over the winter, so good drainage is critical. In sandy or heavy soil, dig in organic material such as well-rotted compost or leaf mold. Loosen the soil to about twelve to fourteen inches deep and remove weeds and debris. When planting tulips, choose a site that is not irrigated in the summer; this will help extend their life.

There are several ways to add a fertilizer specifically made for bulbs or a general-purpose fertilizer. If putting fertilizer in individual holes, dig the holes deeper and mix fertilizer well with the soil to avoid burning the bulbs. With a larger bed, incorporate the fertilizer into the entire area before planting, or scratch it into the surface afterward.

Many bulbs are best planted in drifts; others, such as tulips, are appropriate for more formal designs. Check each entry in this section for suggestions. Avoid planting bulbs in single file.

Planting depth depends on bulb size. The general rule is to plant so the base of the bulb is three times as deep as the bulb is wide, although tulips may be planted deeper to extend their life. It can be tempting to cheat on this step if you're planting dozens of bulbs, but best results will be achieved when the bulbs are planted at the proper depth. Make sure no air pockets remain under the bulb. Once the bulbs are planted, replace the soil, firm it, and water the area well.

The biggest threat at planting time is from squirrels, which enjoy digging up and eating certain bulbs. Put an old window screen or wire mesh over the newly planted bed for a few weeks, until the soil settles, and clean all bulb debris, such as the papery outer skins, from the ground around the planting site. Commercial repellents may be applied. Dutch gardeners plant crown fritillarias (*Fritillaria imperialis*) around bulb beds in the belief that rodents are put off by the skunky scent.

After planting the bulbs, continue watering when the soil is dry until the soil freezes. Then the newly planted bulbs may be mulched with shredded bark, evergreen boughs, or shredded leaves.

Caring for Hardy Bulbs

When the first shoots appear in spring, gradually remove the mulch and expose the emerging bulbs. Hardy spring bulbs will not be harmed by a sudden dip in temperatures.

During the first year, the bulbs won't need extra fertilizer. In subsequent years, an early spring fertilizer may be beneficial, especially in soils with poor fertility. Bulbs planted in beds with other flowering plants that are fertilized generally don't need extra feedings.

After the bulbs bloom, leave the foliage on the plants until it turns papery and yellow or brown. While it is still green, the leaves are producing nutrients that aid the bulb in its production of next spring's flowers.

The hardy bulbs' yellowing or ripening foliage, left intact to nourish the bulbs for next year's show, can be hidden by growing perennials and annuals. Hostas and daylilies are often used for this purpose. Their leaves emerge at just the right time to cloak the declining leaves of daffodils and tulips.

Most bulbs will continue flowering for years. Certain tulips, however, may bloom well for only one or two years, then show only leaves thereafter. When flower production declines, these bulbs should be dug and discarded.

Hardy bulbs generally have few pest or disease problems. In spring, deer and rabbits may nibble bulb foliage and flowers; fencing is about the only permanent solution. Daffodils are usually unappealing to deer.

A Smart Investment

Hardy bulbs are a smart gardening investment. They are relatively inexpensive by the dozens or even hundreds. In the right location, many hardy bulbs will multiply and bloom for years, and many make attractive cut flowers.

Like annuals, bulbs are an excellent choice for a splash of color in a beginner's garden, and they are equally capable of providing sophisticated effects.

Autumn Crocus

Colchicum autumnale

The wispy goblet-shaped flowers of autumn crocus emerge on bare stems in late summer and fall. This oddity of timing and form explains some of this curious plant's nicknames: wonder bulb and naked boys. Colchicum grows from a large irregular corm. It produces surprising flowers as autumn approaches, and the following spring it sprouts glossy leaves in mounds ten to fifteen inches high and wide. The leaves present a challenge to gardeners. Although initially attractive, the coarse green foliage turns yellow by early summer, and it must remain in place until the leaves die back naturally. The best place for colchicum is where the ripening foliage won't be an eyesore. This plant is not a true crocus, but the rosy-purple cup-shaped flowers are similar in appearance to those of crocus.

Bloom Period and Seasonal Color
Pink, lavender, and white in late summer and fall.

Mature Height × Spread
4 to 6 in. × 6 in.

Zones
To Zone 4

When, Where, and How to Plant
Autumn crocus corms are sold June to late August. Plant them immediately. Don't delay, or they may flower aboveground. Plant autumn crocus in average, well-drained soil in sun to part sun or shade. Follow the general directions for planting bulbs on page 63. Plant the corm so the base is 3 to 4 in. deep, and space them 6 to 9 in. apart. Once planted, colchicum sends up its flowers within weeks.

Growing Tips
Water after planting. Care is minimal. Water the spring foliage if rain is scarce. Colchicum seldom needs fertilization.

Care
Colchicum are usually free of pests and disease. Let the hosta-like foliage mature fully. This gives the plant the opportunity to make and store nutrients for flowers later in the season. The plants will slowly form colonies if left undisturbed, or they may be lifted, divided, and replanted after three years. The time to do this is after the foliage matures. Note that this plant is considered toxic—use gloves when digging corms.

Companion Planting and Design
Colchicum is also an excellent bulb for rock gardens, under perennials, and among groundcovers. For a fall surprise, plant pink colchicum with multicolored 'Burgundy Glow' ajuga or white autumn crocus with lamb's ears and blue spirea. A groundcover backdrop both sets off and supports the fragile colchicum flowers, which can fall over and get dirty after rainstorms. Colchicum also makes an effective display in groundcover at the edge of a woodland or an area of mixed shrubs. The maturing foliage is not as noticeable in less-formal areas.

We Recommend
Colchicum autumnale is a rosy lilac color and 8 in. tall. *C. autumnale* 'Album' is a subtly beautiful white form. 'Alboplenum' is a spectacular double white form. Many showy colchicums selections are hybrids. 'Lilac Wonder', a very free-flowering selection, has large pink-purple blossoms. As you might expect, the white-centered rosy lilac flowers of 'The Giant' are even larger.

Crocosmia

Crocosmia × crocosmiiflora 'Lucifer'

When, Where, and How to Plant

Plant container-grown plants in the spring to early summer. Corms (sometimes available in summer-flowering bulb catalogs) can be planted in the spring around the frost-free date. Plant 'Lucifer' crocosmia in full sun and fertile, well-drained soil. Plants will tolerate some shade but not poor drainage. For corms, dig holes and plant 5 in. deep. Plant groups of five to seven corms, spaced 2 in. apart, for attractive results. Container-grown crocosmia should be planted in the garden following the general directions for planting perennials on page 102.

Growing Tips

After planting, water thoroughly. Add no special fertilization beyond what is provided for your other perennials. Although somewhat drought-tolerant, crocosmia will be healthier with adequate moisture. Mulch to keep the roots cool and to protect for winter.

Care

Crocosmia is generally pest- and disease-resistant. Spider mites may attack the foliage, but control measures are usually unnecessary. If the population is out of control, use an insecticidal soap according to the directions on the product. Don't be too quick to remove the spent flowers; the seedpods remain attractive until the stalks begin to yellow. Cut back the foliage in the fall after the foliage has matured completely. Divide large clumps in early spring if desired.

Companion Planting and Design

Combine 'Lucifer' with the hot colors of summer—sneezeweed, coreopsis, sunflower heliopsis—or temper the red with a backdrop of bronze fennel or ornamental grasses. Although montbretia mingles successfully with other tall plants, it shines on its own where its architectural presence can be appreciated. Try it in a prominent location rising up from a frothy mass of lavender-blue 'Six Hills Giant' catmint.

We Recommend

In Zones 3 and 4, corms should be lifted in the fall and overwintered indoors. Pack the corms in peat or vermiculite, and store them for the winter in a dark and cool location (about 50 degrees Fahrenheit). Other montbretias are available, but most are not hardy this far north.

The fiery red flowers of Crocosmia 'Lucifer' steal the show from mid-July through August. 'Lucifer' quickly grows from a smallish corm to create a bold season-long presence in the garden. Montbretia appears tropical, and in fact, many catalogs will tell you it isn't hardy in Michigan. It's true that most montbretia can't handle our cold winters, but 'Lucifer' is reliable and easy to grow in Zones 5 and 6. Gardeners in colder areas can lift and store the corms for the winter. The flowers are this plant's most spectacular asset. Arranged in zigzags high on upward-arching stems, the bright tubular trumpets attract hummingbirds. Meanwhile, the plant's swordlike pleated foliage, unusual in the sunny garden, provides a bold accent.

Other Name
Montbretia

Bloom Period and Seasonal Color
Scarlet-red in mid- to late summer.

Mature Height × Spread
3 to 4 ft. × 1 to 2 ft.

Zones
To Zone 5

Crocus

Crocus vernus hybrids

The large flowers of Dutch crocus are the most familiar and most loved of the early-spring bulbs. In glowing shades of yellow, purple, and white, crocuses symbolize springtime, even if the temperature outdoors still feels like winter. Plant crocuses where you will pass them often, such as along a driveway or near a doorway. And plant generously. Five dozen butter-yellow crocuses planted around the base of a tree will soon grow into a swath of color bright enough to boost the spirits of an entire spring-starved neighborhood. Crocuses can be naturalized in lawns if you're willing to mow after the narrow leaves die back on their own. With the right selections, the crocus season can span several weeks in March and April.

Bloom Period and Seasonal Color
Yellow, white, purple, lavender in early spring.

Mature Height × Spread
5 to 6 in. × 4 to 6 in.

When, Where, and How to Plant
Plant the corms in September. Crocuses do well where they receive sun in spring. They may be naturalized or planted randomly under shade trees because they will finish flowering and their leaves ripen before the tree leaves appear. Crocuses prefer well-drained soil. Amend heavy clay before planting. Follow the general instructions for bulb planting on page 63. Plant large-flowered Dutch crocuses about 4 in. deep and 4 in. apart.

Growing Tips
Water after planting to settle the soil. In poor soils, mix bulb fertilizer with the soil before planting. Dutch crocus may be fed again in the fall if performance has dwindled.

Care
Crocus foliage must ripen in place, but this is a much faster process, and the grasslike leaves are less noticeable, than with larger bulbs. The bulbs are usually disease-free, but squirrels and mice find them irresistible. Cover the newly planted area with mesh screening or chicken wire, apply a commercial repellent, or enlist the patrol assistance of a cooperative cat or dog. Crocuses require no additional care.

Companion Planting and Design
Use crocuses for early-spring flowers in borders, rock gardens, and spots you walk or drive by every day, such as near doorways and drives. They look best in clusters of at least seven corms; more is better, and crocuses are available by fifties or hundreds at substantial discounts. Crocuses are charming coming up through groundcover. Make them part of a succession of spring bulbs, including snowdrops, squills, daffodils, tulips, and ornamental onions.

We Recommend
Choose your favorite Dutch crocus from the bulb catalogs. Consider extending the crocus season by planting a range of crocus species. The cheery little flowers of snow crocus, *Crocus chrysanthus*, appear several weeks earlier than those of Dutch crocus. Many selections are available. Another early small crocus, *Crocus tommasinianus*, comes in shades of purple and red-violet. You'll like it, but squirrels don't, and it self-sows to form large colonies.

Daffodil
Narcissus spp. and hybrids

When, Where, and How to Plant

Plant daffodil bulbs in September or early October at the latest. They need about a month to establish roots before the ground freezes. The ideal site is in full sun in spring and dappled shade in summer. Daffodils want plenty of moisture in spring. The soil should be well drained and average to rich in organic matter. Follow the general directions for planting bulbs on page 63. The bulb merchant should have specific instructions on how deep to plant the type purchased.

Growing Tips

Water the bulbs well after planting. If you are using a bulb fertilizer, incorporate it well in the soil before planting to reduce the chance of burning the bulbs. In fall, apply a bulb fertilizer if desired, particularly to mature and crowded clumps.

Care

Daffodils usually withstand diseases and pests. Snap off the seedpod after flowering, but let the foliage mature fully. With daffodils, this can take six weeks or even longer. Some people braid the fading leaves to make them less noticeable—don't do it! It impairs the plants' ability to make food and ensure plentiful blooms for next year. Every five to ten years, the bulbs may be dug and divided to increase stock or reduce crowding.

Companion Planting and Design

Daffodils may be arranged formally, but they have a more natural appeal when planted in quantity as sweeping drifts in beds or at the edge of a wooded area. They also work well in beds and groundcover, near doors, and as an underplanting for shrubs.

We Recommend

Trumpet daffodils, the traditional favorite, have center trumpets that are at least as long as their petals. 'King Alfred' is the prototype. Especially welcome are the early-season cyclamineus hybrids, with their long trumpet and turned-back petals. They are less hardy than the trumpet types. If you garden in Zone 3 or 4, check local sources for daffodils that are hardy in your area.

Dancing in the wind on a brisk spring day, a crowd of bright-yellow daffodils nods and sways in a ballet celebrating the new season. They are the quintessential spring flowers. Narcissus or daffodils are equally at home in natural settings such as under tall trees as well as in more formal landscapes. Daffodils are easy bulbs to grow where the soil is well drained and they can receive full to part sun. Thousands of cultivars are available, and most will increase in number each spring. These bulbs are all classified as narcissus, and there are confusing distinctions among those called narcissus, daffodils, and jonquils. But whatever you call them and however you use them, plant these hardy bulbs. No yard can have too many daffodils.

Other Names
Narcissus, Jonquil

Bloom Period and Seasonal Color
Yellow, pink, peach, and white in spring.

Mature Height × Spread
6 to 18 in. × 6 to 8 in.

Dwarf Iris
Iris reticulata

The miniature blooms of Iris reticulata *invite close exam-ination. Because blooms appear in early spring, this can lead to cold, wet knees—but that's a small price to pay to discover the sweet fragrance and to admire these exquisite flowers. The distinctive iris flowers, with upright standards and downward falls in shades of deep purple and blue, are nestled among the linear four-angled foliage. The falls are often blotched with white or yellow. One of the earliest plants to flower, dwarf iris competes with snowdrops and crocus for first place. It isn't as dependable as crocus, as it needs sharper drainage and sun—but where it finds a suitable home, it will flourish. Plant groupings of dwarf iris for best effect. The more, the merrier!*

Other Name
Reticulated Iris

Bloom Period and Seasonal Color
Blue, purple in early spring.

Mature Height × Spread
4 to 5 in. × 6 in.

Zones
To Zone 4

When, Where, and How to Plant
Plant the teardrop-shaped bulbs of dwarf iris in September through mid-October. Dwarf iris prefers well-drained soil in full sun. It will bloom in partial shade, but it won't thrive. Poor drainage will doom these bulbs. Follow the general directions for planting bulbs on page 63. Plant the bulbs 4 to 5 in. deep, measured from the base of the bulb to the soil surface. Space bulbs 1 to 2 in. apart in natural-looking groups.

Growing Tips
Water the bulbs after planting to settle and moisten the soil. Dwarf iris doesn't require any watering or fertilization.

Care
Dwarf iris has no significant pest or disease problems. Let the foliage mature; it's narrow, grows to almost 12 in. tall, and disappears quickly.

Companion Planting and Design
Plant dwarf iris in the front of a sunny border, on top of a rock wall, near a front walk, or wherever good drainage can be provided. A gravelly free-draining spot or a rock garden is ideal. Combine it with other early-blooming bulbs, or use it to add spring interest to a planting of low-growing sedums and thymes. The dark-purple selections don't stand out well against dark soil and mulch. Use them to better effect in areas with a gravel mulch.

We Recommend
The original species is deep purple. Cultivars are available with sky blue, indigo blue, and a range of color variations. Many cultivars of *Iris reticulata* are available, differing in color and markings. 'Cantab' is pale sky blue with a yellow blotch. 'Purple Gem' is dark purple with a white blotch. *Iris histrioides* has larger blue flowers, which appear slightly earlier than *I. reticulata*. Hybrids exist between the two, such as 'Harmony', a two-tone sky blue and royal blue with a yellow blotch.

When, Where, and How to Plant

Plant the small bulbs of glory-of-the-snow in September through early October. Glory-of-the-snow grows well in all but poorly drained soils. It prefers full sun but tolerates light shade with ease. It will grow through groundcovers and turfgrass and under trees. Follow the general guidelines for planting bulbs on page 63. Plant the bulbs so that they are 3 to 4 in. deep, from the base of the bulb to the soil surface. Space bulbs 1 to 3 in. apart in natural-looking groups.

Growing Tips

Water bulbs after planting. Incorporating bulb fertilizer (9-9-6) into the soil at planting will give the plants a boost. This is an extra step and unnecessary when planting in turf or adding a few bulbs to beds or borders.

Care

Glory-of-the-snow is pest- and disease-free and needs no special care. If naturalizing *Chionodoxa* in lawns, let the foliage mature before mowing.

Companion Planting and Design

Use large quantities, at least 50 to 100 bulbs, for the best effect and economy. Glory-of-the-snow provides an extra layer of interest under small trees and shrubs. Plant naturalistic groupings—not perfect circles—under small trees such as star magnolia and serviceberry or shrubs such as Korean rhododendron. Use sweeps of its blue flowers to add interest to perennial gardens and shrub beds. Glory-of the-snow, while superb on its own, also combines well with other early-spring bulbs. Try it as a complement for species tulips or small early daffodils such as 'Jack Snipe'.

We Recommend

A few cultivars of *Chionodoxa forbesii* are available, offering larger flowers and different colors, but it's hard to beat the delicate form and white-eyed lavender-blue flowers of the species. *Chionodoxa luciliae* (formerly *C. gigantea*) has larger upward-facing flowers. 'Alba' is its white counterpart. *Chionodoxa sardensis* has 3/4-in. flowers in a beautiful shade of clear bright blue with a tiny white eye. It naturalizes freely; a large mass can stop you in your tracks.

As befits their name, the cheery flowers of glory-of-the-snow often get caught by an early-spring snow, a fairly common occurrence in Michigan. Glory-of-the-snow comes on the heels of snowdrops and winter aconites, and all three are a delight to the winter-weary. Glory-of-the-snow has lilac-blue to sky blue star-shaped flowers. The arching stem's relaxed habit causes the flowers to face skyward, revealing the distinctive white eye that distinguishes Chionodoxa *from* Scilla, *the Siberian squill, with which it is sometimes confused. It naturalizes both by seed and offsets to form a memorable blue carpet. For an early-spring lift, try a few dozen in your rose beds or in a perennial herb garden. The starry-eyed presence of glory-of-the-snow is welcome almost anywhere.*

Bloom Period and Seasonal Color
Blue, pink, and white in early spring.

Mature Height × Spread
4 to 5 in. × 4 in.

Zones
To Zone 4

Grape Hyacinth

Muscari armeniacum

Clusters of tiny purple-blue urns top the leafless stems of grape hyacinth, a dependable easy-to-grow bulb. Each tapered cluster of flowers resembles a bunch of grapes. They make a spectacular contrast when grown in front of yellow daffodils or pansies, or under a star magnolia. In Dutch gardens, "rivers" of grape hyacinth run through the landscape, where they set off the flaming hues of tulips. Grape hyacinths multiply readily if they have ample sun, and the stems and foliage die back after flowering. In early fall, the narrow grasslike leaves sprout again; they remain evergreen, though somewhat disheveled, for much of the winter. Although they are native to the Mediterranean region, grape hyacinths thrive in Michigan gardens. Plant these by the dozens, fifties, or hundreds—create your own blue river.

Bloom Period and Seasonal Color
Blue, pink or white flowers in mid-spring.

Mature Height × Spread
6 to 8 in. × 6 in.

Zones
To Zone 4

When, Where, and How to Plant
Grape hyacinths are planted in September. They should be planted immediately because the foliage will begin to grow in the fall. Any site in full sun to partial sun with average well-drained soil is suitable. In poor soils, amend the area as necessary with compost, shredded leaves, or other organic material. Plant the bulbs 3 in. deep and 3 in. apart. Follow the general planting directions on page 63.

Growing Tips
Mix in a bulb fertilizer before planting, or topdress with fertilizer afterward. Water after planting and during dry periods until the ground freezes.

Care
Grape hyacinths need little additional care and are easy to grow. Self-sowing is the best way to establish large drifts. Deadhead if you wish to prevent them from self-sowing, although this is impractical for a large planting. If squirrels are a persistent problem in your garden, protect newly planted bulbs by covering the area with screening or chicken wire, or using a commercial repellent. To propagate, lift and divide the clump after the foliage matures in summer. Grape hyacinths are generally disease-free.

Companion Planting and Design
Use generous quantities of these small bulbs to ensure they are visible and appreciated in mid-spring. Plant them in curving sweeps or drifts under trees and shrubs where they can spread and remain undisturbed. They are useful at woodland edges, in rock gardens, or along a path. Combine them with yellow daffodils and red tulips for spectacular contrast. Grape hyacinths are excellent bulbs for naturalizing in landscapes along with daffodil and squills.

We Recommend
Of this genus, *Muscari armeniacum* is the most widely planted and the best for naturalizing. Cultivars are available in several shades of blue to bluish-purple. 'Early Giant' has deep-blue flowers rimmed in white. *Muscari botryoides* is smaller but hardy to Zone 3. It has sky blue flowers and does not spread as quickly. Pretty pink and white forms are available.

When, Where, and How to Plant

Plant the bulbs in late October or as soon as they are received from the grower. Spring planting is a second choice. Lily bulbs can dry out quickly, so get them in the ground fast. Most lilies prefer moist but well-drained humus-rich garden soil, and full sun. Many will tolerate partial shade. Drainage is of critical importance. Lilies don't compete well with aggressive spreading ground-covers or perennials; plant them in the gaps between clumping perennials. Plant bulbs 5 to 8 in. deep, depending on the size of the bulb, following specific instructions that arrive with it. Incorporate bulb fertilizer into the hole. For attractive groupings, plant bulbs of the same variety in triangular groups of three, spaced 12 to 18 in. apart.

Growing Tips

Lilies should be fertilized for best results. Apply a well-balanced granular fertilizer such as 10-10-10 in the spring as the shoots emerge. Or use a dilute liquid feed or a generous application of well-rotted manure. Water lilies during dry spells.

Care

Lilies are generally pest- and disease-free. Dead-head hybrid lilies before seeds form, but leave as much foliage as possible. Divide clumps as they start to lose vigor, usually every five or six years. Do this in the fall after the foliage has died back. Lift the bulbs, separate, and replant.

Companion Planting and Design

Use lilies in perennial gardens, mixed borders, and gaps in a shrub planting. Choose a lily to enhance a summer-blooming combination or add excitement to an area where little else is in bloom.

We Recommend

The Asiatic hybrids—easy, long-lived, and less fussy about drainage—are the best place to start. 'Enchantment' and 'Connecticut King' are undemanding. The later-blooming Oriental hybrids are more difficult to cultivate. A good one to try is the gorgeous white 'Casa Blanca'. For the gardener mainly interested in lilies and lots of them, the widely available naturalizing mixtures are a great value.

This is the real lily, not a wannabe like the daylily, water-lily, or others that attempt to raise their stature by association with this most exotic and beautiful of garden flowers. Lilies suffer from a reputation of being difficult, tracing back to when bulbs arrived in Europe, dry and desiccated, from the far reaches of Asia. But now lilies are available fresh and ready to plant from growers in the United States. It's true that some species can be tricky, but after years of breeding, easy-to-grow hybrid lilies are well adapted to garden culture. Pendant trumpets, upward-facing stars, ruffled, spotted, fragrant—lily flowers are dazzling. A group of lilies in a garden raises the ordinary to the extraordinary.

Bloom Period and Seasonal Color
White, yellow, gold, orange, pink, or red flowers in summer.

Mature Height × Spread
18 in. to 6 ft. × 1¹/₂ to 2 ft.

Ornamental Onion

Allium aflatunense

Everyone knows that onions, garlic, shallots, and chives are indispensable in the kitchen. But many people don't realize that scores of onions (Allium *spp.*) are grown in the garden for their ornamental value alone. Allium aflatunense, *one such ornamental onion, shows off dense, spherical flower heads held high on strong, straight stems. Its rose-purple flowers in four-inch-wide balls, highly prized for cut flowers, are a superb accent. Each flower bursts from the bud to form a perfect globe that lasts for close to three weeks. After the flowers pass, the attractive seedheads persist for months. No trouble to grow, this ornamental onion complements other spring-flowering perennials and then disappears, as bulbs do, only to return the following spring for a repeat performance.*

Bloom Period and Seasonal Color
Lilac-purple flowers in late spring to early summer

Mature Height × Spread
20 to 30 in. × 12 in.

Zones
To Zone 4

When, Where, and How to Plant
Plant the rounded, white-skinned bulbs in late September to early October. Plant in full sun, although a bit of shade may be tolerated. They prosper in average to rich, well-drained soil. Follow the general instructions for planting bulbs on page 63. Plant bulbs so the base of the bulb is 5 in. below the soil surface. Plant at least three in each group, spaced 3 to 5 in. apart.

Growing Tips
Water-in newly planted bulbs. In poor soils, mix bulb fertilizer (9-9-6) into the planting hole to improve performance. Alliums are carefree; no watering or additional fertilizing is necessary.

Care
In well-drained soil, ornamental onion should not have pest and disease problems. The leaves are attractive as they appear but begin to look shabby as the flower matures. Grow this allium up through other perennials; this creates a double-tier effect that masks the browning foliage. Cut back the flowering stems at the point you feel they are unattractive. Ornamental onion will often self-sow. This can be prevented by removing the heads before they scatter their seed.

Companion Planting and Design
The globular heads of flowers are best used in groups of at least five, but a dozen is even better. Groups of ornamental onion placed at regular intervals provide an interesting accent to a perennial border. A memorable planting from Cranbrook House in Bloomfield Hills featured the spherical flowers of ornamental onions as an accent among purple perennial salvias, pink petunias, gray artemisia, and ornamental kale.

We Recommend
The 3- to 4-ft. giant onion, *Allium giganteum*, is the large purple globular flower often seen towering over an admiring child in bulb catalogs. It's gorgeous but expensive, and not so easy to grow. The drumstick allium, *Allium sphaerocephalum*, has a lithe habit; tall (15 to 30 in.), with elliptical, dark rose-purple flowers, this onion works well growing up through 'Autumn Joy' sedum.

Siberian Squill
Scilla siberica

When, Where, and How to Plant
Plant squills in late September. Although squills need sun in spring, they tolerate shade in summer; it is fine to plant them beneath deciduous trees because the squills will be finished with their show by the time the trees leaf out. These bulbs prefer areas with sun to part sun and well-drained soil. Follow the general directions for planting bulbs on page 63. Plant them 3 in. deep and space them 3 in. apart.

Growing Tips
A bulb fertilizer may be mixed into the area before the bulbs are planted. After planting, water the area well. The area where squills are planted may be fertilized in the fall or dressed with a top layer of compost in the fall every few years.

Care
Squills make few demands. They are generally disease- and pest-free. Let the squill foliage fully ripen before removal. If squills are planted in the lawn, do not mow the grass until the foliage matures. Until that time, the plant is making food that will fuel the bulb and next year's flowers. In a suitable location, *Scilla* will multiply by bulblets and seed into colonies. When the seedpods mature, you can collect and scatter the seeds. The seedlings will reach blooming size after three to five years.

Companion Planting and Design
Use squills generously at woodland's edge, in lawns, in rock gardens, and along paths. Play up their diminutive size to edge a path or patio, to encircle a star magnolia or redbud, or to use at the front of a planting of bulbs or perennials.

We Recommend
'Spring Beauty' is large and vigorous with more blue flowers per stem than others. Twinleaf squill, *Scilla bifolia*, is an excellent choice for naturalizing. Its starlike blue flowers are arranged loosely on graceful 6-in. stems. Even if you can't pronounce *S. mischtschenkoana*, you'll appreciate its pale-blue flowers that appear in very early spring before other squills.

The electric blue of Siberian squills is almost bold enough to send out shock waves. This early bloomer won't be ignored. When planted thickly along walkways or scattered in lawns, these small hardy bulbs grow into a mat of rich color so intense that it nearly sparkles, accounting for their long popularity with gardeners. Some squill plantings have remained viable for a half-century or longer. Their pendant star-shaped flowers are among the earliest to open, following snowdrops. Whether they are found at the edge of a woodland or in a rock garden or lawn, squills are favorites for mass plantings over large areas where they will multiply to form huge colonies. For a relatively low-cost spring thrill, plant squills by the hundreds.

Bloom Period and Seasonal Color
Blue flowers in early spring.

Mature Height × Spread
4 to 6 in. × 4 in.

Snowdrop
Galanthus nivalis

Few sights any time of the year bring more joy to gardeners than the first snowdrop. Undaunted by cold weather, these petite beauties pop up as early as February and March, often while there is still snow on the ground. Their white pendant flowers are small but distinctive, with three flaring petals and a central notched tube marked with green. A woodland native, snowdrops can be planted in part to full shade, such as under trees or in a shady border. They thrive in well-drained moisture-retentive soil where they will eventually multiply. According to bulb historian Scott Kunst of Ann Arbor, snowdrops are immensely popular in the United Kingdom, with enthusiasts eager to buy and grow named varieties that show even the slightest variation.

Bloom Period and Seasonal Color
White flowers in early spring.

Mature Height × Spread
6 in. × 3 to 4 in.

When, Where, and How to Plant
Plant snowdrops with other minor bulbs in September. They may take a year or two to get established. For faster results, plant snowdrops "in the green." After they flower in the spring, snowdrops may be dug and spread around your garden. Snowdrops prefer light to partial shade and moist but well-drained soil that is high in organic matter. Sandy soils should be amended with organic matter. Don't plant in hot, dry areas. Follow general directions for planting bulbs on page 63. The bulbs should be 3 to 4 in. deep and spaced 4 in. apart.

Growing Tips
Water the newly planted bulbs. In poor soils, mix in bulb fertilizer (9-9-6) to improve performance. When properly sited, snowdrops are easy to grow and should not require additional watering beyond melting snow and spring rains. A light organic mulch is beneficial.

Care
Snowdrops are not troubled by pests and diseases. They may be dug and divided when they form large, vigorous clumps as the bulbs finish flowering and the foliage is still green. Separate the clump into single bulbs and replant immediately.

Companion Planting and Design
Use quantities of snowdrops planted randomly in a woodland setting or at the front of a shady border. One of the best places for snowdrops is with low-growing groundcover under the shade of deciduous trees. Snowdrops are particularly lovely with the yellow flowers of winter aconite. Or plant snowdrops and hellebores under an 'Arnold Promise' witchhazel. Add golden snow crocus to balance the yellow petals of the witchhazel and create your garden's first blooming combination.

We Recommend
Galanthus nivalis (4 to 5 in.) is the common or garden snowdrop. It generally opens late February to March and is not damaged by snow or freezing temperatures. The cultivar 'Flore-Pleno' has double flowers. It's interesting but has lost the elegance of the single form. *Galanthus elwesii*, the giant snowdrop at 8 to 10 in., has distinctive gray-green leaves.

Species Tulip
Tulipa tarda

When, Where, and How to Plant

Plant the bulbs of species tulips in October through November, leaving them for last when planting bulbs in fall. They prefer cool temperatures. Plant in well-drained soil and full sun. Good drainage is important for success; most species tulip bulbs like to be warm and dry in the summer. *Tulipa tarda* will tolerate partial shade, but some botanical tulips won't. Follow the planting instructions on page 63. Plant the bulbs so that the base is 4 to 5 in. below the soil surface.

Growing Tips

Water the bulbs after planting. In poor soils, incorporate bulb fertilizer (9-9-6) into the soil at planting time. Don't skimp on the planting depth. As with all tulips, the best results occur when bulbs are planted at the full depth recommended. Avoid planting species tulips in areas that receive summer irrigation.

Care

After planting, species tulips are carefree. *Tulipa tarda* will self-sow and spread in ideal locations. Provided with good drainage, it should not have pest or disease problems.

Companion Planting and Design

Plant these small tulips in groups of at least a dozen for the best effect. Use them in the front of perennial beds, by sunny patios, along front walks, or combined with sun-loving-but-not-too-aggressive groundcovers like sedum or thyme. Ideal locations are rock gardens or the tops of stone retaining walls. Try *Tulipa tarda* growing through woolly thyme and the downy nodding purple flowers of pasqueflower for an early-spring association.

We Recommend

Buy species tulips from reputable merchants; be sure the bulbs are commercially propagated and not collected from the wild. Try some of these: *T. kaufmanniana*, the waterlily tulip, is creamy yellow brushed with red on the exterior of the petals. *T. bakeri* 'Lilac Wonder' has soft-pink flowers with yellow centers. The candy-stripe tulip, *T. clusiana* 'Lady Jane', has white flowers stained rose-red on the outside. Try a few. You'll get hooked!

Tulipa tarda, a starry little tulip with yellow petals tipped in white, is only one example of the numerous species tulips available. These aren't the grand hybrids, massed by the truckload and underplanted with pansies. These are small and unpretentious, but with the underlying appeal that sparked the hysteria of Tulipomania and resulted in the hundreds of showy Darwin, cottage, and triumph tulips that are now commonplace. Dozens of species tulips are offered in the trade, and not all are easy to grow. Some are native to high rocky hillsides in central Asia and require specialized treatment, but others are an easy garden addition. With sun and good drainage, these tiny charmers will perennialize and return to your garden long after the fancy hybrids have disappeared.

Other Name
Botanical Tulip

Bloom Period and Seasonal Color
Yellow petals with white points in spring.

Mature Height × Spread
3 to 4 in. × 4 to 6 in.

Zones
To Zone 4

Star-of-Persia
Allium christophii

Star-of-Persia opens like a starburst—first a few star-shaped flowers appear, then the whole thing explodes to a tremendous sphere of celestial lavender flowers. These perfect starry globes, each close to ten inches wide, are a novelty in perennial beds and cottage gardens. Each flower head holds close to a hundred six-pointed flowers. The amethyst stars have a silvery luster, each with a small green center. In bloom for many weeks, the large spheres remain attractive in the garden for months. The loose flower heads on stout stems provide interest at ground level, harmonizing with the silvery foliage of lavender, lamb's ears, and woolly thyme. Sun and adequate drainage are all this wonderful ornamental onion needs to return and bloom year after year.

Bloom Period and Seasonal Color
Silvery lilac flowers in late spring to early summer.

Mature Height × Spread
10 to 20 in. × 12 to 18 in.

When, Where, and How to Plant
Plant the white-skinned bulbs of star-of-Persia in late September to mid-October. Star-of-Persia and other alliums should be planted in full sun (a bit of shade may be tolerated) in average to rich, well-drained soil. Follow the general directions for bulb planting on page 63. Plant so the bottom of the bulb is 5 in. below the soil surface. Plant at least three in each group, spaced 8 to 12 in. apart.

Growing Tips
Water the newly planted bulbs. In poor soils add bulb fertilizer (9-9-6) to the planting hole and mix in to improve performance. Although drought-tolerant later in the summer, while the star-of-Persia is in bloom, give it adequate moisture. In soils of average fertility, this ornamental onion will not require extra fertilization.

Care
In well-drained soil, star-of-Persia should not be troubled by pest or disease problems. The seedheads of star-of-Persia, if cut before they begin to deteriorate, can be used as an everlasting. *Allium christophii*, when ideally situated, will self-sow. The seedlings will take two or three years to reach flowering size. Remove unwanted seedlings.

Companion Planting and Design
Use them in perennial beds, cottage gardens, and mixed plantings. Plant star-of-Persia in groups of at least three. A dozen creates a spectacular display. Star-of-Persia makes a great accent when planted to come up through sun-loving groundcovers such as thyme or lamb's ears. Take advantage of the flowers' metallic purple cast by planting them with steely blue oat grass and silvery veronica. Add the dusky plum 'Vera Jameson' sedum for an effective color echo.

We Recommend
An expensive but spectacular onion, 'Globemaster', is the result of a hybrid between star-of-Persia and another ornamental onion. It has huge (almost volleyball-sized) flowers of a sparkling pinkish-purple and grows 30 to 36 in. tall. The Turkistan onion, *Allium karataviense*, has pale lilac, globular flowers set off by attractive ribbed gray-green leaves, edged with purple.

Summer Snowflake

Leucojum aestivum

When, Where, and How to Plant

Plant the daffodil-like bulbs of summer snowflake in late September through early October. Summer snowflake flourishes in rich, well-drained soil, but—unusual among bulbs—it also grows well in moist and less-than-perfectly-drained sites. Moist soil, not sodden, and full sun to light shade are ideal. Follow the general directions for planting bulbs on page 63. Plant so that the base of the bulb is 4 to 5 in. below the soil surface. Space bulbs 3 to 5 in. apart in natural-looking groups.

Growing Tips

Incorporate a bulb fertilizer (9-9-6) into the soil at planting. Summer snowflake likes moist soil. Water the bulbs after planting, and during extended dry periods as well.

Care

Summer snowflake is pest- and disease-free and needs no special care. Let the foliage mature fully before removing. You can carefully move snowflakes while in leaf, and this is a useful way to establish the plant elsewhere. If plants become congested and blooming decreases, dig and separate them into single bulbs. Replant as recommended above.

Companion Planting and Design

Use summer snowflake in perennial beds and cottage gardens, as an accent for groundcover plantings, and naturalized in a sunny, moist location. It's a great choice for adding interest to a moist, partly shaded location at the edge of a shrub bed. Try summer snowflake with the spotted foliage of Bethlehem sage, flowers of blue woodland phlox, and ferns in a corner of the garden with filtered shade.

We Recommend

Look for 'Gravetye Giant', a taller and more floriferous selection that grows 20 to 24 in. tall. It was named for Gravetye Manor, home of William Robinson, the 19th-Century English gardener and garden writer who was one of the first to promote the naturalization of bulbs. The spring snowflake, *Leucojum vernum*, is often confused with the snowdrop; they are a similar size and prefer similar growing conditions. Snowflakes have bell-shaped flowers touched with green, but not the distinctive central tube of the snowdrop.

Summer snowflake dangles white bell-shaped flowers, each petal marked with green, from upright stems and glossy straplike leaves. Despite its common name, this snowflake actually blooms in late spring, flowering for two to three weeks in May. Summer snowflake is graceful, not flashy. Its dainty, nodding flowers, produced among robust foliage, add subtle beauty to the garden. The overall effect is one of green foliage decorated with small white bells. Summer snowflake, native to wet fields, woods, and swamps of Europe and western Asia, tolerates and possibly prefers moist soils. The fresh white bells are particularly attractive reflecting in the water of a pond or gracing the bank of a stream. The graceful nodding flowers are a pleasant addition to flower arrangements.

Bloom Period and Seasonal Color
White flowers in late spring.

Mature Height × Spread
14 to 24 in. × 6 to 10 in.

Zones
To Zone 5

Tulip
Tulipa hybrids

Stately and formal in a geometric massed planting or casual and cheery in a clump near the front door, tulips are a colorful staple unparalleled in the spring garden. Even a modest grouping of two dozen bulbs can jazz up the view from a window or walkway. Tulips start coming into bloom at the end of April. Most of them open in May after the minor bulbs finish flowering and toward the end of the daffodils' show. Tulips display an immense range of colors, shapes, bloom periods, and heights. These hardy bulbs have been grown in the United States since the earliest European settlers arrived. They continue to be among the most widely planted today, especially in mass displays that herald spring.

Bloom Period and Seasonal Color
Spring in a kaleidoscope of colors.

Mature Height × Spread
6 to 30 in. × 6 to 12 in.

When, Where, and How to Plant
Plant tulips late in October to November or as long as the soil can be worked. Tulips need sun and a well-drained soil. Choosing the right location will prevent problems. In heavy clay soils or poorly drained locations, tulips will perform poorly and will eventually rot. Before planting, loosen the soil to a depth of 12 in. Plant bulbs 6 to 8 in. deep, and space 4 to 6 in. apart. Follow the general instructions for bulb planting on page 63. It is important to plant tulips to the full recommended depth. A deep planting will be longer lived and less likely to be invaded by rodents.

Growing Tips
Fertilize tulips at planting by working bulb food into the soil. Water newly planted bulbs. Regular fertilization will increase bulb longevity. Feed lightly as the first leaves emerge; fertilize again in fall with bulb food, or topdress with compost.

Care
After tulips finish blooming, allow the foliage to mature until it turns yellow. Leave the bulbs in place, or dig them up, divide, and store in mesh bags in a cool, dry place to replant in fall. In formal beds, some gardeners treat tulips as annuals, discarding the bulbs after flowering.

Companion Planting and Design
Tulip displays are most dramatic when the bulbs are planted in quantity or drifts. Use groups of one color for a sophisticated effect, or mixed colors for an informal party of color. Unlike daffodils, large hybrid tulips are not suited to naturalizing since the bulb display cannot be counted on for more than a year.

We Recommend
With so many tulips to choose from, the best way to select is to spend time with a bulb catalog. If you want tulips with staying power, choose carefully. Some, like the emperor tulips, and others sold as "perennial tulips," will bloom well for three to five years or longer. For more tulips, see the separate entry on species tulips.

Windflower

Anemone blanda

When, Where, and How to Plant

Plant the small brown bumpy tubers from late September until mid-October. Windflower prefers moist, well-drained soil that is high in organic matter. The ideal location is sunny in early spring and partially shady later, such as a woodland garden, borders under high trees, and the edges of shrub beds. Windflowers will also grow in full sun with adequate moisture. Soak purchased tubers in water overnight. Dig holes and plant the tubers so that the base is 2 to 3 in. below the soil surface. Look carefully for eyes or buds, and plant them facing up. If you can't determine which end is up, plant the tubers on their sides. Space bulbs 2 to 3 in. apart in natural-looking groups.

Growing Tips

Mix bulb fertilizer with the soil before planting the bulbs, and water well after planting. Watering may be necessary in an extended dry period. A loose organic mulch will help overwinter windflower in the colder parts of Zone 5. Before investing in large quantities, grow a few to be sure they will be hardy in your garden.

Care

Windflowers need no special care and are virtually trouble-free. They can also be split and moved after flowering—or, for that matter, while in flower. Dig them up, disturbing the roots as little as possible, and replant in the desired location. This is a good way to spread windflowers to other parts of the garden.

Companion Planting and Design

Plant windflowers in drifts under river birch, crabapple, or corneliancherry trees. Add daffodils to enliven the show. Many beautiful combinations can be devised; try white emperor tulips underplanted with pink windflowers, or red tulips with mixed blue shades.

We Recommend

Purchase only nursery-propagated windflowers; choosing cultivated selections ensures this. 'Blue Shades' is a mix of blue hues. 'White Splendor', with its beautiful flowers against dark foliage, lights up woodland gardens. 'Radar' is flashy with magenta flowers and a white bull's-eye.

The daisylike flowers of windflower are uniquely appealing in early spring. Perhaps the yellow-centered daisies, resembling asters, suggest the lush growing season to come. Or maybe it's just that daisy flowers, so common in high summer, are uncommon in early spring. Whatever the reason, a carpet of windflowers is a delight on a sunny Michigan spring day. Windflowers are among the earliest bulbs—combining with snowdrops, winter aconite, and squill—and they hang on for weeks, remaining in bloom for the daffodils and early tulips. Windflower is impressive when planted in a mass; it's not enough to plant just a few. Windflower can often be purchased in lots of fifty or a hundred for a substantial price break. The tubers are easy to plant. Come spring, you won't regret the effort.

Bloom Period and Seasonal Color
Blue, white, and bright-pink flowers in early spring.

Mature Height × Spread
3 to 4 in. × 2 to 3 in.

Zones
To Zone 5

Winter Aconite
Eranthis hyemalis

Once you know where winter aconites grow, watching for them becomes a favorite early-spring ritual while the tall trees are still bare and the ground is covered with patches of snow. Impatiently, you look and look again and finally, one day, you spot these bright-yellow flowers poking up toward the sun, blooming proof that winter is over. The inch-wide flowers resemble buttercups and appear surrounded by a rufflike collar of green. Winter aconites are cohorts of squills, crocuses, and snowdrops in that they fall into the category of the so-called minor bulbs, even though that label can be misleading. Winter aconites and their fellows are small in size, but they have a major impact on gardeners because they come so early in the season.

Bloom Period and Seasonal Color
Yellow flowers in early spring.

Mature Height × Spread
4 in. × 3 to 4 in.

Zones
To Zone 4

When, Where, and How to Plant
Plant winter aconites along with the other small bulbs in September or as soon as they are available. They profit from extra time to get established before the ground freezes. The best site for winter aconite is a shady area that remains cool and moist in summer. Here they will have spring sun but will be finished maturing by the time the trees and shrubs leaf out. The bulbs require well-drained moisture-retentive soil. Soak the dried tubers in water overnight before planting. Space the tubers 3 in. apart and plant 3 in. deep. Seed from the ripening seedheads can be scattered in areas of a woodland garden where you want winter aconites to spread. These will take three or four years to reach blooming size.

Growing Tips
Winter aconite is carefree and will spread rapidly in ideal conditions. Mix bulb fertilizer with the soil before planting the bulbs, and water well after planting; if sited correctly, they will not need additional watering. A loose organic mulch like shredded leaves is beneficial.

Care
If rodents regularly ravage bulbs in your yard, cover a new planting with wire screening or chicken wire, or apply a commercial repellent. Winter aconite has no serious diseases, although it does have a well-deserved reputation for being difficult to establish. The small brown tubers are often too desiccated to prosper. A more reliable way to obtain winter aconite is to dig and divide established plantings in spring, while the plants are still green.

Companion Planting and Design
Plant winter aconite by the dozens or hundreds under deciduous trees or in shrub borders, woodland gardens, and beds. Create a carpet of buttercup yellow on a wooded slope. The bright yellow makes a colorful contrast with white snowdrops and creates spring's earliest floral display.

We Recommend
Once you're hooked on *Eranthis hyemalis*, you'll want to try *E. cilicica*. This aconite has a similar yellow flower with deeply divided bronzy green leaves. Unfortunately, it doesn't form large colonies.

Lawns *for Michigan*

For many people, having and maintaining a healthy green lawn is an important part of home ownership. Turf is attractive and functional, soft and inviting. Its textured, horizontal surface sets off the rest of the landscape—flowers, trees, and shrubs. It is relatively easy and inexpensive to install and maintain.

Questions and Answers

The question is, how much grass—and how much work—should there be? There are many choices. Part of the populace loves to tend turf on the weekend. Others choose to replace lawn with groundcovers, pavers, or mulch, cutting down on maintenance as well as the water and fertilizers required to maintain a healthy lawn.

To figure out what kind of lawn you want and need, consider how the area will be used. Will it get lots of traffic? Will children play on it? Will its main function be to serve as a visual link to the flower borders or the vegetable garden?

Then assess how much sun the area receives. Turf requires exposure to sun for most of the day. Soil drainage and fertility are also considerations, although they can be improved with the incorporation of organic materials such as compost. Take a soil test to see what nutrients are needed before beginning a new lawn.

Planting and Caring for Your Lawn

The best time to establish a lawn from seed or to renovate bare patches is mid-August to mid-September, or about two weeks earlier in northern Michigan. By then the nighttime temperatures are beginning to cool, the days are still warm, rainfall is increasing, and weeds are not growing as actively as they were earlier in the year. All these conditions are good for grass seed germination. If you can't do the work at that time, the next best period to sow grass seed is mid-April to mid-May.

Besides sowing seed, another way to begin is by hydroseeding. In this process, grass seed is mixed with mulch and fertilizer and then sprayed on the soil. Hydroseeding is best done in spring or fall.

Sod may be laid from April through late fall as long as the soil temperature is above 40 degrees Fahrenheit. Before installing sod, moisten the soil to a depth of six inches, and keep the area watered afterward until roots are established.

Starting a lawn from seed is the least expensive way to begin a new lawn. It also requires more work and takes longer to achieve good results. Sod, while more costly, provides the fastest results.

When you undertake a new lawn or want to seed bare patches, evaluate the existing conditions. If the soil and grade are acceptable, the only preparation required is to scratch or roughen up the surface to a depth of at least two inches.

Heavy clay or infertile or sandy soil may be improved by adding well-rotted compost, aged manure, and other organic materials. These will improve the soil's ability to drain as well as its capacity to retain moisture.

Dig up any weeds or kill them with a herbicide. In a new lawn, this is the time to install an in-ground irrigation system if desired.

Choosing Grass Seed

Some seed packages contain more filler than others, so check the label of the seed mixtures or blends to see what percentage is selected seed. When buying grass seed, it's a better bargain to pay more for higher quality.

Although it is sometimes advertised for sale, zoysia grass is not a good choice for Michigan lawns. It is a warm-season grass that thrives in hot weather but turns brown when temperatures drop, both in spring and in fall. Bentgrass is another type to avoid for residential lawns. It is beautiful on golf course greens but requires a higher level of maintenance than most homeowners can provide.

The Players

There are four main turfgrasses used in Michigan:

Fineleaf fescues (*Festuca* species) perform better in shady areas than do other turfgrasses recommended for Michigan lawns. They may be mixed with Kentucky bluegrass to increase shade tolerance and used in

a low-care utility lawn that tends to stay dry and includes some shade. The fine fescues require less fertilizer per growing season than do Kentucky bluegrass or perennial ryegrass. Fine fescues need one to two pounds of actual nitrogen per 1,000 square feet each season; apply one pound of nitrogen per application around Memorial and Labor Days. In open sun, fine fescues perform better with some irrigation. Sow seed at three to five pounds per 1,000 square feet of turf. If you decide to later use a herbicide, wait at least six weeks after seeding, since fine fescues are susceptible to injury if treated any earlier. Fine fescues are prone to develop leaf spot disease during humid, wet summers, so plant only on well-drained soil. If possible, select a cultivar with moderate disease resistance because it contains endophytes, a fungus that helps repel chinch bugs, billbugs, sod webworms, and aphids. Mow with the blade set to two-and-a-half inches or higher.

Kentucky bluegrass (*Poa pratensis*) is the most widely planted lawn grass in Michigan. It has a deep-green color and carpetlike texture. Use Kentucky blue in lawns in full or nearly full sunlight. This grass requires more watering (supplemental irrigation is needed) and fertilizing (no more than one pound of nitrogen per 1,000 square feet of turf per application around Memorial Day, Fourth of July, Labor Day, and Halloween) than most other grasses. Lawns planted in Kentucky bluegrass are planted with several cultivars in a blend or combined with perennial ryegrass or fine fescue. The best choices for high-quality lawns in full sun are the improved bluegrass cultivars, which have names like 'Baron' or 'Touchdown'. Sow seed at a rate of one to two pounds per 1,000 square feet. Kentucky bluegrass is slow to begin growing. If you will be using a herbicide, wait until the grass has been mowed three or four times. Mow with the blade set to two-and-a-half to three-and-a-half inches.

Perennial ryegrass (*Lolium perenne*) germinates and grows quickly. Mixed with Kentucky bluegrass, it forms the basis of a tough, attractive lawn for high-traffic areas. It is best in well-drained soils of average fertility, in sun or part shade. Perennial ryegrass needs lots of moisture and goes dormant in extreme heat and drought. Its water and fertilizer needs are similar to those of Kentucky bluegrass, described above. Annual ryegrass, *Lolium multiflorum*, is not recommended for lawns in Michigan. It is coarse, may out-compete other grasses, and does not usually live more than a year. Perennial ryegrass cultivars are reasonably cold hardy. Use improved types, which better withstand the cold and have a finer texture. Look for cultivars enhanced with endophytes, which help repeal some turf pests. Sow at the rate of four to five pounds of seed per 1,000 square feet of lawn. After sowing, wait at least until the grass has been mowed three or four times to apply a herbicide. Perennial ryegrass needs one pound of actual nitrogen per 1,000 square feet of turf applied three to five times a year for irrigated lawns or twice a year for non-irrigated turf. Mow at $2^1/2$ to $3^1/2$ inches.

Turf-type tall fescues (*Festuca arundinacea*) are coarse grasses that grow in bunches or clumps. When planted alone or as the main grass in a mix, tall fescues form a good uniform sod with wide leaf blades and prominent veins. Tall fescues may be mixed with a smaller percentage of Kentucky bluegrass or

perennial ryegrass seed. Avoid older types of tall fescues, which are coarse and not reliably winter hardy. Newer cultivars have narrower leaves and can withstand dry periods, heat, and traffic. They tolerate some shade and resist pests and disease to some degree. Tall fescues make resilient lawns that have proven hardy in southeastern Michigan. Some seed is enhanced with endophytes, which helps it resist turf pests. Use tall fescues on banks subject to erosion and elsewhere for a low-care lawn. They may be planted in sun or shade and in many soils, including sand. Sow at the rate of four to eight pounds per 1,000 square feet of lawn. After sowing, wait at least until the third or fourth mowing to apply a herbicide. Tall fescue requires infrequent but deep watering. Mow at the highest setting, three to four inches. Tall fescues need one pound of nitrogen per 1,000 square feet applied three times a season—at the end of May, in early July, and in early September.

Post-Planting Care

Lightly roll or firm the area so seed makes contact with the soil. Water, and then cover the surface with a mulch such as clean straw. A light application of fertilizer (half the normal recommended rate) may be made at seeding.

The main reason grass seed fails is that it dries out. If the weather is warm and windy, it may be necessary to water the newly seeded area several times a day. After about three weeks, the straw mulch may be removed. Mow when the new grass is three inches tall.

Mowing Tips

Lawn experts recommend mowing high—two-and-a-half, three, or three-and-a-half inches. With more surface area, the grass can manufacture more nutrients to nourish its roots and stems. Longer blades also shade the soil surface, making it harder for crabgrass seeds to germinate. Mow frequently enough so that no more than the top third of the grass blade is removed at one time. Mowing is easier if beds are defined with edging and there is a circle left free of grass around the base of trees. This also protects the tree trunks from close encounters with a lawn mower.

In addition to mowing high, turf experts advise leaving the grass clippings to disintegrate where they fall on the lawn. The cut pieces are mostly water. As they break down, they return nutrients to the soil and the grass roots.

The Lawn Diet

Nitrogen is the most important nutrient in a fertilizer for lawns.

Organic fertilizers, which are made from natural products such as animal manures, are less concentrated, so more fertilizer will be needed to apply the recommended rate of nitrogen. This can make organic fertilizers more expensive to use, but their lower concentration means there is less danger of runoff, and they rarely burn the grass.

Synthetic fertilizers are mixtures of chemical salts and inert substances that break down quickly when they are watered into the soil. They are concentrated, so less of the product is needed, but they must be used at the proper rate to avoid burning, and should not be used around rivers or lakes.

Slow-release fertilizers, which release the nutrients gradually over several months, are a better choice for waterside locations because there is less chance of pollution from runoff. As a precaution, leave unfertilized a strip at least twenty feet wide next to the water.

Controlling Crabgrass and Weeds

Crabgrass control is a traditional concern for those who maintain lawns. In the past, seeing the forsythia in full bloom meant it was time to apply pre-emergent herbicides. The forsythia flowers signaled that the soil had almost reached the temperature when weed seeds would start growing.

Now, rather than blanket the entire lawn with a pre-emergent each spring, the emphasis is on figuring out how to outsmart crabgrass. Determine why crabgrass is a problem, and then work to tip the balance to favor turf growth instead.

Crabgrass seeds need sunlight to germinate. That means they germinate most efficiently in bare spots in the lawn. If you can get grass to grow strongly, it will shade the soil surface and make it difficult if not impossible for crabgrass to grow. Look around for bare or thin spots in the turf and reseed with high-quality grass seed.

The best way to prevent crabgrass and other lawn weeds is to keep the lawn healthy through mowing at the right height, watering, and fertilizing. These steps keep the grass dense and tall, shading the soil so

crabgrass can't germinate. Tests at Michigan State University show that simply using the right amount of fertilizer significantly reduced the number of weeds in lawns.

Rather than spread a pre-emergent over the entire lawn, treat crabgrass on a spot basis. Dig it out and sow with high-quality grass seed.

If perennial weeds like dandelions are a problem, dig them with a long fork, pull by hand or, if desired, treat them on a spot basis with an herbicide.

These approaches reflect the principles of IPM, or integrated pest management. The idea is to figure out why a problem is occurring, then start to remedy it with the least toxic method first. For more on the IPM approach and how you can use it in your own home landscape, turn to page 245.

Cool Grasses in Hot Weather

Cool-season grasses, the kind recommended for Michigan lawns, grow most vigorously when the temperature is 60 to 85 degrees Fahrenheit. They go dormant in hotter weather. This is a natural process and does not harm the grass, which will green up again when the weather turns cooler.

If you choose to keep the grass from going brown and dormant, you will have to water often in hot, dry weather. Turfgrasses require about one inch of water a week during the growing season, from rain, a sprinkler, or an irrigation system. The current recommendation is to water every day for short periods rather than to wait several days and then provide a longer soaking. Watch the lawn for signs of drought stress such as wilting or a blue-gray color.

More on Lawn Care

Aerating a lawn helps keep grass vigorous, especially in heavy clay or compacted soils. Core aerators are heavy large drums covered with spikes. As they pass over the turf, they cut out round sections several inches deep and throw them on the surface. This process creates thousands of small holes in the lawn, exposing the root area to additional air, water, and nutrients. It also helps reduce thatch or accumulated debris around the base of the grass plants. If the aeration is done in spring, the grass will recover fairly quickly. Aeration does not have to be done each year.

In fall, keep tree leaves from forming a thick mat on the grass. The usual way to remove leaves is with a rake or blower. Another option is to mow the leaves and let them stay on the lawn. If they are cut finely with a mulching mower or two passes of a regular lawn mower, the leaves will decompose and will not contribute to thatch. In a study at Michigan State University, a six-inch layer of leaves was mowed and left on a lawn without harmful effect. As a result, many Michigan golf courses are now mowing the leaves and letting them stay on the grass each fall.

Getting Grubby

There's a lot of talk—and a plethora of TV commercials—these days about grubs and lawns. Grubs are beetle larvae. As soon as the soil begins to warm in spring, the white C-shaped larvae start chomping on the roots of turf plants.

Nearly every lawn has some grubs, but, when they reach a certain level, the damage can become severe enough to be noticed as dead, easily lifted patches of turf. There may also be lots of bird activity as they pick at the turf to get the grubs.

To lessen grub damage, keep the lawn regularly irrigated. Damage is much worse on dry soil. Most healthy lawns will recover from minor grub damage.

Consider using an insecticide only if the grub population is more than 5 per square foot on non-irrigated lawns, or more than 15 to 20 grubs per square foot on irrigated lawns. To count the grubs, cut a square foot from the turf and peel it back. Dig down a few inches into the soil and look for white larvae. When you are finished, reposition the cut section and water it so it will continue growing.

Timing is the key to effective grub control. Though damage is most noticeable in spring, wait until early July to apply a growth regulator insecticide. This is just before the time that the next generation of grubs will be hatching, so the treatment will stop grub injury in the fall and the following spring. Researchers are also experimenting with beneficial nematodes to see if the tiny worms can be used to combat grubs.

The Big Picture

Many people enjoy maintaining their healthy lawn as a lush green backdrop for other plants. If mowing, watering, fertilizing and worrying about weeds or grubs become too big of a chore, reduce the size of the lawn and plant groundcovers or install hard surfaces instead.

Ornamental Grasses *for Michigan*

Why don't more gardeners grow ornamental grasses? Perhaps some people overlook them because their flowers aren't bright and showy. Others may be leery of grasses in general, fearing they will become weedy, like crabgrass.

In fact, ornamental grasses that are selected and sited correctly add elegance, a rustling sound, and graceful movement to the garden in a way few other plants can. Plant ornamental grasses in drifts or swaths or as accents in the shrub or perennial border, where their fine texture will make for dramatic contrast.

Grasses and spring bulbs make a happy pairing. The bulbs bloom while the grasses are still dormant. By the time the bulb foliage starts to yellow, the grasses start to grow. Cut back the grasses in late winter, and the bulbs are ready to start the cycle again.

Ornamental grasses play an important role in the New American Garden, a style of landscaping that uses grasses massed with other perennials. They are used extensively at the Horticultural Demonstration Gardens and elsewhere on the campus of Michigan State University. Ornamental grasses are showing up in fashionable plantings around the state.

How Ornamental Grasses Grow

Most ornamental grasses are perennials. They grow in two different ways. Running grasses spread quickly by vigorous rhizomes. Clump-forming grasses increase in size slowly. Clump-formers are the best choice for home gardeners.

Grasses are categorized according to the temperatures in which they grow best. Cool-season grasses prefer temperatures of 60 to 75 degrees Fahrenheit, and they produce foliage in spring or early summer. Some go dormant in hot weather, then resume growth in the fall.

The warm-season grasses, which thrive when it is 75 degrees Fahrenheit or warmer, stay dormant until late spring and then grow rapidly, flowering in late summer. They often turn color in the fall and add interest to the winter garden.

Most grasses do best in full sun, although some will tolerate part shade. Grasses are adaptable to different soil types. Many prefer rich, loamy soil, but some perform well even on poorly drained sites. Once established, most ornamental grasses will withstand drought. They rarely require fertilizer.

Important Tips for Michigan Gardeners

The ideal time to observe ornamental grasses is late summer and fall, when they are at their peak. Plant in the spring so grasses have time to get established before the heat of summer. They often take two years to achieve their mature effect.

Space the grasses adequately to allow them room to grow. Moving them closer together in a mass planting creates the effect of an ocean of grass. Spacing them farther apart emphasizes each plant's form.

When planting, set the grass so it is growing at the same depth it was in the pot. If a plant is pot-bound, loosen the rootball. Water thoroughly and keep the grass moist until it is established. Mulch to help conserve soil moisture.

Cutting back the foliage of ornamental grasses is the most important maintenance activity. Most grasses are cut back in late winter to early spring, before new growth begins. Cut back small clumps or individual plants with pruners or loppers. Large clumps and/or mass plantings may require hedge shears. Wear gloves and long sleeves to avoid scratches. Tying the grass clump with twine before cutting back facilitates cleanup.

If your grass clump begins to die out in the middle or split open, it may need division for rejuvenation. Large clumps require significant effort to divide. Grasses may be divided in early spring, as the foliage emerges. Lift clumps out of the ground and split them apart with a sharp spade, saw, or ax. Discard the unproductive center and replant healthy sections from the outside of the clump. Keep the divisions well-watered; lack of water is the main reason that new grass divisions fail.

We selected these grasses because they are reliable performers for Michigan gardens and none has fast-running roots. All are hardy to Zone 5. This attractive and diverse group can open new design possibilities for the garden.

Ornamental grasses are among the easiest perennials to grow, and they are unbeatable for multi-season impact. Their beauty is natural, never contrived, and their appearance is reminiscent of prairies and meadows.

Blue Oat Grass

Helictotrichon sempervirens

The metallic foliage of blue oat grass shimmers in the garden. A cool-season grass, Helictotrichon sempervirens gets a jump on the season by producing foliage in the early months of spring. Spiky tufts of blue leaf blades highlight the pink, purple, and magenta flowers of the spring garden. While most ornamental grasses save their flowers for late summer, the delicate blue-gray flowers of blue oat grass rise above the foliage to dance in the spring breeze. Grown primarily for its foliage, blue oat grass nevertheless puts on quite a floral display. When planted in the foreground of a garden bed, the tall flowering stems add unexpected height, and their delicacy allows a see-through effect.

Bloom Period and Seasonal Color
Blue-gray flowers turn to beige in late spring; silver-blue foliage is attractive all season.

Mature Height × Spread
3 ft. × 2 to 2 1/2 ft.

Zones
To Zone 4

When, Where, and How to Plant
Plant blue oat grass in spring or September. It prefers full sun and well-drained, fertile soil. It tolerates a range of soils but not heavy, wet conditions, and will tolerate light shade for part of the day. Plant blue oat grass plants 2 1/2 to 3 ft. apart. Follow the general directions for planting grasses on page 91.

Growing Tips
Water thoroughly after planting and keep clumps moist until established. Blue oat grass doesn't need any special fertilization. Plants appreciate water during dry spells

Care
In hot, humid summers, foliar rust may occur. Avoid this problem with wide spacing and good air circulation. Blue oat grass needs some grooming, but not the ground-level cutback given to many grasses. For the best spring show, cut only to the top of the clump or tussock, in the fall or early winter. An alternative is to groom the plants in spring when clumps have a mixture of blue and beige leaf blades. Gently tug and remove the old foliage. Remove the flowering stems when they are no longer appealing. Plants occasionally need division, which is best done in the spring. Follow the general directions for dividing grasses on page 91. Divisions often take several years to develop their characteristic tufted form.

Companion Planting and Design
Blue oat grass is at its best alone or in groups of three as an accent plant among perennials or shrubs. Enjoy the steely blue foliage of blue oat grass with a profusion of June bloom. Plant it with lavender-blue catmint, purple 'May Night' salvia, magenta cheddar pinks, and 'White Swirl' Siberian iris. Add the purple globes of ornamental onion, or star-of-Persia for extra interest.

We Recommend
'Sapphire Fountain' has bright blue foliage and improved rust-resistance. We also like *Festuca glauca* 'Elijah Blue' (10 in.), a smaller grass with a similar blue landscape effect. 'Elijah Blue' is the best of the blue fescues, which can be short-lived.

Feather Reed Grass

Calamagrostis × acutiflora 'Karl Foerster'

When, Where, and How to Plant

Plant feather reed grass in the spring to establish roots before the heat of summer. It prefers full sun but will tolerate some shade. Too much shade will decrease flowering, and clumps may flop. Feather reed grass is very adaptable, tolerating drier and heavier soils but preferring moist, well-drained conditions. Plant feather reed grass in the garden 2 to 2½ ft. apart, following the directions on page 91. If plants are potbound, loosen the rootballs.

Growing Tips

Water thoroughly, and keep moist until established. Mulch will help conserve moisture. Fertilizer is unnecessary.

Care

Feather reed grass requires little care. Cut back clumps to 6 in. from the ground in midwinter, a month or so earlier than warm-season grasses, to avoid removing the tips of new foliage. Feather reed grass doesn't need frequent division. If clumps start to die in the center, follow the general directions for dividing grasses on page 91. Rust will occasionally appear on the foliage, particularly in areas with poor air circulation. It doesn't warrant treatment. The tall stalks never need staking. Rain and snow may weigh them down, but they always resume their vertical posture.

Companion Planting and Design

Use drifts of feather reed grass in perennial beds, with shrubs, as a screen, or in meadowlike mass plantings with other grasses and perennials. Although tall, feather reed grass is not a giant, and its lithe nature and vertical habit make it appropriate for even small gardens. A horizontal golden swath of feather reed grass sets off all the flowers of fall.

We Recommend

For small gardens, we recommend *Calamagrostis* 'Overdam'. It possesses all the attributes of feather reed grass but is smaller (3 to 4 ft.) and has attractive cream-striped foliage. The Korean feather reed grass, *Calamagrostis brachytricha*, is an attractive addition to the garden but isn't a superstar like 'Karl Foerster'. It blooms in September, and has self-sowing tendencies.

Few herbaceous plants offer the ever-changing interest of feather reed grass. It transforms itself for almost ten months in the garden. If you're unsure about adding ornamental grasses to your yard, start with this natural beauty. Feather reed grass is well behaved in every way. A naturally occurring hybrid, it is sterile and never self-sows. A cool-season grass, it quickly forms fresh green clumps, maturing at about three feet. By late spring and early summer, when many grasses are just starting, feather reed grass sends forth tall loose plumes of bronzy purple-tinged flowers. Next the flowers turn a golden wheat color and stiffen into an architectural vertical form. Moving with the slightest breeze, the upright flowers literally form amber waves.

Bloom Period and Seasonal Color

Purplish-green flowers changing to gold, effective late spring through late winter.

Mature Height × Spread

5 to 6 ft. × 2 to 2½ ft.

Zones

To Zone 5

Little Bluestem
Schizachyrium scoparium

Michigan is known as a place that has wonderful forests and beautiful sand dunes that grace our expansive coastlines. Within the dunes and also in remnant prairies, the little bluestem makes its home. The common name bluestem comes from the glaucous blue leaf blades that are often touched with purple. Nursery growers have recently recognized the beauty of this native grass and named selections with steely blue foliage or exceptional autumn color. Gardeners who hate to pay high water bills will delight in the drought-tolerance of this plant and combine it with other tough natives to create more care-free gardens. The diminutive flowers emerge with little fanfare, but as they fade they take on a silvery appearance that shimmers in the autumn sun. If you cannot locate S. scoparium, another botanical name for little bluestem is Andropogon scoparium.

Bloom Period and Seasonal Color
Grown for its bluish foliage and orange fall color.

Mature Height × Spread
2 to 4 ft. × 2 to 3 ft.

When, Where, and How to Plant
Container-grown plants are best planted in late spring after the foliage appears, but they can also be planted in early fall. Choose locations with full sun. Bluestem tolerates a wide range of soils from clay to sand. Plant according to the general directions for planting grasses on page 91. Space at 2 to 3 ft.

Growing Tips
Keep new plants moist, but avoid overwatering. Bluestem is drought-tolerant once established. Plants that receive too much water will flop over. Do not mulch. Fertilization is not recommended for this tough native grass, which performs best in lean soils.

Care
Little bluestem is rarely bothered by insects or disease. Cut back the grass in late fall. The foliage does not generally remain upright throughout the winter months. In large-scale planted prairies where burning is an option, the little bluestem will recover and flourish after early or late fall burns. Do not conduct burns without first checking on local or municipal ordinances. Division can be used to rejuvenate or control plants that have become too large in size and have begun to flop over.

Companion Planting and Design
Little bluestem looks wonderful planted in masses or mixed with other flowering prairie plants. Combine it with black-eyed Susan and purple coneflower. For a drought-tolerant prairie all-star planting, plant bluestem with the aromatic aster, *Aster oblongifolius* 'October Skies', and the 'Shenandoah' switch grass. This tough plant will work in tough spots that receive little water and bake in full sun.

We Recommend
'The Blues' is a particularly fine blue-leaved form that makes a wonderful addition to a prairie garden planting or a colorful perennial border. 'Blaze' is a seed-grown cultivar notable for its intense red fall color.

Miscanthus

Miscanthus sinensis

When, Where, and How to Plant

Plant miscanthus in the spring. Moist, rich soil is ideal, but this grass tolerates a wide range of conditions, from wet to somewhat dry. Plants prefer full sun but will take some shade; in too much shade, clumps will sprawl open. Space miscanthus at least 3 to 6 ft. apart depending on the cultivar. Don't crowd this grass; let it have room to display its elegant form. Follow the directions for planting on page 91.

Growing Tips

Keep moist until established. Water clumps during drought; the leaf blades will roll, indicating stress, when they need moisture. Mulch will help conserve moisture. Fertilizer is unnecessary.

Care

In late winter or early spring, use a hedge trimmer or loppers to cut clumps to several inches from the ground. Wear long sleeves and gloves because miscanthus leaves are sharp and can scratch and irritate your skin. Plants may need rejuvenation every five to seven years. Divide following the instructions on page 91. Keep in mind that division is a considerable undertaking. Keep new divisions well watered; desiccation is the leading cause of death for new grass divisions. Clumps planted in partial shade or those in need of division may split open and require staking. In Michigan, it is pest-free.

Companion Planting and Design

Miscanthus is superb as a specimen and an excellent choice for planting by a pond or water feature. Take advantage of its fiery fall color by combining it with fall bloomers like 'Snowbank' boltonia and lavender-blue asters.

We Recommend

The following cultivars have performed well in mid-Michigan. 'Purpurascens', called flame grass (to 5 ft.), flowers in August and has striking fall color. 'Graziella' (5 to 6 ft.) has early flowers and orange fall color. 'Morning Light' (5 to 6 ft.) is grown for its finely variegated foliage, which appears silvery. The tropical-looking porcupine grass, 'Strictus' (5 to 7 ft.), has leaves horizontally striped with yellow. Visit the gardens at Michigan State University to discover more.

Tall and poised, miscanthus has the noble bearing of a garden aristocrat. Cultivated in Japan for centuries and fairly common in American gardens at the turn of the century, Japanese silver grass is back in vogue, and its attractive shape, adaptability, fall color, gleaming plumes, and winter presence are just a few of the reasons. Scores of cultivars are now available with striped, banded, fine-textured, and coarse-textured foliage; for a Michigan garden, however, choose hardy early-flowering selections to avoid disappointment. The name silver grass refers to the silvery plumes, breathtaking against a blue autumn sky. If the flowering stalks are frosted before they emerge, you've lost its raison d'être. Miscanthus provides unfailing winter interest—the fluffy plumes catch the snow, and the plants remain attractive until spring.

Other Names
Japanese Silver Grass, Maiden Grass

Bloom Period and Seasonal Color
Purplish-bronze changing to silver white, effective from late summer through winter.

Mature Height × Spread
5 to 8 ft. × 3 to 4 ft.

Zones
To Zone 5

Pennisetum

Pennisetum alopecuroides

Fountain grass attracts attention with elegance, not flamboyance. Truly resplendent, the glossy narrow foliage and pinkish foxtail flowers cascade loosely, catching the summer light to mimic a sparkling fountain. A warm-season grass, pennisetum is not much to look at in spring, but by early summer the graceful bright-green foliage clumps are an attractive addition to the garden. By midsummer, the pinkish-purple bottlebrush flowers appear on the stems. The foliage bleaches to an almond tan by December, catching snow and adding volume to the winter garden. Use pennisetum as a specimen plant to show off its full, cascading habit, or use several plants as anchors for a bed of summer annuals. Note that hardiness can be a concern with pennisetum.

Other Name
Fountain Grass

Bloom Period and Seasonal Color
Pinkish-green to whitish-tan in midsummer through early fall.

Mature Height × Spread
3 to 4 ft. × 3 to 4 ft.

Zones
To Zone 5

When, Where, and How to Plant
Plant in the spring so that the roots will have a chance to develop before the heat of summer. Pennisetum appreciates full sun and moisture-retentive, well-drained soil. It is adaptable to a wide range of soil conditions. Space the plants at least 3 to 3 1/2 ft. apart; closer spacing will crowd them and obscure their splendid form. For planting instructions, follow the advice on page 91.

Growing Tips
Water thoroughly, and keep moist until established. Mulch will help conserve moisture. Fertilizing is unnecessary.

Care
Pests and disease aren't problematic. Cut back pennisetum any time from late fall to early spring to several inches from the ground. A hedge trimmer will facilitate the process. Clumps may require division every three to five years. Follow the guidelines on page 91. Division takes significant exertion, so recruit an assistant. Pennisetum is not completely hardy in Zone 5; in unusually cold winters and exposed locations, the plant may winterkill. Fountain grass will self-sow to some extent, and seedlings should be pulled before their root systems develop. In warmer areas of the country, self-sowing is a nuisance. Because of this, we don't recommend planting pennisetum in natural areas.

Companion Planting and Design
Use fountain grass to provide contrast with coarser-textured perennials such as sedums and 'Goldsturm' rudbeckia. This combination has been used extensively as a component of the New American landscape style and is often seen in Michigan public plantings. Plant daffodils to add spring interest around the late-developing foliage.

We Recommend
A smaller cultivar of pennisetum called 'Hameln' (2 1/2 to 3 ft.) is hardier but not as dramatic. A good choice for massing, it has creamy-white bottlebrush flowers. We don't recommend the black-seeded cultivars like 'Moudry'. They are less hardy and are prolific self-sowers. Purple fountain grass, *P. setaceum* 'Rubrum', is a tender grass with burgundy foliage and purplish plumes. It makes a spectacular centerpiece for a container.

Prairie Dropseed
Sporobolus heterolepis

When, Where, and How to Plant

Plant dropseed in the spring, in well-drained soil in full sun. Soil type is not as important as good drainage. Plants will take some shade but tend to flop open. Follow general directions for planting grasses on page 91. Space plants at 18 to 24 in.; spacing too closely will obscure their form.

Growing Tips

Prairie dropseed is easy to grow and requires little care. Keep newly planted grasses moist until established. Prairie dropseed is quite drought-tolerant once established, and fertilization is unnecessary. If you are using mulch to control weeds, avoid piling it around the base of the clump.

Care

Insect pests and disease rarely bother prairie dropseed. Dropseed tends to be slow-growing and clumps will take about three years to develop their full effect. Cut back clumps in early December to about 3 in. from the ground; this plant doesn't provide reliable winter interest. Plants may self-sow, but this is rarely a nuisance. Prairie dropseed doesn't need frequent division; if clumps start to die in the center, follow the general directions for dividing grasses on page 91. Divide plants in the spring. New divisions, like new plants, take several years to reach their full potential.

Companion Planting and Design

Prairie dropseed may be used in sunny perennial beds or naturalistic prairie gardens, and as edging or groundcover. A mature clump makes a wonderful accent plant. Use it in the foreground of beds; the delicate flowers are a "see-through," and the glistening finely textured foliage provides welcome contrast to a host of perennials. In summer it is a beautiful foil for butterfly weed and black-eyed Susan. For a gorgeous fall combination, plant dropseed with 'Fireworks' goldenrod, 'Bluebird' smooth aster (*Aster laevis*), and calamint.

We Recommend

There aren't any named selections of prairie dropseed, but we highly recommend you try this wonderful native.

Prairie dropseed is startling in its simple beauty. Its upright arching clumps produce a fountain of shimmering bright-green foliage. Later, the airy flowers push above the foliage on long graceful stalks. When backlit by the sun, they create a glowing translucent veil that trembles in the breeze. A surprising feature of this prairie native is its fragrance. When in bloom, the flowers emit a light herby fragrance reminiscent of cilantro. If that was not enough, prairie dropseed ends the year with a smoldering orange hue. Dropseed's low height makes it easy to use in smaller gardens and its extremely fine texture complements almost everything. It's easy to please, too: Full sun and good drainage will ensure success. This grass deserves more appreciation.

Bloom Period and Seasonal Color
Delicate flowers midsummer through fall; orange fall color.

Mature Height × Spread
18 to 24 in. × 2 ft.

Switch Grass
Panicum virgatum

Switch grass, an American native, is highly adaptable. It grows in almost every state, occurring in tall-grass prairies, dunes, and open, moist woodlands. Switch grass creates a diaphanous pinkish cloud when in bloom. In the autumn, its fall color—often yellow, orange, and purplish-red—adds an incendiary glow to the garden. By winter its leaves bleach to straw, and its sturdy silhouette contributes to the garden until early spring. Full sun is all you need to grow switch grass; it is not particular about soil type or drainage. The species varies in height, habit, and fall color, and it is best used in meadows or prairie-style gardens, or for wildlife cover. Gardeners should look for cultivars, which offer compact uniform size, upright habit, and attractive autumn color.

Bloom Period and Seasonal Color
Pinkish-green to burgundy in midsummer.

Mature Height × Spread
4 to 7 ft. × 3 ft.

Zones
To Zone 4

When, Where, and How to Plant
Plant in the spring so that the roots will have time to grow before the heat of summer. Switch grass is very adaptable and will grow in a wide range of soil types and conditions. It prefers full sun and moist, fertile soil but accepts dry and moist situations. In very dry sites, plants will be stunted. Plant switch grass in the garden at least 3 ft. apart, following directions for planting grasses on page 91.

Growing Tips
After planting, water thoroughly, and keep moist until established. Mulch will help conserve moisture. Fertilization is unnecessary.

Care
Pests and diseases are not usually a problem. Cut back switch grass in late winter or early spring to 4 or 5 in. If plants begin to split open in late summer, the clump should be divided or moved to a sunnier location. Divide clumps in spring following the instructions on page 91.

Companion Planting and Design
Use switch grass as a specimen, or in small groups or large sweeps. Switch grass makes an excellent backdrop for fall-blooming perennials. In a moist, sunny bed, red switch grass dramatically sets off the fresh white flowers of 'Whirlwind' anemone with a haze of deep color. If you have the space, add Joe-pye weed 'Gateway' for more drama. Switch grass is well suited to massing in meadow-style gardens with prairie plants such as purple coneflower, blazing star, and Culver's root.

We Recommend
Many cultivars are available. They differ by foliage color, size, and fall color. 'Shenandoah' and 'Rotstrahlbusch' are cultivars with foliage that develops early burgundy coloration; these are sometimes called red switch grass. 'Heavy Metal' (4 to 5 ft.) is a selection with an upright narrow habit and bluish foliage. 'Cloud Nine' is a particularly large selection with blue-green foliage that turns yellow in the fall; it tops out at 6 to 8 ft.

Tall Purple Moor Grass
Molinia caerulea ssp. *arundinacea*

When, Where, and How to Plant
Plant tall purple moor grass in the spring. Choose locations with full sun for best growth and flowering; some light shade is acceptable. Moor grass is tolerant of a range of soil types, although moist well-drained soil is preferred. Avoid dry sites, and plant following the general directions on page 91. For mass planting, space at least 3 ft.

Growing Tips
Keep newly planted grasses moist until well established. Apply a 2-in. layer of organic mulch to conserve moisture. Tall moor grass is not especially drought-tolerant, so water deeply during dry spells. Fertilizer is generally unnecessary for ornamental grasses.

Care
Like most grasses, tall moor grass is seldom troubled by pests or disease. This grass is not invasive and rarely self-sows. By early winter, the foliage and flower stalks of tall moor grass shatter. To avoid a mess, tie up the clump with twine in late fall and cut through the bottom with a lopper or hedge trimmers; you can then dispose of the foliage in one neat package. Divide moor grass in the spring following the instructions on page 91; larger divisions will mature faster.

Companion Planting and Design
Though tall purple moor grass works well in a mass, it makes a noteworthy freestanding specimen plant. Use it to add summer-through-fall interest to perennial gardens, island beds, and mixed plantings. It's effective as a repetitive element along a walkway, where the arching flowering stems provide excitement. Tall purple moor grass adds sparkle and movement to a combination of sedums, hybrid anemones, and Joe-pye weed.

We Recommend
Our favorite selection is 'Transparent'. Its graceful flowering stems rise to about 6 ft. It has a delicate see-through effect and can be used even in small gardens. If you have the space, 'Skyracer' towers over the garden at 8 to 9 ft. The shortest selection is 'Staefa'; it is a good choice for massing.

Ornamental grasses bring movement to the garden. Tall purple moor grass is like a kinetic sculpture, constantly in motion. From arching clumps of green foliage two to three feet tall, the flowers, on flexible stems, rise three to four feet high above the foliage. In full bloom, a mature clump has a strong architectural form, and its graceful flower stalks play in the slightest breeze. Though this grass's height is lofty, its delicate character never overwhelms. In the fall, tall moor grass turns a rich golden yellow. Put tall purple moor grass to its best use by using it as a spectacular focal point. It may take a few years to reach maturity but then will never fail to earn admiration.

Bloom Period and Seasonal Color
Airy flowers from late summer through fall; yellow fall color.

Mature Height × Spread
Foliage 2 to 3 ft., flowers to 6 ft. × $2^1/_2$ to 3 ft.

Zones
To Zone 5

Tufted Hair Grass
Deschampsia caespitosa

From a modest one-foot clump of arching dark-green foliage, tufted hair grass generates a tremendous cloud of delicate flowers almost three feet high. The flowers emerge in late spring a soft silky bronze-green, but, as they mature, they stiffen to form a billowing mass of yellow or gold. Tufted hair grass is in its glory in midsummer when its bright airy flowers create a remarkable backdrop for perennials. A cool-season grass, it's well suited to Michigan's chilly spring and sometimes-cool summer. The clumps of slender foliage are an early presence in the garden, when many ornamental grasses still appear lifeless. Unlike most grasses, tufted hair grass will grow in partial shade. A large drift creates a cloud of color when in bloom.

Bloom Period and Seasonal Color
Pale green changing to golden yellow in later spring to early summer.

Mature Height × Spread
2 to 3^1/$_2$ ft. × 2 ft.

When, Where, and How to Plant
Plant tufted hair grass in early spring or in September. It prefers light shade but will thrive in full sun with adequate moisture. It is one of the few grasses that will grow in shade, although too much shade will decrease flowering. It prefers moist, rich soil and tolerates fairly wet, heavy soils. It will not survive in a hot, dry location. Plant tufted hair grass in the landscape 2 to 3 ft. apart, following the general directions for planting grasses on page 91.

Growing Tips
Water thoroughly, and keep moist until established. Mulch will help conserve moisture. If sited correctly, no fertilizer is necessary. In full sun, tufted hair grass will need watering during dry spells.

Care
Tufted hair grass is usually pest- and disease-free. Remove the flowering stems in late summer or early fall when the inflorescences begin to break up and look disheveled. In fact, shearing the whole clump back in late summer is often the best option. New foliage will appear to form a fresh green clump by mid-fall and will remain evergreen through the winter. After three or four years, clumps of hair grass may need rejuvenation; follow the directions for dividing grasses on page 91.

Companion Planting and Design
Use tufted hair grass in perennial beds and in groundcover plantings. Plant it under shrubs or on the edges of a woodland garden or massed on a bank. Hair grass is not at its peak in late summer and early fall; at that point, the flowers are beginning to deteriorate. Keep this in mind when planning mass plantings in high-use areas. Superb in moist soil, it should be tried pondside with the dramatic foliage of big-leaf ligularia, *Ligularia dentata* 'Desdemona', and the yellow flag iris.

We Recommend
There are many easy cultivars, but the names are difficult. 'Bronzeschleier' ('Bronze Veil') has bronze-green flowers changing to bronze-yellow. 'Goldschleier' ('Gold Veil') has brighter golden yellow flowers. 'Northern Lights' is a dramatic variegated selection with cream-and-green-striped leaves sometimes suffused with pink.

Wild Oats

Chasmanthium latifolium

When, Where, and How to Plant

Plant wild oats in the spring to allow time for its roots to grow before summer's heat. Wild oats prefers moist, well-drained, humus-rich soil and partial shade. With adequate moisture, plants will thrive in full sun; the foliage will be lighter green. It is somewhat drought-tolerant but will not thrive in a hot, dry location. Plant wild oats in the landscape 1^1/$_2$ to 2 ft. apart, following the directions on page 91.

Growing Tips

After planting, water thoroughly, and keep clumps moist until established. Unless in moisture-retentive soil, plants located in full sun will need regular watering. Mulch will help conserve moisture. If properly sited, fertilizer will be unnecessary.

Care

Pests and disease are negligible. Cut wild oats back to the ground in early spring. Self-sowing is the biggest concern. It may be welcome and the extra plants can be moved to enlarge your planting, but in some situations it can be a nuisance. A thick layer of mulch will discourage self-sown seedlings—or you can deadhead plants to remove the spikelets in the fall, although you'll sacrifice the winter interest. To divide clumps, follow the directions for dividing grasses on page 91.

Companion Planting and Design

Plant wild oats in woodland gardens or shady perennial beds, and by streams and ponds. Take advantage of wild oats' bamboolike foliage in shade-garden combinations. Contrast its wide flat leaf blades with the airy flowers of Bowman's root, dark-leaved heucheras, and the heart-shaped foliage of Siberian bugloss; or accent a ground-cover planting of bigroot geranium with wild oats' upright form and nodding spikelets.

We Recommend

Wild oats makes a wonderful cut flower and everlasting. The drooping stems and flattened spikelets create an elegant outline in a large vase. Stems can be harvested at any stage. If cut while young, they will maintain a greenish cast; later, the stalks will be coppery brown.

Few perennials have the winter appeal of wild oats. Their copper-tan spikelets, when backlit by the low winter sun, create a garden picture as memorable as peonies in June. Wild oats excels in three seasons—with foliage and flowers in summer, with bronze color in autumn, and with a vase-like form and persistent spikelets in winter. Native to woodlands and riverbanks of the eastern United States, its natural range just reaches into the southwest corner of Lower Michigan. Owing to its woodland origins, wild oats is one of the few grasses that prefers partial shade. The flowers, excellent for arrangements, start out green and gradually change to a copper brown. Spangle grass, another common name, alludes to the dangling spikelets as they sway in the slightest breeze, reflecting light.

Other Name
Spangle Grass

Bloom Period and Seasonal Color
Green changing to coppery brown in midsummer.

Mature Height × Spread
2 to 3 ft. × 2 ft.

Zones
To Zone 5

Perennials *for Michigan*

With careful planning, a perennial garden can glow with color and beauty from early spring to late fall. And unlike annual flowers, which look the same all season, perennials are constantly changing as new plants come into their prime. Part of the gardener's pleasure comes from orchestrating a whole year of interest and planning seasonal combinations of flowers as well as foliage. Attractive leaves add a charm and texture all their own and form a unifying ribbon that ties the garden together.

The plants chosen for this chapter have proved to be superior for Michigan gardens. They are generally long-lived and adaptable, and they resist pests and diseases if planted in the right site and properly maintained. Bed preparation is especially important since perennials often remain in place for many years. Before planting, test the soil and amend it as required.

Grow What You Like

With new and beautiful perennials coming on the market all the time, it's tempting to want one of each. Certain qualities can help you identify which ones will be hardy and high achievers in your garden.

The easiest ones will be those that seldom need staking or special treatment for diseases or pests. Those that spread moderately or stay in clumps will blend well with the rest of the garden without trying to take over.

Seek out perennials with attractive foliage. Many bloom for just a week or two, but their leaves can be an important element in the garden all season long.

Instead of looking for low-care perennials, you may be looking for plants that will offer a wider range of diversity and be more challenging to grow.

Many gardeners find that caring for perennials is relaxing and a good way to tap into their creative and artistic talents.

Either way, maintaining your garden should be a pleasure and an expression of your personality. Grow what you like, experiment, and learn.

Planting Your Perennials

Container-grown perennials can be planted from spring to fall, although extra watering will be necessary as they become established for those planted in the heat of summer.

Pay special attention to the light requirements of the plants on the following pages. Plants that require sun will struggle in shady spots, and vice versa. There are so many perennials available for various light conditions that it should not be difficult to choose one to match your site.

The best soils for most perennials are of average or better fertility with plenty of organic matter, although the following entries include some plants that thrive on poor or sandy soil. Work in compost, aged manure, shredded leaves, or other material if needed before planting to improve soil fertility or drainage.

When digging the planting hole, make the opening at least as deep as the container and twice as wide. Position the plant so the soil level is the same as it was in the pot. Fill in with soil around the roots about halfway up, firm gently, and water well. Add more soil to fill the hole completely. Water regularly until plants are established. Mulch to conserve soil moisture.

Post-Planting Care

In a well-prepared bed with average or better soil, perennials will need infrequent fertilization. More is not better when fertilizing perennials; overfertilization can lead to soft, leggy growth. Take your cue from the plants. A plant that needs fertilizer may appear stunted, exhibit chlorosis, or show lack of vigor.

Perennials that have been growing in a bed for many years or heavy feeders like garden phlox will profit from fertilization. In the spring, apply a two-inch topdressing of compost, or a light application of a general-purpose fertilizer (10-10-10, 12-12-12, or 5-10-5). Organic fertilizers may be used in place of chemical fertilizers. Sprinkle the fertilizer around the base of the plants and, if the soil is dry, water it in. If a plant needs a midseason boost, use a foliar feed with a water-soluble chemical or organic fertilizer.

Grooming and Dividing

Gardeners should inspect the foliage of perennials every fall. Some leaves, like those of peonies and iris, should be removed and disposed of offsite if possible, since they may harbor pests or disease. But most other perennials may be left until late winter. The old stalks and seedheads are interesting as they catch the snow and may provide food or shelter to wildlife.

Many perennials require periodic division for rejuvenation. Watch how they grow over the years. Those that die in the middle, produce fewer flowers than they used to or those that are splitting open are ready to be divided. In most cases, the plants should be dug out of the garden and cut apart. A sharp flat spade (not a shovel!) and garden forks are invaluable tools for digging and dividing perennials. Don't be afraid to work with your perennials. Most are tough and forgiving. When you divide them, take the opportunity to dig compost into the planting hole, then replant the healthy portions. Caring for newly divided plants is critical while they get established.

Plants that bloom in spring and early summer can usually be moved or divided in late summer or early fall. Those that bloom later in the season can be moved or divided in spring. The idea is to give the plant plenty of time to re-establish before it comes into bloom again.

In the fall, while your memory of the season is still fresh, make notes about your garden to review during the winter and spring. Jot down what plants are splitting open or spreading out of bounds, and put them on the list for division. Note which plants to move in order to improve seasonal combinations or fine-tune design.

Designing with Perennials

When beginning a new perennial garden, it can be overwhelming to choose a few plants from the thousands available. It may help to make a chart showing various

characteristics of the plants. There should be plants in a range of heights, flower colors, and foliage shapes and textures. By underplanting with spring bulbs and making careful perennial selections, you can have something in bloom from April through November.

The best perennial gardens include not only these herbaceous plants but also shrubs such as caryopteris and shrub roses, and evergreens for year-round interest. Ornamental grasses bring movement during winter, at a time when most perennials are brown and lifeless.

Designing a successful perennial garden isn't difficult if you follow a few simple guidelines.

First, **follow the "right plant, right place" principle**. Analyze your site and choose plants that are hardy in your zone and well suited to your growing conditions.

Next, **develop a concept**. This could be a theme, color scheme, look, or season of interest. Defining your personal goals helps you narrow your plant choices.

Create seasonal combinations. The most compelling perennial gardens have plants that bloom together, creating beautiful pictures. Try some of the combinations in the Companion Planting and Design sections. Visit other gardens to make note of the perennials that bloom together in your area. Add bulbs and annuals for extra color.

Use perennials with attractive foliage that lasts throughout the growing season. Foliage is the backdrop that unifies a garden. Add some perennials and ornamental grasses for their foliage effect alone.

Finally, **fine-tune your garden** by changing what doesn't work. If two perennials are blooming in isolation, make a note to move them closer together to create a combination.

Experiment with perennials. Try the combinations in the following pages, as well as others that occur to you. As you gain experience, you will want to try additional effects. The amazing thing about perennials is how they can be used to express the gardener's own unique vision and personality.

Perennials bring variety, color, and romance to the garden. They entice the gardener to try new tactics, to move and experiment, to extend the season of bloom. For these reasons, as well as for sheer beauty, growing perennials is satisfying and rewarding—as more gardeners are discovering every year.

Artemisia
Artemisia ludoviciana

In the garden realm, the royal pair 'Silver King' and 'Silver Queen' are not the best-behaved of monarchs. Though they are not exactly tyrants, their spreading ways strike some gardeners as overbearing. Still, they're worth planting. These artemisias offer silvery foliage that calms nearby bright colors. They provide texture, and they shine in their own right. Use artemisia to create a backdrop for other plants or to fashion a ribbon of silver that ties together a summer planting. 'Silver King' grows to about three feet tall and has slender stems and fine-textured narrow silvery leaves. It creates a billow of silver-gray in the garden. 'Silver Queen' is more variable. It is generally shorter, about two feet, and has wider leaves with jagged edges.

Other Names
White Sage, Wormwood

Bloom Period and Seasonal Color
Grown for its silvery foliage.

Mature Height × Spread
2 to 3 ft. × 2 to 3 ft.

Zones
To Zone 4

When, Where, and How to Plant
Artemisia can be planted from spring into summer. Choose locations in full sun and any soil. Though tolerant of heavy soil, plants will sprawl if the site is too moist. Plant it in informal areas where its spread will be welcome. Follow the general directions for planting perennials on page 102. Space plants 2 to 3 ft. apart.

Growing Tips
Water regularly until plants are established. Artemisia does not need extra watering or fertilization. Too much fertility will lead to soft sprawling growth. Mulch is unnecessary.

Care
Plants are rarely bothered by insects, but rot can be a problem where the drainage is poor. Every spring, evaluate your planting and remove unwanted sections. Underground runners may have spread several feet from the main clump. Take a sharp spade and cut down to sever all roots. Pull up and remove. When the clump starts to die in the middle, dig it up and replant vigorous pieces from the outside edges. White sage may be pruned back at any time to shape its growth, tame floppy stems, or eliminate flowers.

Companion Planting and Design
Perhaps these plants shouldn't be used in small or formal gardens, but they come into their own when planted in drifts as part of a large, sweeping display. 'Silver Queen' sparks the already vibrant combination of yellow yarrow and violet-blue salvia. 'Silver King' can set off orange daylilies, 'Lucifer' crocosmia, and gloriosa daisies.

We Recommend
'Valerie Finnis' has wide silver foliage and a spreading but not aggressive habit. It almost creates a white effect in the garden. Wormwood, *Artemisia absinthium*, is a semievergreen shrublike artemisia with silvery gray, finely divided foliage. 'Lambrook Silver' (2½ ft.) is one of the best ferny silver plants for Michigan gardens. Also look for *A. versicolor* (8 to 10 in.), sometimes called sea foam. It is a wonderful low-growing artemisia with silvery curled foliage.

When, Where, and How to Plant

Plant container-grown astilbe in the spring so the roots become established before summer's heat. Choose moist, humus-rich soil in partial shade. Astilbe will tolerate sun, but only if it has almost constant moisture. Plant astilbes 1 1/2 to 2 ft. apart following general directions on page 102.

Growing Tips

Water regularly until plants are established. A layer of mulch will conserve moisture. Keep plants moist—in extended dry periods, the leaves will brown and die. Feed in the spring by topdressing with well-rotted compost or an application of general fertilizer such as 10-10-10.

Care

Astilbe is resistant to pests and diseases. After about three to five years, clumps will start to lose vigor. For rejuvenation, divide plants in the spring as the foliage is emerging. Dig up the clumps, and split apart the woody fibrous-rooted crowns with a sharp spade or large knife. Before replanting, enrich the soil with organic matter. Keep new divisions well watered and mulched. Deadheading astilbe is a judgment call. Tidy gardeners often find the browning flowers unappealing and remove them from the plant. Flowering stems left in place will provide an effective contrast with snow. Remove them in early spring.

Companion Planting and Design

Plant astilbe in shady, moist beds, in borders and woodland gardens, and by ponds and water features. A mass display of assorted astilbe cultivars provides more bright color in the shade than any other perennial. Plant ribbons of astilbe with hostas, 'Palace Purple' heuchera, and Solomon's seal for an interesting groundcover.

We Recommend

There are many cultivars. 'Ostrich Plume' (3 ft.) is favored for its tall pink arching flowers. 'Fanal' (2 ft.) is renowned for its deep-red flowers and bronzy leaves. *Astilbe simplicifolia* 'Sprite' (12 in.), with shell-pink flowers and bronzy foliage, creates a delicate effect. For a bolder statement, plant *Astilbe chinensis* var. *taquetii* 'Superba' (4 ft.); it blooms in mid- to late summer with tall upright spires of rose-purple.

The "right plant, right place" message can be clearly demonstrated with astilbe. When planted in partial shade and humus-rich, moist soil, astilbe is beyond compare, and clouds of feathery plumes float above glossy divided foliage. In sun and dry soil, though, astilbe bakes, the foliage sears, and the flowers are stunted. Grow astilbe in the sun if you must, but be prepared to make frequent runs for the hose. Hybrid garden astilbes are esteemed plants for light shade and moist soil. They adorn the shady garden with color and long-lasting handsome foliage. The flowers appear above the foliage in open feathery sprays or slender upright plumes. They can be subtle, in shades of cream, pale pink, or peach, or obvious with deep reds, intense whites, or bright pinks.

Bloom Period and Seasonal Color

White, red, pink, or peach flowers in late spring and summer.

Mature Height × Spread

1 1/2 to 3 1/2 ft. × 18 to 24 in.

Beebalm
Monarda didyma

The vivid colors of this mint relative and Michigan native earn it a place in the sunny border, where it attracts bees and hummingbirds in July. In the past, many gardeners grew discouraged with beebalm because its foliage often became covered with powdery mildew by midsummer. Proper siting and selection of resistant cultivars, however, improve the odds of enjoying good-looking leaves as well as the distinctive beebalm flower heads, which are really clusters of long tube-shaped flowers. According to the Chicago Botanic Garden, some of the most disease-resistant cultivars are 'Jacob Cline' (deep-red flowers), 'Marshall's Delight' (pink), and 'Raspberry Wine' (purplish red). Beebalm is a native plant that early settlers—including some near Oswego, New York—used for tea. Crushed leaves are fragrant.

Other Names
Oswego Tea, Bergamot

Bloom Period and Seasonal Color
Red, purple, pink, white flowers in July and August.

Mature Height × Spread
2 to 5 ft. × 2 to 3 ft.

When, Where, and How to Plant
Plant beebalm in spring or early fall. *Monarda* does best in full sun and where there will be good air circulation so foliage does not stay wet. The soil should be moist and well drained. Remove the plant from its container and tease apart the roots gently to encourage outward growth. Plant it at the same depth it was growing in the pot, and water it well and regularly. Space so air can circulate around plants.

Growing Tips
Water regularly; *Monarda* is not drought-tolerant and requires regular moisture to thrive. A soaker or drip hose will deliver water to the base of the plant, keeping the foliage dry while providing the moisture that beebalm needs. Mulch to conserve soil moisture, keeping a mulch-free circle about 3 in. wide at the base of the plant. Fertilizer is unnecessary.

Care
Deadhead the old flowers. Powdery mildew and rust can disfigure beebalm, especially older cultivars grown in overcrowded conditions. Plants in dry soil are also more prone to mildew. If mildew turns plants gray after they flower, cut down and destroy the old stalks. Any foliage that remains should be removed and destroyed in fall to avoid overwintering spores. Beebalm can be cut back in May to encourage smaller, more compact growth. Divide *Monarda* at least every three years, in spring or early fall, to keep it within bounds and healthy. Dig up the clump and divide the outer portion into rooted sections. Discard the older, center part.

Companion Planting and Design
Monarda peaks in July. Enjoy the splash with the Shasta daisy cultivar 'Becky', blazing star, garden phlox, and daylilies. Beebalm has a somewhat coarse effect. Enlist the stately and finely-textured 'Karl Foerster' feather reed grass to tone down this rowdy midsummer crowd.

We Recommend
'Raspberry Wine' beebalm is a wonderful wine-red color with many flowers and excellent mildew resistance.

When, Where, and How to Plant

Plant bellflower in the spring. Choose locations in moist, well-drained soil in full sun or light shade. Hot, dry sites will not do; evenly moist soil with a bit of afternoon shade is best. The Carpathian bellflower needs good drainage to survive. Follow the general planting directions on page 102. Space peach-leaf bellflower $1^1/2$ ft. apart and Carpathian bellflower 1 ft. apart.

Growing Tips

Water regularly until plants are established, then water plants during drought. Apply a 2-in. layer of organic mulch to conserve moisture. Avoid piling mulch around the tussocks of Carpathian bellflower. In poor soils, fertilize with a sprinkling of 10-10-10 in the spring.

Care

Bellflowers are rarely troubled by insects or disease. For peach-leaf bellflower, deadhead by cutting back the whole stem to encourage rebloom on new stems. The tall stems of some peach-leaf bellflowers may succumb to wind and rain; to avoid this, staking is an option. Bellflowers may become crowded and lose vigor over the years and can be divided or replaced. Add organic material to the soil after division. Bellflower can self-sow. Flowers may or may not come true from seed.

Companion Planting and Design

Plant bellflowers in perennial beds and borders, and in cottage gardens. Peach-leaf bellflower is a welcome addition to a mixed planting of shrub roses, annuals, and perennials. Try a white-flowered selection with the purple-blue of catmint and a pink rose such as 'Carefree Wonder'. The Carpathian bellflower 'Blue Clips' looks sweet on a rock wall with pink 'Red Fox' veronica and 'Vera Jameson' sedum.

We Recommend

'Telham Beauty' (3 to 4 ft.) is a tall, vigorous cultivar of peach-leaf bellflower with large China-blue flowers. White forms are attractive with blue- and purple-flowered perennials. 'Alba' is $2^1/2$ ft. tall with delicate white bells. One of the best Carpathian bellflowers is 'Blue Clips'; 'White Clips' is its white counterpart. Both are 6 to 8 in., compact and floriferous.

Bellflowers are full of old-fashioned charm. Their appealing bell-shaped flowers appear for weeks or, with deadheading, even longer. The bellflowers represent a large group of plants; some grow to over two feet while others reach just eight inches. The peach-leaf bellflower, Campanula persicifolia, is a cottage garden staple. Its delightful cup-shaped bells in blue or white rise several feet above its neat mats of bright-green leathery leaves. The Carpathian bellflower, C. carpatica, is a best-seller at Michigan perennial nurseries. This cutie flowers like crazy, smothering its low six-inch tussocks of foliage with lavender-blue or white bells. Use Carpathian bellflower for the front of the border, edging, or a rock wall. Plant drifts of the peach-leaf bellflower for the June garden.

Bloom Period and Seasonal Color
Blue or white flower in early to midsummer.

Mature Height × Spread
8 to 24 in. × 8 to 14 in.

Black Snakeroot

Cimicifuga racemosa

So many woodland plants hug the ground, soaking in sunlight as it hits the forest floor. Tall and bold plants add much-needed contrast that brings the shade garden to life. For handsome foliage and lofty flowers, black snakeroot, Cimicifuga racemosa, is a dramatic choice. A woodland native at home in rich soil and open shade, black snakeroot is at the northern edge of its range in Michigan. At maturity, it forms large, beautiful three-foot clumps of dark-green dissected foliage. In summer, slender stems topped with white bottlebrush-shaped flowers rise above the foliage, reaching more than six feet. The wandlike stems of black snakeroot bend and lean with grace. On a shady slope, black snakeroot can form a memorable groundcover planting all on its own.

Other Name
Bugbane

Bloom Period and Seasonal Color
White flowers in midsummer.

Mature Height × Spread
5 to 6 ft. × 3 to 4 ft.

When, Where, and How to Plant

Plant black snakeroot in the spring. Choose a location with moist, humus-rich soil in partial shade. Add organic matter to sandy or clay soils. Snakeroot will grow in full sun with ample moisture but is at its best in light shade. Plant following the general directions on page 102, spacing 3 ft. apart.

Growing Tips

Water regularly until plants are established. Spread a 2-in. layer of an organic mulch to conserve moisture. Snakeroot needs moist soil to thrive, so water deeply when natural rainfall is scarce. In the spring, fertilize mature clumps with a sprinkling of 10-10-10 fertilizer or a topdressing of compost.

Care

Snakeroot is rarely bothered by insects or disease. The tall flower stalks have a tendency to lean; tidy gardeners often secure each stalk with a slender green stake. Don't hurry to deadhead; the seedheads are ornamental. Snakeroot's clumps increase slowly, and division is rarely necessary. For propagation, the large fibrous-rooted crowns can be divided in the spring. Plants of snakeroot take several years to reach their full potential.

Companion Planting and Design

Use snakeroot as a vertical accent in shade gardens and woodland edges or as an elegant addition to the moist, lightly shaded perennial border. It makes an effective tall groundcover. Black snakeroot's dark divided foliage makes for interesting contrast with variegated hosta, heuchera, astilbe, and woodland wildflowers.

We Recommend

Native to Siberia, the Kamchatka bugbane, *Cimicifuga simplex* (3 to 4 ft.), is the last of snakeroots—or, for that matter, the last of the perennials—to flower. 'White Pearl' is the cultivar usually offered. Often the white airy wands catch brightly colored foliage as it drops from the trees in October. This garden vision is fraught with risk, though; flowers can get nipped by the first frost. *C. ramosa* 'Hillside Black Beauty', an extraordinary cultivar of a Japanese bugbane, has deep-purple foliage and tall creamy-white spires.

Blazing Star
Liatris spicata

When, Where, and How to Plant

Plant blazing star in the spring to early summer. Choose locations with average to rich, moist soil in full sun. *Liatris spicata* tolerates moisture better than other blazing stars. Avoid poorly drained sites. Plant following the general directions on page 102, spacing plants 2 ft. apart. Blazing star corms are sometimes sold in the spring unpotted like summer-flowering bulbs. These should be planted so that the pinkish buds are 2 in. below the soil surface. Firm the soil lightly, and water.

Growing Tips

Water regularly until new plants are established. Water during extended dry spells as well; although drought-resistant, spiked blazing star grows best in moist soils. A layer of organic mulch helps conserve moisture. Fertilization is generally unnecessary.

Care

Blazing star is easy to grow and pest- and disease-free. Prevent rot by choosing well-drained soils. In formal plantings, deadhead the spikes as they fade; in more natural areas, leave the seedheads for the birds. Tall plants may need to be staked. Division is seldom needed, but corms can be lifted and separated or cut apart in the spring to increase stock.

Companion Planting and Design

Blazing star is at its best in prairie and meadow plantings where the lanky (close to 3 ft.) stems are supported by grasses and other meadow flowers such as Culver's root, sunflower heliopsis, and black-eyed Susan. Blazing star and purple coneflower are a natural combination. In all but the largest perennial borders, plant blazing star in groups of three or as a single specimen. The bold form is too extreme in larger groups.

We Recommend

The cultivar 'Kobold' (15 to 18 in.), also called 'Gnome', is a good choice. It has bright red-violet flower spikes and a more compact habit, eliminating the need for staking. 'Floristan White' (2$^{1}/_{2}$ to 3 ft.) is an excellent white-flowered cultivar. Its partner 'Floristan Violet' (3 ft.) is a taller rose-purple selection. These were bred for cut-flower production.

Blazing star is a spectacular perennial with long, fat spikes of rose-purple flowers. Often seen in florists' bouquets, this native wildflower is more at home on the prairie. The spiked blazing star, Liatris spicata, is the easiest to grow and the best for gardens. Blazing star's thick spires are made up of clustered, wispy rose-purple flowers held on stems clothed with narrow grasslike foliage. Spiked blazing star grows in the southern third of Michigan's Lower Peninsula in meadows, wet prairies, and other moist, open places, although its natural habitat is diminishing. A label on a herbarium specimen collected in 1896 states "thousands of acres covered with it about Lake St. Clair." That image alone is reason enough to try this plant in your garden.

Other Name
Gayfeather

Bloom Period and Seasonal Color
Rosy-purple flowers in early to late summer.

Mature Height × Spread
2 to 3 ft. × 2 ft.

Bleeding Heart
Dicentra spectabilis

Common names are often descriptive, and "bleeding heart" depicts the distinctive pink heart-shaped flowers of Dicentra spectabilis, *with inner petals that resemble a drop of liquid. Turn them upside-down to see the "lady in the bathtub," a lighthearted common name that is a favorite of preschoolers for this old-fashioned beauty. A full-grown clump of bleeding heart, one yard high and equally wide, creates a magnificent display. The arching stems dangle pink-and-white flowers like heart-shaped lockets. Bleeding heart needs only the right location— rich, moist soil and partial shade—to flourish. It has one significant flaw, the tendency for the foliage to yellow and die by late summer. That is easily accommodated, however—plant it with ferns, large-leaved hosta, or bluestar to fill in the gap.*

Bloom Period and Seasonal Color
Pink and white flowers in mid-spring.

Mature Height × Spread
2 to 3 ft. × 18 to 24 in.

When, Where, and How to Plant
Plant bleeding heart in the spring. Choose a location with moist, well-drained, humus-rich soil in partial shade. Bleeding heart tolerates sun with adequate moisture, but the foliage will go dormant prematurely. Add organic matter to light soils. Don't choose hot, dry, or windy locations. Follow the general directions for planting perennials on page 102, spacing plants 18 to 24 in. apart.

Growing Tips
Water regularly until plants are established. In the spring, spread a 2-in. layer of organic mulch to conserve moisture. Water during dry spells; adequate moisture prevents the foliage from declining. In the spring, fertilize mature clumps with a sprinkling of 10-10-10 fertilizer or a topdressing of garden compost.

Care
Bleeding heart is rarely troubled by insects or disease problems. Early dieback of the foliage is normal and not a reason for concern. When the foliage starts to deteriorate, cut it down to the ground. Bleeding heart shouldn't need dividing, but it can be divided to yield more plants in early spring. If you can spare them from the garden, the arching sprays of bleeding heart are a superb cut flower.

Companion Planting and Design
Bleeding heart is a traditional part of the spring perennial border, and can also be tucked in with spring-flowering shrubs and groundcovers. Fill a lightly shaded north or east corner near the house with a bleeding heart, and underplant it with bigroot geranium. Or try a white bleeding heart among the dark-green foliage and blue forget-me-not blooms of Siberian bugloss.

We Recommend
The white-flowered types of bleeding heart are 'Alba' or 'Pantaloons'. A related plant of high merit is the fringed bleeding heart, *Dicentra eximia*. Growing to a height of 9 to 18 in., this forest native of the eastern United States forms carpets of lovely blue-gray dissected foliage. The pink flowers have an elongated heart shape. These plants flower heavily in spring and continue sporadically through October.

When, Where, and How to Plant

Plant blue false indigo in the spring. Choose a permanent location in full sun with moist, well-drained, average to fertile soil. Clumps will tolerate light shade but will flop in too much. Give each plant ample room. Plant following the general directions on page 102, spacing 3 to 4 ft. apart.

Growing Tips

Water regularly until established; plants are drought-tolerant once established. In the spring, fertilize mature clumps with a sprinkling of 10-10-10 fertilizer or a topdressing of garden compost.

Care

Blue false indigo needs little care. Plants are slow to establish and best left alone. In adequate sun, plants will not need staking. In too much shade, clumps may split open and flop. It's almost impossible to stake them unobtrusively. Better to plan a spring move to a sunnier part of the garden or try lightly pruning back the foliage after flowering to keep plants compact. Because it resents disturbance to its large root system, division is not recommended. If you must divide them, however, dig clumps in the spring as early as possible. It is mainly pest- and disease-free. But voles relish the roots, and rabbits may eat young foliage.

Companion Planting and Design

Blue false indigo is versatile and may be planted in formal borders, informal cottage gardens, island beds, or even massed as a shrub for hedges or foundation plantings. Try blue false indigo as part of a late-spring combination. Add the vertical form and lovely flowers of Siberian iris, blue or magenta hardy geraniums, Bowman's root, and blue star. Add drifts of hybrid anemones and red switch grass for late-season interest.

We Recommend

Look for *Baptisia australis* var. *minor*, a plant with all of blue indigo's good qualities but smaller stature. White false indigo, *Baptisia alba*, hardy to Zone 5, is a choice plant with creamy-white pealike flowers on dark stems and blue-gray foliage. *Baptisia lactea*, also called white or prairie false indigo, has beautiful gray-green foliage and a tall, shrublike habit. It grows on prairies and dry open roadsides in southern Michigan.

Blue false indigo combines strength and beauty. The tall spires of blue-violet flowers add grace to the late-spring garden, and the mounds of soft gray-green foliage create an elegant backdrop right into autumn. The stems of blue false indigo push up quickly in the spring garden. It has its big moment in June, when the intense blue pealike flowers open on tall stalks that are a handsome complement to peonies. Later, the three-lobed cloverlike foliage adds soft gray-green color, textural form, and structure to the garden. Once established, the clumps will last a lifetime with no special care. In the garden, it couldn't be easier. Plant it once, give it a few years to grow, and enjoy.

Bloom Period and Seasonal Color
Blue-violet flowers in late spring.

Mature Height × Spread
3 to 4 ft. × 3 to 4 ft.

Blue Star

Amsonia tabernaemontana

Blue star, a plant of considerable yet subtle beauty, is underappreciated or even unknown by many gardeners. When in bloom, the icy blue celestial flowers of blue star are attractive and refreshing but not scene-stealers. Some plants play supporting roles that are just as important as the lead. Blue star makes other plants look good. The starry domed clusters push up quickly on stems with slender leaves. As the flowers pass, the willowy foliage grows to form a two- to three-foot shrublike mass that contributes structure to the perennial border all season. The shiny green foliage later changes to a rich yellow, enhancing the autumn garden. Few perennials offer reliable fall color, and amsonia is one of the best.

Bloom Period and Seasonal Color
Pale-blue flowers in late spring.

Mature Height × Spread
2 to 3 ft. × 2 to 3 ft.

Zones
To Zone 4

When, Where, and How to Plant
Plant container-grown blue star in the spring, in moist, well-drained soil of average to rich fertility and full sun or partial shade. Deep, moist soils and sun are ideal. Avoid hot, dry sites. Plant blue star 2 1/2 to 3 ft. apart, following the general directions on page 102.

Growing Tips
Water regularly until plants are established. It is drought-tolerant, although some water during dry spells is beneficial. A 2-in. layer of organic mulch will conserve moisture. If sited correctly, fertilization is unnecessary.

Care
Blue star needs little care. We have never experienced a pest or disease problem with this plant. Plants in partial shade have more of a tendency to sprawl, and can be pruned to create dense, compact growth. Use pruners (don't shear) to cut back by about half after flowering. Plants will produce new shoots. Long-lived with a woody, fibrous-rooted crown, this plant will not usually require division, but, if it is desired, division to increase stock may be done in spring.

Companion Planting and Design
Use blue star in perennial beds or borders, in mixed plantings, with shrubs, or in natural areas. Mass it for a low-maintenance but tall ground-cover or foundation plant. Blue stars are excellent companions for peonies, blue false indigo, Oriental poppies, and other late-spring flowers. Capitalize on blue star's fall color by planting clumps with ornamental grasses, asters, and Japanese hybrid anemones.

We Recommend
There are few, if any, cultivars of this native of the southern United States, but several other species and forms are available. The var. *montana* is lower growing, reaching only 2 to 2 1/2 ft., and has a more lax habit. The Arkansas amsonia, *Amsonia hubrectii*, is worth seeking out. It has fine-textured, almost feathery foliage, reaching a height of 3 ft., and beautiful orange-yellow fall color. It has survived in Michigan's Zone 5 but may not be hardy in Zone 4.

When, Where, and How to Plant

Plant container-grown boltonia in the spring. Choose a location with moist, average to fertile, well-drained soil in full sun. Boltonia tolerates some light shade, but plants won't be as upright. Plants grow tallest in moist soil. Follow the general directions for planting perennials on page 102, planting 2 ft. apart. The species should be spaced at 3 ft.

Growing Tips

Water regularly until plants are established. Somewhat drought-tolerant, clumps will be shorter in dry soils. Water during dry spells for more lush growth. Special fertilization is not needed.

Care

Boltonia is resistant to pests and disease. The cultivar 'Snowbank' is usually self-supporting. The species may grow too tall and require staking, particularly in rich soil or light shade. To avoid staking, cut back the plants by about half in late spring or early summer. Divide clumps every three or four years to restore vigor and control spread. This is easily accomplished in the spring. Dig clumps, split into sections, and pull apart the pieces. Replant vigorous divisions. Water well until established.

Companion Planting and Design

This easy-to-grow perennial is an excellent addition to formal and informal perennial gardens, to meadows, or to a rustic fence. Boltonia's willowlike foliage is handsome, but the stiff upright habit is best softened by lower-growing plants. A striking late-season combination is bluebeard and boltonia in front of the silvery plumes and fiery hues of flame grass (*Miscanthus sinensis* 'Purpurascens').

We Recommend

'Snowbank' (3 to 4 ft.) is a superior compact, although still tall, selection. 'Pink Beauty' (4 ft.) has tousled pale-pink daisies and blue-gray foliage. It has a sprawling habit even in full sun. Cut it back in early summer to promote compact growth, or plant it tightly with more upright plants such as feather reed grass. The soft pink and wispy nature of the plants is more delicate than a pink aster.

The white one-inch daisies of boltonia engulf its foliage with flowers from late summer into fall. This asterlike plant is called false aster in some field guides, and the two are quite similar. Boltonia's flowers are more delicate, however, and the foliage—gray-green and willowlike—doesn't succumb to the diseases that attack some asters. Like many asters, boltonia is a North American native. It occurs south of Michigan, although it has been found in a few of our southernmost counties. With adequate moisture and sun, plants can reach close to six feet tall. Given its tremendous height, the species isn't suitable for most gardens; a cultivar called 'Snowbank' is a better choice. 'Snowbank' grows to three or four feet and is smothered with shaggy daisies when in bloom.

Bloom Period and Seasonal Color
White flowers late summer through fall.

Mature Height × Spread
3 to 6 ft. × 3 to 4 ft.

Zones
To Zone 4

Bowman's Root
Gillenia trifoliata

Bowman's root, an overlooked North American native, offers ever-changing beauty throughout the growing season. Never flashy, although it has its brilliant moment in the fall, Bowman's root is always noteworthy for its refined presence. The season begins with the patterned texture created by the thrice-divided leaves. In summer a lacy display of delicate white flowers veils the foliage. In fall, an extra surprise is the wonderful color, a warm combination of yellow, orange, and red all on the same plant. Bowman's root may be a bit hard to find, but it is worth seeking out. Try it first in a lightly shaded garden or woodland edge. Once it wins you over, you'll be adding this plant to other parts of your garden. Bowman's root is sometimes listed under the botanical name Porteranthus trifoliatus.

Bloom Period and Seasonal Color
White flowers in summer.

Mature Height × Spread
2 to 4 ft. × 3 ft.

Zones
To Zone 4

When, Where, and How to Plant
Plant Bowman's root in the spring. Choose locations with moist, fertile soil and partial shade to full sun. Plants do best in moisture-retentive soil in full sun. Add organic matter to light soils. Follow the general directions for planting perennials on page 102, spacing plants about 2 ft. apart.

Growing Tips
Water regularly until plants are established. Although drought-tolerant, water the plants, especially those in full-sun locations, during drought. Spread a 2-in. layer of organic mulch around plants to conserve moisture. In the spring, fertilize mature clumps with a sprinkling of 10-10-10 fertilizer or a topdressing of garden compost. In rich soils, fertilization is unnecessary.

Care
Bowman's root needs little care if sited correctly and it is rarely troubled by insect and disease problems. In rich soil, plants may sprawl and benefit from staking. Division of the deep, thick roots is seldom needed but can be attempted in the spring.

Companion Planting and Design
Use the plant in a lightly shaded woodland garden, a sunny, moist perennial bed, or a cottage garden. It also softens the edges of walks and patios. Its airy texture is accentuated by massing, but a single clump creates a lovely detail among lower, ground-covering perennials. The airy flowers add light to the shady garden. A refined combination for partial shade pairs an elegant specimen or drift of Bowman's root with blue-leaved hostas, 'Palace Purple' alumroot, and the drooping spikelets of wild oats. Add Siberian bugloss and Bethlehem sage for spring flowers. In a moist, sunny perennial bed, try Bowman's root with peonies and blue star for a dramatic foliage effect right into fall. Cottage gardeners combine it with shrub roses and hardy geraniums.

We Recommend
Gillenia stipulata, a similar plant but not as showy, is sometimes available.

Butterfly Weed
Asclepias tuberosa

When, Where, and How to Plant

Plant container-grown butterfly weed in the spring, in full sun in poor to average, well-drained soil. Sandy loam is ideal; good drainage is paramount. Plants are tolerant of dry soils and drought. Avoid poorly drained or heavy clay sites. Follow the general directions for planting on page 102. Avoid disturbing the root and space clumps of butterfly weed 1 1/2 to 2 ft. apart.

Growing Tips

Water new plants regularly until established. Butterfly weed is drought-tolerant and shouldn't need additional watering. Fertilization is generally unnecessary. It is one of the last perennials to appear, and it's easy to damage its roots while working in the spring garden. Mark its place with a label, or leave 6 in. of stem to remind you of its location.

Care

Butterfly weed needs little special care and is rarely bothered by insects or disease. Avoid poorly-drained sites to prevent root rot. The deep, fleshy taproots resent disturbance; young plants should be left alone to develop into mature clumps, which will take at least two to three years. Plants often self-sow if seed is allowed to disperse. Division is usually unnecessary.

Companion Planting and Design

Use in beds, borders, and meadow plantings. One clump of orange butterfly weed creates a remarkable focal point. Try butterfly weed interplanted with lavenders and the tall rose-purple spires of Brazilian verbena. Or front ornamental grasses and the yellow-orange sunflowers of heliopsis with butterfly weed, yellow coreopsis, and 'Butterfly Blue' pincushion flower. Watch out for the butterflies!

We Recommend

'Gay Butterflies Mix' (24 to 30 in.) is a seed-grown strain with showy flowers in shades of deep red, orange, and yellow. The swamp milkweed, *A. incarnata*, grows throughout Michigan. Typically, the flowers are a deep rose. It prefers heavy, wet soils and grows to 4 ft. A beautiful white-flowered selection, 'Ice Ballet' (4 to 5 ft.), makes an unusual addition to a perennial garden. Try it with turtlehead in a moist, sunny spot.

Bright orange grabs your attention. That's why butterfly weed, the flamboyant star of the milkweed family, is one of the most recognizable summer-blooming wildflowers. Native to a vast area of the United States, butterfly weed grows in most of Michigan's Lower Peninsula in woodland openings, sandy roadsides, old fields, and grassy meadows. It gets noticed even at sixty-five miles per hour. Butterflies also take note: this plant is a magnet for monarchs. Butterfly weed has unusual flowers shaped like a crown above flaring reflexed petals. It is easy to grow in full sun and average to sandy soil where drainage is good. Although a milkweed, it doesn't have milky sap. Its long, tapered seedpods open to release the standard milkweed seeds, each with a fluffy parachute.

Bloom Period and Seasonal Color
Orange flowers in early to midsummer.

Mature Height × Spread
18 to 24 in. × 18 to 24 in.

Calamint

Calamintha nepeta ssp. *nepeta*

A workhorse perennial is one that pulls its own weight in the garden, performing all season with little care. Hosta, daylily, 'Autumn Joy' sedum, Russian sage, and 'Goldsturm' rudbeckia are well-known workhorse perennials. But you may not yet be familiar with calamint, another plant that deserves a spot in this group. Compact and aromatic, calamint produces a haze of tiny pale bluish-white flowers from summer until fall. It's a delicate addition to the garden, but it's a tough plant. It's easy to grow in well-drained soil in full sun or light shade and blooms for months. The masses of tiny flowers turn pale lavender when cool temperatures arrive. Try calamint where you need an outstanding plant that thrives with no effort.

Bloom Period and Seasonal Color
White flowers in midsummer through fall.

Mature Height × Spread
12 to 18 in. × 18 to 24 in.

Zones
To Zone 5

When, Where, and How to Plant
Plant calamint any time from spring to late summer. Choose locations with well-drained soil. Full sun is preferred, but calamint will tolerate some shade. Consult page 102 for tips on planting perennials. Space 15 to 18 in. apart.

Growing Tips
Calamint is easy to grow and requires little care. Keep new plants moist until established. Calamint is drought-resistant and seldom needs water. A layer of mulch will help conserve water but is not critical with this plant. In average or better soils, fertilizer will not be necessary.

Care
Calamint is rarely troubled by pests and disease. Plants may be pruned back as needed. Calamint becomes somewhat woody at the base; in the spring, cut back the woody stems to make way for new growth. Division is rarely needed for rejuvenation, but the plant can be easily divided in spring.

Companion Planting and Design
Calamint is versatile and can be used anywhere sun and good drainage can be provided. Use it for a frothy effect at the front of a perennial border. It's a nice addition to island beds, mixed plantings, and dry gardens. In a sunny aspect, calamint works well as a groundcover or edging plant. Its fine texture makes for dramatic contrast with plants like sedum 'Matrona' or lamb's ears. It makes a subtle pairing with the silvery 'Morning Light' miscanthus or 'Snowbank' boltonia.

We Recommend
Sometimes gardeners need persuading to try a new plant. They get familiar with the old crowd, knowing how each one behaves and the kind of care it needs. If that describes you and you haven't yet tried calamint, buy a plant at the beginning of the next growing season. Put it in full sun. By season's end, we predict you too will be a member of the calamint fan club. 'White Cloud' is a descriptive cultivar name for a selection with pure-white flowers.

When, Where, and How to Plant

Plant catmint in the spring. Choose locations with well-drained to sandy soil of average fertility in full sun. In heavier or richer soils or partial shade, plants will split open; wet sites will lead to rot. Plant catmint 2 to 3 ft. apart depending on the selection. Follow the general directions for planting perennials on page 102.

Growing Tips

Water regularly until plants are established. Catmint shouldn't need additional watering or fertilization.

Care

Catmint is carefree and needs only a little pruning. After the first flush of bloom, cut back the stems to tidy the plants and to encourage rebloom. Clumps that split open in the middle are a signal that the catmint needs dividing or a sunnier exposure. Divide in early spring as the fuzzy foliage is just emerging. Dig clumps, and split into sections with a sharp spade. Replant, and keep watered until established. The true *N. × faassenii* won't self-sow. If your plants are *Nepeta mussinii*, self-sown seedlings will appear and may be weeded out where unwanted. There are no pests to bother it.

Companion Planting and Design

Use catmint in borders or beds or as a sun-loving groundcover. It is often seen bordering herb, vegetable, and rose beds in British gardens, but its romantic, billowing form can be a nuisance next to lawns. Place it farther back in the bed, or plant it where it will border brick or stone. Let it intermingle with other perennials such as iris, daylilies, or 'Lucifer' crocosmia. Plant a grouping as a misty lavender-blue complement to a clump of yellow hybrid lilies.

We Recommend

One of the best hybrid catmints is a new selection called 'Walker's Low'. It forms spreading mounds of lavender-blue flowers and needs no pruning to maintain bloom and its shape for the whole season. 'Six Hills Giant', a fine garden plant, is bigger than other cultivars, growing to close to 3 ft. tall.

Long-flowering perennials are favorites of garden designers. Their steady presence bridges the gap between seasons, allowing the creation of many garden "pictures." Hybrid catmint, Nepeta × faassenii, is such a perennial. This easy plant for sun and well-drained soil has grayish-green foliage and clouds of blue-purple flowers creating a soft, misty appearance. It opens its first flowers in late spring, but its lavender haze continues through midsummer or even beyond. At first catmint is upright, growing to two to three feet. Then stems begin to flop as the season progresses. The polite way to describe this tendency is to identify the plant as a weaver, which means its natural habit is to sprawl. Site plants where this relaxed habit will be welcome.

Other Name

Faassen's Catmint

Bloom Period and Seasonal Color

Lavender-blue flowers in later spring through midsummer.

Mature Height × Spread

2 to 3 ft. × 3 ft.

Cheddar Pinks
Dianthus gratianopolitanus

Cheerful and fragrant, the cheddar pinks begin blooming in late spring with 1-inch-wide flowers in various shades of pink and rose. These are easy-to-grow perennials with abundant fragrant flowers over an evergreen mat of narrow, grasslike blue-gray foliage. A particularly nice cultivar is 'Bath's Pink', which has pale-pink fringed flowers and a scent of clove. Combine the cheddar pinks with other gray-foliaged plants such as salvias, lamb's ears, lavender, blue oat grass, and catmint. They are also effective with creeping thyme, blue flax, and hardy geraniums. The cheddar pinks called 'Tiny Rubies' has half-inch double flowers in a deep shade of rose. This is an apt cultivar name because the flowers sparkle like jewels over the clumps of blue-gray foliage.

Bloom Period and Seasonal Color
Pink flowers in later spring to midsummer.

Mature Height × Spread
9 to 12 in. × 12 to 16 in.

Zones
To Zone 4

When, Where, and How to Plant
Plant cheddar pinks in the spring. Choose locations with average to sandy, well-drained soil in full sun. Pinks dislike acid soils. Add organic matter to heavy soils. Avoid poorly drained sites, which will lead to rot. Follow the general planting directions for perennials on page 102, spacing 2 ft. apart.

Growing Tips
Water regularly until plants are established. Properly sited in areas of the garden with good drainage, cheddar pinks will not need any special care. Although they are somewhat drought-tolerant, water them during extended dry spells. Avoid piling mulch around the mats of foliage because this can lead to rot. Plants will not need extra fertilization.

Care
Cheddar pinks are generally pest- and disease-free. Site plants correctly to avoid problems with rot. After they finish flowering, deadhead the flowering stalks, removing them back to the basal foliage. The mats of foliage are evergreen. Do not attempt to cut off the plants at ground level during fall cleanup. Divide clumps when they begin to die out in the middle. In spring, just as the new growth begins, lift mats, and split into healthy, vigorous pieces each with ample roots. Replant, taking care not to set the plants too deep. Keep watered until established.

Companion Planting and Design
Use in perennial beds and borders, in rock gardens, and along edges of brick or stone patios. Combine cheddar pinks with other perennials, and place them in the front of borders and beds. Lining a walkway, cheddar pinks form a low-growing mat that invites visitors into your garden.

We Recommend
The maiden pinks, *Dianthus deltoides* (6 to 18 in.), form very low, spreading clumps, and their small bright flowers create mats of color. 'Brilliant' has deep rose-pink flowers and 'Zing Rose' has deep rose-red flowers. The China pinks or annual pinks, *Dianthus chinensis*, sold as bedding plants, also behave as short-lived perennials in Michigan. These plants have excelled in annual trials at Michigan State University.

Clematis

Clematis spp. and cultivars

When, Where, and How to Plant

Plant clematis in spring, when they are available both growing in containers and bareroot in plastic and cardboard sleeves. The spot should be well-drained and situated so the top of the clematis will get sun but the base will be shaded by plants or mulch to keep the root zone cool. Avoid hot sites. Provide support for climbers. Dig a hole as deep as the container and twice as wide, and mix in organic matter. Remove the plant from its container carefully to avoid damaging the brittle stems. Gently tease apart roots to encourage outward growth. The crown of large-flowered cultivars should be planted 2 to 3 in. deeper than it was growing in the pot. Keep the transplant watered regularly. Plants may not bloom the first year or two.

Growing Tips

Fertilize in spring with a fertilizer such as 5-10-10, or use a liquid feed. Water during dry weather.

Care

Clematis are often pruned to remove dead stems and, if space is limited, to control their growth and habit. When to prune clematis depends on when it blooms. One approach is to wait until the plant leafs out in spring and remove any deadwood. For specific information, ask at the nursery where you buy the plant, or consult a book such as Lee Reich's *The Pruning Book*. Clematis wilt is a problem on some large-flowered hybrids. It strikes just as buds are ready to open, turning the plant suddenly limp. Remove dead stems, give the plant water and fertilizer, and it will usually recover. Sweet autumn clematis self-sows and can be invasive.

Companion Planting and Design

Plant vining clematis to grow up roses, trees, and shrubs as well as fences. The fluffy seedheads remain attractive for months.

We Recommend

Clematis × jackmanii is a prolific bloomer and resists wilt. Let it climb with the Canadian Explorer rose 'William Baffin'.

The genus Clematis *includes beautiful woody climbing vines as well as some shrubby perennials. Most familiar are the showy vines like the velvety purple* Clematis × jackmanii, *whose blooms smother countless lampposts and fences every summer. Plant vining clematis to run up and into the tops of small trees and woody shrubs, where its blooms are a pleasant surprise. Many of the large-flowered hybrids like the flashy bicolor 'Nelly Moser' have five-inch-wide blooms, but also worthy are the species and cultivars with more diminutive flowers. For instance, tube clematis (*Clematis heracleifolia*) is a shrubby perennial with blue tube-shaped flowers. And sweet autumn clematis (*Clematis terniflora*) throws a cloud of vanilla-scented blooms in September. Clematis are excellent cut flowers to float in a shallow bowl.*

Bloom Period and Seasonal Color

Purple, pink, or white flowers in late spring to fall, depending on type.

Mature Length

6 to 20 ft. or more

Culver's Root
Veronicastrum virginicum

With its sheer vertical form and elegant, airy effect, Culver's root is a native plant that successfully makes the transition to the garden. It can be found in southern Michigan's prairies, fens, and meadows, along rivers, and in deciduous woodlots. The roots were formerly used for medicines. Culver's root has a tall, lofty presence, making it a strong character in the perennial garden or in a shrub border. It is easy to grow in sun, where it will achieve the best form. The tapered spikes, appearing in mid- to late summer, are most often white but occasionally pale lavender. The stems are encircled by clusters of five narrow, toothed leaves. These horizontal leaves create an interesting texture below the elegant branched spires. Another botanical name for Culver's root is Veronica virginica.

Bloom Period and Seasonal Color
White flowers in mid- to late summer.

Mature Height × Spread
4 to 6 ft. × 3 to 4 ft.

When, Where, and How to Plant
Plant Culver's root in the spring. Choose locations with full sun to light shade and moist but well-drained, average to fertile soil. Avoid deep shade; clumps grown there may lose their vertical habit and need staking. Avoid windy or shady spots, which may cause the plant to flop. Plant Culver's root 2 to 3 ft. apart, following the general directions on page 102.

Growing Tips
Water regularly until plants are established. Spread a 2-in. layer of organic mulch around clumps to conserve moisture. Culver's root needs no special care, although it should be watered during times of drought. In the spring, topdress mature clumps with garden compost or sprinkle with 10-10-10 fertilizer and scratch in.

Care
Insects and disease are hardly ever a concern. Plants grown in too much shade will need to be staked to maintain their upright posture. The clumps rarely need division but may be divided in the spring. Dig up the clumps, and split them apart with a knife. Replant them at the same level, and keep the plants moist until they are established.

Companion Planting and Design
Use Culver's root in back of a perennial border or at the center of an island bed. It is also suitable for sunny, moist meadows, for woodland edges, by ponds, and in natural areas. Culver's root is a frequent accent plant in European perennial borders, where its distinctive form contrasts with Joe-pye weed, asters, and purple coneflower for a striking architectural effect. Play up the tall, vertical habit of Culver's root by combining it with the mounded form and chubby bright gold-orange daisies of sneezeweed.

We Recommend
Pink and lavender forms of Culver's root are available. 'Roseum', a pale-pink selection, is very attractive and makes an excellent show with 'Prairie Blue Eyes' daylily, rose-pink obedient plant (*Physostegia virginiana*), and the paler pink 'Brilliant' showy stonecrop.

Cushion Spurge
Euphorbia polychroma

When, Where, and How to Plant
Plant cushion spurge in the spring. Choose locations with average well-drained soil in full sun or partial shade. Cushion spurge tolerates poor sandy soils and dislikes heavy soils or wet sites. In rich soil and partial shade, the mounded foliage may sprawl. Plant according to the general directions on page 102, spacing 12 to 18 in. apart.

Growing Tips
Cushion spurge, when sited correctly, is long-lived and needs no special care. Water regularly until established. Spurges usually do fine without fertilization.

Care
Spurges are generally untroubled by insects and disease, and clumps do not require division. In moist soil and partial shade, plants may become overgrown and split open to reveal the center. With most perennials, this is the signal to divide, and, although this can be attempted in spring with cushion spurge, the large rootstock resents disturbance. Self-sown seedlings may appear in some locations and are easily pulled. All spurges produce a milky sap that can be irritating to the skin. Wear gloves when handling plants.

Companion Planting and Design
Put this accommodating perennial to good use by placing it in perennial beds and borders, in cottage gardens, or in large drifts as a groundcover in a sunny area. Its early bloom sets off spring bulbs and is particularly pretty with tulips. Later, let ornamental onions grow up through the foliage. Try it with blue dwarf bearded iris, lamb's ears, and moss phlox in a well-drained, sunny area.

We Recommend
A great plant with a similar texture and mounded habit, but with the addition of rich purplish foliage, is *Euphorbia dulcis* 'Chameleon'. Try it in a lightly-shaded location with Japanese sedge and lady's mantle or *Heuchera villosa* 'Autumn Bride' for an interesting contrast of leaf shape and color. Add the purple globes of ornamental onions for extra interest. Like most spurges, 'Chameleon' will self-sow.

Cushion spurge's neatly mounded foliage is brightened in spring with early green-to-yellow, almost fluorescent flowers that add zest and fresh color to the garden. The eye-catching bloom is actually a bract, or modified leaf, similar to the red bracts of the cushion spurge's relative, the poinsettia. This group of plants has no petals or sepals. After the flowering period, the foliage remains attractive all season and turns a warm orange-red in the fall. Cushion spurge thrives in areas that enjoy full sun and well-drained, even dry, soils. It may be used as a specimen or planted among other perennials. The high-quality foliage makes it invaluable in the garden.

Bloom Period and Seasonal Color
Yellow flowers in mid-spring.

Mature Height × Spread
18 to 24 in. × 2 ft.

Daylily
Hemerocallis hybrids

Daylilies are among the easiest and most attractive of all perennials to grow. Although each blooms for just one day, the plant continues to produce flowers for weeks. By choosing early, midseason, and late daylily cultivars, it is possible to extend the season of bloom for much of the summer. Thousands of hybrid cultivars exist, and hundreds more are being introduced each year. Perhaps the most well-known of these is the long-flowering 'Stella d'Oro', with flowers the gaudy yellow of egg yolks and sporadic rebloom all season. As with hostas, it is possible to spend a considerable amount of money on a rare daylily cultivar. Other daylilies are available for more modest prices, however, allowing them to be used in quantity in the landscape.

Bloom Period and Seasonal Color
Yellow, orange, red, pink, or lavender flowers in early to late summer.

Mature Height × Spread
1 to 4 ft. × 2 to 3 ft.

When, Where, and How to Plant
Container-grown daylilies can be planted anytime from spring through early fall. Bareroot divisions are usually shipped in spring or early fall. Daylilies tolerate a range of soils and full sun to light shade. For the best results, choose moist, well-drained, average to fertile soil in full sun. Follow the general directions for planting perennials on page 102. Space plants 2 to 3 ft. apart, depending on the cultivar.

Growing Tips
Water regularly until plants are established. If planting in hot weather, provide ample water, and shade the clumps with cardboard boxes or bushel baskets. Mulch to conserve moisture. Although they are drought-tolerant once established, they prefer moist soil, so water during dry periods. In poor soils, sprinkle 10-10-10 fertilizer or a light topdressing of well-rotted compost in spring.

Care
Daylilies are generally free of insect and disease problems. Remove faded flowers daily to keep the plants well groomed. Daylilies rarely need division but are so durable that they may be divided at almost any time. The best time is in spring, when the foliage is just emerging. Dig them up, and pull or slice them apart. One way to do this is with two spading forks held back to back. Add organic material to enrich the soil, then replant divisions and keep them well watered.

Companion Planting and Design
Use daylilies in island beds, perennial borders, and mixed plantings. Plant in drifts or groups of three for the best effect. Daylilies can also be used to cover banks, to edge driveways, and to deal with problem areas where a tough plant is needed. Interplant with daffodils for an extra season of interest. Team daylilies with fine-textured plants such as purple fennel, Russian sage, catmint, and threadleaf coreopsis.

We Recommend
There are hundreds of daylilies from which to choose. When making your choice, consider color, size of flower, stem height, and time of bloom. More repeat bloomers are appearing on the market. 'Happy Returns' is a popular long-flowering daylily with yellow flowers.

When, Where, and How to Plant

Plant phlox in the spring. Choose locations with moist, well-drained, fertile soil in full sun. Add organic matter to improve poor or heavy soils. Plant garden phlox 2 to 3 ft. apart; plant taller selections farther apart. Don't crowd plants. Follow the general directions for planting on page 102.

Growing Tips

Phlox needs special attention to be an asset in the garden. To avoid powdery mildew, provide ample moisture, and water deeply during dry spells. Fertilize clumps in early spring with an application of general fertilizer (10-10-10) or a layer of compost. Additional fertilizer later in the season will promote strong growth and flowering. A 2-in. layer of mulch is beneficial.

Care

Powdery mildew is the biggest impediment to growing phlox. One strategy to reduce mildew is thinning to improve air circulation. When foliage is about 6 in. tall, remove the weak stems, and thin the remainder to about five to eight stems. Deadhead to avoid self-sown seedlings, which won't resemble the parent plant. Phlox clumps should be divided every two to four years. Dig clumps, and divide the crowns into sections. Take only vigorous divisions from the outside of the clumps. Augment the soil with plenty of compost or other organic soil amendments. Replant at the same level at which they were growing, and keep well watered.

Companion Planting and Design

Phlox is a gorgeous addition to the summer border or cottage garden. Combine it with Shasta daisies, daylilies, coreopsis, heliopsis, sneezeweed, and purple coneflowers.

We Recommend

If you wish to grow phlox, seek out resistant cultivars that will perform best in your garden. In Lansing, 'Mt. Fujiyama' was mildew-free in some years; other years it was unsightly. A gardener with a view of Lake Superior reports no problems there with mildew. In other words, it's impossible to make blanket recommendations. The Chicago Botanic Garden lists 'Katherine' as the best all-around performer in its trials.

Garden phlox is the flamboyant prima donna of the summer garden. With its bright colors and large pyramidal heads, phlox is often considered the backbone of the summer border. It does require some tending, however. It is often hit hard by powdery mildew, which turns its leaves gray and dusty-looking and can make it a garden liability rather than an asset. Use thinning, proper spacing, frequent division, watering at ground level, and the selection of resistant cultivars to minimize disease. If these measures don't solve the mildew problem, try another perennial in that location. If garden phlox grows well for you, exploit its colorful July and August blossoms and let it take center stage in your summer garden.

Bloom Period and Seasonal Color

Pink, white, lavender, orange, or red flowers in early to late summer.

Mature Height × Spread

$2^1/_2$ to $3^1/_2$ ft. × 3 ft.

Goat's Beard
Aruncus dioicus

A fine North American native, goat's beard has splendid foliage; its sheer size makes it an imposing addition to any shady garden. In summer, goat's beard produces an impressive display of creamy-white flowers on tall branches, a graceful addition to a distinctly shrubby plant. The ultimate size of goat's beard (four to seven feet) makes it ideal for a grand accent. The frothy blooms brighten the shady garden. Male and female flowers appear on separate plants and have different bloom characteristics. The male flowers are more showy. The female blooms are pretty but bend with the weight of newly developing seeds. When you purchase a goat's beard, you take your chances—there is no way to identify the sex from a clump of foliage!

Bloom Period and Seasonal Color
Creamy-white flowers in early to midsummer.

Mature Height × Spread
4 to 7 ft. × 4 to 5 ft.

When, Where, and How to Plant
Plant goat's beard in the spring or fall. Choose a location with partial shade and a moist, well-drained, humus-rich soil. While goat's beard tolerates sun, it will languish in a hot, dry site and require frequent irrigation. Put it to best use in a lightly shaded garden or a rich, moist location that receives morning sun and afternoon shade. Follow the general directions for planting perennials on page 102, spacing the plants 4 to 5 ft. apart.

Growing Tips
Water regularly until plants are established. Add a 2- to 3-in. layer of organic mulch to conserve moisture. Topdress mature clumps with garden compost, or scratch in a sprinkling of 10-10-10 fertilizer.

Care
Sited correctly, goat's beard is rarely troubled by insects or disease. It forms a tough, woody crown and generally does not need division. Mature clumps are difficult to move, so choose a permanent location. Female plants produce numerous seedlings that can be transplanted to other areas of the garden if desired. Flowers can be cut and dried for arrangements.

Companion Planting and Design
Use it as a bold accent plant in a woodland garden or shady border, or as a foundation plant near the house, or mass it with shrubs. The dark foliage contrasts well with the bold blue-scalloped leaves of hosta 'Halcyon' and the vase-shaped hosta called 'Krossa Regal'. Nothing can compare to its best use as a tall highlight for the woodland border.

We Recommend
'Kneiffii' is an exceptional cultivar with finely divided foliage and a smaller stature, reaching only 2¹/₂ to 3 ft. tall. It has creamy-white plumes in early summer. *Aruncus aethusifolius*, a diminutive Korean goat's beard reaching only 1 ft. in height, has finely dissected foliage and creamy-white flowers. Place it in partial shade in the front of a border or with other woodland plants. This dwarf goat's beard develops brilliant fall color where it receives some sun.

Goldenrod
Solidago spp. and hybrids

When, Where, and How to Plant

Plant goldenrod in the spring. Choose locations in average, well-drained soil in full sun. Sandy or loamy soil is preferred; rich soil may lead to rampant spread and floppy growth. Most species and hybrids of goldenrod are drought-tolerant. Follow the general directions for planting on page 102. Space goldenrod 18 to 36 in. apart, depending on the species or cultivar.

Growing Tips

Goldenrod properly sited will need no special care. Watering and fertilization can lead to soft, weak growth, and plants will need staking to stay upright. A few goldenrods, native to moister areas, appreciate water during dry spells.

Care

Insects and disease are rarely a concern. Many goldenrods produce self-sown seedlings. Weed them out in spring. Most of the cultivars are not rapid spreaders, but goldenrod may need division to rejuvenate the plant or control its spread. Do this in the spring. Dig clumps, and split them into pieces with a sharp spade or old kitchen knife. Replant vigorous pieces from the outside of the clumps, and discard the unproductive center. Keep new divisions well watered until established.

Companion Planting and Design

Grow it as the Europeans do in formal perennial beds, or use it in island beds, natural areas, or meadow or prairie gardens, or along rustic fences. Goldenrod combines naturally with aster, boltonia, and ornamental grasses.

We Recommend

The stiff goldenrod, *Solidago rigida*, growing to 3 to 5 ft., is one of the best species of goldenrod for the garden. It has large flat-topped clusters of golden-yellow flowers and reddish fall color. Showy goldenrod, *S. speciosa*, has long wands of golden yellow. We love 'Fireworks', a cultivar of rough-leaved goldenrod, *S. rugosa*. It has an airy horizontal blooming habit. Many hybrid goldenrods are suitable for Michigan gardens. They have compact habits, restrained growth, showy flowers, and less tendency to self-sow. A few good choices are 'Goldenmosa', 'Cloth of Gold', and 'Crown of Rays'.

More than thirty-five species of goldenrod grow in Michigan, creating a golden glow over meadows and hillsides late in the season. With all the beauty it brings to our natural landscape, goldenrod is often maligned as a weed that causes hay fever. It doesn't. Reconsider this natural beauty, and welcome goldenrod into your garden. Many hybrid cultivars are excellent garden plants. They offer compact habits and showy plumed clusters of golden yellow. Species of goldenrod are well suited for planting in meadows, "wild" borders, and naturalized areas. When choosing a species goldenrod, find out if it has a clumping or running habit. Some goldenrods are well behaved, but others can be assertive spreaders. Nonetheless, many of our native goldenrod species are fit for garden use.

Bloom Period and Seasonal Color

Yellow flowers in later summer through fall.

Mature Height × Spread

2 to 5 ft. × 2 to 4 ft.

Hardy Geranium
Geranium sanguineum

Though the flower structure and finely cut foliage of this hardy geranium sometimes are delicate, the blossoms pack a punch, opening to a bright magenta that smolders like an ember in the garden. This tough hardy geranium, sometimes called the bloody cranesbill, spreads out eagerly, forming low, wide-spreading, mounded clumps that turn dark red in the fall. Use it as a filler plant with other perennials such as the yellow-green flowers of lady's mantle, the cheery pastel flowers of hybrid columbine, and the clear blues of Siberian iris. Hardy geranium's weaving habit makes it an effective groundcover and accent around taller perennials. Bloody cranesbill and other hardy geraniums are easy-care, hardworking additions to the garden.

Other Name
Bloody Cranesbill

Bloom Period and Seasonal Color
Magenta or red-purple flowers from late spring through early summer.

Mature Height × Spread
12 in. × 12 to 18 in.

When, Where, and How to Plant
Plant in the spring. Hardy geranium can be planted later with adequate moisture during hot weather. Choose locations with moist, well-drained, average to humus-rich soil. Full sun with adequate moisture is ideal, but partial shade is readily tolerated. Its form will be looser in shade. Bloody cranesbill is fairly drought-tolerant due to its fleshy roots. Plant following the general directions on page 102, spacing 1^1/$_2$ to 2 ft. apart.

Growing Tips
Hardy geranium is very easy to grow. Water regularly until plants are established, and provide water during drought. Fertilization is generally unnecessary.

Care
Insect and disease problems are rarely a concern with hardy geranium. After the first flush of bloom, plants may be sheared back to remove the seedpods and to promote rebloom. Clumps seldom need division, but, in tight situations, division may be needed to keep the spreading growth in check. Dig clumps, and pull them apart into sections. Replant, and water well until established. Add some organic matter to replenish the soil before replanting. To increase your supply of plants, you don't even have to dig up the whole clump of bloody cranesbill. Just use a sharp spade to cut off pieces from around the edge.

Companion Planting and Design
Bloody cranesbill is quite versatile. It's wonderful in perennial gardens, cottage gardens, and rock gardens and in other parts of the landscape as groundcover or edging. Use drifts of this hardy geranium to knit together Siberian iris, wild blue indigo, and lady's mantle.

We Recommend
Hardy geraniums are lovely and easy garden plants. *Geranium sanguineum* var. *striatum* is a very low grower with ferny foliage and light-pink flowers etched with rose. Striatum makes an excellent groundcover or edging plant. 'Album' is a white selection with an open form. Other cultivars exist and are not dramatically different from the species. 'New Hampshire Purple', with deep reddish-purple flowers, has been a good performer.

When, Where, and How to Plant

Plant heliopsis in the spring. Choose locations with full sun and well-drained, average soil. Heliopsis is adaptable to a wide range of soils including clay, sand, and poor soils. Clumps may sprawl in moist, rich soil. Follow the general directions for planting on page 102, spacing $2^{1}/2$ to 3 ft. apart.

Growing Tips

Water regularly until plants are established. Plants are fairly drought-tolerant, but will appreciate water during extended dry spells. A 2-in. layer of organic mulch is beneficial. Extra fertilization is unnecessary.

Care

Aphids will sometimes bother sunflower heliopsis. Treatment is rarely called for, but spraying aphids with a stream of water will knock down their numbers. Deadheading is necessary to improve the plant's appearance and to lengthen the flowering period. Taller forms may profit from staking in windy locations. Clumps need division when stems become crowded and flower production decreases. In the spring when the foliage is just emerging, dig up the clumps, and split them into pieces with a sharp spade. Lifting large clumps out of the ground can be moderately difficult. Replant vigorous pieces at the same level at which they were growing. Water well until established.

Companion Planting and Design

Plant sunflower heliopsis for intense color in perennial borders and island beds, meadow plantings, and cut-flower gardens. Add to parts of the garden that peaked in June. The vibrant flowers add late color to plantings of blue false indigo and blue star. To mimic the yellow-orange and purple combination found in prairies, use it with blazing star and purple coneflowers. Temper these combos liberally with ornamental grasses.

We Recommend

Choose cultivars for the best garden performance. 'Summer Sun' (3 to 4 ft.) has a long blooming period and comes true from seed. 'Karat' (3 to 4 ft.) is another gorgeous single-flowered selection. 'Golden Plume' (3 to $3^{1}/2$ ft.) is a selection with full double flowers.

For a blast of eye-popping yellow-orange, plant heliopsis in a sunny border or island garden. This plant—native to Michigan prairies, meadows, and roadsides—has sunflower-like blooms over a long season, from July to September. Heliopsis has gold-orange daisy flowers with raised centers. Like the bold and brassy shades of 'Goldsturm' rudbeckia and the other bright daisies of summer, it can be tricky to combine with the garden's more subdued colors without blasting them out of the water. Still, it is useful to provide long-lasting and bright color to the summer garden. Specific cultivars of heliopsis are preferable for garden use because they are more compact and upright and less coarse in appearance.

Other Name
Ox-eye Sunflower

Bloom Period and Seasonal Color
Yellow-gold flowers in summer.

Mature Height × Spread
3 to 4 ft. × 3 to 4 ft.

Heuchera

Heuchera spp., hybrids, and cultivars

Back when Henry Ford sold cars in any color as long as it was black, coralbells were pretty much limited to grayish-green leaves. Now cars come in all colors, and so, it seems, does heuchera foliage. There are dozens of showy alternatives—purples, browns, reds, even those with silvery overlays. The color floodgates opened with 'Palace Purple', which is a dark bronze-purple, and many others have followed. Heuchera foliage stays attractive all season. In fact, some gardeners prefer it to the flower stems, which they remove. But the slender stems can be charming, too. Tall and delicate, they hold the dainty bell-shaped flowers like tiny balls suspended high above the foliage. Although newer heucheras are alluring, don't overlook the appeal of green-leaved ones.

Other Names
Alumroot, Coralbells

Bloom Period and Seasonal Color
Red, pink, magenta, or white flowers in late spring to fall, depending on variety.

Mature Height × Spread
12 to 24 in. × 12 in.

When, Where, and How to Plant
Plant heuchera plants in spring. They need time to establish before winter, when they are prone to heaving. They require moist, well-drained soil rich in organic matter in part sun or light shade. Avoid a spot exposed to hot afternoon sun, where foliage will burn. Space plants 12 in. apart, following the general directions for planting perennials on page 102.

Growing Tips
Water regularly as plants become established, then water during dry weather. The plants require little if any fertilizer. Apply 2 in. of an organic mulch.

Care
Remove the finished flowering stalks to promote rebloom. In well-drained soils, heucheras are usually free of pests and disease, although they profit from division every three to five years. Dig up the clump and gently pull it apart. Discard old, woody sections and plant young, vigorous pieces, each with a rosette of foliage, woody root, and some attached fibrous roots. Bury the piece to the level of the foliage. In fall, let the foliage remain in place since it stays evergreen all winter. After the soil freezes, mulch with evergreen boughs or pine needles; this will help prevent the repeated freezing and thawing that causes heucheras to heave or pop out of the soil.

Companion Planting and Design
The dark heucheras make a lovely contrast with lady's mantle and a small gold-edged hosta like 'Grand Tiara' along a walkway. Or plant drifts of heucheras with Siberian irises, columbine, and hardy geraniums. Although heuchera flowering stalks can reach 24 in., they are so slender and delicate that the plants may be placed near the front of the border.

We Recommend
'Autumn Bride' is a particularly nice selection of maple-leaved alumroot, *Heuchera villosa*. It has large apple-green leaves and long wands of white flowers in late summer through frost. 'Purpurea' has bronzy-purple foliage.

When, Where, and How to Plant

Plant bareroot plants in spring. Plant container-grown hosta at any time during the growing season. Choose locations with moist, well-drained, humus-rich soil in partial to full shade. Some hostas will tolerate more sun, but most do best in partial shade. Follow the general planting directions on page 102. Space hostas according to potential size.

Growing Tips

Water regularly until plants are established. Use mulch to conserve moisture. Water hosta during hot, dry weather. Leaves can develop sun scorch caused by too much sun or too little water. Spread a 2-in. layer of organic mulch to conserve moisture.

Care

Hostas are disease-resistant but may be troubled by slugs. Set out traps such as moist newspaper, an old board, or cabbage leaves. Check the undersides daily, and destroy the prisoners. Although hostas rarely need it, division is an inexpensive way to increase your supply of plants. Dig up the clumps in the spring, and cut them into pieces with a large sharp knife. Replant at the same level at which they were growing. Water new divisions frequently. Flower stalks can be removed after bloom in highly visible areas if desired.

Companion Planting and Design

Hostas are bold additions to woodland gardens, shady perennial beds, foundation beds, and edges of ponds and pools. They may also be used as edging plants and groundcovers. Large specimens create a dramatic accent. Hostas make a valuable cover for early spring bulbs and spring woodland plants, which often disappear after they flower.

We Recommend

There are hundreds of hostas to choose from. Here are two with a Michigan connection: 'Krossa Regal', a vase-shaped beauty with bluish-gray-green foliage, was named for the late Gus Krossa of Saginaw; 'Gold Standard', introduced by the late Pauline Banyai of Madison Heights, has gold leaves edged with green. And consider the old-fashioned fragrant plantain lily, *Hosta plantaginea*, with its shiny green leaves and large, fragrant white flowers.

Hostas are getting plenty of attention these days as easy-to-grow, dependable perennials for Michigan gardens. Although they have attractive, sometimes fragrant flowers on tall stems, they are usually more prized for their foliage and the ability to bring interest to shady corners of the garden. With leaves in greens, blues, chartreuse, and variegated colors as well as various textures, hostas form clumps ranging from just a few inches to several feet wide. Some leaves are puckered or veined; edges may be smooth or wavy. They are long-lived and rarely require division. Their clumps enlarge, but they are never invasive. The variegated forms, especially, bring light into the garden. From the array of plants suitable for shade, hostas emerge as among the best.

Other Name
Plantain Lily

Bloom Period and Seasonal Color
White or lavender flowers in midsummer to late summer.

Mature Height × Spread
6 to 48 in. × 1 to 4 ft.

ese Anemone

e × hybrida

Japanese anemones add an element of surprise to the garden. For most of the year, they remain a low clump of foliage, but, just when the garden is gearing down, hybrid anemones burst on the scene with startlingly beautiful flowers in shades of pink, rose, and white. The most useful perennials display attractive foliage, even when flowers are nowhere to be seen, and hybrid anemones are a good example of this. The divided leaves are handsome, bold, and textured. In late summer, Japanese anemone's three- to four-foot-tall branching stems push up, topped with round silvery-furred buds. These open to reveal the elegant, yet simple, flowers, single or double, surrounding a green button and yellow stamens. The flowers sway in the breeze from late summer until frost.

Other Name
Hybrid Anemone

Bloom Period and Seasonal Color
White or pink flowers in late summer to early fall.

Mature Height × Spread
3 to 4 ft. × 2 ft.

Zones
To Zone 5

When, Where, and How to Plant
Plant anemones in the spring. Container-grown plants can be planted later if given adequate moisture. Choose a location with rich, moist soil in sun or light shade. Avoid hot, dry sites. Too much shade will cause the flowering stalks to lean. Consult page 102 for planting tips, and space plants 14 to 16 in. apart. Water regularly until plants are established.

Growing Tips
Water anemones during dry spells. Spread a 2-in. layer of organic mulch to conserve moisture. In humus-rich soils, fertilization may not be necessary. In poorer soil, a light application of 10-10-10 fertilizer is beneficial. A winter mulch, applied after the ground freezes, may allow some Zone 4 gardeners to overwinter hybrid anemones.

Care
Anemones are seldom bothered by insects or disease. Hybrid anemones have a spreading habit. In the spring, remove any shoots that have overgrown their boundaries. Clumps can also be divided at this time. Often the soil falls away from the roots and you are left with smallish pieces. Enrich the soil with organic matter and replant. These divisions take a few years to develop into mature clumps. An early frost will occasionally nip the flowers of hybrid anemones.

Companion Planting and Design
Use anemones in perennial gardens or mixed plantings, or as a groundcover or edger. Their attractive foliage is always an asset. Hybrid anemones are excellent for providing fall bloom to a spring garden. Try the elegant white 'Honorine Jobert' in front of the rich fall color of switch grass, or pink 'Queen Charlotte' with blue asters, turtlehead, and the abundant pink daisies of 'Clara Curtis' chrysanthemum.

We Recommend
The following cultivars have performed well in Michigan: 'Honorine Jobert' (3 to 4 ft.) is a single white cultivar that has been unsurpassed for more than 100 years. 'Whirlwind' (3 ft.) produces a cloud of semidouble white flowers. 'Queen Charlotte' (3 ft.) has silvery pink semidouble flowers.

Joe-pye Weed

Eupatorium maculatum

When, Where, and How to Plant

Plant container-grown Joe-pye weed in the spring in sun, humus-rich soil, and a moist site. It grows naturally in wetlands and appreciates plenty of moisture, although it will survive in drier conditions. Follow the general planting directions on page 102. Allow at least 4 ft. in diameter for it to grow.

Growing Tips

Water well and regularly while the plant becomes established. After that, Joe-pye weed is more tolerant of dry conditions, but water if it shows sign of drought stress. In spring, apply a 2-in. layer of organic mulch. In average soil, it should not require fertilizer.

Care

Joe-pye weed is relatively free of pests and disease. Insects occasionally chew holes in the leaves in summer, but this causes only cosmetic damage. Division is rarely necessary, but plants may be divided in spring if desired. Pinching out the growing tips in late spring will produce a more compact plant with smaller flowerheads.

Companion Planting and Design

Use Joe-pye weed as a magnificent specimen plant in perennial borders, island beds, or naturalistic gardens, and with shrubs. This tall native, beautiful in its own right, makes a great backdrop for other perennials. It can loom over other plants, so consider scale when planning your combinations. A perfect companion is red switch grass, which has burgundy leaves. Add lavender-blue Russian sage and white boltonia. Feather reed grass is also a nice complement.

We Recommend

Eupatorium maculatum 'Gateway', with wine-red stems and reddish-purple flowers, is a choice cultivar that supposedly tops out at about 5 ft. In real life, though, it reaches close to 6 to 7 ft. by its third year in the garden. A new cultivar, 'Purple Bush', has entered the market and it is supposed to reach 4 to 6 ft. 'Atropurpureum' is a beautiful form with large domes of mauve-purple flowers and dark purple stems.

Several North American natives like goldenrod, asters, and sneezeweed achieved popularity among European gardeners before they did at home. Joe-pye weed is a classic example. Twenty years ago, the only place you'd notice it growing in Michigan was in meadows and roadside ditches. Now it is finally recognized as having a place in the garden, where its incredible beauty and stature are appreciated. It is one of the tallest perennials you can grow; in moist conditions, it skyrockets to more than seven feet. Joe-pye weed forms huge domed flowerheads in a shade of dusky rose. Its tall stems, often wine-red, have large whorled leaves that give the plant a tiered effect. Plant it where you have the room for drama. Butterflies find it irresistible.

Other Name
Boneset

Bloom Period and Seasonal Color
Mauve-purple flowers from late summer through fall.

Mature Height × Spread
4 to 8 ft. × 3 to 4 ft.

Lady's Mantle
Alchemilla mollis

Lady's mantle is a gracious garden companion. Its attractive mounds of scalloped foliage and airy chartreuse flowers are rarely out of place. Its frothy flowers extend spring right into summer. The color, a fresh yellow-green reminiscent of the early flowers of some trees, complements any nearby plant. The foliage is just as appealing as the flowers. Rounded light-green leaves emerge pleated and enlarge to form lobed fans with wavy edges. The surface is softly hairy. Raindrops bead up on the fuzzy foliage and shine like jewels. Their overlapping shapes and lax habit create an intriguing patterned carpet that sets off other perennials. Adaptable and easy to grow, lady's mantle will thrive just about anywhere except in hot, dry sites.

Bloom Period and Seasonal Color
Chartreuse flowers in later spring to early summer.

Mature Height × Spread
12 to 18 in. × 2 ft.

When, Where, and How to Plant
Plant lady's mantle in the spring. Choose locations with moist, well-drained, average to fertile soil in partial shade or sun. Add organic matter to sandy soils. Avoid hot, dry, sunny sites; the foliage will scorch. Following the general directions for planting perennials on page 102, space lady's mantle 2 ft. apart.

Growing Tips
Water regularly until plants are established, and water in full sun during dry spells. Place 2 in. of an organic mulch around plants to conserve moisture. Fertilization shouldn't be necessary.

Care
Lady's mantle is pest- and disease-resistant and needs little special care. If clumps begin to look unkempt, remove the tattered foliage; in several weeks, new foliage will grow. Lady's mantle self-sows abundantly in moist, partly shaded locations. Remove the flowering stems before they set seed to prevent this sometimes annoying trait. Clumps rarely need division. The flowers of lady's mantle are excellent for cutting and for drying. Pick stems before the flowers begin to brown, and hang them upside down in a well-ventilated location until dry.

Companion Planting and Design
Lady's mantle is an attractive addition to perennial beds and borders, herb gardens, lightly shaded woodland gardens, and cottage gardens. A cloud of lady's mantle is a fine companion for Siberian iris and 'Johnson's Blue' hardy geranium. Mass it as a groundcover with other perennials, or use it as an informal edging for a paved path. Edge a stone walk with lady's mantle, purple-foliaged heuchera, and 'Sprite' astilbe in partial shade. The flowers billow onto stone and brick walks; if planting next to turf, leave room to accommodate this trait.

We Recommend
'Auslese' is a cultivar said to be "tidier"—its flower sprays are more upright. For enthusiasts, there are other small lady's mantles that make an interesting addition to the garden. Look for *Alchemilla alpina* and *A. conjuncta*; both have silver-edged foliage.

Lamb's Ears
Stachys byzantina

When, Where, and How to Plant

Plant container-grown lamb's ears in the spring. Choose locations with light, sandy soil and full sun for the healthiest growth. Lamb's ears will also grow well in average to rich loamy soil but will be prone to rot in heavy, poorly drained sites. Plants are drought-tolerant. Consult page 102 for tips on planting perennials, and space them 1 to 2 ft. apart.

Growing Tips

Water regularly until plants are established. Lamb's ears are drought-tolerant and rarely require irrigation. When watering, avoid getting the foliage wet, which can promote foliar disease. Fertilization is unnecessary.

Care

Insects rarely trouble lamb's ear. In hot and humid summers, the plant can be prone to rot, although it performs well most years in Michigan. Deadhead the flower stalks whenever you feel they detract from the silvery foliage. In the spring, plants will need a little grooming to look their best. Gently pull out any brown foliage. Divide clumps when they become woody and unproductive in the center or are spreading into areas where they are not wanted. Pieces of lamb's ears can be separated easily from the mother plant without lifting the entire clump. Just use a sharp spade to sever a piece, and fill in the hole with soil.

Companion Planting and Design

Use lamb's ears in perennial gardens, dry gardens, and cottage gardens, under shrub roses, and as edging for a brick or stone path. It flatters any plant with a silvery sheen like star-of-Persia, Russian sage, and catmint.

We Recommend

'Silver Carpet' (4 to 6 in.) is a nonflowering selection that forms a dense, felt-like silver mass. A fabulous lamb's ears, 'Helene von Stein', is sometimes called 'Big Ears' in the trade. It forms a 12-in. clump of broad foliage that is not as silver-white as typical lamb's ears but a very soft silvery gray-green. Combine with almost any sunloving perennial. It is more adaptable to hot, humid weather.

Who can resist petting the fuzzy silver leaves of lamb's ears? They form dense, woolly velvet mats that almost glow in some lights, beckoning both youngsters and grownups to touch. The alternate common name— lamb's tongue—perhaps more aptly describes the shape of the leaves, which remain attractive all season, although the foliage is at its best in spring. As spring turns to early summer, the square flowering stalks bear small rosy-purple flowers in furry, chunky clusters. The stems may turn floppy and need to be removed. If you find the flower stalks unattractive, look for selections that are free, or nearly free, of flowers. Use lamb's ears, which spread by creeping fibrous-rooted rhizomes, with other plants that have silvery foliage, such as lavender or creeping thyme.

Bloom Period and Seasonal Color

Red-purple flowers in later spring, but grown for silvery foliage.

Mature Height × Spread

12 to 15 in. × 12 to 18 in.

Lavender
Lavandula angustifolia

Lavender has been cultivated for thousands of years for its fresh, singular fragrance. It doesn't always make it into the perennial books—it is often included with the herbs or the shrubs. Whatever its classification, lavender is an indispensable addition to the sunny garden. It forms shrubby mounds of needlelike gray-green foliage. In early summer, hundreds of purple spikes transform the plants into a fragrant swell of purple. Lavender likes it hot and dry. To grow it in Michigan, the soil must be light and well drained. Plants will not prosper in heavy, wet soil. On its edge of hardiness in the colder parts of Zone 5, lavender offers northern gardeners more of a challenge. Good drainage seems to be the key for winter hardiness.

Other Name
English Lavender

Bloom Period and Seasonal Color
Lavender or purple flowers in early to midsummer.

Mature Height × Spread
18 to 30 in. × 2 to 3 ft.

Zones
To Zone 5

When, Where, and How to Plant
Plant container-grown lavender in spring. Choose locations with sandy, well-drained soil and full sun for best performance. It will also grow in average, loamy, well-drained soil. Good drainage is critical; avoid wet areas. Lavender grows very well in raised beds. Follow the general directions on page 102, spacing plants 2 to 3 ft. apart.

Growing Tips
Lavenders grown in well-drained soil and sun are very long-lived and trouble-free. They don't require watering, mulching, or fertilization.

Care
Lavender is rarely bothered by insects or disease. In mid-spring when new growth is breaking, clip the shrubs back to live wood. In harsh winters, this could mean cutting the clumps back to 1 or 2 in. above the ground. In mild winters, you still may wish to trim the plants way back to promote compact growth, particularly for a formal edging. Shear flowering stalks when the flowers are no longer attractive. Plants are more susceptible to winterkill in heavy, wet soils. They have survived in Zone 4 of the Upper Peninsula where there is sandy soil and deep snow cover. Division is not advised; the stems become thick and woody and the plant is difficult to divide successfully.

Companion Planting and Design
Use lavender in perennial beds and borders, cottage gardens, herb gardens, and dry gardens. It can be planted as an edging for a rose garden or stone path, combined with other perennials, or massed as a groundcover. A gardener with a home near Lake Lansing planted a sandy slope with lavender and butterfly weed; in midsummer, the planting is a breathtaking sea of deep purple-blue punctuated by brilliant orange.

We Recommend
The plain English lavender, *Lavandula angustifolia*, is the best choice for massing, herbal harvests, and dry gardens. The differences among the plants add interest. The cultivars are especially useful when you need uniformity as for an edging, low hedge, or grouping in a perennial border. 'Hidcote' is a famous deep-purple selection.

Lenten Rose

Helleborus orientalis

When, Where, and How to Plant

Plant Lenten rose in the spring, in a moist, humus-rich soil in shade to partial shade. Hellebores will not tolerate hot, dry conditions. Follow the general directions on page 102, spacing plants $1^1/2$ to 2 ft. apart.

Growing Tips

Water regularly until new plants are established. Mulch with 2 in. of organic mulch to conserve moisture. Water plants during extended dry periods. When the plants are sited properly, additional fertilization may not be needed.

Care

Remove any brown foliage in early spring to allow for the development of new leaves. Be careful; avoid clipping or damaging the flowerbuds that rest close to the ground. Insects are rarely a concern. Hellebore black spot can be an occasional problem. Dark spots appear on the leaves, stems, and flowers, causing leaf yellowing, foliage loss, and wilted flowers. Chemical controls are not recommended. Instead, remove and discard infected leaves and flowers to control the spread of the disease. Lenten rose expands slowly over time and takes a few years to develop an impressive clump of evergreen foliage. Division is possible but not recommended. Lenten rose resents disturbance, and may take years to recover.

Companion Planting and Design

Hellebores may be planted in groupings or grown as a single accent plant. Plant them where they'll be noticed in early spring. The attractive evergreen foliage, when planted in mass, makes an appealing groundcover. Add Lenten roses to shady borders and woodland gardens, and tuck them under shrubs and small flowering trees. Create an interesting foliage collage with Lenten rose, fringed bleeding heart, and the silvery foliage of the Japanese painted fern.

We Recommend

New hybrids of Lenten rose, offering a range of flower colors from yellow to pink to burgundy, are arriving on the market with much fanfare. Time will tell which selections are ultimately adaptable to our northern climate. The white-flowered Christmas rose, *Helleborus niger*, can also be grown in Michigan.

Each year, gardeners watch and wait for signs of spring, and one of the plants greeting us early is the Lenten rose. In late February and early March, you can push the snow off the evergreen leaves of hellebore to discover the thick, tight flowerbuds patiently waiting for warmer temperatures. In due time, the flowers appear as nodding waxy blooms emerging directly from the crown. The flowers are made of petal-like sepals. The colors vary from soft white to rose to deep purple and are often stippled with crimson and maroon. The bloom period of the Lenten rose can extend beyond eight weeks, as the cool spring air preserves the flowers. Plants are slow to develop, but once they are established, they are tough customers.

Other Name

Hellebore

Bloom Period and Seasonal Color

White to purple flowers in early spring to summer.

Mature Height × Spread

15 to 18 in. × 1 to 2 ft.

Zones

To Zone 4

New England Aster
Aster novae-angliae

In late summer, asters are a familiar sight along Michigan's roadsides. More than twenty-five different asters are native to Michigan, many worthy of cultivation. The purple New England aster grows native in meadows and fields, as well as our wet prairies and fens. In nature, these asters can be gangly, growing to five feet, but they are capable of generating a profusion of bloom. In the garden, New England asters are not carefree. They need fairly frequent division, some are susceptible to mildew, and taller types may flop without pinching or staking. Early in the season, their appearance is sometimes coarse. Still, their stellar performance in the late summer and fall eclipses these shortcomings. Selections of New England aster are available that overcome some of the flaws.

Bloom Period and Seasonal Color
Lavender-blue, pink, purple, or white flowers in later summer to fall.

Mature Height × Spread
18 in. to 5 ft. × 2 to 4 ft.

When, Where, and How to Plant
Plant asters in the spring or early summer. Choose locations with moist, normal to fertile soil in full sun. Asters like moist soil and tolerate heavier clay soils. Consult page 102 for planting tips, and space them 3 to 4 ft. apart. Smaller cultivars can be spaced closer. Don't crowd them; asters need good air circulation.

Growing Tips
Water regularly until plants are established, then water during dry spells. Always water at the base of the plant; wet foliage creates a favorable environment for foliar disease. A 2-in. layer of organic mulch is beneficial. Asters do better without fertilizer.

Care
Asters are pest-resistant but can be prone to foliar diseases. Plant resistant selections, space plants adequately, and water as directed above to prevent disease. You may also thin plants as described in the entry on garden phlox. Tall asters may need to be staked, but this should be unnecessary with full sun and the right plant choice. Pinching out the growing tip of each stem when it reaches 6 in. high will make plants more compact. Division is necessary every two to four years to keep the plants vigorous. In the spring, dig up the clump and divide into healthy sections. New divisions bloom the first year.

Companion Planting and Design
Plant asters in borders, mixed plantings, and meadow or prairie-style gardens. The taller types are suitable for natural gardens and the back of the border; shorter types can be used in the front. Bring the Michigan meadow to your garden— plant goldenrod and asters together.

We Recommend
'Purple Dome' is a mass of purple on compact plants. 'Alma Potschke' has brilliant magenta flowers. 'Honeysong Pink' has clear rich-pink flowers. Many other native Michigan asters are appealing garden residents. We highly recommend the following: smooth aster, *A. laevis* 'Bluebird'; calico aster; *A. lateriflorus* 'Lady in Black'; heath aster, *A. ericoides*; and aromatic aster, *A. oblongifolius*.

Peony

Paeonia lactiflora and hybrids

When, Where, and How to Plant

Plant peonies in September in full sun and moist, well-drained soil that is rich in organic material. Dig a large hole, about as big as a bushel basket. Mix the removed soil with a handful of fertilizer that is high in phosphorus and low in nitrogen. Firm some of this soil into the hole to make a mound. Place the crown on it so the buds or eyes face upward. The buds should be no more than 1 to $1^{1}/_{2}$ in. below the soil surface. Peonies planted too deeply will not flower, and those planted too near the surface are prone to winter damage. Continue filling the planting hole and water. Space peonies at least 3 ft. apart.

Growing Tips

Water regularly, especially in spring as flowerbuds develop. Peonies may be fertilized in early spring with a general food such as 10-10-10. Avoid high-nitrogen fertilizers that stimulate leaf growth but not flowers. For the first winter after planting, mulch the peony after the ground freezes. Remove the mulch in early spring, taking care not to damage the new growth.

Care

Peonies are rarely bothered by insects but are susceptible to a disease called botrytis. To control it, remove any streaked or discolored foliage. In fall, cut back and destroy old foliage. Peonies can remain in place undisturbed for many years. If necessary, move or divide in September. Plants may take three years to reach peak flower production. Deadhead or remove faded flowers. Peony cages or supports should be placed around the plants in spring.

Companion Planting and Design

Use peonies as specimens, as an herbaceous hedge, or integrated into perennial borders. Their attractive foliage makes them an asset all season.

We Recommend

Stretch the peony season with fernleaf peony, *Paeonia tenuifolia*, which has finely dissected foliage and bright-red flowers and is among the earliest to bloom. Among the last is 'Elsa Sass', a white fragrant double peony.

Peonies are fragrant old-fashioned perennials that celebrate the arrival of early summer. The exquisite flowers may be single, semidouble, or double and full as fluffy petticoats. Even after the herbaceous peonies finish flowering, the glossy deep-green foliage remains attractive into fall. Newer cultivars as well as single peonies tend to bloom earlier and stand up better to wind and rain than do older and double types. One of Michigan's biggest plantings of old peonies is at Nichols Arboretum in Ann Arbor. Established in 1922, the beds are now renovated and filled with bloom in June, but for several decades the peonies were ignored and actually mowed. Fortunately, many original plants survived and recovered, a testament to this sturdy perennial's tenacity.

Bloom Period and Seasonal Color

White, pink, or crimson flowers in later spring to early summer.

Mature Height × Spread

2 to 3 ft. × 3 ft.

Pulmonaria
Pulmonaria spp.

In the shade garden, foliage plants with unusual variegation or leaf colors stand out and draw the attentive eye of
the gardener. The pulmonarias, also called lungwort or
Bethlehem sage, are a group of spectacular foliage plants
offering tremendous variation in foliage markings and
highlights that can brighten dark corners in the shade
and make spectacular contrasts in a mixed planting. The
lungworts form mounding, low-growing clumps of foliage
with a diversity of silvery patterns on dark-green leaves.
Different pulmonarias have varying degrees of silver,
from spots to splatters to completely drenched. The foliage
certainly carries this plant through the seasons, but the
early spring flowers are beautiful in a range of colors
from pure white to pink to the deepest azure.

Other Names
Lungwort, Bethlehem Sage

Bloom Period and Seasonal Color
Pink, blue, or white flowers in early to late spring.

Mature Height × Spread
9 to 12 in. × 9 to 12 in.

When, Where, and How to Plant
Plant pulmonaria in the spring or fall. The lungworts prefer moist, well-drained, humus-rich soil
and partial to full shade. This is not a plant for dry
shade. In full sun, plants experience leaf burning,
and the attractive foliage turns crispy brown.
Consult page 102 for tips on planting perennials.
Space pulmonarias 12 to 18 in. apart.

Growing Tips
Water regularly until plants are established. Apply
a 2-in. layer of organic mulch to conserve moisture. Water deeply in times of prolonged drought
to avoid the foliar scorch and stress that can leave
plants susceptible to powdery mildew. In humus-
rich soil, extra fertilization won't be needed.

Care
Lungwort is seldom bothered by insects but is susceptible to powdery mildew that can ruin its
appearance. Choose resistant selections and keep
the soil moist to avoid foliar disease. Deadhead the
flowering stalks when the flower display is over. In
midsummer, the older foliage may deteriorate;
remove it to make way for new, fresh foliage.
Clumps rarely need division but may be split easily
for propagation.

Companion Planting and Design
Plant lungworts in woodland gardens and shady
beds and under shrubs. Few shade plants can compare in foliage and flower. Combine with spring
bulbs, woodland wildflowers, and other shade-
lovers such as Siberian bugloss and barrenwort.
The silvery-spotted foliage adds interest to plantings of astilbes, hostas, and ferns. Pulmonaria
makes a fine groundcover, but only where adequate moisture can be supplied.

We Recommend
The catalogs are flooded with new pulmonarias.
Choose cultivars with the amount of silver you
prefer, but remember that powdery mildew can
destroy the foliage effect. The Bethlehem sage,
Pulmonaria saccharata, is more prone to mildew
than is the long-leaved lungwort, *P. longifolia,* and
its hybrids. One of the best is 'Roy Davidson'. This
hybrid has dark-green leaves spotted with silver,
and sky blue flowers.

When, Where, and How to Plant

Plant purple coneflower in the spring. It tolerates a wide range of soil types, including both dry and heavy soils, but moist, well-drained, average to rich soil is ideal. Full sun is best, although it will tolerate light shade for part of the day. Consult page 102 for tips on planting perennials. Space plants at least 2 ft. apart; crowding may increase disease.

Growing Tips

Water regularly until plants are established. Purple coneflower is an undemanding garden resident. Plants are heat- and drought-tolerant and seldom need water. Fertilization is usually unnecessary.

Care

Purple coneflower is not often bothered with pests. Avoid potential problems with rot by choosing well-drained locations. Occasionally, in wet humid weather, plants will be troubled by foliar disease. Remove and destroy any infected foliage. Deadheading will prolong bloom. Plants often self-sow, and these seedlings may not be identical to the parent plant. To prevent volunteer seedlings, remove faded flowers before seed dispersal. The clumps rarely need division.

Companion Planting and Design

Use purple coneflower in perennial beds, mixed plantings, cutting gardens, and meadow-style gardens. A favorite combination is purple coneflower with a lavender-blue cloud of Russian sage. Add the narrow gray-green foliage and airy white flowers of boltonia for even greater contrast. The orange center cone allows purple coneflower to both clash and blend with hot-colored flowers. In a meadow-style garden, the pink blooms add zip to the multitudes of yellow-orange daisies such as sunflower heliopsis, sneezeweed, and black-eyed Susan.

We Recommend

The flowers of purple coneflower typically form a shuttlecock shape, but some cultivars have spreading petals, which give the flower a flat daisy look. The cultivars are less variable than the species. 'Magnus' is a reliable form with open carmine-rose flowers. 'Kim's Knee High', at 2 ft., is compact and produces weeks of brilliant pink flowers with reflexed petals. 'White Swan' is a stunning white form with copper-orange centers.

The purple coneflower isn't really purple at all. The large eye-catching flowers are bright rose-pink. Each flower has a bristly iridescent orange center cone that provides lively contrast with the reflexed petals and a feeding station for butterflies. Growing on moist prairies and open woods, this American native was collected in southern Michigan more than 150 years ago but typically occurs in the prairies of the Midwest. Purple coneflower isn't a graceful plant. The flowers are big and bold, the form stiffly upright, and the foliage coarse. It may not be tame, but it's wildly bright, easy to grow, and dependable. Native Americans have long used purple coneflower relatives for medicine, and today echinacea is enjoying a renewed popularity in health food stores.

Bloom Period and Seasonal Color
Rose-pink or white flowers in early to late summer.

Mature Height × Spread
2 to 4 ft. × 2 ft.

dbeckia

udbeckia fulgida ssp. *sullivantii*

In horticultural books and botanical field guides, Rudbeckia fulgida is called orange coneflower, but anyone who sees its brilliant yellow-orange daisies and chocolate-brown centers can't help thinking "black-eyed Susan." Whatever you decide to call this perennial—we chose rudbeckia—it is among the very best for Michigan gardens. It produces masses of dark-centered yellow-orange flowers from midsummer until frost and lends a sunny meadow feeling to any garden. The species, a Michigan native occurring in the Lower Peninsula's meadows, wet ground, swamps, and prairie fens, is a worthy garden plant in its own right. 'Goldsturm', a German selection that flowers for two or even three months, is more compact and has dark-green, boldly textured foliage and a greater number of larger flowers.

Other Names
Black-eyed Susan, Orange Coneflower

Bloom Period and Seasonal Color
Orange-yellow flowers in mid- to late summer.

Mature Height × Spread
2 to 3 ft. × 2 ft.

When, Where, and How to Plant
Plant rudbeckia in the spring and early summer, choosing a location with full sun and average soil. Plants prefer moist, well-drained soil and are tolerant of heat but not extended drought. Some light shade is tolerated, but plants will flower less profusely. Plant black-eyed Susan following the general directions on page 102, spacing 2 to 2$^{1}/_{2}$ ft. apart.

Growing Tips
Water regularly until plants are established. Rudbeckia responds dramatically to moisture—clumps in moist areas will be taller and outperform those in dry areas. Water plants during dry periods. Fertilization is usually not needed. A 2-in. layer of organic mulch is beneficial.

Care
Rudbeckia is rarely troubled by insects and disease. It is a vigorous grower, and clumps will need to be divided about every three or four years as the centers die out. This chore isn't difficult. Lift the clumps and amend the soil in which the plants were growing with well-rotted compost. Separate them into pieces, and discard the worn-out middle sections. Replant at the same level at which they were growing, and water well. Divisions often bloom the first year.

Companion Planting and Design
Rudbeckia 'Goldsturm' is an excellent addition to perennial borders, island beds, and mixed plantings. A standard component of the New American Garden style of landscaping, it is often seen in combination with 'Autumn Joy' stonecrop and ornamental grasses. If you want to try a different combination, use the bright yellow-orange daisies set off by blue asters and softened by the subtle haze of switch grass.

We Recommend
Many other gardenworthy rudbeckia are available. Where there is room, the tall (6 ft.) *Rudbeckia* 'Herbstonne' (translated to 'Autumn Sun') is spectacular. It has drooping petals and a greenish central disk. For hundreds of plump yellow-orange daisies, try the three-lobed coneflower, *Rudbeckia triloba*. A Michigan native of wet prairies and marshy ground, this short-lived perennial will self-sow and come back each year.

Russian Sage
Perovskia atriplicifolia

When, Where, and How to Plant
Plant Russian sage in spring. Russian sage thrives in full sun. Some shade is tolerable, but plants will lean toward the light and may sprawl. Choose locations with well-drained soil—good drainage is essential. Follow the general planting directions on page 102, spacing plants 2 to $2^1/2$ ft. apart.

Growing Tips
Water regularly until established; after that, plants are quite drought-tolerant. They prefer soil on the lean side, so extra fertilization isn't necessary. Russian sage may also be grown in Zone 4 with the protection of a winter mulch. It will die back to the ground.

Care
There are no serious pest and disease problems. Good drainage and full sun will lead to healthy plants. Wait to cut back Russian sage until signs of new growth appear in the spring. At that time, remove with pruners any dead or weak branches, and cut remaining branches back, leaving four to six healthy buds. In an unusually cold winter, plants may die back to the ground and resprout from below soil level. Due to its semiwoody habit, division of Russian sage is inadvisable. Sometimes prostrate stems will root. These can be severed from the plant and planted.

Companion Planting and Design
Plant drifts of Russian sage in perennial borders, landscape beds, or mixed plantings of annuals, perennials, and shrubs. Try them by a sunny patio or behind a bench with a full-sun exposure. At its best in drifts of three or more, Russian sage's extended blooming period, among the longest of any perennial, allows for a wide range of successful plant combinations.

We Recommend
Several cultivars are available, offering uniformity and improved characteristics. 'Blue Spire' grows to 3 ft.; it has bluer flowers, deeply cut foliage, and a more erect habit. 'Filagran' has delicately filigreed foliage. 'Longin', a very upright selection, has silvery leaves that are not as divided. It's more formal but not as graceful in the garden.

The delicate flowers of Russian sage create a lavender-blue haze above gray-green foliage in the garden. The flowering effect lasts for months, providing a light and airy backdrop for purple coneflower in July and later with ornamental grasses in September. Russian sage's graceful three- to four-foot stems hold thousands of small flowers, but its delicate appearance belies its ease of culture. Russian sage needs full sun and good drainage for optimum growth; it is adaptable to a wide range of soil types. It is a subshrub, which means it doesn't die back completely as do most herbaceous perennials. It grows each year from woody branches near the base of the plant. The silvery white stems provide winter interest in the garden until spring.

Bloom Period and Seasonal Color
Lavender-blue flowers in early summer through fall.

Mature Height × Spread
3 to $4^1/2$ ft. × 3 ft.

Zones
To Zone 4

Salvia

Salvia × superba

Red, orange, and yellow flowers vie for attention in the garden. Hybrid perennial salvia doesn't use a hot-tempered display to get noticed; it coolly attracts admiring glances with its deep violet-blue pools of color. Perennial hybrid salvia provides months of saturated purple-blue. In late spring, its flowers are early enough to complement peonies or Siberian iris. A few weeks later, the purple flowers are at their peak, providing dramatic contrast for the yellow daisies of threadleaf coreopsis or the golden flat-topped clusters of 'Coronation Gold' yarrow. Like these two, violet sage needs full sun to perform its best. The dense spikes arise by the score from mounds of gray-green foliage and retain an attractive red-violet cast even after the flowers drop.

Other Name
Perennial Salvia

Bloom Period and Seasonal Color
Violet or purple flowers in late spring to midsummer.

Mature Height × Spread
18 to 24 in. × 18 in.

Zones
To Zone 4

When, Where, and How to Plant
Plant perennial salvia in the spring so the roots can become well established before winter. Choose locations with average to fertile, well-drained garden soil. Full sun is preferred, but light shade is tolerated. Plants in heavy soil and partial shade will not achieve their full potential and will sprawl. Avoid poorly-drained sites. Follow the general directions for planting perennials on page 102, spacing plants $1^1/2$ to 2 ft. apart.

Growing Tips
Water regularly until established. Salvia is drought-tolerant and will survive without supplemental irrigation, but water during dry spells will improve performance. Deep snow cover—or, where it can't be relied upon, a winter mulch of evergreen boughs applied after the ground freezes—will help overwinter plants in Zone 4. Additional fertilizer is unnecessary.

Care
Salvia is rarely troubled by insects or disease. Correctly sited, hybrid perennial salvia will need little care other than removing the spent flower stalks. This deadheading will encourage a second flush of bloom. Cut back hard to the basal foliage. Clumps seldom need division but may be divided in the spring.

Companion Planting and Design
Use salvia in formal and informal perennial borders and cottage gardens. Salvia's rich purple-blue is stunning with magenta, pink, and lavender, and it makes silver foliage shine. Try salvia 'May Night' with the intense pink flowers of bloody cranesbill, 'Bath's Pink' cheddar pinks, catmint, lamb's ears, and 'Valerie Finnis' artemisia.

We Recommend
There are many selections of hybrid salvia. 'May Night' is a wonderful garden plant with deep violet-blue flowers on long spikes for an extended period. A new cultivar, 'Caradonna', has dark purple-black stems that complement its purple flowers. Another nice perennial sage, *Salvia verticillata* 'Purple Rain' (18 to 20 in.), has smoky purple flowers in whorls over wavy, heart-shaped gray-green foliage. Although not as showy as hybrid salvia, it flowers over a long period and has a spreading habit.

When, Where, and How to Plant

Plant sedum from spring through early fall. Choose locations with full sun and average soil. Plants will grow in fertile soil but will be taller and more prone to split open. Avoid poorly drained sites; good drainage is the key to success. Follow the general planting directions on page 102, spacing plants according to selection.

Growing Tips

Keep new plants well watered, particularly in hot weather, until established. After establishment, stonecrop is heat- and drought-tolerant. It does better without fertilizer.

Care

Although basically carefree, sedums may sometimes attract aphids. In general, control is not needed. Keep populations in check by washing off aphids with a direct stream of water. Cut back the dried sedum seedheads in early spring to make way for new growth. If clumps get overcrowded and split open in the center, they need division. In the spring, lift the clumps and split them apart with a sharp spade. Remove the unproductive center and replant vigorous pieces from the outside of the clump. Keep well watered. Even small pieces will establish with little care.

Companion Planting and Design

Sedums are versatile and can be used in many ways. Low types are suitable for dry gardens, rock walls, edging, and groundcover. The taller ones are suitable for the perennial border, island beds, mixed plantings, landscape beds, and massing as in the New American Garden style. Take advantage of their wonderful color and texture in combination with ornamental grasses and perennials.

We Recommend

There are too many great sedums to list them all here, but here are a few favorites: 'Matrona' is similar in size to 'Autumn Joy' but has blue-green foliage, red stems, and broad heads of pale-pink flowers. 'Vera Jameson' is lower-growing with dusky plum foliage and bright-pink flowers. 'Ruby Glow', a low-spreading type, has blue-gray foliage and vivid ruby-red flowers.

Stonecrops, or sedums, offer the gardener a wide range of useful and easy-to-grow plants. Some are wonderful border plants, and others are suitable for groundcovers and rock walls. Perhaps the most famous stonecrop is 'Autumn Joy', which is truly a joy to the gardener. It's attractive all year—as well as almost indestructible—as it transforms itself from green to pink to russet. It delights in winter when dusted with snow. Once you have grown 'Autumn Joy', you'll be eager to discover how other stonecrops can uplift your garden. Even when not in flower, stonecrops are texturally interesting; their succulent leaves vary in color from green to plum to burgundy. If you've got sun, there is a stonecrop for you.

Other Name
Stonecrop

Bloom Period and Seasonal Color
Pink, white, or yellow flowers in summer to fall.

Mature Height × Spread
2 to 24 in. × 12 to 24 in.

Bugloss

...ophylla

Opening with the daffodils, the sky blue starry flowers of Siberian bugloss deserve to be a standard feature in every spring garden. They resemble forget-me-nots held aloft on thin stalks, and the flowers continue to be attractive for weeks. Unlike some other spring charmers, Siberian bugloss continues to play a role in the summer garden even after its flowers are gone. The plants grow as clumps in partial shade, and their showy, coarse dark-green leaves gradually enlarge, reaching up to eight inches across by summer's end. The leaves are shaped like hearts. Easy to grow in partial shade, Siberian bugloss requires little care. It excels in a wooded setting, as a groundcover under shrubs, and in any place where it can naturalize.

Bloom Period and Seasonal Color
Sky blue flowers in mid- to late spring.

Mature Height × Spread
12 to 18 in. × 12 to 18 in.

When, Where, and How to Plant
Plant Siberian bugloss in spring. Choose locations with moist, well-drained, humus-rich soil in partial shade. Siberian bugloss will tolerate some sun but may need more frequent watering in sunny locations. Plant $1^{1}/_{2}$ to 2 ft. apart following the general directions for planting on page 102.

Growing Tips
Water regularly until plants are established. In the spring, apply a 2-in. layer of organic mulch to conserve moisture. Water plants during dry spells; foliage will brown if conditions are too dry. Sited correctly, yearly fertilization is unnecessary.

Care
Siberian bugloss is rarely troubled by insects or disease. It self-sows in moist, shady gardens. Seedlings may be moved to other locations, weeded out, or allowed to grow. Where self-sowing is prevalent, this plant will spread to form large masses. Eventually, clumps may split open in the center and need dividing, which is easily accomplished in the spring. Dig up the clumps, and split them apart with a sharp spade or large knife. Discard the unproductive center, and replant the healthy pieces. Water new divisions frequently until established. Mulch new divisions to conserve moisture.

Companion Planting and Design
Use Siberian bugloss in woodland gardens, shady borders, and foundation beds, and as a groundcover under trees and shrubs. The dark-green, heart-shaped leaves make a striking contrast with hardy spring bulbs. The clear blue flowers are especially lovely when interplanted with bright-yellow daffodils. The coarsely-textured foliage functions as does that of hosta, providing contrast with the more common finely textured foliage of other shade-loving plants such as ferns, astilbes, and fringed bleeding hearts.

We Recommend
Some interesting cultivars exist, but they may be difficult to find. 'Variegata' has large leaves that are mostly to partly white; it requires a shady, moist location. The leaves of 'Hadspen Cream' are light green with off-white margins. 'Langtrees' has foliage marked faintly with silvery spots.

Siberian Iris
Iris sibirica

When, Where, and How to Plant
Plant container-grown Siberian iris from spring into early fall. Choose locations with moist, humus-rich soil in full sun to partial shade. Siberian irises are very tolerant of moisture but don't like having their roots submerged. Plant 1¹/₂ to 2 ft. apart following the guidelines on page 102.

Growing Tips
Water regularly until plants are established. Apply a 2-in. layer of organic mulch to conserve moisture. Water the plants during dry spells if they are planted in sandy soil. Clumps may be fed lightly with a sprinkling of 10-10-10 fertilizer in the spring.

Care
Siberian iris is much more resistant to the pests that affect bearded iris. Eventually, the clumps will produce fewer flowers and become dead in the center. Divide them in spring when the foliage is 4 to 6 in. high. Split a clump into pieces with a sharp spade, or even a saw. Discard the woody center, and replant vigorous pieces from the outside of the clump. Add organic material to the soil and keep divisions moist until established. If clumps are splitting open, divide them or move them to a sunnier location. Cut back the foliage of Siberian iris in the fall. Foliage left standing for the winter will flop, providing a hiding place for rodents, which love to eat the roots.

Companion Planting and Design
Plant Siberian iris in perennial beds, mixed plantings, and cottage gardens, and in drifts by water features. Use as an accent plant among peonies, blue false indigo, lady's mantle, hardy geraniums, and tufted hair grass.

We Recommend
Many cultivars of Siberian iris are available, and some of the older selections that have stood the test of time are still worth considering. 'Caesar's Brother' (2¹/₂ ft.) is a deep dark purple with graceful flowers. 'Ego' (2 ft.) is a medium blue, and 'Super Ego' (2 to 2¹/₂ ft.) is a delicate pale-blue beauty with falls veined deep blue-violet.

The exquisite flowers of Siberian iris add grace to the garden. With their upright standards and downward falls, the blooms have classic, clean lines that are both beautiful and elegant. The falls, often with intricate veining and a marking called a blaze, are smooth, unlike those of their more flouncy and demanding relative, the tall bearded iris. When in bloom, the blue, purple, or white flowers of Siberian iris dance aloft, looking almost as if they could take flight against the blue sky. After the blooming period, the iris's arching foliage adds vertical structure to the garden all summer long. Siberian iris is easy to grow. Moist, well-drained soil and sun ensure success, but these long-lived, disease-resistant plants also tolerate wet sites and partial shade.

Bloom Period and Seasonal Color
Blue, purple, red-violet, or white flowers in later spring to early summer.

Mature Height × Spread
2 to 4 ft. × 2 ft.

Sneezeweed

Helenium autumnale

Sneezeweed produces mobs of bright chubby daisies lighting up the summer border. But with a name like sneezeweed, it's hard to achieve popularity. Some perennial catalogs have taken to calling it Helen's flower in a marketing attempt to upgrade sneezeweed's image. The common name "sneezeweed" describes not an allergic reaction but the use of the dried flowerheads to produce a sort of snuff. In field guides, Helenium autumnale is sometimes called the swamp sunflower, and a swamp, wet meadow, or a riverbank is where you might find it growing in the Great Lakes state. This lanky native, often growing to five feet, has been civilized and hybridized by European growers into a range of beautiful, floriferous, and more compact garden plants.

Bloom Period and Seasonal Color
Yellow or orange flowers in early to late summer.

Mature Height × Spread
3 to 5 ft. × 2 to 3 ft.

When, Where, and How to Plant
Plant sneezeweed in the spring, in locations with moist, average to fertile soil in full sun. Plants are tolerant of wet soils, and adequate moisture promotes healthy growth. Avoid dry sites. Plant following the general directions on page 102, spacing 2 to 3 ft. apart.

Growing Tips
Water regularly until establishment and mulch to conserve moisture. Water plants during dry spells if they are not planted in a moisture-retentive site. Regular moisture is the key to growing this plant well. If plants need it, fertilize in the spring with a sprinkling of 10-10-10.

Care
In moist soils, sneezeweed is usually pest- and disease-free. Deadhead flowering stems to encourage more bloom, or take the shears to clumps and cut back plants by half. Although often relegated to the list of plants needing frequent division, sneezeweed clumps can often go for four to six years without it. Always take your cue from the plants. If flowering diminishes and clumps begin to die out in the center, divide the following spring. Pinching out the growing tips when the shoots are about 6 in. high will delay flowering and promote stockier growth.

Companion Planting and Design
Use sneezeweed in moist, sunny perennial beds and borders, wet areas, cottage gardens, and natural meadow-type plantings. The bright, rich color of sneezeweed adds life to the summer garden. It is often seen in large British perennial borders with other North American natives such as Culver's root, Joe-pye weed, asters, and goldenrod.

We Recommend
The cultivars are preferred over the species for garden use. The heights are lower, the stems are stronger, and the flower colors range from bright yellow to warm copper-orange and mahogany-red. Choose the shorter selections to avoid the need for staking or pinching. 'Butterpat' ($3^1/2$ to 4 ft.) is a gorgeous sunny yellow selection. Another favorite is 'Moerheim Beauty' (3 ft.), which has rich copper-red flowers with dark centers.

Spiked Speedwell
Veronica spicata

When, Where, and How to Plant
Plant spiked speedwell in the spring, in a location with average, well-drained soil in full sun. Sun and good drainage are important for success. Consult page 102 for tips on planting. Space plants 1 to 2 ft. apart depending on the selection.

Growing Tips
Water regularly until plants are established. Apply a 2-in. layer of organic mulch to conserve moisture. Although somewhat drought-tolerant, speedwell appreciates water during dry spells. Don't overfertilize—too much fertilizer will lead to flopping.

Care
In full sun and well-drained soil, speedwell is pest- and disease-resistant. Remove the flowering spikes to promote rebloom. When flowering decreases, about every four or five years, divide clumps for rejuvenation. This is easily accomplished in the spring. Dig clumps, and split apart with a knife or sharp spade. Replant vigorous pieces from the outside of the clumps. Keep new divisions watered until established.

Companion Planting and Design
Plant spiked speedwell in perennial beds and borders, and rock gardens, and use for edging. Woolly speedwell is an attractive groundcover. The vertical spires of spiked speedwell are a natural complement to the rounded form of many perennials. The soft-yellow mounded form of 'Moonbeam' coreopsis makes an attractive pairing with the dark-blue 'Goodness Grows' or the lighter 'Blue Charm'. Spiked speedwell is welcome in mixed plantings and cottage gardens. Try it under shrub roses, with hardy geraniums, lady's mantle, and cheddar pinks.

We Recommend
A superior selection is 'Blue Charm' (18 to 24 in.); it produces months of blue flower spikes. 'Icicle' (18 to 20 in.) is a fine white cultivar with deep-green foliage and spires of white flowers over a long period. 'Goodness Grows' veronica is a low-growing (to 12 in.) perennial for the front of the border; it has narrow spires of dark indigo-blue from June through October. A cultivar of woolly speedwell called 'Silver Slippers' doesn't flower at all!

Yellow flowers abound in the summer garden, but blue flowers are all too rare. Spiked speedwell, often just called veronica, sends forth tapering spikes of deep or light blue, adding vertical lift to the mounds and mats of the garden's foreground. The long, graceful spikes bloom for almost six weeks, appearing in profusion atop neat clumps of green foliage. Some, such as 'Blue Charm', are fairly tall—almost two feet—and are suitable for the middle of a perennial bed; the upward spires provide visual relief from the chunky trusses of phlox or the flat-topped clusters of yarrow. Others are more diminutive; the woolly speedwell, Veronica incana, is grown not only for its ten-inch blue-violet spikes but also for its prostrate mats of silvery foliage.

Other Name
Veronica

Bloom Period and Seasonal Color
Blue, pink, or white flowers in early to midsummer.

Mature Height × Spread
1 to 2 ft. × 18 to 24 in.

Threadleaf Coreopsis
Coreopsis verticillata

Many perennials are transitory in the garden, blooming only a few weeks at most. The threadleaf coreopsis 'Moonbeam', though, blooms on and off from early summer into fall, peaking at midsummer. In addition to its long season of bloom, 'Moonbeam' is unusual for its pale, almost icy yellow color that blends harmoniously with blues, purples, and whites without being intense. Other types of threadleaf coreopsis are a brighter golden-yellow. The finely-textured foliage is airy and attractive before and during flowering. Threadleaf coreopsis, a native to the southeastern United States, needs little care. In light soils and full sun, it spreads quickly. Leave it uncut in late fall, and the small dark-brown buttonlike seedheads will remain attractive all winter over the tangle of stems.

Other Name
Tickseed

Bloom Period and Seasonal Color
Yellow flowers in early summer to fall.

Mature Height × Spread
18 in. to 3 ft. × 2 to 3 ft.

When, Where, and How to Plant
Plant threadleaf coreopsis in spring or early summer. Choose locations with full sun and moist but well-drained, average soil. Clumps tolerate light shade. Threadleaf coreopsis is drought-tolerant once established. Follow the general information for planting perennials on page 102, spacing the plants 2 to 3 ft. apart depending on the selection.

Growing Tips
Threadleaf coreopsis needs little care. Water regularly until plants are established. Additional watering and fertilizing are rarely needed.

Care
The clumps are pest- and disease-resistant. After about four years, plants will begin to die in the middle, flower less profusely, or spread into areas where they are unwelcome. This is the time to divide. In the spring, lift the mats of spreading rhizomes and fibrous roots, and cut into sections. Replant healthy, vigorous pieces. Water well until established. 'Moonbeam' forms clumps more slowly and is less likely to need division. Cut back the brown stems to the ground in the spring. The dark-brown seedheads, particularly of 'Moonbeam', can be quite ornamental in the winter.

Companion Planting and Design
The fine-textured foliage and starry flowers of threadleaf coreopsis are a welcome addition to perennial borders and island beds, or use it for massing as edging, as a groundcover, or with grasses in a landscape design. It makes a fine groundcover combined with other spreading perennials such as common yarrow, 'Silver King' artemisia, and hardy ageratum (*Eupatorium coelestinum*).

We Recommend
'Moonbeam' (12 to 18 in.), which is probably a hybrid, forms a mound of dark-green foliage and pastel yellow flowers. Gardeners in colder zones may find that 'Moonbeam' is less hardy than the other selections. Bright-gold 'Golden Showers' (2 to 3 ft.) is larger and more vigorous. 'Zagreb' (12 to18 in.) is a similar but smaller form. The large-flowered tickseed, *Coreopsis grandiflora*, has yellow-orange flowers and simple leaves. 'Sunray' is a pleaser with multitudes of double golden-yellow flowers.

Turtlehead
Chelone obliqua

When, Where, and How to Plant
Plant turtlehead in the spring. Choose locations with moist, humus-rich soil in full sun or light shade. Turtlehead is not tolerant of dry soils; moisture is the key to success. Consult page 102 for tips on planting perennials, spacing plants 2 to 3 ft. apart.

Growing Tips
Water regularly until plants are established. Apply a 2- to 3-in. layer of organic mulch to conserve moisture. In well-drained areas, water to keep soil moist. If sited correctly, extra fertilization should be unnecessary.

Care
Turtlehead is rarely troubled by insects or disease. If sited in moist soil, it will need no special care. If plants grow too tall and flop, relocate to a sunnier position. Thriving clumps will increase quickly. To control spread or for propagation, divide the fleshy rooted crowns of turtlehead in the spring when the foliage is just emerging. Some gardeners pinch the shoot tips when the stems are about 6 in. tall to promote branching. In full sun, this shouldn't be required.

Companion Planting and Design
Use turtlehead in moist perennial borders, along ponds and streams, and in wet spots and natural areas. If the plant is to succeed in the perennial border, the soil must be moisture-retentive and humus-rich. Turtlehead is well adapted to a place by a stream or a pond. In a naturalized damp garden, plant rose turtlehead with the tall smoky-purple clusters of Joe-pye weed and the white flowers of 'Ice Ballet' swamp milkweed. Lavender-blue asters and burgundy-tinted switch grass would be an attractive addition.

We Recommend
The pink turtlehead, *Chelone lyonii*, is also suitable for garden culture in moist sites. A selection called 'Hot Lips' was chosen for its attractive dark-red stems. The white turtlehead, *C. glabra*, grows throughout Michigan on low ground along streams and rivers. It has dark-green narrow foliage and the same snapdragon-like arrangement of flowers. With rich soil and consistent moisture, turtlehead will thrive.

Rose turtlehead has a fascinating appearance due to the unusual structure of its flowers. Each deep-rose tubular bloom resembles a turtle's head with lower lip protruding and mouth agape. It's a strange image, but the satiny pink flowers arranged in spikes like snapdragons are gorgeous. The lush dark-green leaves provide the perfect complement. Native to but rare in southeastern Michigan, rose turtlehead can occasionally be found along rivers and in wet places blooming at the end of summer. Healthy plants will produce a large number of stems blooming over an extended period from late summer into fall. In locations where moist soil can be found—a condition not uncommon in Michigan gardens—turtlehead is an easy, long-lived, and engaging garden plant.

Bloom Period and Seasonal Color
Rose-pink flowers in midsummer to early fall.

Mature Height × Spread
2 to 3 ft. × 2 to 3 ft.

Yarrow
Achillea 'Coronation Gold'

Radiating the warm glow of summer, the mustard-yellow flat-topped floral clusters of Achillea 'Coronation Gold' catch the sun's rays and reflect them. This striking hybrid yarrow is one of the very best for the garden. The upward-facing flowerheads are produced on strong stems over aromatic feathery gray-green foliage. The color glows against the soft muted leaves. As the flowers develop, the woolly buds are silvery white, opening to the radiant gold for which this cultivar is named. For cutting and drying, these bright flat-topped flowerheads are beyond compare. Some yarrows sprawl and require staking, some have flowers that fade in the sun, and others spread aggressively, requiring yearly division. With sun and average soil, the 'Coronation Gold' stands tall and bright in the summer garden.

Bloom Period and Seasonal Color
Golden-yellow flowers in early to late summer.

Mature Height × Spread
$2^{1}/_{2}$ to 3 ft. × $2^{1}/_{2}$ × 3 ft.

When, Where, and How to Plant
Plant yarrow in the spring. Choose locations with well-drained, average soil in full sun. Yarrow is tolerant of sandy soils and drought. Avoid shade and locations with moist, rich soil. Following the advice on page 102 for planting tips, space plants 2 to $2^{1}/_{2}$ ft. apart.

Growing Tips
Water regularly until plants are established. Yarrow is drought-tolerant and shouldn't need additional watering. Fertilizer is generally unnecessary, and high nitrogen levels will lead to weak floppy growth. Avoid heavy layers of mulch.

Care
Yarrows are seldom bothered by insects or disease. Prevent rot by choosing well-drained locations. Plants in rich soil may require staking. Deadhead the flower heads when they become brown. After three or four years, clumps will need division for rejuvenation. In the spring, dig clumps and split with two spading forks or a sharp spade. Take vigorous pieces from the outside of the clumps. Replant and keep watered until established. For drying, cut the stems when the flowers are just beginning to open and before the pollen develops. This will preserve the bright-yellow color.

Companion Planting and Design
Use hybrid yarrow in perennial beds and borders, cottage gardens, cut-flower gardens, and mixed plantings. Combine this gold yarrow with the purple spires of perennial salvia for an eye-catching contrast of form and hue. For a drought-tolerant grouping, plant yarrows with purple fennel, shrubs of lavender, and lamb's ears.

We Recommend
Another valuable hybrid yarrow is 'Moonshine'. It has softer yellow flowers, and a more compact size, growing to 2 ft. It needs more-frequent division to look its best, often every two to three years. 'Anthea' is a similar, and reportedly better, selection. The Galaxy hybrids are a group of cultivars developed in Germany. Most open one color in early summer and fade to a softer tint, giving the plant a two-tone appearance. Many are quite beautiful but not as sturdy as 'Coronation Gold'.

Shrubs *for Michigan*

Flower and fragrances, colorful stems and fruits, exfoliating bark—shrubs offer all these attractions and more. With the right selection, a shrub provides four-season appeal in a relatively compact size.

Shrubs are an important design element in the garden. Trees and shrubs define space, creating a framework in which to fit other plants. They add form and texture while providing a backdrop for annuals and perennials during spring, summer, and fall. In winter, when many branches are bare, the strong shapes of trees and shrubs are at their most distinct. Shrubs give your garden structure.

This chapter includes shrubs with outstanding attributes that are among the easiest to grow in Michigan gardens.

Selecting Shrubs

Shrubs are typically sold in one of three ways: container-grown, bareroot, or balled-and-burlapped.

Container-grown plants have spent most of their lives in pots. These shrubs may be planted at any time during the growing season, but spring and fall planting is preferred. There should be signs of new leaves. Lift the plant gently from the pot so you can see the rootball. If roots are circling tightly inside the container, the shrub will have a difficult time making the transition to your garden.

Bareroot shrubs have been grown in a nursery field. They are dug up while dormant in early spring or late fall and offered for sale. When you receive these plants, look them over immediately and examine the roots for damaged portions. Cut and remove broken or damaged roots back to healthy tissue before planting, which should take place as soon as possible.

Balled-and-burlapped shrubs are also field-grown. They are dug with a ball of soil left intact around their roots and are usually the largest shrubs available. The rootball is wrapped in burlap or other material to hold it together. Because this takes more labor, these plants are usually the most expensive. They are also heavy, so enlist a friend to help plant your shrub.

Balled-and-burlapped shrubs may be planted in March, April, and May, or in September, October, and November. Spring planting is often preferred because the roots have time to grow before the heat of summer sets in.

Planting Shrubs

Dig a hole as deep as the rootball or container and two to three times as wide. With containerized shrubs, remove the plastic pot before planting. Hose off the rootball to expose the roots and, if possible, gently loosen the roots with your fingers. With rootbound plants that have built up a large mass of circling roots at the bottom of the ball, score the roots with a utility blade or old kitchen knife. Four or five cuts spaced evenly around the ball will break roots free and encourage their healthy development in the soil. When planting balled-and burlapped shrubs, place the plant in the hole and remove the top one-third of the burlap before backfilling the hole with soil.

Position the shrub so it is growing at the same depth it was in the container or field. Replace the soil around the rootball, water well to moisten and to eliminate air pockets, and then check again to see if additional soil is needed. Mound up the soil in a ring around the new plant. The ring creates a retention reservoir that holds water in place so it can slowly percolate into the soil.

After planting, prune out any dead or broken branches. Apply a two- to three-inch layer of mulch, such as shredded bark, around the shrub. During the first season, water the shrub during dry periods, continuing until the ground freezes.

Pruning can be used to control shrub size, to promote flowering, and to remove overcrowded growth. It also rejuvenates plants that have lost vigor and need a jump start to get growing again. Many shrubs, though, need very little yearly pruning.

Shrubs that bloom on last season's growth, such as lilacs and forsythia, should be pruned after they flower. Those that bloom on the current season's growth, such as the panicle hydrangea and summer-sweet, should be pruned in February or March while the plant is dormant.

Maintaining Good Health

The health and vigor of your shrubs will be enhanced if you periodically apply fertilizers. It is generally not recommended that you fertilizer shrubs for the first year after planting. During the first year, new roots have not developed to the point where they can absorb the nutrients and feed the plant.

After that, look for clues from your shrubs that they need additional nutrients. Plants that lack nitrogen have pale green, rather than dark green, leaves. The leaves may be undersized and the overall growth of the plant slow or stunted. Shrubs that lack iron will have yellow leaves, with only the veins within the leaves displaying a dark green color. This is often the case on high pH or alkaline soils.

If you're unsure about the nutrient capacity of your soil, have the soil tested. After a sample is analyzed in a laboratory, you will receive a detailed nutrient profile of the soil that will better inform your decision on what type and amount of fertilizer to apply. The tests are generally inexpensive. Your county extension office can tell you how to submit a soil sample.

If you determined that your shrub needs fertilizer, the best time to apply it is in late April or early May, or in late fall once plants are dormant.

There are so many fertilizers available, it can be hard to decide which one to use. First, read the package to determine if the product is for use on shrubs. Select a fertilizer that contains slow-release forms of nitrogen. These release nutrients gradually and are less likely to leach from soils or burn the plant. They are also much easier to handle, apply and store than liquid fertilizers.

Follow the recommended rates listed on the package. Nitrogen-based fertilizers should be used in response to the specific symptoms described above. For plants exhibiting iron deficiencies, slow-release fertilizers containing sulfur-coated urea provide nitrogen with the added benefit of sulfur. They help lower soil pH and allow for increased iron absorption. This is particularly valuable in high pH or alkaline soils. Adding compost and other organic material such as shredded leaves to the soil around

your shrubs provides beneficial nutrients and improves soil characteristics such as moisture retention. This may lower or even eliminate your need for fertilizers.

Whatever the need, there is a shrub for every purpose. Look through the following pages to find the perfect choice for your garden.

Annabelle Hydrangea

Hydrangea arborescens 'Annabelle'

In July, just when the shrub border is getting boring, Annabelle hydrangea comes to the rescue. Its round white flower clusters, which are called corymbs, have a startlingly bright effect. In fact, one man who glimpsed the eight- to twelve-inch balls at dusk in a wooded setting initially thought the flower heads were some kind of electric landscape lights. About six weeks after the flowers open, the heavy heads turn chartreuse, and they remain attractive for months. Annabelle hydrangea usually dies back to the soil level during Michigan winters. In late March, cut down the stems; soon, new ones will begin to grow. Light up your shrub border with Annabelles. They thrive in partial shade or even a sunnier location if you give them extra water.

Other Name
Smooth Hydrangea

Bloom Period and Seasonal Color
White flowers, becoming chartreuse in summer through fall.

Mature Height × Spread
3 to 5 ft. × 4 to 5 ft.

When, Where, and How to Plant
Plant container-grown 'Annabelle' in spring, summer, or early fall. The best location is in well-drained but moist soil in partial shade, although plants will tolerate more sun if they receive sufficient moisture. Dig a hole as deep as the rootball and twice as wide. If necessary, work in organic matter. Before planting, check to see if the plant is potbound. If it is, make vertical slices around the perimeter of the rootball to encourage outward growth. Replace the soil so the plant is growing at the same depth it was in the pot. Allow 4 ft. between plants. Water well and often.

Growing Tips
Water frequently during dry periods. If the plant doesn't get enough water, the leaves will droop. Fertilize with 10-10-10 or a similar balanced product as new growth begins in spring, or mulch with shredded leaves to provide nutrients and to conserve soil moisture.

Care
Cut down or mow off the old stems in late winter to early spring, before new growth starts. 'Annabelle' hydrangea is relatively free of insects and disease.

Companion Planting and Design
Mass 'Annabelle' hydrangeas to light up a partly shady corner of the landscape. Their flowers radiate a cool brilliance that is spectacular at twilight against a dark backdrop like a hemlock hedge. A cultivated variety of a native species, 'Annabelle' flower heads add interest to the garden beginning in midsummer. Use these shrubs in a mixed shrub border with viburnums and with purple-leaved specimen plants like 'Velvet Cloak' smokebush.

We Recommend
The relatively easygoing nature of smooth hydrangeas like 'Annabelle' will be a refreshing change for those who have only grown the more temperamental (at least in Michigan) bigleaf types. Another good one to try is *Hydrangea arborescens* 'Grandiflora'. It is also showy, with flower clusters similar to those of 'Annabelle' but with fewer and larger flowers.

When, Where, and How to Plant

Plant in spring or early fall. Yews can be planted from full sun to shade and in most soil types, but avoid wet conditions, where they become susceptible to root rot, and avoid exposed windy locations, where needles brown out from water loss. Plant as a container-grown or balled-and-burlapped shrub following the instructions on page 154.

Growing Tips

Keep newly planted yews moist when going into the winter season. Read page 154 for advice on fertilization.

Care

Yews can be kept under control by reserved pruning—don't get carried away with the shears. Prune to accentuate your yew's natural habit by taking back selected branches to the main body of the shrub, using handpruners if possible. Vary the depth of the cuts to avoid creating a straight line. Prune in the winter or early summer. Two pests sometimes pose a problem for yews. The taxus mealybug sucks sap from the plant, causing needle drop and loss of vigor. A dormant oil application is the recommended control for mealybug. Black vine weevil feeds on roots, causing needles to yellow; the adult weevil feeds at night, notching the needles. This is most noticeable on needles in the center of the plant. Orthene™ is the recommended control for the black vine weevil. *Caution: seeds are poisonous.*

Companion Planting and Design

Plant yews to add winter color to your landscape. They make effective hedges or screens, but pay attention to the ultimate size and spread of the cultivar as you plan your hedge. Plants placed too closely will immediately require pruning and will have poor form.

We Recommend

'Ward' or 'Wardii' is a low-spreading selection with dark-green foliage. It is slow-growing, with a twenty-year-old plant reaching 6 ft. in height and 19 ft. in width. The 'Ward' yew is a female selection. 'Brownii' is a male plant with attractive dark-green foliage and a rounded habit, staying below 6 ft. in height and responding well to pruning.

The yew is a beleaguered plant, a shrub that Rodney Dangerfield might say "can't get no respect." Overused, hacked, butchered, and vying each year for the unofficial title of "the state shrub of Michigan," yews are caught in an ugly conundrum of versatility versus abuse. It is certainly true that they appear all too frequently in Michigan landscapes, but they are (and should be!) extremely important shrubs for homeowners looking for green relief in the often gray days of winter. The anglojap yew offers several cultivars with a low, spreading habit, and it is particularly useful for foundation plantings, evergreen screens, or hedges, or in mass plantings as a backdrop to other colorful trees or shrubs. Female plants have brightly-colored fleshy fruit.

Bloom Period and Seasonal Color

Dark evergreen needles, fleshy red fruit in fall.

Mature Height × Spread

Recommended forms are under 6 ft. × 6 to 8 ft.

Zones

To Zone 4

Arborvitae

Thuja occidentalis

Arborvitae grows naturally in the wet cedar swamps in northern Michigan and the sandy dunes that border the Great Lakes. This shrub's adaptability to both wet and dry sites makes it a valuable addition to the landscape where poor soils are a challenge and limit the plants you can use. Numerous arborvitae selections are available, offering a myriad of shapes and sizes with a tremendous range of evergreen foliage colors, from soft green to intense dark tones. While arborvitaes are perhaps over-used in landscapes, they are extremely versatile, which accounts for their popularity. The greatest challenge is selecting the right arborvitae to suit your needs. The variety is overwhelming, but over time a few selections have proven superior for northern climates.

Other Name
White Cedar

Bloom Period and Seasonal Color
Evergreen foliage in a range of greens.

Mature Height × Spread
Dwarf selections to 5 ft.; hedge types to 10 to 20 ft. × 4 to 6 ft.

When, Where, and How to Plant
Arborvitae can be planted in spring or fall. It tolerates a wide range of soils and moisture. Keep plants away from roof lines, where sliding snow may break branches. Follow the general directions for planting shrubs on page 154. With container-grown plants, be sure to pull apart compacted or circling roots.

Growing Tips
Arborvitaes do not tolerate prolonged drought, so water well in dry periods. See page 154 for general information on fertilization. With fall planting, keep the rootball moist going into winter. Use a burlap screen to protect the foliage from winterburn in exposed sites. Fall watering and winter screening will help new plants survive the critical first winter season.

Care
Tall plants may need staking during the first few seasons while they establish roots. Arborvitae leafminer is a pest that may need control. Leafminers feed on the inner portion of the foliage, causing it to become translucent or papery in appearance. Light infestations will not seriously threaten the plant. Should heavy infestations occur, spray with an application of Sevin™ following the manufacturer's recommended rates.

Companion Planting and Design
Dwarf cultivars of arborvitae can be used as foundation plants or as a low-growing hedge. Larger types make effective hedges or screen plantings. Use columnar or narrow selections to make unusual vertical accents. Arborvitaes are the ultimate evergreen plant for creating hedges because they respond well to shaping.

We Recommend
When choosing from the many cultivars of arborvitae, find out each one's mature size and shape. For instance, 'Globosa' will never respond well to pruning intended to make it into a box. 'Globosa', a dwarf (5 ft.) shrub, maintains a perfectly round shape with minimal pruning. 'Smaragd' (often sold as 'Emerald' or 'Emerald Green') is an extreme upright form with beautiful bright-green foliage. 'Techny', also known as 'Mission', has a large pyramidal form reaching 10 to 15 ft., with dark-green foliage.

Arrowwood Viburnum

Viburnum dentatum

When, Where, and How to Plant

Plant in spring or fall. This viburnum tolerates a range of soil types and full sun to partial shade. Avoid deep shade. Moist locations where other plants would struggle are acceptable. When planting in groups, space at least 8 to 10 ft. apart to increase air circulation and prevent individuals from shading out each other. Follow the general instructions for shrub planting on page 154.

Growing Tips

Keep plants moist until established. For general advice on fertilizing shrubs, see page 154. Mulch plants to conserve moisture.

Care

Remove older wood periodically to encourage the development of new growth. Shrubs sprout new stems from underground or from the bottom branches. Prune peripheral outside branches that have expanded beyond their boundaries. Generally pest- and disease-free, downy mildew is sometimes a problem in deep shade and where air circulation is poor. Leaves become off-colored and eventually turn brown and fall off. Wet weather encourages the development of downy mildew. To avoid the problem, site plants correctly.

Companion Planting and Design

The arrowwood is suitable for a variety of situations—it can be used as a single specimen, planted in mass, used for a hedge or screening, or incorporated into the shrub border. Use it in natural gardens to provide food and cover for birds.

We Recommend

The Chicagoland Grows® plant introduction program has released some improved selections of arrowwood viburnum. 'Chicago Lustre' has dark-green glossy foliage, creamy-white flowers, and metallic blue fruits. 'Morton', also known as Northern Burgundy™, has an upright-rounded habit with dark-green foliage that turns burgundy in the fall. Abundant blue-black fruits are produced in late September through October. The mature size is 10 to 12 ft. in height and spread. 'Ralph Senior', also known as Autumn Jazz™, has an upright graceful habit that is enhanced by its slightly pendulous dark-green foliage with colorful red stems. The fall color is a blend of yellow, orange, and red.

Viburnums are some of the most serviceable shrubs for Michigan gardens, and the native North American arrowwood viburnum is no exception. Beautiful in foliage, flower, and fruit, this little-known shrub has seen vast improvement in recent years with new selections adaptable to northern climates. It's a moderate-sized shrub with delicate branches forming a dense, rounded habit. The arrowwood has lustrous dark-green leaves that turn to reddish-purple or burgundy in the fall. The creamy-white flowers appear in June in flat-topped blooms that last for about two weeks. In late summer, large crops of blue-black fruits attract birds to the garden. The twiggy framework of this shrub makes it highly recommended for wildlife plantings because birds find it a suitable shrub to nest in.

Bloom Period and Seasonal Color

Creamy-white flowers in June, blue-black fruits in late summer.

Mature Height × Spread

10 to 15 ft. × 8 to 12 ft.

Bayberry
Myrica pensylvanica

Once in a while you come across a plant and cannot fathom why it is not used more often. The bayberry is in this category. Aromatic glossy green foliage and branches bearing masses of waxy gray berries invite the gardener to use this plant in areas where a naturalistic look is wanted. The bayberry reaches up to ten feet in height and slowly colonizes by underground stems. It is native to the Atlantic coastline, where it endures saline conditions. Its salt tolerance, drought resistance, and rugged beauty make it a valuable urban landscape shrub. At Michigan State University it is used along walkways that are heavily salted to melt ice for pedestrian traffic. Bayberry's waxy fruit was used to produce bayberry candles.

Bloom Period and Seasonal Color
Insignificant flowers in spring; waxy gray fruit.

Mature Height × Spread
9 to 12 ft. × 9 to 12 ft.

When, Where, and How to Plant
Plant in spring or fall as a container-grown plant. Choose locations in full sun or partial shade. Shrubs in full sun will have more fruits. Bayberry is unique in that it can fix its own nitrogen, using special bacteria in association with its roots. This helps the plants survive in low-nutrient, sandy soils. Remarkably, plants also adapt well to heavy clay soils that are frequently waterlogged or wet. Follow the general directions for planting shrubs on page 154.

Growing Tips
No special requirements are needed for bayberry. It transplants easily and is very drought-tolerant. In high pH soils, use an acid-based fertilizer in spring following the directions on page 154.

Care
Bayberry tends to sucker and form large colonies. Pruning is recommended if plants have grown too tall or are escaping into other areas. Remove large straggly branches that have grown out of proportion. To reduce the height of mature plantings, cut right back to the ground in spring just before new growth begins. New growth will quickly emerge and begin to fill in again. Yearly pruning will be necessary to keep bayberry growing as a compact foundation shrub. Male and female flowers appear on separate plants, and you must have both for fruit set. In the nursery, plants are not often labeled male or female. The best solution is to buy plants in fall when the fruits are apparent. Choose at least one plant with fruits and one without. Bayberry has no pests or diseases to bother it.

Companion Planting and Design
Bayberry is effective in mass plantings. Use it on steep hillsides, where you want to forget about growing grass and instead establish shrubs. Bayberry has a rugged character that makes it hard to use in more formal landscapes. Combine it with evergreen shrubs like arborvitae and red-twigged dogwood to create an interesting textural contrast in winter.

We Recommend
There are not many widely available cultivars; select the species.

Bottlebrush Buckeye
Aesculus parviflora

When, Where, and How to Plant

Early spring or fall is the best time to plant buckeyes. Container-grown plants often come with suckers ready to spread when you place the plant in its hole. Plants are rarely offered balled and burlapped. Buckeyes prefer a rich, loamy soil and will thrive in sun and shade. If your soil is sandy, work in organic matter. Plant according to the directions on page 154.

Growing Tips

Bottlebrush buckeye is not drought-tolerant, so keep the root zone moist, especially when newly planted. Fertilize plants in spring following the directions on page 154.

Care

This relatively maintenance-free plant will not ask for much if properly sited. Pest and disease problems are negligible. Mature plants can be cut back to the ground to control their size or to rejuvenate. Keep rabbits away from the new growth. Protect young plants by placing chicken wire cages around them as they adjust to their new surroundings.

Companion Planting and Design

The bottlebrush buckeye is well suited to a naturalistic or woodland setting where the underground stems can spread freely. It's an excellent lawn specimen for large landscapes. Keep it away from the foundation of your house or it will eventually obscure windows. Take advantage of its colonizing nature to screen an ugly view or form an attractive privacy barrier.

We Recommend

Bottlebrush buckeye can be difficult to find in nurseries due to low seed production. Demand creates supply. If you can't find this plant at your local nurseries, encourage them to stock it. The suckering underground stems around the shrub's periphery can be dug as divisions in spring or fall. Dig a large portion of roots to ensure successful establishment in its new site. The red buckeye, *Aesculus pavia*, is a medium-sized tree that reaches 10 to 20 ft. in height and produces beautiful red flowers in late June in Michigan.

Bottlebrush buckeye is an unusual and exotic-looking southeastern native that is perfectly adaptable to Michigan gardens. The shrub forms a large mound as much as fifteen feet wide, spreading by underground stems to form a dense colony. Its large, textured, five-part leaves hang downward in a lazy fashion. By midsummer, tall beautiful spikes of tiny white flowers appear over the foliage in a billowing mass. These upright blooms light up the garden at a time when few woody plants are showing color. The fall season is showtime again as the foliage turns a beautiful yellow before dropping. Although a southern native and rare in the wild, the bottlebrush buckeye is hardy to Zone 4 and is not bothered by our frigid winters.

Bloom Period and Seasonal Color
White flowers in midsummer; yellow fall color.

Mature Height × Spread
8 to 12 ft. × 8 to 15 ft.

Zones
To Zone 4

Boxwood

Buxus 'Green Velvet'

You can't help thinking of the colonial South when garden talk turns to boxwood. Although boxwood has enjoyed southern hospitality for years, its presence in the North has been rife with trials and tribulations. The main problem occurs when winter sun and drying winds turn the lush green foliage to a sickly yellowish-brown. Nurserymen have tried for years to develop superior selections adaptable to northern climates. A hybrid cross of the common boxwood, with the hardier Korean boxwood, has resulted in a new generation of boxwoods valued for their winter toughness and dwarf habit. 'Green Velvet' is a cultivar with a compact, mounded habit, reaching only three feet. The bright-green new growth in spring is a sight for sore eyes after a long winter.

Bloom Period and Seasonal Color
Dark evergreen foliage all season.

Mature Height × Spread
3 ft. × 3 ft.

Zones
To Zone 5

When, Where, and How to Plant
Early spring is the best time for planting. Avoid late fall; the roots will not develop sufficiently, resulting in winterburn. Boxwood prefers full sun or light shade and is adaptable to most soils except those that are too wet or dry. Despite its hardier constitution, 'Green Velvet' should be protected from strong westerly winds and winter sun. Plant on the east side of the house to protect against these winds. Plant following the directions on page 154.

Growing Tips
Keep the root zone moist, particularly going into winter. Read page 154 for information on fertilization. Mulch boxwood to conserve moisture and reduce root zone temperatures. This also protects the roots, which are easily damaged by digging around the base of the plant.

Care
Prune boxwood in early May. For a formal look, use hedge shears. Avoid creating a top-heavy plant that will shade the lower section, limiting growth. Use handpruners to cut back leggy stems to the main body of the shrub. Under certain conditions 'Green Velvet' may produce a late-summer growth that will become scorched in the winter season. Prune out these late flushes in fall. Two pests that can be a problem with boxwoods are spider mite and the boxwood psyllid. To avoid the conditions that favor pests, mulch and water during dry times of the year. Contact your county extension agent for specific controls.

Companion Planting and Design
'Green Velvet' makes the ultimate low hedge and can be used to define pathways and create topiary or a medieval knot garden. These shrubs take readily to shearing and are particularly valued for the formal element they give to the landscape.

We Recommend
'Green Mountain' is a pyramidal shrub with growth that is more vigorous than that of 'Green Velvet'. It grows 4 ft. wide and just over 3 ft. tall and has green foliage and a burgundy cast during the winter months. It is a hybrid selection of the common and Korean boxwoods.

Carolina Allspice
Calycanthus floridus

When, Where, and How to Plant
Plant in spring or fall. Choose a location with sun or partial shade and moist fertile soil. Carolina allspice is easy to transplant; follow the general planting instructions on page 154.

Growing Tips
Water in times of drought. Sweet shrub may show signs of chlorosis in high pH soils. The foliage turns a sickly yellow in color, and the output of green healthy leaf tissue will diminish. To lower pH, use an acid-based fertilizer.

Care
Carolina allspice is generally disease- and insect-free. *Calycanthus* may become straggly after many years in your garden but can easily be rejuvenated by cutting to the ground immediately after flowering. Young shoots will sprout from the base and within a few years produce a dense, full-sized shrub. Prune after flowering to encourage new flowering wood for next spring. Winterkill or dieback of selected branches occurs in very cold years. Remove any dead branches in early spring. The Carolina allspice spreads from underground stems, which can be dug from the periphery of the bush and planted elsewhere in your garden. Perform division in spring while the plant is still dormant.

Companion Planting and Design
Plant sweet shrub around outdoor living areas or on the windward side of your house to catch the sweet breezes that roll off this shrub as it flowers. Use as a specimen plant, in shrub borders, or as a hedge. In mass plantings, space plants at least 8 ft. apart to allow room to grow.

We Recommend
Seed-grown *Calycanthus* in the nursery trade will vary in its flower fragrance; purchase a plant that passes your nose test to be sure it's the right one for your garden. 'Edith Wilder' has burgundy flowers that are extremely fragrant and a more open habit that may need pruning to keep it compact and manageable. 'Athens' is a unique form with showy yellow blooms, great fragrance, and a dense and mounded habit.

Although botanically imprecise, common names are often very descriptive, as is the case with the Carolina allspice, also called sweet shrub. Its bark, branches, flowers, and fruits are highly aromatic. While fragrance abounds both spicy and sweet, the allspice is also a serviceable landscape plant forming a rounded bush with attractive, glossy, dark-green foliage. Fall color varies from year to year but can be a beautiful yellow. The flowers of the allspice are unusual, with numerous reddish-brown petals that emit a fruity fragrance. The odor is pervasive on hot sunny days and varies from strawberry to banana to pineapple, ending with cider as the flowers fade. The dark flowers are hidden, but the smell makes you come closer to discover the mysterious bloom.

Other Name
Sweet Shrub

Bloom Period and Seasonal Color
Dark-maroon flowers in late spring to early summer; variable fall foliage.

Mature Height × Spread
6 to 9 ft. × 6 to 12 ft.

Zones
To Zone 5

Caryopteris
Caryopteris × clandonensis

The bluebeard is a versatile shrub that finds a natural spot in the garden in combination with late-blooming herbaceous perennials. The long arching branches are covered with aromatic silver foliage. Later in the summer, light to dark blue flowers emerge at a time when few other woody plants are in bloom. Butterflies love the late-season flowers. Because of its size and arching habit, and the textural quality of the foliage, this shrub combines particularly well with ornamental grasses. Gardeners treat the bluebeard like a herbaceous perennial since it is not stem-hardy in the North. Caryopteris is a dieback shrub. Each year, the branches die back to the woody center or crown of the plant; however, they quickly grow back with the onset of warmer temperatures.

Other Names
Bluebeard, Blue Spirea

Bloom Period and Seasonal Color
Blue flowers in late summer through fall.

Mature Height × Spread
2 to 3 ft. × 3 to 4 ft.

Zones
To Zone 5

When, Where, and How to Plant
Spring is the best time for planting. If you decide to plant in fall, water well and mulch after the ground freezes. This will keep the plant from heaving or lifting out of the ground due to soil temperature fluctuations. Space plants $2^1/2$ to $3^1/2$ ft. apart. Plant in full sun and loose, well-drained soil following the general directions on page 154.

Growing Tips
While reputedly drought-tolerant, the bluebeard will suffer in sharply drained soils during dry periods. Water when shrubs start to flag or wilt. Plants normally do not require fertilizer in average soils. Rich soils or unnecessary fertilization will cause rank growth that will not produce flowers.

Care
Bluebeard is generally carefree. Spider mite is occasionally a problem in drought conditions. Remove any seedlings that appear; they are generally inferior to the mother plant in foliage and flower. You may worry about bluebeard in spring. Its new growth is slow to sprout while nearby plants are well on their way. This is a time for patience. Eventually, the bluebeard will show signs of life. Prune back to live wood in spring. In mild winters, cut back to 1 ft. to keep plants compact. If the plant does not dieback or is not cut back, it will become leggy.

Companion Planting and Design
The bluebeard, with its low stature and wispy branches, does not make a strong hedge plant. Instead, use it where the late-summer blooms will add color to a dull spot in your garden. The foliage and flowers are attractive with pink and magenta asters, ornamental grasses, and the white blooms of 'Honorine Jobert' anemone. Attractive butterfly plantings combine the bluebeard with purple coneflower and the blazing star.

We Recommend
'Dark Knight' produces striking dark-blue flowers from late July to mid-August. 'Blue Mist' has powder-blue flowers that combine well with sedum 'Autumn Joy'. 'Arthur Simmonds', with purplish-blue flowers, is one of the hardiest selections.

When, Where, and How to Plant

Plant juniper as a container-grown plant in spring or fall. Plant in full sun to avoid the leggy, weak growth that develops in shade. It prefers full sun and tolerates a wide range of soil conditions with the exception of excessively dry or wet soils. Plant following the instructions on page 154.

Growing Tips

Keep newly planted junipers moist until established, especially going into winter. For information on fertilization consult page 154.

Care

Prune the Chinese juniper during the winter months with handpruners. Remove long branches back to the main framework. Avoid shearing junipers because it creates a rough look. Prune topheavy growth that shades out the bottom portion of the shrub. With large-scale plantings comes the threat of disease. A fungus called juniper twig blight is a common problem, particularly in wet weather. The tips of the branches become a reddish brown, eventually turning an ash gray as needles die. To avoid infection, plant in open, well-drained areas and do not use overhead irrigation. If disease strikes, prune out and destroy infected branches.

Companion Planting and Design

Use as a specimen, screen, groundcover, or foundation plant. Junipers are quite tolerant of shaping and make excellent hedge plants. Pair them with other winter-interest plants. On the campus of Michigan State University, Chinese junipers are often found at the base of crabapples. The red fruits provide bright contrast with the blue-green juniper foliage.

We Recommend

When you select a juniper, ascertain its ultimate height and spread. The popular Pfitzer juniper, installed as a small foundation shrub, can become a menacing giant. Plant lower-growing selections where space is limited. 'Sea Green' has a fountain-like form with dark-green foliage. It grows 4 to 6 ft. high and 6 to 8 ft. wide. The sargent juniper, *Juniperus sargentii*, is a low-growing blue-green selection with long trailing branches. It grows 2 ft. high and up to 10 ft. wide.

In Michigan and other colder areas of the country, evergreen shrubs play an integral part in almost any landscape design, adding continuity and color to the long winter season. Junipers represent a large group of utilitarian shrubs that withstand not only bitterly cold conditions but also hot, dry conditions and windy exposed sites. Their salt tolerance makes them valuable around sidewalks and entrances. With their inherent toughness comes their widespread overuse in our landscapes, but their value cannot be underestimated. When selecting a cultivar of the Chinese juniper, think of new ways to use this old standby shrub. Many selections have outstanding foliage with intense coloration ranging from green to blue-green to grayish-green. Several varieties offer the beautiful fragrant juniper berries on female plants.

Bloom Period and Seasonal Color
Blue-green evergreen foliage.

Mature Height × Spread
4 to 12 ft. × 6 to 8 ft.

Climbing Hydrangea
Hydrangea petiolaris

The climbing hydrangea is a vine unrivaled for its four-season appeal. It has soft-green, lustrous leaves and beautiful clusters of large white flowers. In the winter, the tan peeling outer bark reveals the beautiful orange-tan underbark. The climbing hydrangea's early performance, however, often disappoints gardeners. They wait anxiously to see this vine cover a brick wall or cascade over a trellis, but nothing much happens for the first few years. This vine is slow to establish, taking several years to adjust to its new home. When roots finally become established, it grows vigorously, forming shoots that expand horizontally from the main stems. Large-sized older specimens are majestic in their height and beauty and are truly worth the early years of doubt and worry.

Bloom Period and Seasonal Color
White flowers in late spring to early summer.

Mature Length
To 75 ft.

Zones
To Zone 5

When, Where, and How to Plant
Plant in spring or fall. The climbing hydrangea requires a rich, moist soil with good drainage, or its roots will suffer. Plants can be placed in full sun or partial shade. Follow the general instructions for planting on page 154. Be careful not to disturb the root system while planting.

Growing Tips
Keep the rootball of a new planting moist. Water plants in prolonged periods of drought. Mulch with an acidic compost, like pine bark, to cool the root zone and conserve moisture. Fertilize in spring with an acid-based fertilizer according to the instructions on page 154.

Care
Climbing hydrangea is generally pest- and disease-free. Small aerial roots called holdfasts emerge from the undersides of the stems, anchoring the vine and making it upwardly mobile. Young plants need encouragement to become attached to brick or stone. Use a small wood trellis to train stems up and onto the desired surface. Plants don't adhere well to aluminum siding. Periodically check your vine to see that it is in contact with the wall and on its way to developing holdfasts. Large-sized plants may become top-heavy over time and can have sections that detach from their growing surfaces. When this situation develops, prune or cut back lengthy sections to reduce the load.

Companion Planting and Design
Climbing hydrangea is primarily a specimen plant for brick and stone walls and structures. You can also grow climbing hydrangea on boulders or on an old tree stump, where the low-spreading branches and flowers produce a beautiful shrublike effect.

We Recommend
If you can find it, try the Japanese hydrangea vine, *Schizophragma hydrangeoides*, a closely related vine with the same clinging habit but larger, less lustrous leaves and spectacularly large, drooping white flowers. It requires the same conditions for growth as the climbing hydrangea. 'Moonlight' is a selection featuring silver mottling on each heart-shaped leaf. Flowers are pure white with a lacy, graceful habit.

Diabolo® Ninebark

Physocarpus opulifolius 'Monlo'

When, Where, and How to Plant

Plant as a balled-and-burlapped shrub or containerized plant in spring or fall. The ninebark can grow in acid or alkaline soils and can withstand dry situations for short periods. Plant in full sun for the best dark-foliage effect. Follow the general directions for planting shrubs on page 154.

Growing Tips

Keep newly planted shrubs moist until established. Water during drought. Spread a 2- to 3-in. layer of mulch around the base of the plant to conserve moisture. In spring, fertilize your shrub before new growth begins if it appears to lack vigor or you are planning to rejuvenate the plant by cutting it back. Consult page 154 for advice.

Care

This shrub is seldom troubled by pests or diseases. Ninebarks produce rapid growth each season and can become twiggy and overgrown in appearance. Rejuvenation by cutting back all stems to 6 in. will promote new growth with increased vigor and better color. Prune in the winter months without worry that this plant will lose its flowers, as they are produced on new growth each year.

Companion Planting and Design

Diabolo® ninebark commingles well with other native shrubs including Carolina allspice, gray dogwood, and Michigan holly. Diabolo® works well as a color accent in a perennial garden. The ninebark will eventually lose some of its lower leaves, so it is important to combine it with annuals, perennials, or low-growing shrubs at its base. The 'Purple Wave' petunia looks striking in contrast with the foliage, as does the pinkish bottlebrush blooms of fountain grass. Shell-pink peonies and icy bluestar would make a stunning June picture. There are lots of possibilities.

We Recommend

Another ninebark with ornamental color is 'Nugget'. It has a compact habit, growing to 6 ft., and fine-textured foliage that emerges yellow in spring and matures to a lime green.

Plants with dark foliage create a unique focal point and provide contrast to other plants in your garden. While most dark-foliaged plants are in the herbaceous perennial realm, a recent new introduction of our native ninebark called Diabolo® is a large, upright arching woody shrub with remarkable reddish-purple foliage. The early-summer flowers are creamy-white and contrast well with the dark foliage. As the shrub matures, the bark begins to peel in brown papery strips, adding interest to the winter garden. This ninebark is perfect for single-specimen use as a punctuation mark in the garden or planted in mass, where it really makes a statement.

Bloom Period and Color
White flowers with a pinkish tinge in June.

Mature Height × Spread
8 to 10 ft. × 8 ft.

Fragrant Winter Hazel

Corylopsis glabrescens

Spring is a time of anticipation in Michigan as we wait patiently for the bloom of forsythia, cherries, and crab-apples. In the midst of this colorful parade, the fragrant winter hazel blooms with pale-yellow, scented flowers that hang gracefully like tiny bells from a string. This subtle display could go unnoticed as showier plants take center stage, but observant gardeners know the fragrant winter hazel is unrivaled in its simple beauty. It forms a twelve-foot-high spreading shrub with a dense oval habit. Its dark-green leaves turn a clear yellow in fall, and the zigzag nature of its slender twigs give it a unique winter artistry. If placed in a prominent spot, it becomes a true showstopper.

Bloom Period and Seasonal Color
Pale-yellow flowers in spring; yellow fall color.

Mature Height × Spread
8 to 12 ft. × 8 to 12 ft.

Zones
To Zone 5

When, Where, and How to Plant
Plant in spring or fall. The early spring bloom of *Corylopsis* is susceptible to hard freezes, particularly in exposed sites where the warm winter sun causes precocious bud swell. Choose a site with partial shade, or sun if there is adequate moisture. Avoid a warm southern exposure and sites where strong winter winds and wide temperature fluctuations may occur. Fragrant winter hazel prefers a moist, well-drained, slightly acidic soil. In alkaline soils, add peat and leaf mold to the planting hole to lower the pH and increase the soil's moisture-holding capacity. Plant shrubs according to the instructions on page 154.

Growing Tips
Keep plants moist until established. Use a mulch to conserve moisture, and water deeply during extended dry spells. In spring, fertilize with an acid-based formula following the instructions on page 154.

Care
Winter hazel is generally disease- and pest-free. Pruning is not recommended because it might destroy the unique form of this plant. It can be cut and forced for indoor display. Branches cut in March usually take a couple of weeks to open in a vase placed in a sunny window.

Companion Planting and Design
Plants are used to best effect against an evergreen backdrop, which illuminates their pale-yellow flowers and yellow fall color. When planting under winter hazel, use groundcover plants that will fit below its low-spreading horizontal branches. The spring bloom coincides with the 'Cornell Pink' Korean rhododendron. An underplanting of the blue windflower, *Anemone blanda*, would be delightful.

We Recommend
The word "dainty" most accurately describes the habit and bloom of the buttercup winter hazel, *Corylopsis pauciflora*. It grows to 4 to 6 ft. high with an equal or greater spread. The pale-yellow flowers hanging from slender twigs are both delicate and showy. This plant is hardy only in Zone 6 and prefers partial shade. In full sun, leaf scorch may turn leaf margins a papery brown. If your local climate can support it, by all means, grow it!

Gray Dogwood
Cornus racemosa

When, Where, and How to Plant

Gray dogwood is easy to transplant in spring or fall. It grows best in a moist, well-drained situation and tolerates both wet and dry sites. Site in full sun or shade, and be prepared to let gray dogwood run. The shrubs spread by underground stems and should be kept away from confined spaces or areas you wish to remain open. Plant as a container-grown or balled-and-burlapped plant following the instructions on page 154.

Growing Tips

Keep new plants watered until established. Fertilizing is unnecessary.

Care

Gray dogwood is generally a carefree shrub that adapts well to both poorly-drained and dry soils. Plants occasionally develop leaf spot, a fungal disease that produces dark irregular blotches on the foliage. Leaf spot may be unattractive but is usually not a serious health threat. Plants can be rejuvenated easily by cutting them back right to the ground. This will result in vigorous growth and the development of numerous colorful stems.

Companion Planting and Design

Use this shrub in naturalistic plantings. Gray dogwood is extremely valuable in both wet, swampy and extremely dry sites. Use it on difficult hillsides or eroding banks. A mass planting can create a screen or privacy barrier. Effective in large-scale plantings and invaluable for use in both poorly-drained soils and excessively dry soils, gray dogwood is truly a versatile shrub. Plant it with the redosier dogwood, *Cornus stolonifera*. The contrast of gray and red twigs creates a colorful winter collage. Combine with other winter-interest plants to create fantastic winter vistas.

We Recommend

The silky dogwood, *Cornus amomum*, is a closely related shrub that is not as ornamental in many respects but has beautiful porcelain-blue fruits in the fall. It grows in wet sites, reaching an ultimate height and spread of 6 to 10 ft.

A real pleasure of the Michigan winter is driving along the road and coming upon thickets of gray dogwood. Often they are found in a marshy area cavorting with the Michigan holly. This beautiful pairing of native plants illustrates why we should use these shrubs more in our cultivated landscapes. Gray dogwood has four-season appeal. The dark-green foliage takes on purplish coloring in fall, creamy-white flowers appear in late spring, and white fall fruits are relished by birds, while the attractive reddish-pink fruit stalks are persistent. A combination of old gray stems and brownish new growth terminating with the colorful fruit stalks creates a distinctive winter character of great beauty. With a little ingenuity, you'll find the right spot for gray dogwood.

Bloom Period and Seasonal Color
White flowers in late spring to early summer; persistent reddish-pink fruit stalks.

Mature Height × Spread
10 to 15 ft. × 10 to 15 ft.

Zones
To Zone 4

Hazelnut
Corylus americana

A nursery owner once told Tim he considered hazelnut in the "quiet native" category. What he meant by that was that hazelnuts, like many other natives, are subtle plants. They are beautiful, yet they don't scream for attention. The hazelnut sits quietly most of the year, then puts forth its beautiful ephemeral spring catkin flowers. The long, graceful male flowers hang like strings from the branches in late March, harkening the arrival of warmer temperatures. The tiny nuts produced by the plant are a favorite of squirrels. In its native habitat, hazelnut can be found in the shady understory of an oak-hickory forest, or colonizing old fields and abandoned prairies.

Other Name
American Filbert

Bloom Period and Seasonal Color
Flowers in early to mid-spring.

Mature Height × Spread
12 to 15 ft. × 12 ft. or more

When, Where, and How to Plant
Plants are generally available as container-grown or balled-and-burlapped, and both types can be planted in spring or fall. Hazelnut will spread by underground stems to form a colonizing shrub, so give it plenty of room. It grows best in moist, well-drained soils but tolerates heavy clay soils. Plant hazelnut following the general directions for planting shrubs on page 154.

Growing Tips
Keep newly planted shrubs moist until established. Once established, plants are drought-tolerant. To improve the soil- and moisture-holding capacity of your new planting, mulch with well-rotted leaf mold, which will break down over time to help feed the plant. See page 154 for more information on shrub fertilization.

Care
Hazelnut is pest- and disease-free, and is a carefree plant after establishment. Occasional pruning of dead wood will be required as the plant matures. Two methods of pruning can be employed, thinning or complete rejuvenation. Thinning involves cutting out a third of the older branches each year by removing them to ground level with lopping shears or a small handsaw. Complete rejuvenation of the shrub can be accomplished by cutting it back to 6 in. above the ground level to encourage new vigorous growth. This is best done after flowering in the early spring. A chain-saw or loppers can be used for this process.

Companion Planting and Design
The hazelnut is best used for naturalizing; its spreading habit and large size make it unsuitable for smaller properties. Plants placed in full sun at times produce a striking reddish fall color. This shrub is also quite drought-tolerant and can be paired with other tough customers such as the bayberry or the exceptional native sweetgum tree. If you have a moist site, consider underplanting with some of our native ferns, particularly Christmas fern or maidenhair fern.

We Recommend
Grow the species as there are not any cultivars available.

Hydrangea
Hydrangea spp.

When, Where, and How to Plant
Plant in spring or fall, in full sun for vigorous growth and flowers. It prefers moist, well-drained soil but is quite urban-tolerant. Plant following the general instructions for shrub planting on page 153.

Growing Tips
Water well in drought periods. Mulch annually to conserve moisture, and cool the root zone. Consult page 154 for information on fertilizing shrubs.

Care
Pests and disease are generally not a problem. Hydrangeas need pruning to keep them tidy. The panicle hydrangea should be pruned in winter or early spring because it forms flowerbuds on the new growth each season. Prune out older wood periodically, cutting it to ground level. Some gardeners prefer to prune the panicle hydrangea each year to prevent straggly old wood from developing. This will work if your soil is fertile enough to support strong new growth each year. Prune the oakleaf hydrangea after flowering, as it produces flowerbuds on growth from the previous season. Underground stems will emerge in great numbers to form a solid framework over time. Remove dead wood as needed. To preserve the flowers for dry arrangements, cut them at their peak and hang upside down in a dry, cool area.

Companion Planting and Design
These shrubs are excellent planted in a large mass or as a single specimen. They work well in an old-fashioned shrub border.

We Recommend
The panicle hydrangea has two exceptional cultivars. 'Unique' has an upright habit and large white flowers that turn pink in midsummer. 'Kyushu' has an exceptionally long flowering period, from July through September. The oakleaf hydrangea, *Hydrangea quercifolia*, a southern native hardy to Zone 5, requires a protected site that has enough sunlight for development and adequate moisture. It has coarse-textured foliage, large showy flowers, and wonderful burgundy-red fall color. On older specimens, the bark peels in winter to reveal a handsome cinnamon color. 'Snow Queen' is a popular selection.

It's fun to watch old-fashioned plants undergo a revival. The panicle hydrangea (Hydrangea paniculata) has been criticized as overused along the East Coast, but it is slowly regaining the popularity it once had. Its beautiful pyramidal panicles of pure-white flowers appear in July or August and gradually fade to pink. The panicle hydrangea can reach tree size under certain conditions but generally grows to ten feet. Many cultivars are available today and will keep the panicle hydrangea an enduring part of the cultivated American landscape. Consider the oakleaf hydrangea as well (see We Recommend). This North American native is a real four-season performer with immense seven- to thirteen-inch conical flowers composed of pure-white sterile petals fading to a dusty rose and gorgeous burgundy fall color.

Bloom Period and Seasonal Color
White flowers in midsummer.

Mature Height × Spread
10 to 25 ft. × 10 to 20 ft.

Korean Lilac

Syringa patula 'Miss Kim'

The beautiful 'Miss Kim' lilac is often difficult to find at your local nursery, as it disappears quickly if witnessed in bloom. It's irresistible! The sweetly fragrant lavender-pink flowers float over the stems in a mass and fade to an ice blue. This is a diminutive lilac compared with the larger common lilac. It grows slowly, reaching a height of four to seven feet. The summer foliage of 'Miss Kim' is a dark green that later turns to mauve-purple. This is one of the few lilacs you can count on for fall color. Use it as a foundation plant; its compact size makes it perfect for placement beneath a first-floor window. The spicy fragrance will permeate your house through open windows, clearing out old winter air.

Bloom Period and Seasonal Color
Lavender-pink flowers in mid- to late spring.

Mature Height × Spread
4 to 7 ft. × 4 to 6 ft.

When, Where, and How to Plant

Plant as a container-grown and balled-and-burlapped plant in spring or fall. Bareroot plants should be planted in spring while dormant. Site in full sun in an open area with good air circulation. Choose moist, well-drained soil, and avoid dry areas. When planting, space shrubs at least 6 to 8 ft. apart to prevent overcrowding. Follow the general instructions for planting shrubs on page 154.

Growing Tips

Mulch to conserve moisture. Water during dry spells by letting a hose slowly trickle at the base for fifteen to twenty minutes, giving your plant a deep watering. Do not use overhead water because this may promote the development of the leaf disease powdery mildew. For information on shrub fertilization, consult page 154.

Care

Pruning is generally not needed, but you may decide to remove spent flowers, which otherwise eventually move onto seed production, reducing the vigor of your plant. Powdery mildew does not afflict 'Miss Kim' as often as it does the common lilac. This leaf disease occurs most commonly in wet seasons, and its likelihood is increased when shrubs are planted in shady locations. Site plants correctly to avoid mildew attack.

Companion Planting and Design

'Miss Kim' is a fine lilac for small gardens, shrub borders, and massing. Be sure to plant it close to your house or an outdoor living space to enjoy its fragrant flowers and attractive fall color. 'Miss Kim' works well planted on slightly sloping hillsides, creating a cascade of billowing blooms.

We Recommend

Syringa meyeri 'Palibin' is another outstanding small lilac whose size and spread are similar to those of 'Miss Kim'. Deep-purple buds open to pink-white to violet color. 'Palibin' is less cold hardy than 'Miss Kim', and its flowers are sometimes susceptible to late frosts. It is hardy to Zone 4. 'Bailibelle' or Tinkerbelle™ is another dwarf lilac with deeper-pink petals and the same luscious fragrance.

Korean Rhododendron
Rhododendron mucronulatum 'Cornell Pink'

When, Where, and How to Plant

Plant in spring in part sun or partial shade in a well-drained soil. Good drainage is important. 'Cornell Pink' is moderately tolerant of alkaline soils but performs best in slightly acidic conditions. Modify heavy clay soils by adding well-rotted compost or leaf mold to the backfill soil. Plant according to the instructions on page 154. If containerized plants have a buildup of fibrous roots, break up the root mass, and spread it out in the planting hole.

Growing Tips

Keep the root zone of new plantings moist. 'Cornell Pink' is not drought-tolerant and will need watering in the hot, dry times of the year. Yellowing foliage indicates soil alkalinity. Fertilize in spring with an acid-based fertilizer according to instructions on page 154. Mulch each year with an acidic fertilizer to help reduce the pH of your soil.

Care

If sited correctly, plants are pest- and disease-resistant. Removing the faded flowers will encourage new flowering wood for the next spring season. Break off spent flowers by hand; pruning shears are not needed. Grasp the old flowers and remove at the base of the flower stalk just before emerging leaf buds. Good cultural practices will help keep your rhododendron healthy.

Companion Planting and Design

Use 'Cornell Pink' as a foundation plant and in doorway gardens. It makes a delightful spring combination with early-spring bulbs such as the Siberian squill and glory-of-the-snow. In Zone 6, plant 'Cornell Pink' with the buttercup winter hazel, *Corylopsis pauciflora*, for a beautiful spring pairing.

We Recommend

Another rhododendron to try in a midwestern garden are the hybrid azaleas in the Northern Lights™ series. These hardy plants have beautiful flowers and are compact, reaching a height and spread of 6 to 7 ft. A wide range of colors exists within the series. Some of the more subtle colored flowers are found on 'Orchid Lights', 'Golden Lights', and 'White Lights'.

The rhododendrons are a captivating group of shrubs with numerous species, hybrids, and cultivars available to choose from, but growing azaleas and rhododendrons well is a difficult proposition in Michigan. Heavy clay soils combined with alkalinity (high pH) are two forces working against these beautiful shrubs here. The 'Cornell Pink' Korean rhododendron makes the fight worthwhile. With a little help, it will reward you with years of great beauty in your garden. 'Cornell Pink' has flowers that emerge a lovely light pink before its foliage in late May. The flowers contrast well with the shrub's straw-colored branches. The leaves are a pleasing soft green during the growing season but change from yellow to crimson in a marvelous fall color parade.

Bloom Period and Seasonal Color
Light-pink flowers in early spring; great fall color.

Mature Height × Spread
4 to 8 ft. × 4 to 8 ft.

Zones
To Zone 4

Koreanspice Viburnum
Viburnum carlesii

Viburnums are among the most valuable groups of shrubs for midwestern gardeners. They are hardy and offer species and cultivars that meet various landscape needs. Among the best for bloom and fragrance are the Koreanspice and burkwood viburnums. The clove-scented fragrance of Koreanspice viburnum is unmatched by other woody plants. In spring, pink buds open to form white flower clusters. They release a wildly intoxicating fragrance that causes people to stop in their tracks to take in the heady bouquet. The foliage is a pleasant soft green. The burkwood viburnum, Viburnum × burkwoodii, flowers before the Koreanspice, and it, too, has a heavenly aroma. The foliage is a dark, shiny green. Both shrubs get up to ten to fifteen feet tall and eight feet wide.

Bloom Period and Seasonal Color
Pink buds and white flowers in later spring.

Mature Height × Spread
To 10 ft. × 8 ft.

Zones
To Zone 4

When, Where, and How to Plant
Plant in spring or fall. Choose full-sun locations for best habit and flowering. Plant far enough apart to allow room to grow. Plants placed close together will shade each other out, reducing overall growth and flower production—space at least 10 ft. apart. Follow the general directions for shrub planting on page 154. Container-grown plants may have circling or congested roots at the bottom of the pot; they should be teased apart before placing in the hole.

Growing Tips
Keep plants moist until established. Water in prolonged periods of drought. Consult page 154 for information on fertilizing shrubs.

Care
These viburnums are generally pest- and disease-resistant. To increase flowering, remove old flowers as they fade. As plants mature, selective pruning is needed to remove old, dead, or dying wood. Removal of older wood allows sunlight into the inner portions of the plant, encouraging new growth. Plants placed too close together will become bare at the bottom, and foliage and blooms become confined to the upper portions of the plant. If this situation develops, thin out plants nearby to increase the amount of light reaching the lower portions of the plant. New growth will soon sprout to fill in bare spots.

Companion Planting and Design
Both the Koreanspice and burkwood viburnums make excellent single specimens and are effective in mass. Plant near a window or by a door or a walkway so that you can experience the fragrant blooms that appear as the warm temperatures of summer approach. Combine with daffodils.

We Recommend
The cultivar of the Koreanspice viburnum called 'Compactum'—despite the name—grows up to 8 ft. in height. 'Mohawk' is a wonderful cultivar with deep-pink flowers in bud, opening with a strong spicy fragrance. It is a compact shrub growing to a height and spread of 6 to 8 ft. with orange-red fall color.

Leatherleaf Viburnum

Viburnum rhytidophyllum

When, Where, and How to Plant

Plant in spring or fall, siting plants in full sun or partial shade. Well-drained soil is important, and plant with protection from drying winds and winter sun for best leaf retention. For mass plantings, space plants at least 12 ft. apart. Follow general directions for planting on page 154.

Growing Tips

Keep plants moist until established, especially going into winter. Mulch to conserve moisture. Consult page 154 for information on fertilization.

Care

There are no significant pests or diseases. In exposed situations, these shrubs will have wind-burned leaves that turn brown and can be unsightly in winter. Fortunately, as new growth emerges in spring, these leaves fall from the plant. Individual flowers within the flat-top clusters will also dry out in exposed situations. Rejuvenate older shrubs by selectively removing older wood and allowing young shoots to develop in their place.

Companion Planting and Design

Landscapers frequently plant these viburnums at the edge of a building, anchoring down a corner and softening an edge. Single specimens work well combined with perennials or other woody shrubs that offer unique contrasts in foliage. Combine the dark, crinkled leaves of the leatherleafs with the silvery foliage of bluebeard and the red-pink variegated foliage of 'Rose Glow' barberry for a contrast of foliage color and texture.

We Recommend

The lantanaphyllum viburnums have tight flower-buds that form attractive clusters that provide winter interest. The fruits are quite showy and a favorite of birds. Two excellent selections have proved popular in Michigan landscapes. 'Willowwood' has excellent lustrous foliage and an arching habit. 'Alleghany' is a superior form with a dense, rounded habit, reaching a height of 11 ft. at maturity. The fruit is brilliant red in the fall. Both shrubs make outstanding plants as screens or as single specimens. Reaching a height of more than 15 ft. with a similar spread, these shrubs need room to develop and are not appropriate for gardens with limited space.

Ubiquitous yews and ever-present junipers—these true evergreen shrubs play an important role in our winter landscapes. For something new, try the semievergreen leatherleaf viburnums. Some years, the leatherleaf viburnum has leaves that persist throughout the winter months, depending on how low temperatures drop. In summer, you'll appreciate the foliage. The attractive leaves are large, dark, and heavily textured. In spring, masses of yellowish-green flat-top blooms are followed by a display of red and black fruits. You may wish to try the lantanaphyllum viburnum, Viburnum × rhytidophylloides, a related shrub of hybrid origin. It is similar to the leatherleaf but has broader leaves that are not as heavily textured. The new growth of both shrubs has a feltlike covering on the stems and undersides of the leaves.

Bloom Period and Seasonal Color
Yellow-green flowers in late spring.

Mature Height × Spread
10 to 15 ft. × 10 to 15 ft.

Zones
To Zone 5

Lilac

Syringa vulgaris

It is undeniable that the lilac is an enduring shrub, part of our past and ever-popular today. How many of us can recall the sweet smell at an old homestead or at a relative's home? With their glorious flowers' fragrance, lilacs are still in demand. The bloom of lilac is its most important feature, and, after the flowers are gone, this shrub fades from the scene with little to offer beyond large, heart-shaped leaves. Numerous trials and evaluations have helped define what makes a good lilac and how we should grow them to best effect in Michigan. With their popularity and overuse in certain instances, the lilac has been plagued by pest and disease problems that can be overcome by proper selection and planting.

Bloom Period and Seasonal Color
Purple, lilac, pink, and white flowers in spring.

Mature Height × Spread
8 to 15 ft. × 6 to 10 ft.

When, Where, and How to Plant
Plant lilacs in spring or fall. Plant in full sun in a site with good air circulation to avoid powdery mildew. Plant as a container-grown or balled-and-burlapped shrub, following the general instructions on page 154.

Growing Tips
Keep a new planting moist until established. Follow the general directions for fertilizing shrubs on page 154.

Care
The common lilac is not considered a low-maintenance shrub; it requires work to keep it healthy and beautiful. Powdery mildew, a fungus, generally appears in late summer, forming cottony masses on the foliage. The fungus does little long-term damage to the shrub, and its control is usually not necessary. An insect called the lilac stem borer can be a serious pest of lilacs, causing large branches to die. Borers attack branches that are 1 in. or more in diameter, so periodic removal of these older branches reduces the likelihood of attack. Pruning is an important maintenance chore. Removing older branches opens up the shrub to sunlight and air circulation, which discourages powdery mildew and lilac stem borer and increases the production of flowering wood. Remove the vigorous growth of underground stems (suckers) as well, because they crowd the interior of the plant, blocking light and limiting air movement.

Companion Planting and Design
Lilacs can be planted in groupings or as single specimens and are most valuable along pathways or spots that you frequently pass so that you can enjoy their remarkable fragrance. *Syringa* makes an effective privacy screen and, when properly pruned, a nice, informal hedge.

We Recommend
There are over 400 selections of lilac. A few fragrant favorites follow. 'Krasavitsa Moskvy' or 'Beauty of Moscow' is a doubled-flower form with lavender-rose buds opening to creamy-white with a hint of pale lilac. 'Miss Ellen Willmott' has large flower clusters composed of pure-white double flowers. 'Edith Cavell' has sulfur-yellow buds that open to pure-white double flowers. All of these selections are extremely fragrant.

Michigan Holly

Ilex verticillata

When, Where, and How to Plant

Plant in spring or fall in full sun to partial shade. Choose moist, slightly acid soils high in organic matter. The winterberry can take long periods with its roots submerged in water. Space according to selection. These shrubs are thicket-forming plants that will extend their area by producing spreading stems underground. Plant as a container-grown or balled-and-burlapped shrub according to the advice on page 154.

Growing Tips

While their tolerance for wet soils is well documented, these shrubs have also been promoted for their adaptation to dry soils. In general, they will suffer in long periods of drought and should be watered. Fertilize in spring with an acid-based formula following the directions on page 154. New shrub plantings will benefit from a layer of organic mulch that will help conserve moisture, cool the root zone, and discourage weeds.

Care

If sited correctly, plants are generally pest- and disease-free. To prevent problems with spider mites, avoid planting too close to brick or cement walls that absorb heat, intensifying drought conditions and creating the optimal conditions for infestation. Prune older stems of overgrown plants.

Companion Planting and Design

Plant masses of hollies for an effective winter display. The fruiting display is enhanced by a backdrop of dark-needled evergreen spruces. Create a beautiful winter scene by combining the winterberry with dark-needled evergreens or the native river birch. The red berries of the hollies stand out against the flaky cinnamon-brown peeling bark of the river birch.

We Recommend

Among the best performers so far in Michigan landscapes is 'Afterglow', which has glossy green leaves and orange-red fruits that can last into February. It makes a multistemmed shrub reaching 10 ft. in height and width and appears to be more drought-tolerant. A dwarf cultivar of exceptional merit is 'Red Sprite', with a mature size of 3$^{1}/_{2}$ ft. by 4 ft. wide, for smaller landscapes. You need male plants for fruit set. The male pollinator for 'Afterglow' and 'Red Sprite' is 'Raritan Chief'.

When we think of hollies, we think of the evergreen red-berried boughs of the Christmas season. Consider, though, that native deciduous hollies are found throughout Michigan in wet situations bordering marshes, bogs, and lakes. Michigan hollies have outstanding colorful fruit displays that persist on naked branches in the winter. The flowers of winterberry appear in May or June along dark-brown stems. There is now a dazzling array of cultivated deciduous hollies with red, orange, or yellow berries. It is important to select cultivars that have proved superior in Michigan landscapes. Male and female flowers appear on separate plants, so both must be present for fruiting to result. When purchasing plants from a nursery, insist that the cultivars will form a fruitful pairing.

Other Name

Winterberry

Bloom Period and Seasonal Color

Orange, red, or yellow berries in late summer to fall.

Mature Height × Spread

6 to 10 ft. × 6 to 10 ft.

Zones

To Zone 4

Redtwig Dogwood
Cornus stolonifera

When developing a garden, you should plan for year-round interest. Winter, the time between autumn's colorful good-bye and spring's green awakening, is the toughest. With the right plants, however, winter can be a vibrant season of colorful barks, stems, and fruits. Cornus stolonifera *offers a group of cultivars with varia-tions in stem color and summer foliage. These plants also produce creamy-white spring flowers, white summer fruits, and reddish-purple fall color. The shrub spreads by underground stems and takes on a multistemmed, rounded shape. The principal asset of the redtwig dog-wood is the stem coloration, which varies from light red, reddish-purple, and dark red to vibrant yellow. The color-ful stems played off newly fallen snow make the redosier dogwood the ultimate winter-interest shrub.*

Other Name
Redosier

Bloom Period and Seasonal Color
Creamy-white flowers in late spring; colorful winter stems; reddish-purple fall color.

Mature Height × Spread
6 to 8 ft. × 10 ft.

When, Where, and How to Plant
Plant in spring or fall. This shrub transplants easily and is adaptable to a wide range of soil conditions, especially wet sites. Plant in full sun for best stem coloration. To prevent disease, avoid planting in deep shade and in areas where air movement is limited. Plant shrubs following the general instruc-tions on page 154.

Growing Tips
Keep plants moist until established. Water during extended dry spells. Fertilize in spring following the directions on page 154.

Care
To maintain the colorful stems on redtwig dog-wood, adopt a regular April pruning routine. The most colorful stems are one to three years in age. On older shrubs, you have two choices. One is to remove 1/3 of the older stems each year, cutting them to the ground. After a three-year period your plant will look great, and you will have maintained its natural form throughout the process. A more drastic approach is to cut all the stems back to the ground. New growth will quickly fill the void you've created. The redtwig dogwood is occa-sionally bothered by disease, especially during wet weather. A twig blight fungus produces cankers, causing portions of the stem to die back. Prune out diseased wood by removing the entire stem or branch. A leaf spot fungus produces irreg-ular dark blotches on the leaf surfaces. It is generally not life-threatening.

Companion Planting and Design
Place redtwig where the winter sun will illuminate the colorful stems. Its colonizing habit makes it a valuable shrub for steep hillsides or low, wet areas. Redtwig dogwood combines well with perennials in a mixed border. Plant with the Lenten rose; the white flowers and evergreen foliage complement the dogwood's dark-red stems.

We Recommend
'Silver and Gold' is a newer introduction with yel-low winter stems. The variegated leaves have cream-colored margins. 'Cardinal' is a cherry red-stemmed selection that looks fantastic placed around the peeling bark of river birch.

Rugosa Rose

Rosa rugosa

When, Where, and How to Plant

Plant bareroot roses as early in spring as the soil and weather allow. Container-grown plants should be planted in spring or early summer. Plant rugosa roses in moist, fertile, and well-drained soil. They also tolerate sandy soils. Locate in full sun for the best performance. Follow planting directions on page 242. Look for rugosa roses grown on their own roots. If the rose is grafted, it should be positioned so the bud union is level with the surrounding soil or, in northern parts of the state, slightly below.

Growing Tips

Keep newly planted roses well watered, and apply a 3-in. layer of mulch. Rugosa roses have low fertility requirements; in fact, they are widely naturalized on the rocky, sandy eastern coast of the United States.

Care

Rugosa roses are pest- and disease-resistant and usually need little pruning. In spring, remove any dead or damaged canes or any that are out of scale with the plant. Removing older woody branches encourages young vigorous growth.

Companion Planting and Design

Rugosa roses are suitable for hedges and shrub borders, and in combination with perennials and annuals. Use them in difficult sites for their tolerance of sandy and saline soils. Create a garden picture with a rose as the focal point. Try 'Frau Dagmar Hastrup' with perennials such as Russian sage or 'Hameln' fountain grass. Or plan for late-season color by complementing its autumn beauty with the fiery hues of perennials such as bluestar, Bowman's root, and flame grass. Add the boltonia 'Snowbank' for its white flowers.

We Recommend

The disease-tolerant and hardy rugosa roses 'Jens Munk' and 'Henry Hudson' are both introductions from the Canadian Explorer series. 'Henry Hudson' has white fragrant double flowers and grows 2 to 3 ft. high and wide. 'Jens Munk' has semidouble vibrant pink flowers. Flowering repeats until frost, followed by red hips. This shrub rose reaches 4 to 5 ft. tall.

A wonderful shrub for the Michigan landscape happens to be a rose. Shrub roses, beautiful and useful, shouldn't be relegated to a rose garden. Hybrid rugosa roses are tough, disease-resistant, and extremely winter hardy. The fragrant flowers appear all summer, and many form ornamental orange hips the size of large crabapples. Rosa rugosa, a Japanese species rose, has been replaced with hybrids called the hybrid rugosas. 'Frau Dagmar Hastrup' is one of the best. It has silky pink fragrant flowers on compact four-foot bushes and resists common rose diseases. The bronzy fall color complements the red hips. Rugosa roses can also be used for hedging, softening a fence, or lining a drive. Every sunny Michigan garden should be home to at least one.

Bloom Period and Seasonal Color
Rosy-purple, pink, or white flowers in early summer, continuing sporadically until frost.

Mature Height × Spread
4 to 6 ft. × 4 to 6 ft.

Spicebush
Lindera benzoin

The deep, rich, moist woods of Michigan are an inviting place in the early spring before mosquitoes arrive to chase us out. Take a walk to see emerging spring wildflowers and the showy yellow blossoms of spicebush. A large shrub that grows happily in deep to partial shade, it produces cheery blossoms while other woody plants remain in a deep sleep. These wonderful flowers on the female plants produce beautiful bright-red fruits in fall that are relished by wildlife. Tim and his children like to camp at a state park along Lake Michigan, where the campsites are enveloped by masses of the spicebush. A gentle rub of the plants' twigs reveals a wonderful spicy scent that gives this shrub its moniker.

Bloom Period and Seasonal Color
Yellow flowers in spring.

Mature Height × Spread
6 to 12 ft. × 12 ft.

Zones
To Zone 4

When, Where, and How to Plant
Plant as a containerized plant in spring for best results. Spicebush prefers moist, well-drained soils in partial shade. It will grow in full sun if given adequate moisture. Plants placed in shade will have an open horizontal branching pattern as they search for filtered sunlight; plants in full sun have a more rounded character and will produce a more intense fall-color showing. Plant following the general instructions on page 154, spacing 6 to 8 ft. apart.

Growing Tips
Keep new shrubs moist until established. Mulch with several inches of well-rotted leaf mold to conserve moisture and enrich the soil. Water in drought situations, and be careful not to disturb the roots after planting. See page 154 for information on shrub fertilization.

Care
Spicebush has no serious insect or disease problems. It has a natural multistemmed habit, which requires little or no pruning. To ensure pollination and fruiting, be sure to purchase male and female plants and plant them together. Male plants are reportedly showier in flower. An option is to buy them in fall when the fruit is set, although spring planting is preferred.

Companion Planting and Design
The spicebush is at home in the woodland garden and in large-scale naturalistic landscapes. It mingles well with wildflowers like Solomon's seal, columbine, wild ginger, and our native ferns. The splendid golden-yellow fall color combines well with the wine-red fall color of the pagoda dogwood. Plant spicebush outside a window to catch the seasonal beauty that this underutilized native shrub can bring to your garden.

We Recommend
The Japanese spicebush, *Lindera obtusiloba*, is a rare shrub in commerce sought out by the discerning plantsperson. Similar in habit and flower to our native spicebush, it differs mainly by its unusually lobed mitten-shaped leaves. It has the same cultural requirements but is generally available only from small specialty mail-order firms. Plants are shipped in small sizes but grow very quickly if given an appropriate location.

When, Where, and How to Plant

'Grefsheim' spirea is easy to transplant as a balled-and-burlapped or containerized shrub. Plant either in fall or spring. This shrub dislikes waterlogged soils, so place it where you have adequate drainage in full sun. Follow the general directions for shrub planting on page 154. Space at 5 to 6 ft. to enjoy the full cascading form of this plant. Overcrowding obscures the form and prevents sunlight from fully reaching the shrub.

Growing Tips

New plantings will require watering in drought periods. If plants lack vigor or a healthy foliage color, apply fertilizer. Plants that have recently been rejuvenated by renewal pruning will benefit from fertilization as well. Refer to page 154 for more information. A layer of organic mulch is beneficial.

Care

Aphids occasionally attack spirea. For severe infestations, treat with an insecticidal soap according to package directions. The old flowers can be removed if the look is distracting, but most gardeners let them remain. Renewal pruning is recommended on older shrubs that are not as vigorous or as reliable in their flower production. To keep the graceful billowing form of this plant, selectively thin out older stems to the ground, removing 1/3 of the older wood over a three-year period. After the third year, you will have young flowering wood in abundance.

Companion Planting and Design

'Grefsheim' spirea blooms when tulips and other spring bulbs are in flower. Consider making a spring-blooming section of your garden by incorporating this shrub as a single specimen or in a mass planting. The cool blue foliage is a pleasant foil to the dark foliage of the purple alumroot, *Heuchera villosa* 'Purpurea'.

We Recommend

The compact thunberg spirea, *Spiraea thunbergii* 'Compacta', is a beautiful dwarf flowering shrub that works well where space is limited. It has the same wonderful white blooms of the 'Grefsheim' spirea, all in a much smaller package.

On old farmsteads and in gardens throughout Michigan, bridal veil spirea, Spiraea × vanhouteii, is a mainstay. Its cascading pure-white blossoms erupt from the branches to signify summer's approach. For all its charm, though, it also has problems. Fireblight, a bacterial disease, attacks flowers and stems, causing them to shrivel as if they had been torched. Vanhoutte has a gangly habit, which causes it to become a mess over time. The hybrid 'Grefsheim' spirea is smaller and more disease-resistant than Vanhoutte spirea, but it has the same distinct spring blossoms that appear a week or two earlier. The cool blue color of the foliage takes over after flowering, adding a distinct leaf shade that works well in a mixed shrub border with perennials.

Bloom Period and Seasonal Color
White flowers in mid-spring.

Mature Height × Spread
4 to 5 ft. × 5 to 6 ft.

Staghorn Sumac
Rhus typhina

Several of our finest native shrubs are sometimes labeled "garden thugs" due to their wild character. Taking an informed look at native shrubs, we can reevaluate their perceived faults and use them judiciously, allowing their beauty and utility to come through. The native staghorn sumac is often considered a coarse, untamed plant with limited garden appeal, but this is simply not true. It has large green compound leaves that change to a spectacular array of yellow, orange, and red in the fall. The fall foliage, red fruits, and picturesque branching habit of this colonizing shrub are among its chief ornamental assets, and it is also is tolerant of hostile growing conditions. It's the perfect plant to transform a difficult site into a beautiful vision.

Bloom Period and Seasonal Color
Yellow, orange, and red fall color.

Mature Height × Spread
15 to 25 ft. × 15 to 20 ft.

When, Where, and How to Plant
Plant in spring or fall, in full sun or partial shade, in a place where you can let it spread but not get out of control. Avoid planting in deep shade, or it will become straggly and leggy. While the staghorn adapts well to dry soils, it is intolerant of extremely wet sites. Plant as a container-grown or balled-and-burlapped plant according to directions on page 154.

Growing Tips
Keep a new planting moist. Once established, it is fairly drought-resistant and shouldn't need watering or fertilization.

Care
Staghorn sumac is pest- and disease-resistant. It is a rambunctious plant, so you may occasionally need to temper its vigorous growth habit. To lower or rejuvenate an overgrown plant, cut back to ground level in the early spring. New vigorous growth will quickly result, leading to the reestablishment of its territorial hold.

Companion Planting and Design
It is tolerant of drought situations and prospers in areas where little else will survive or that are difficult to maintain. These include steep banks or hillsides and waste areas with poor soil. It makes a wonderful privacy screen when planted in a mass. When planted as a single specimen, sumac can be pruned into a tree form, which results in a wide-spreading open crown with a picturesque branching habit. Proper siting is important with this shrub, which can reach treelike proportions. Do not use as a foundation plant, where it may consume your home and become a problem.

We Recommend
'Dissecta' and 'Laciniata' are two cultivars with finely dissected leaflets, producing an incredible ferny foliage effect. The fall color is outstanding. Both of these selections are female and need a male plant placed nearby to produce fruits. The shining sumac, *Rhus copallina* (20 to 30 ft.), is a large colonizing shrub with glossy green leaves and scarlet-red fall color.

Star Magnolia
Magnolia stellata

When, Where, and How to Plant

Plant as a container specimen in spring. Magnolias can be difficult to transplant and are notorious for their thick, fleshy roots that are easily damaged and slow to produce laterals. Fall planting is not recommended. Magnolias prefer well-drained, slightly acidic, moist soils. Add leaf mold or peat moss to your planting hole. Plant in full sun, but avoid a warm southern exposure—plant in a northern exposure to keep the buds tight and protected until the danger of late frosts has passed. Magnolias dislike root competition, so place in a space where roots can grow unimpeded. Follow the planting directions on page 154. Do not plant too deeply.

Growing Tips

Under the right conditions, your magnolia will thrive with minimal care. Mulch the root zone, and water in prolonged drought situations. Fertilize with an acid-based formula according to the instructions on page 154.

Care

Prune in early summer after flowering. Do not remove the lower branches; its full habit is better left alone. Remove vigorous branch shoots that grow straight upward off older limbs. These deplete the main branches of energy and threaten the natural form. Star magnolia is susceptible to attack by magnolia scale. Adult scale looks like dark brown, round bumps on twigs and causes plants to weaken. Dormant oil sprays applied before growth begins in spring will suffocate scales. The crawler stage of the insect can be controlled by Orthene™ applications. Light scale infestations can be removed by hand.

Companion Planting and Design

Magnolias are effective as single specimens or in group plantings. Create a heartwarming spring scene by underplanting star magnolia with early spring-blooming bulbs such as the grape hyacinth and squill.

We Recommend

'Royal Star' is pink in bud, opening to large white flowers that are 6 in. across with up to thirty petals. It blooms a week later than normal for the species, which gives it some extra protection against late frosts.

In winter, the smooth gray bark of star magnolia is handsome, and its fuzzy flowerbuds are a unique feature both beautiful to look at and useful as they protect the quiescent flowers within. Then, in April, the flowers are a spring wake-up call! The fragrant star-shaped blooms cover the plant completely before its leaves emerge. Magnolias, for all their beauty, still have limitations to their performance in Michigan landscapes. Their early-blooming habit can get them in trouble. Flowers that push their luck on a warm spring afternoon may get zapped by a hard freeze. Some steps can be taken when siting your star magnolia, increasing the odds that you can enjoy the rousing spectacle of its radiant blooms on a yearly basis.

Bloom Period and Seasonal Color
White, pink, or rose in early spring.

Mature Height × Spread
5 to 15 ft. × 5 to 15 ft.

Zones
To Zone 4

Summersweet
Clethra alnifolia

Native North American shrubs are currently hot items in the horticultural world, and deservedly so. While some of these plants are cumbersome or difficult to incorporate into home landscapes with limited room, the summersweet fits right in with outstanding year-round appeal. Clethra alnifolia is a moderate-sized shrub reaching up to nine feet in height but with many cultivars available at smaller sizes. In midsummer the glossy green summer foliage is topped by intensely fragrant pink, rose, or white flowers. Summersweet's flower spikes form persistent seed capsules, which are attractive in the winter months. The fragrant blooms are the main calling card for this shrub, appearing at a time when most woody plants have already bloomed and are content to ride out the summer heat wave.

Other Name
Sweet Pepperbush

Bloom Period and Seasonal Color
White or soft-pink flowers in midsummer.

Mature Height × Spread
5 to 9 ft. × 4 to 6 ft.

Zones
To Zone 5

When, Where, and How to Plant
Plant in spring or fall, in full sun for the most vigorous growth and flowers, and better fall color. Summersweet is tolerant of partial shade. It tolerates both dry and wet sites but prefers a moist, slightly acidic soil. Plant as container-grown or balled-and-burlapped plants following the general directions on page 154. Allow 4 to 5 ft. between plants.

Growing Tips
Water in periods of prolonged drought to avoid the stressful conditions that predispose plants to spider mite attack. Mulch with pine needles or an acid-based bark mix. Summersweet will develop leaf yellowing or chlorosis in soils with a pH over 7.5. Fertilizers with an acidic reaction may bring your plant back to health. See page 154 for more on fertilizing shrubs.

Care
Spider mites can sometimes be a problem. See above for the best control approach. Rabbits are especially fond of summersweet as a winter food source; protect new plants with chicken wire if rabbits are a problem in your area. Winter is an excellent time to prune your plants. Rejuvenate an older shrub by selectively cutting back the branches to ground level, allowing young stems to develop and take their place. Be careful not to remove new suckering stems.

Companion Planting and Design
Summersweet can be planted as a foundation plant or shrub border, or in mass plantings. Its upright habit makes it useful for narrow areas where few woody shrubs can fit. Due to its shade tolerance, it can be used effectively on the edge of a woodland or as an understory shrub.

We Recommend
The smaller selection 'Hummingbird' is perfect beneath a first-floor window. A low-mounded shrub, it reaches 4 ft. and has fragrant white blooms. It may have some winter dieback. 'Paniculata' has large white flowers and is known for its strong growth. 'Rosea' and 'Pink Spire' are often confused in the trade; you may think you're getting one but end up with the other. Both are exceptional pink-flowered forms.

Weigela
Weigela florida

When, Where, and How to Plant
Plant weigela in spring or fall, in full sun. It is adaptable to most soil types except those with poor drainage. Plant as a container-grown or balled-and-burlapped plant following the general directions for planting shrubs on page 154.

Growing Tips
Water well after planting, and mulch shrubs to conserve moisture and discourage weeds. Water in prolonged periods of drought. Consult page 154 for information on fertilizing shrubs.

Care
Weigelas need cosmetic pruning every year. Remove branches that have died back or appear damaged. The entire shrub can be rejuvenated by cutting it completely back to the ground or selectively removing older wood over a three- to five-year period. Prune after flowering in June or July. Weigela is generally not bothered by serious insects or diseases.

Companion Planting and Design
Use weigela in grouped plantings or as a single specimen. Dwarf selections can be used for foundation plantings. This shrub has an extremely coarse winter habit; place it in an area where it will draw little attention, or obscure it with better winter-interest plants. Once the flowering has passed, this shrub needs to blend in with the crowd, so plant in a mixed border with other woody or perennial plants.

We Recommend
Many new cultivars of weigela are appearing at nurseries. Perhaps the best of the bunch is 'Alexandra', sold as Wine & Roses™. It has incredibly dark burgundy-purple foliage that holds its best color in full sun. Rosy-pink flowers contrast well with the foliage, and its small stature of 4 to 5 ft. makes it exceptional as a foundation planting. It also combines well with colorful perennials in a mixed shrub border. 'Polka', reaching 5 to 6 ft., has been proclaimed "the best pink weigela" by many nursery catalogs. It has soft-pink flowers over an extended period, from June to September.

Some shrubs for one reason or another carry with them a strong feeling of nostalgia. Many of us remember a favorite plant in a grandparent's garden as if it were an old friend. The old-fashioned weigela fits into this category as a once-popular plant that has since fallen by the wayside. In the past few years, however, interest in this old-time shrub has picked up again, slowly but surely putting it back into the mainstream. The pink trumpet-shaped flowers are the drawing card for weigela, with blossoms that reliably cover the shrub in June. Weigela was no stranger to criticism for its lanky habit and limited seasonal appeal, but some of the new selections offer compact forms, new flower colors, and attractive purplish leaves.

Bloom Period and Seasonal Color
Red, white, rose or pink flowers in late spring.

Mature Height × Spread
4 to 9 ft. × 9 to 12 ft.

Zones
To Zone 4

'William Baffin' Climbing Rose

Rosa 'William Baffin'

Climbing roses make a large romantic impact. Unfortunately, most climbers aren't hardy in Michigan, but the Canadian Explorer series offers new tough, hardy, and disease-resistant roses that can survive even frigid climates. These roses don't climb on their own; you must tie the long canes to a structure such as a fence, trellis, or arbor. 'William Baffin' is considered the hardiest and heaviest-blooming climbing rose for the North. Its semidouble flowers create a tremendous spectacle. Flowering is heavy in early summer and may repeat through frost. Train this rose to a trellis or grow it as a large shrub. 'William Baffin' is resistant to the usual rose scourges, blackspot and mildew. It flowers with abandon rather than refined elegance.

Bloom Period and Seasonal Color
Deep-pink flowers in early summer, repeating later.

Mature Height × Spread
9 to 10 ft. × 5 ft.

When, Where, and How to Plant

Plant bareroot climbing roses in early spring. Container-grown roses should be planted early to late spring for best results. Avoid container-grown roses that have become potbound because it will be more difficult for the plants to send roots out into your garden's soil. Plant in fertile well-drained soil and full sun. Follow the general directions for planting roses on page 242.

Growing Tips

Regular watering is important for a new rose. Apply a 3-in. layer of mulch to conserve moisture and keep the roots cool. Fertilizer should be applied about two weeks after spring pruning, and once more about six weeks later in the season. When you purchase the rose, inquire about fertilizer recommendations.

Care

'William Baffin' is remarkably resistant to rose diseases. In spring, remove any dead or damaged canes. Loosely tie the canes into the structure with string or fabric strips. In spring and early summer, train the young canes to grow in the direction you desire. A fan-shaped pattern is best for an arbor or trellis. Remove canes heading in the wrong direction. After four or five years, remove old woody canes and tie in new ones. 'William Baffin' is extremely vigorous, and tying in the spiny canes can be a difficult task. Be sure to wear heavy gloves.

Companion Planting and Design

Grow 'William Baffin' as a climber, tying canes into a trellis, or use it as a freestanding shrub or tall hedge. Climbers like to have the bottom of their canes shaded, so underplant with perennials or annuals. Plant a Jackman's clematis along with the rose for a flowering combination.

We Recommend

Another Canadian Explorer series climber is 'John Cabot'. It has deep pink, almost red flowers and a long blooming season. Growing to about 8 ft., it can be trained to a trellis or fence or grown as a large arching shrub.

Hamamelis × intermedia 'Arno

When, Where, and How to Plant

Transplant in spring or fall as container-grown or balled-and-burlapped plants. Plant in full sun or partial shade, in areas with moist, well-drained soil. Avoid planting under eaves where vertical space is limited. Follow the general instructions for shrub planting on page 154. 'Arnold Promise' is typically a grafted shrub. When planting, be careful not to disturb the graft union, a weak point that can be easily damaged.

Growing Tips

Keep the soil moist until the shrub is established. Fertilize in spring with an acid-based fertilizer according to the guidelines on page 154.

Care

Witchhazel is insect- and disease-free. Protect it from rabbits the first few seasons by surrounding the base of the plant with a screening of chicken wire. Witchhazels develop a strong and attractive framework and do not require regular pruning. Do not try to shear a witchhazel or reduce it drastically in size. A problem can occur with grafted plants when the understock (the rootstock portion) sprouts below the graft union. Eventually it can overtake the top portion of the plant. Remove these vigorous sprouts as soon as they start to grow. These shoots are normally rank in growth and keep their leaves attached long after the leaves have dropped in autumn.

Companion Planting and Design

Witchhazels are too large for a foundation planting. Instead, place them within view of a window or near a well-traveled path. 'Arnold Promise' is beautiful accompanied by the yellow flowers of winter aconite.

We Recommend

'Arnold Promise' is a hybrid shrub resulting from a cross between the Japanese and Chinese witchhazels. The vernal witchhazel, *Hamamelis vernalis*, is native to the central United States but is fully hardy in Michigan. It blooms as early as February with smaller orange to yellow flowers. We can look within our own state borders to find another beautiful witchhazel, *H. virginiana*. Common in the Lower Peninsula, this tree-sized shrub flowers in October.

With their scented, spidery blooms, beautiful fall color, and architectural branching habit, witchhazels are enchanting. The witchhazels are a group of North American and Asian species. 'Arnold Promise' is the showiest of the bunch, with spectacular early flowers that are both long-lasting and fragrant. The deep-yellow flowers are composed of thin straplike petals that open in the first warm days of March. The petals have a curious habit of unfurling on warm days, only to roll back in again as temperatures decline. Witchhazels can be hard to find at the local garden center. If this is true in your area, ask your garden center to stock the plant. It blooms before most people are out shopping for trees and shrubs and is therefore sadly neglected.

Bloom Period and Seasonal Color
Yellow flowers in early spring.

Mature Height × Spread
15 to 20 ft. × 15 to 20 ft.

Zones
To Zone 4

Trees *for Michigan*

Trees are a living link between the past and the future. One of life's most satisfying and humbling experiences is to plant a sapling and see it grow in twenty or thirty years into a fine, mature tree. Yet these days, many people demand instant results, including—and perhaps especially—in their gardens. So why plant trees?

First, trees are beautiful all year long. They intensify our awareness of the changing seasons, from their first pale-green leaves in spring through their lush summer foliage and fall colors. In winter, deciduous trees are dramatic and sculptural and evergreens become more conspicuous, bringing cheer to the otherwise stark landscape.

Trees shade us in summer and allow winter sunlight and warmth to reach us when we need them most. Trees remove carbon dioxide and furnish oxygen to the air we breathe. They provide a sense of emotional comfort and stability for people as well as habitats for birds and other wildlife.

Selecting Your Tree

Trees may be purchased with the rootballs wrapped in burlap. These trees have been grown in fields, dug, and then wrapped with burlap and sometimes wire baskets. Remove at least the top third of the burlap and wire at planting. Synthetic burlap will not decompose and must be removed entirely. Balled-and-burlapped trees may be planted March through May and September through November.

Bareroot trees are grown in a field, then dug when dormant, in very early spring or late fall. Once dug, these trees must be planted immediately so the roots don't dry out.

Trees that have been grown in containers are also available. Look for signs of healthy new growth. If roots have grown into a dense, encircled ball, they should be teased or cut at planting to encourage lateral growth. Container-grown trees may be planted at any time during the growing season, but spring and fall are preferred. Take a tree out of its container before planting.

Planting

A soil test will tell you what nutrients, if any, should be added before you plant a tree. If you have matched the tree to the site, you should not have to add many or any amendments to the soil.

Dig the planting hole as deep as the container or rootball and three times as wide. Fill the hole with water, and let it stand for an hour. If water remains, drainage is poor and you will need to plant the tree higher than the existing soil level.

If that is the case, put some of the soil back in the planting hole, creating a mound that will elevate the top one-third (or three to four inches) of the rootball above grade. Mound up the soil around the base of the trunk so the tree is at the same depth it was in the container or field. Gently slope the sides of the mound back toward the ground. Water the tree well and keep it watered regularly while it gets established. Apply a three-inch layer of mulch; this will help conserve moisture and protect the trunk if the tree is planted in a lawn area. Make sure the mulch is not in contact with the trunk of the tree.

Post-Planting Care

The most critical factor for tree growth the first two years after planting is water. The tree will need at least one inch of water a week during the growing season.

Fertilizer is usually not needed for the first year or so. If the tree has poor stem or leaf development, you may choose to fertilize. The best time to fertilize trees is in late fall after the leaves have dropped or early spring before the leaves have emerged. Rather than applying it routinely, watch for clues that your tree needs fertilizer, such as pale-green leaves, undersized leaves, or overall slow growth. The plant may require more nitrogen. If a tree lacks iron, only the leaf veins may be dark green. This sometimes occurs on high-pH soils, as in heavy clay. Slow-release fertilizers containing sulfur-coated urea help lower soil pH and allow for increased iron absorption.

There are many fertilizers available. Check any product's label to make sure it is suitable for use on trees. Choose a fertilizer with slow-release forms of nitrogen to deliver nutrients gradually so the fertilizer won't burn the plant or leach from the soil.

Applying organic material such as finely shredded leaves or compost around the base of the tree can improve the soil and provide nutrients, which may be all the fertilizer your tree needs.

American Smoketree
Cotinus obovatus

The American smoketree has been called one of our most spectacular fall-color plants, and this is no exaggeration. Few trees can match the fall foliage of this handsome native that is too rarely seen in our landscapes. In fact, every season puts forth an exciting feature. Spring begins with bronze new growth that develops into attractive dark blue-green summer foliage. Early summer flowers erupt from the terminals of the tree in a distinctive plume that creates a smoky or hazy effect. As the blooms progress into seed formation, they take on a magnificent rosy color in contrast to the blue-green foliage. The show continues as the summer foliage goes through a fall color spectacle of yellow to orange to reds and purples. Fantastic!

Bloom Period and Seasonal Color
Hazy-green flower changing to pink with seed development in summer; rich fall color.

Mature Height × Spread
30 ft. × 15 to 20 ft.

Zones
To Zone 4

When, Where, and How to Plant
Plant in spring or fall. Site in full sun to partial shade. The smoketree adapts well to high-pH soils and also tolerates compacted soils. It will not tolerate wet soils for any length of time, so avoid low, poorly drained locations. Plant trees following the instructions on page 190. In heavy or poor soils, plant the top of the root system three to four inches above the surrounding grade.

Growing Tips
Keep the root zone moist until established. Mulch after planting with 2 to 3 in. of organic material. For information on fertilizing trees see page 191. Smoketree is quite drought-tolerant after a few years of establishment.

Care
The smoketree is slow-growing and takes several years to get established. The wood of the tree is fragile and susceptible to ice and storm damage. Trees are also susceptible to *Verticillium* wilt, a fungus that is found in the soil and enters the plant through its roots. The fungus moves into the tissues that conduct water and food, disrupting their function and normally causing portions of the tree to wilt. Branches of the tree slowly die out as the fungus spreads. Remove all infected branches, and burn them. Encourage healthy growth by watering during droughts and fertilizing in late fall.

Landscape Merit
The American smoketree is the perfect choice for small landscapes, forming an upright dense rounded crown reaching a maximum height of 30 ft. Trees make great specimens when placed against a wall or evergreen background, where their flowers and fall foliage really come alive.

We Recommend
Cotinus coggygria, the common smoketree or smokebush, is a large shrub with similar but smaller leaves and flowers with the same distinctive smoky effect. Many cultivars are available, including several purple-leaf forms that are spectacular in combination with herbaceous perennials in a mixed shrub border. We recommend 'Velvet Cloak' and 'Royal Purple'.

Amur Chokecherry
Prunus maackii

When, Where, and How to Plant
Plant in the spring of the year; fall transplanting will be less successful. Plant in full sun in a well-drained soil. Chokecherry does not tolerate hot, dry conditions, so keep away from hot concrete and dry sites where plants will suffer. Follow the general planting directions on page 190.

Growing Tips
Keep the root zone of newly planted trees moist until established. After planting, apply a 2- to 3-in. layer of organic mulch. Consult page 191 for general information on fertilizing trees.

Care
This is one of the few ornamental cherries that bloom on wood set from the previous season's growth. In general, you should avoid pruning your tree. Tree wounds will take away from the winter beauty of this tree, so prune only to remove dead, diseased, or broken branches. Prune after flowering. Most cherries are extremely shallow-rooted, so avoid planting groundcovers or shrubs in the immediate vicinity of the tree. This will help prevent competition for water and nutrients and limit possible damage to the roots. Mulching around the root zone encourages a healthy root system. Amur chokecherry is occasionally troubled by fireblight; see the shadblow entry for details on treatment.

Landscape Merit
The tree has a dense, rounded form and reaches 35 to 45 ft. in height. Plant in a prominent position where the handsome bark can be viewed along a walkway or from a window. The shiny brown bark looks spectacular when surrounded by the extraordinary violet fruits of the purple beautyberry, *Callicarpa dichotoma*.

We Recommend
Demand creates supply. If you can't locate this plant at your local nurseries, encourage them to stock it. Several small mail-order nurseries carry a nice selection of ornamental cherries. See the source guide on page 234. If you can find it, try *Prunus serrula*, a small tree with a rich mahogany-colored bark that glistens in the sun. It reaches a height of 20 to 30 ft. and is hardy to Zones 5 and 6.

The remarkable blooms of ornamental cherries awaken us from our winter doldrums with beautiful white to pink flowers, but the amur chokecherry offers more than just spring blooms. It has remarkable shiny cinnamon-brown winter bark that peels away in strips. This is an extremely hardy tree of moderate size that becomes a prime-time plant each winter season when some other cherry species show little to no winter interest. While the winter season brings out the best in amur chokecherry, it also has a pleasant spring display of flowers. Usually blooming in late May and early June, the flowers are white and borne in profusion. From these flowers black fruits ripen and are carried away by birds.

Bloom Period and Seasonal Color
White flowers in late spring; handsome cinnamon bark.

Mature Height × Spread
35 to 45 ft. × 20 to 30 ft.

Baldcypress
Taxodium distichum

Imagine a swamp in Louisiana and you'll probably picture alligators and tall cypress trees, covered with Spanish moss. Most people don't know that this cypress, brought out of the swamp and placed in our landscapes, makes an outstanding year-round tree of great beauty. In fact, it's even tolerant of urban conditions. More commonly known as the baldcypress, this tree grows naturally into southern Illinois, where it reaches the northernmost point of its natural range. But it is hardy in the southern half of Michigan's Lower Peninsula as well. While it is definitely a cone-bearing tree (a conifer), it is not evergreen. Instead, the needles turn a distinctive copper-brown in the fall and then drop, along with the soft outer twigs.

Bloom Period and Seasonal Color
Soft-green needles turning reddish-brown in fall; deciduous.

Mature Height × Spread
50 to 70 ft. × 30 to 40 ft.

Zones
To Zone 4

When, Where, and How to Plant
Spring planting is recommended for the baldcypress. Plant in full sun for stronger growth and better fall color. It tolerates both extremely wet soils and poor dry soils. Plant according to general instructions on page 190.

Growing Tips
Keep the rootball of newly planted trees moist until established. After establishment, it is drought tolerant. After planting, apply 2 to 3 in. of organic mulch. For information on tree fertilization, see page 191.

Care
Baldcypress is a relatively carefree tree. If chlorosis or leaf yellowing develops as a result of high soil pH, fertilize using mixes that contain sulfur or that are known to have an acidic reaction. Use them according to the manufacturer's instructions. Mulch every year with composted oak leaves and pine needles to lower the pH of your soil. The baldcypress has a natural "church spire" habit that should not be altered by pruning. Remove only dead, diseased, or dying limbs, being careful not to alter the main central trunk or leader.

Landscape Merit
Baldcypress can reach a height of 50 to 70 ft. with a narrow pyramidal habit that makes it a good choice for street tree plantings and for exposed, windy situations. Plant a grove in wet areas along a pond or stream side where standing water presents no problem for the growth of this tree. *Taxodium* is a great plant for providing summer shade for your house. When the needles drop, winter light and warmth will come through when you most need them. Trees are particularly effective as textural contrasts with other woody plants. The fall fruit crop of the Michigan holly sparkles against the copper-brown needles of the baldcypress.

We Recommend
'Shawnee Brave' is a very narrow, upright form of the baldcypress that is particularly useful in street tree plantings or for specimen use where space is limited.

Black Gum
Nyssa sylvatica

When, Where, and How to Plant

Plant in the spring only; fall-transplanted trees are notorious for failure. Plant in full sun to partial shade. *Nyssa sylvatica* is tolerant of shade, but shade does not promote the full-spreading form that is so admirable in this tree. Black gum prefers moist, slightly acidic conditions and will develop leaf yellowing or chlorosis in alkaline (high pH) situations. For best results, plant smaller trees. Avoid transplanting trees larger than 3$^{1}/_{2}$ in. in diameter. Black gum's taproot makes transplanting at larger sizes difficult. Small containerized trees are preferable if you can find them. Follow the general tree-planting instructions on page 190.

Growing Tips

Keep the rootball of newly planted trees moist until established. A yearly topdressing of an acid-based mulch will help keep your tree healthy. Consult page 191 for information on fertilizing trees.

Care

Black gum is generally resistant to pests and diseases. Cankers may develop on stems and branches, causing portions of the tree to die back. Remove infected branches. Chlorosis or leaf yellowing will alert you to alkaline conditions that are detrimental to plant growth. Fertilizers that contain sulfur or that are known to have an acidic reaction may bring your plant back to health. Do not prune or disrupt the main trunk or stem that forms the central leader of the tree; this will damage the natural form of this plant.

Landscape Merit

The black gum is perfect for wet sites or sites where you want to establish a naturalistic planting. It makes an exceptional specimen tree that casts light shade, allowing turf to develop beneath its wide-spreading branches. Black gum has been used to some success in street tree plantings but is generally not tolerant of pollution in urban areas. It is particularly effective with an evergreen backdrop to illuminate its amazing fall color.

We Recommend

Plant the species.

Our North American native trees are the envy of the world when it comes to autumn color. Among the finest is the black gum or tupelo. Found naturally in Michigan in moist bottomlands and wet areas, it develops into a large tree, reaching fifty feet or more in height. The foliage of the black gum is outstanding for its lustrous shiny-green appearance in the summer and incredible yellow-orange to scarlet colors in fall. In winter, the smooth silver bark and horizontal branching habit add architectural beauty to the landscape. While the flowers of black gum are barely noticeable to humans, they provide sweet nectar for bees. Tupelo honey is a popular commodity in southern states.

Other Name

Tupelo

Bloom Period and Seasonal Color

Flowers insignificant; fall color yellow-orange to scarlet-red.

Mature Height × Spread

30 to 50 ft. × 20 to 30 ft.

Corneliancherry
Cornus mas

Every spring as we wait for the appearance of spring bulbs and the disappearance of the last remnants of winter snow, a surprisingly early-blooming dogwood bursts into flower on leafless branches. The corneliancherry's bright yellow flowers cover the tree in mass, making it quite noticeable even from a distance. The summer months offer lustrous green foliage, and by August, red cherrylike fruits appear. In full sun, the fall color is a reddish-purple, and in winter the flaky bark merits notice. The corneliancherry is the perfect small landscape tree. With a round, dense shrublike habit, it reaches twenty to twenty-five feet high and grows fifteen feet wide. The fruits can be made into jam. If you don't eat them, the birds will!

Bloom Period and Seasonal Color
Yellow flowers in spring; reddish-purple fall color.

Mature Height × Spread
20 to 25 ft. × 15 to 20 ft.

Zones
To Zone 4

When, Where, and How to Plant
Spring transplanting is recommended; fall planting is less successful. Plant in full sun for best growth and flower production. One of the easiest-to-please dogwood trees, it is adaptable to most soil types except those that are too wet or dry. When planting in groups, space the trees at least 20 ft. apart to allow room for spread. Follow the general instructions for tree planting on page 190.

Growing Tips
Keep the root zone of newly planted trees moist until established. Mulch after planting with 2 to 3 in. of organic mulch. Consult page 191 for information on tree fertilization.

Care
The corneliancherry is virtually disease- and insect-free. It will generally not require pruning except to remove dead, diseased, or dying branches. You may have to prune older specimens where growth has become too crowded. Nursery plants are available as single-stem trees or multi-stemmed shrubs. Tree forms are good if you want a raised canopy, but shrub forms have better winter interest with numerous branches showing the flaky bark. Cut branches are great to force into bloom; simply place in a vase on a warm windowsill.

Landscape Merit
The corneliancherry is particularly valuable for small landscapes. Plant it as a specimen small tree at the corner of a house, or use a grouping as a privacy screen or windbreak. This early-blooming dogwood is stunning placed against a backdrop of dark-needled evergreens.

We Recommend
'Golden Glory' is an amazing upright form with an incredible flower display. It is perfect as a paired planting on either side of a doorway. It grows 12 to 15 ft. tall with a spread of 8 to 10 ft.. The Japanese cornel dogwood, *Cornus officinalis*, is a closely related tree that is similar in most respects but has a showier bark with rich brown to orange tones and pops its flowers open a few days earlier than corneliancherry.

Dawn Redwood
Metasequoia glyptostroboides

When, Where, and How to Plant

Plant in the spring or the fall, in full sun in a slightly acidic well-drained soil. The dawn redwood likes moisture but does not tolerate excessively wet soils. Avoid planting in low areas because this exposes the tree to a greater likelihood of frost damage. Avoid planting close to sidewalks, for dawn redwood's aggressive roots can lift and crack concrete. Follow the general directions for tree planting on page 190.

Growing Tips

Keep the root zone of newly planted trees moist until established. Mulch after planting with 2 to 3 in. of organic mulch. Trees do not usually require fertilization.

Care

These trees are pest- and disease-free. Dawn redwood seldom needs pruning. The central trunk or leader should be left to develop the distinct pyramidal habit the tree is noted for. If the main leader becomes damaged, a new vigorous shoot normally takes its place. Dawn redwood is known for its impressive annual growth; trees may grow 50 ft. over fifteen to twenty years. They often grow continuously into the fall and have tip dieback with the first hard frosts of autumn. This is nothing to be concerned about, but you should avoid fertilizing trees after midsummer.

Landscape Merit

A tall pyramidal tree that can grow more than 70 ft. tall and 25 ft. wide, the dawn redwood commands a lot of space and should not be shoved into a corner. Use it to great effect in a grove planting. Its unique winter habit and twiggy growth are impressive when the trees are planted in mass.

We Recommend

The selections 'National' and 'Sheridan Spire' are narrower with more upright branches when compared to the species. Dawn redwood is often confused with the baldcypress, *Taxodium distichum*, a close relative. To help distinguish between the two, remember that the dawn redwood has opposite needles or leaves, and the baldcypress has alternate needles or leaves.

Every plant has a story, and the dawn redwood's story is fascinating. This ancient tree was discovered as a fossil in the early 1940s; then a few years later it was found alive and well in central China. The cone-bearing tree drops its needles each year, which sets it apart from the average conifer. Its size makes it unsuitable for a small garden, but it's a great addition to suburban landscapes, adding beauty and a touch of rarity and intrigue to the garden. The soft-green needles have a feathery texture and turn a russet or orange-brown color before dropping. Dawn redwoods are perfect for energy-conscious gardeners, who plant them for shade in the summer and then, after the needles drop, have full sun.

Bloom Period and Seasonal Color
Bright-green needles; russet fall color.

Mature Height × Spread
70 to 100 ft. × 25 ft.

Zones
To Zone 4

Flowering Crabapple

Malus spp.

Flowering crabapples are some of the most popular trees in the nursery trade. Their cheerful blossoms light up the spring landscape and are followed by impressive fruit crops. Not all crabapples were created equal, and certain cultivars are superior in performance when compared to others. The principal diseases associated with crabapples are particularly destructive to their ornamental display in Michigan landscapes. The foliage diseases—powdery mildew, apple scab, and cedar apple rust—wreak havoc on the foliage and fruit quality. Another serious disease, fireblight, can kill a plant. Two of the top-performing crabapples are 'Professor Sprenger' and 'Prairifire'. Both cultivars offer the perfect balance of superior characteristics in crabapples—attractive form, clean foliage, beautiful flowers, persistent fruit, and disease resistance.

Bloom Period and Seasonal Color
Reddish-purple, pink, or white flowers; ornamental fruits summer through winter.

Mature Height × Spread
To 20 ft. depending on selection × 15 to 20 ft.

When, Where, and How to Plant
Crabapples are easy to transplant in spring or fall. Choose full sun in an exposed location. To avoid leaf diseases, avoid stagnant and wind-protected areas. Crabapples will tolerate most soil conditions except poor drainage. Space group plantings at least 20 to 25 ft. apart to avoid overcrowding. Plant according to the general instructions on page 190.

Growing Tips
Keep the root zone of newly planted trees moist. Mulch after planting with 2 to 3 in. of organic mulch. Crabapples will generally not require fertilizer on a regular basis.

Care
Plant resistant selections and site carefully to avoid problems with disease. Prune during the winter months so you can see branches clearly. Almost all crabapple selections are grafted to an understock or rootstock that sometimes sprouts growth off the base of the trunk. Remove these sprouts as soon as they develop or they will quickly overtake your tree, and remove stems that are too closely spaced or are growing back into the center of the tree. Disinfect your pruners after each cut with isopropyl alcohol to prevent the spread of fireblight.

Landscape Merit
With the right selections, crabapples are wonderful four-season plants for gardens, home entrances, and patio plantings. Daffodils are a classic underplanting.

We Recommend
All the cultivars recommended here have good disease resistance. The crimson buds of 'Prairifire' open to red-purple single flowers. The foliage is a deep green with purple tones. Some years the fruit persists into February. 'Professor Sprenger' is an upright tree reaching 20 ft. in height and width. It has white fragrant flowers that emerge from deep rose-pink buds. The persistent fruit changes from a yellow-orange to orange-red. Try 'Sugar Tyme' as well; it's a crabapple selected at Michigan State University by former landscape architect Milton Baron. It forms an upright oval tree 18 ft. high and 15 ft. wide and has pale-pink buds, opening to single white fragrant flowers.

Ginkgo

Ginkgo biloba

When, Where, and How to Plant

Plant in spring or fall in a full-sun location. The ginkgo prefers a well-drained, deep sandy soil but will grow in heavy clay soils as long as they are not waterlogged. Plant according to the general instructions on page 190.

Growing Tips

Keep the root zone of newly planted trees moist until established. Mulch after planting with 2 to 3 in. of organic mulch. Consult page 191 for information on tree fertilization.

Care

The ginkgo is virtually disease- and pest-free. The tree has a main trunk or central leader that provides the framework for the large horizontal branches, giving it a spreading habit at maturity. Do not remove the central leader or a new branch will grow vertically in its place, ruining the form and creating a weak point where the two branches meet. In general, remove only dead, diseased, or damaged branches.

Landscape Merit

Gingko is a large tree that grows 50 to 80 ft. with a pyramidal habit when young to an open spreading habit as it matures. It demands a lot of space and isn't suited to smaller gardens. The tree is generally slow-growing and is frequently used as a street tree because it tolerates urban conditions.

We Recommend

The fruit (naked seed) of the ginkgo is reviled for the horrible smell of its orange pulpy covering. It is truly one of nature's funkiest offerings, even though the seeds are treasured as a delicacy in Asia. Fortunately for those who want to pass on the fruit instead of pass out, male trees are available in the nursery trade. 'Autumn Gold' is a male selection with excellent fall color. 'Fastigiata' is an upright tree well suited for street tree plantings. When purchasing plants, insist on male trees, and buy a named selection to be sure. Seed-grown trees do not produce fruits until twenty or more years of age.

Every fall, youngsters around Michigan capture falling leaves to take home and press between sheets of waxed paper. The leaf collections display oak and maple leaves, but the most prized specimen may be the fan-shaped golden ginkgo leaf. The gingko is known as a living fossil. It appears in the fossil record as far back as 225 million years ago. The distinctive leaves turn a spectacular golden yellow and then drop all at once, creating a carpet of gold around the base. A ginkgo tree is an impressive addition to the landscape. Herbal remedies using various parts of the ginkgo tree abound, adding to its mystery and allure. Though it's unclear if ginkgo will improve your memory, it will definitely improve your view!

Bloom Period and Seasonal Color

Flowers insignificant; unique foliage with golden fall color.

Mature Height × Spread

50 to 80 ft. × 30 to 40 ft.

Hop-Hornbeam

Ostrya virginiana

Some of the finest native trees in Michigan go unnoticed and underappreciated. These trees are not particularly vibrant in flower, so they blend in with the crowd. The American hop-hornbeam has a kind of understated beauty that becomes apparent on close inspection. The first thing you notice about this tree is the gray-brown bark that hangs loosely in longitudinal strips; then you notice the handsome bright-green foliage. The leaves have distinct jagged edges and turn a pleasant yellow in the fall. The male flowers (catkins) are quite noticeable on the tree in the winter months, usually appearing in threes as short brown buds before they open in early spring; the female flowers produce distinctive papery pods that resemble the fruit of the hop vine.

Other Name
Ironwood

Bloom Period and Seasonal Color
Attractive peeling bark; bright-green foliage.

Mature Height × Spread
25 to 40 ft. × 15 to 20 ft.

When, Where, and How to Plant
Plant in the spring, as fall planting is generally less successful. Choose locations in full sun or partial shade. Hop-hornbeam will do quite well on the edge of a woodlot or planted as an understory tree. It prefers a moist, well-drained soil that is slightly acidic. For best results, plant small-sized trees. The hop-hornbeam's taproot makes transplanting large sizes difficult; don't transplant trees whose trunks are larger than 3¹/₂ in. in diameter. Small containerized trees are preferable if you can find them. In poor soils, amend the backfill with organic matter. Follow the general directions for tree planting on page 190.

Growing Tips
Keep the root zone of newly planted trees moist until established. A yearly topdressing with 2 to 3 in. of an acid-based mulch will help keep your plant in a healthy condition. Consult page 191 for information on tree fertilization.

Care
Newly transplanted trees are slow to establish. Trees under stress are sometimes attacked by the two-lined chestnut borer. The larvae of the borer tunnel within the bark of the trees, causing branch dieback that is usually first noticed at the top of the tree. Contact your local extension agent for current recommendations on the control of wood-boring insects. Keeping your trees well watered and vigorous will protect them from attack. Disease is not a problem.

Landscape Merit
Hop-hornbeam is a medium-sized tree reaching a height of 25 to 40 ft. It is useful for naturalistic plantings or as a lawn specimen. It has been used extensively as a street tree in Lansing. With the lower branches removed, its small size makes it suitable for a narrow street lawn. Be aware that although it is used in street tree plantings, it is highly sensitive to salt.

We Recommend
Plant the species; there are not any cultivars. This tree is often in limited supply and may need to be ordered through small mail-order nurseries. See page 234 for mail-order sources.

Katsuratree
Cercidiphyllum japonicum

When, Where, and How to Plant
Plant in early spring for best results; fall transplanting is generally less successful. The katsuratree can be finicky in its transplant requirements. Choose full-sun or partial-shade locations. It prefers a moist, slightly acidic, well-drained soil. Trees grow quickly, so they should be grown only where adequate space is available. Plant following the general directions for tree planting on page 190.

Growing Tips
Keep the root zone of newly planted trees moist until established. Mulch after planting with 2 to 3 in. of organic mulch. The katsuratree will need to be watered over the first few years as it gets established. Consult page 191 for information on tree fertilization.

Care
It has very few insect and disease problems but is sometimes susceptible to bark splitting. The habit of the tree becomes wide-spreading over time, and multistemmed trees can be susceptible to breakage with age. Male and female flowers appear on separate trees. The females produce clusters of tiny banana-shaped fruits that split open and contain numerous seeds, which are easy to germinate and grow. Collect the small fruits in October, and store dry in a paper bag or plastic bowl with a tight-fitting cover in the refrigerator until March. Then plant the seeds just under the surface in a sterile soil mix, and place on a warm windowsill. You will be amazed at the number of trees that sprout.

Landscape Merit
Use this tree as a large lawn tree or a street tree if you can find it as a single-stem form. Underplant katsuratree to play up its elegance. Try red epimedium; its red-flushed early foliage and garnet flowers will echo the reddish blush of the katsuratree's new leaves. Add drifts of blue-gray hosta for contrast.

We Recommend
'Pendula' is a weeping form of the katsuratree. It produces a cascading waterfall effect of blue-green foliage that is spectacular! It is choice and very expensive.

Not many trees can compare to the katsuratree in grace, habit, and year-round beauty. Almost every aspect of the tree seems extraordinarily beautiful. The foliage, its most remarkable asset, emerges reddish-purple in the spring then matures to a blue-green color. The heart-shaped leaves flicker in the summer breeze. In fall, the foliage turns yellow with hints of apricot and brown. The intriguing fragrance of the falling leaves suggests toffee or carmel. Katsuratree typically has picturesque multiple trunks and attractive bark. Its shape is pyramidal when young, but it develops a broad-spreading crown at maturity. This large tree reaches well over a hundred feet in its native Japan and China but will grow to a lesser size in Michigan. A large specimen is unforgettable—in every way.

Bloom Period and Seasonal Color
Small flowers; blue-green summer foliage; yellow to orange fall color.

Mature Height × Spread
40 to 60 ft. × 20 to 50 ft.

Zones
To Zone 4

Kentucky Coffeetree
Gymnocladus dioicus

Some trees are just misunderstood, and the Kentucky coffeetree is one of them. With its stark winter habit, knobby branches, and scaly bark, it looks like a page from a Dr. Seuss storybook. It remains bare for nearly six months of the year; it leafs out late and drops its leaves early in the fall. The time in between is remarkable as new growth emerges with pink tones, changes to a bluish-green, and, finally, a clear yellow. The immense leaves are composed of numerous smaller leaflets. Female trees produce large leathery seedpods that hang from the tree throughout the winter. The seeds, toxic if eaten raw, were roasted by early settlers for a coffee substitute. If you appreciate "character," you'll love this eccentric but beautiful tree.

Bloom Period and Seasonal Color
Attractive green foliage; yellow fall color; unique coarse winter habit.

Mature Height × Spread
60 to 75 ft. × 40 to 50 ft.

When, Where, and How to Plant
Plant in spring or fall, in full sun. It is adaptable to a wide range of soil conditions from moist areas to drought situations, including alkaline soils. Be aware that the coffeetree grows slowly, but it reaches a large size and needs adequate room to develop. Follow the general directions for planting trees on page 190.

Growing Tips
Keep the root zone of newly planted trees moist until established. Mulch after planting with 2 to 3 in. of organic mulch. Consult page 191 for information on tree fertilization.

Care
The coffeetree has few insect pests or diseases. Prune only to remove dead, diseased, or broken limbs. Prune in the dormant season; trees will bleed sap at other times of the year. Remove suckers that emerge at the base of the tree or close to the trunk. The fruits on female trees and large leaf stalks that support the many leaflets drop in mass and require periodic cleanup throughout the year.

Landscape Merit
The large divided leaves cast a light shade, enabling turfgrass to grow beneath its canopy and making Kentucky coffeetree a good suburban lawn tree. A tough tree, it withstands urban conditions and should be planted more extensively.

We Recommend
Plant the species.

Littleleaf Linden

Tilia cordata

When, Where, and How to Plant

Plant in the spring or fall. Choose full-sun locations for best growth and development. This linden is quite adaptable to high-pH soils but prefers a moist, well-drained soil and will not tolerate excessively wet conditions. Plant following the general tree-planting instructions on page 190. In heavy or poor soils, plant so that the top of the root system is 3 to 4 in. above the surrounding grade.

Growing Tips

Keep the rootball of newly planted trees moist until established. Mulch after planting with 2 to 3 in. of organic mulch. See page 191 for information on tree fertilization.

Care

Littleleaf linden is generally trouble-free, with few insect or disease problems. Water in drought periods because spider mites can become a problem on stressed trees. Linden aphid is also a troublesome pest but rarely causes enough damage to warrant control. Japanese beetles have become a problem recently, causing leaves to become an unattractive brown color. For controls, check with your extension agent.

Landscape Merit

Reaching a height of 60 to 70 ft., littleleaf linden is urban-tolerant and thrives in difficult sites where few trees can. While its primary use is as a specimen or street tree, it is good choice for large cement planters. It can be pruned and trained into a remarkable tall hedge for screening or privacy.

We Recommend

'Greenspire' is the most popular selection, with a uniform straight trunk and excellent branching habit. 'Glenleven' is a fast-growing selection with a more open habit, reaching 40 ft. in height and 30 ft. in width. The silver linden, *Tilia tomentosa*, is a spectacular shade tree with large heart-shaped leaves that are dark green on top and silvery white on the bottom. It is a much larger tree than the littleleaf linden, reaching 80 ft. or more in height, and it produces a mass of fragrant flowers in June. The silver linden is hardy to Zone 4.

The best street trees are both resilient and beautiful. A lovely tree often planted along our city streets is the littleleaf linden. Small dark-green heart-shaped leaves grace this rather uniform pyramidal tree, making it an elegant charmer in the urban jungle. Fragrant flowers appear in midsummer, visually hidden by the foliage but easy to find with the nose. The pendulous yellow flowers hang from the tree, perfuming the air and drawing throngs of bees to their nectar. In the fall, clusters of tiny pea-shaped fruits hang delicately from a papery bract, adding another form of ornamentation. The littleleaf linden is the perfect street, lawn, or specimen tree, with many cultivars available that fit easily into the small landscape.

Bloom Period and Seasonal Color

Fragrant yellow flowers in midsummer.

Mature Height × Spread

60 to 70 ft. × 30 to 60 ft.

Norway Spruce

Picea abies

The Norway spruce was once a popular tree for new homesteads and farmhouses, where there was a need for a fast-growing tree that would develop into a tough windbreak. In more recent years, the Colorado blue spruce has become the evergreen tree of choice. This is unfortunate, because the Norway spruce offers grace and beauty beyond that of the metallic blue spruces. Norway spruce is a large, majestic tree, reaching sixty feet or more in height and with a pyramidal habit. Among the finest of evergreen trees for winter color, the dark-green needles are borne on stiff, flat branches. As the tree matures, the needles hang down gracefully from long, arching branches that come off the main trunk in ski-slope fashion.

Bloom Period and Seasonal Color
Dark evergreen needles.

Mature Height × Spread
40 to 60 ft. × 25 to 30 ft.

When, Where, and How to Plant
Plant in spring or fall, in full sun, allowing enough room for this large tree to grow. Norway spruce prefers a moist, slightly acidic soil and will suffer in poor drainage conditions. Avoid planting near sidewalks or along roads. The tree is not tolerant of salt and is easily burned; that is, the salt spray causes a foliar burn. Plant following the general instructions on page 190.

Growing Tips
Water to help new trees become established, especially before the onset of winter. Mulch after planting with 2 to 3 in. of organic material. A well-watered tree in the fall will mean enough moisture for the needles in the winter. Consult page 191 for information on tree fertilization.

Care
The fungus *Cytospora* causes the browning and death of branches. It usually appears on the lower branches and works its way up. Remove infected branches by cutting them back to the main trunk. Help prevent infections of this canker by mulching around newly planted trees to discourage the grass and weed growth that limits air movement. The spruce gall aphid is an occasional pest of Norway spruce, causing a woody cone-shaped growth to form on the branches of the tree. The growths are generally not life-threatening.

Landscape Merit
The Norway spruce still makes a protective windbreak. Space trees 18 to 20 ft. apart. The long, sloping branches will eventually intertwine. The dark evergreen needles of the Norway spruce are an effective backdrop for shrubs with colorful bark, winter stems, or early-spring flowers. Use in combination with the 'Arnold Promise' witchhazel or the colorful twigs of the redtwig dogwood.

We Recommend
The Serbian spruce, *Picea omorika*, is a beautiful evergreen with a slender trunk supporting short, drooping branches with glossy dark-green needles. It reaches a height of 50 to 60 ft. The Oriental spruce, *Picea orientalis*, has the shortest needles of the spruces, forming a dense, narrow tree with very dark-green foliage.

Pagoda Dogwood
Cornus alternifolia

When, Where, and How to Plant

Spring planting is best for the pagoda dogwood. Fall planting is less apt to be successful. Plant in partial to full shade; this plant will suffer in full sun and drought conditions. Morning sun and afternoon shade is ideal. Choose a location with moist, well-drained soil. Pagoda dogwood will not tolerate standing water for long periods of time. Avoid planting in narrow or confined spaces where its horizontal growth would be restricted. Plant trees following the general directions on page 190.

Growing Tips

Keep the root zone of newly planted trees moist. Mulch after planting with 2 to 3 in. of organic mulch to cool the root zone and conserve moisture. The pagoda dogwood will not tolerate drought and hot conditions so water deeply when these conditions prevail. Consult page 191 for general instructions on fertilization. In high pH soil, an acid-based fertilizer would benefit plants.

Care

If sited correctly, pagoda dogwood is pest- and disease-resistant. A canker disease can cause stem and branch dieback. Remove infected branches if they appear. Avoid pruning or you'll risk destroying the elegant branching structure. If you provide sufficient space, no pruning will be necessary.

Landscape Merit

The pagoda dogwood is particularly effective when combined with vertical elements in the garden such as columnar evergreens or upright deciduous trees. It also helps break the starkness of a wall or brick surface. Use this dogwood for planting in a shady woodland setting where it finds itself right at home. Under mature shade trees, combine pagoda dogwood with Siberian bugloss and ferns. Add snowdrops for early spring cheer.

We Recommend

Cornus controversa, the giant dogwood, is a larger-sized version of the pagoda dogwood. It reaches 30 to 45 ft. with the same picturesque horizontal branching habit, large white flat-topped flowers, and bluish late-summer fruits. This Asian dogwood does well in full sun.

A noteworthy tree for its abundance of bloom and picturesque branching habit, the pagoda dogwood is a neglected native that unfortunately plays second fiddle to its close relative, the flowering dogwood, Cornus florida. The most remarkable feature of this Michigan woodland native is its tiered branching habit that reveals itself in the winter season. The horizontal branches, each stretching outward and upward, appear in a sequence of layers. Creamy-white flat-topped blooms appear in the late spring on the upturned ends of branches. By October, they produce bluish fruits that are relished by birds. The fall color is a deep wine-red. With a recent upsurge of interest in native plants and naturalistic gardens, the pagoda dogwood is quickly gaining a devoted following.

Other Name
Alternate-leaf Dogwood

Bloom Period and Seasonal Color
Creamy-white flowers in late spring; wine-red fall color.

Mature Height × Spread
16 to 25 ft. × 20 to 30 ft.

Paperbark Maple
Acer griseum

A rare tree of immeasurable beauty, the paperbark maple is named for its most memorable feature. Paper-thin sheets of bark peel off the tree, revealing cinnamon-orange colors that create an unrivaled winter display. Three-part dark-green leaves are attractive in the summer months and turn bright orange-red in fall. The tree's small size and slow growth are ideal for small landscapes where four-season appeal is desired. Paperbark maple is difficult to propagate because it rarely produces viable seed, and it is difficult to grow by other means. Because of this and the fact that it grows so slowly, it is usually expensive. But paperbark maple is a first-rate plant that will provide years of enjoyment and will make you the envy of your neighbors.

Bloom Period and Seasonal Color
Cinnamon-brown bark; orange-red fall color.

Mature Height × Spread
20 to 30 ft. × 10 to 30 ft.

Zones
To Zone 4

When, Where, and How to Plant
Plant in the spring, as fall planting is generally less successful. Plant in full sun to partial shade, but protect from hot afternoon sun. The tree prefers a well-drained soil and will not tolerate compacted or hard ground beneath its canopy. Follow the general directions for tree planting on page 190.

Growing Tips
Keep the rootball of newly planted trees moist. Water during drought periods, and mulch with 2 to 3 in. of organic mulch around the base of the tree to conserve moisture and protect the maple's shallow root system. Consult page 191 for information on fertilizing trees.

Care
Paperbark maple has no serious pest or disease problems. Pruning should be unnecessary except to remove the occasional dead branch.

Landscape Merit
Reaching a height of 20 to 30 ft., paperbark maple is especially valuable for use on a patio, in a doorway garden, or in a small courtyard. The peeling bark is especially appreciated on multistemmed trees that create fantastic garden focal points with year-round appeal. The pretty foliage of the Alleghany spurge, *Pachysandra procumbens*, makes an elegant groundcover beneath this tree.

We Recommend
Paperbark maple can be difficult to find, but it is often available from small mail-order nurseries (see the source guide on page 234). If you have patience, a small plant will transplant better and be more economical. There are two other beautiful three-leaf maples. The three-flowered maple, *Acer triflorum*, has excellent cinnamon-red bark, and its foliage turns an outstanding orange to carmine-red coloring. It is easier to transplant than the paperbark maple (it is for Zones 5 and 6), but unfortunately, it is just as rare in commerce. The Maximowicz maple, *A. maximowiczianum*, rounds out the "big three" of trifoliate maples. This small tree with a vase-shaped habit and attractive summer foliage turns a brilliant scarlet-red in fall. Reaching a mature height of 20 to 30 ft., this rare tree is perfect for a small garden.

Pawpaw

Asimina triloba

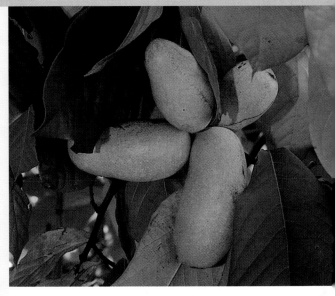

When, Where, and How to Plant

Plant in the spring, as fall planting generally yields poor results. Pawpaws like moist, slightly acidic soils. Partial shade is ideal but sun is tolerated. You will likely have to acquire your pawpaw through mail-order sources; local nurseries do not generally carry them because the taproot makes field-grown pawpaw a risky venture. Mail-order trees should be planted while dormant and given shade and adequate water as they get established. See page 190 for general directions on tree planting.

Growing Tips

Water pawpaw deeply to help establish the long taproot that will later serve the plant well in times of drought. Mulch to conserve moisture. Young trees in the sapling stage need protection from direct sun or their leaves will get sunburned. Provide a burlap screen on the west side of full sun plantings for the first two or more years of development. Consult page 191 for information on tree fertilization.

Care

There are few pests and diseases of pawpaw, in part due to an amazing ability to ward off attack through natural chemical compounds found in the stems and foliage of the tree.

Landscape Merit

Plant pawpaw as an unusual lawn specimen or in a shady shrub border. The natural habit of the tree results in the production of sprouts from its roots. The sprouts form large thickets that are commonly referred to as pawpaw patches. These patches make for a marvelous naturalistic planting for larger landscapes where a privacy barrier or screening is desired.

We Recommend

Plant more than one pawpaw to increase the chances for cross-pollination and fruit set. Lone trees rarely produce fruit. 'Sunflower' is a self-fertile clone with large fruit with butter-colored flesh, reportedly quite tasty. 'Taylor' and 'Taytoo' are cultivated varieties originally collected from the wild near Eaton Rapids, Michigan. These two cultivars have light-green skin and tasty yellow flesh. Their names honor J. Lee Taylor, professor emeritus of the Michigan State University Horticulture Department, and his wife, Jane, founder of the Michigan 4-H Children's Garden.

Michigan's most delectable tree thrives in the rich river basins of the Lower Peninsula. In the wild, a pawpaw tree is amazing to see with its lush tropical-looking foliage hanging downward. The curious reddish-maroon flowers appear in May, nodding like bells from the branches. For over one hundred years, people have sought to domesticate pawpaw for its most famous feature, its large custard-like fruit. The fruit is an acquired taste for some and immediately delicious to others—but the fruit is not the only reason to grow pawpaw. It has wonderful features that make it an exceptional tree for large or small landscapes. It grows into a pyramidal tree reaching up to twenty-five feet tall, and its luxuriant green leaves turn butter-yellow in the fall.

Bloom Period and Seasonal Color

Maroon flowers in spring; yellow fall color.

Mature Height × Spread

15 to 25 ft. × 15 to 20 ft.

Zones

To Zone 5

Redbud
Cercis canadensis

In May, after the shadblow has bloomed, the small pink flowers of the redbud open into a cloud of rosy pink that shines brightly against the tree's dark, leafless branches. The redbud is one of our most beautiful spring-flowering trees. The foliage is elegant and emerges with reddish tones, gradually becoming green with a distinct heart-shaped outline. The leaves have variable fall color, often an attractive yellow. The redbud has a unique feature called cauliflory, which is the ability to produce flower buds on older wood. This is how even old gnarled stems of the tree can produce small reddish-purple flowers every spring. The redbud is a small tree with a short trunk and wide-spreading lower branches that make a spring garden memorable.

Bloom Period and Seasonal Color
Rose-pink flower in spring.

Mature Height × Spread
20 to 30 ft. × 25 to 35 ft.

Zones
To Zone 5

When, Where, and How to Plant
Plant the redbud in spring or fall. It tolerates shady areas and sites that receive a half-day of full sun. Plants in full sun grow with more vigor and produce more flowers. Redbud is highly sensitive to salt, so avoid planting in areas near salted walks or driveways. The tree is pH-adaptable but is not tolerant of poorly drained or heavy soils. Plant following the general advice on page 190.

Growing Tips
Keep the root zone of newly planted trees moist until established. Water during extended dry spells. Mulch after planting with 2 to 3 in. of organic material to conserve moisture.

Care
The redbud grows vigorously as a young tree but slows down with age; its typical life span is thirty to fifty years. Older trees become susceptible to canker that kills larger limbs. Remove infected limbs if they appear. *Verticillium* wilt is a soilborne fungus that results in branch dieback and, eventually, in the tree's death. There is no guaranteed method of control for the fungus at this time. Trees produce papery brown pods that can be a nuisance to clean up on a patio or in an outdoor living area.

Landscape Merit
Redbud makes a wonderful small specimen tree. It reaches a height of 20 to 30 ft. with a slightly greater spread. Underplant with a sweep of groundcover. Try bigroot geranium and dwarf Chinese astilbe to continue a pink theme. It's also a nice addition to a partially shaded mixed border.

We Recommend
Not all redbuds are adaptable to Michigan's climate. When choosing a tree at a nursery, ask about the seed source or region where the tree originated. Plants from Georgia or Tennessee will suffer in our climate. A cultivar called 'Royal White' has large white flowers. It was selected from a wild population in Illinois and is hardy to the southern half of Michigan's Lower Peninsula.

River Birch

Betula nigra

When, Where, and How to Plant

Plant in spring or fall. Plant in full sun for best performance and winter light effects. Moist, fertile, well-drained soils are preferred, but river birch will tolerate drier soils. It can be planted in low, wet areas of the garden and is generally adaptable to most soil types except those that are alkaline with a pH over 7.0. Follow the general instructions for planting trees on page 190.

Growing Tips

Keep newly planted trees moist until established. Mulch with a 3-in. layer of organic mulch to conserve moisture. Plants may experience leaf yellowing or chlorosis in alkaline soils of 7.0 pH or higher. In this event, an acid-based fertilizer would be beneficial. Consult page 191 for information on fertilizing trees.

Care

River birch is resistant to problems that plague the white-barked birches. Nevertheless, birch leafminer is occasionally a pest of the river birch. The adult females lay eggs in the leaves, hatching small larvae that eat the tissue between the upper and lower leaf surfaces. This mining activity causes the leaf surface to turn brown. Orthene™ is the recommended chemical control for leafminer. Apply in mid-May as the larvae begin feeding. Use according to the manufacturer's recommended rates.

Landscape Merit

While many trees need adequate space to develop without competition, the river birch is dramatic in naturalistic grove plantings, where single-stem trees are spaced 20 ft. or less apart and the canopies intertwine. A multistemmed specimen tree looks fantastic in winter with a grouping of red-berried Michigan holly, or surrounded by the evergreen creeping juniper.

We Recommend

Because the degree of exfoliating bark varies from tree to tree, it is best to purchase trees that already exhibit showy bark. Heritage™ is an exceptional tree with handsome peeling bark and dark-green glossy foliage, which, at times, turns to an impressive yellow in the fall.

In the middle of a Michigan winter, the gardener's eye moves upward from the snow-covered plants at ground level to the remarkable architectural beauty of trees that have exceptional form, bark, and structure. The river birch, found along streams and in wet areas in the wild, has a flaky whitish-brown to cinnamon-brown exfoliating bark that is very showy during the winter months. At maturity, this tree can reach forty to seventy feet in height, forming a rounded crown. Multistemmed specimens are particularly effective because you get "more bang for your buck"—that is, more trunks and stems with an attractive winter habit. Use it as a specimen plant in a prime spot in the garden where its warm bark colors will take away the winter chill.

Bloom Period and Seasonal Color
Showy exfoliating bark.

Mature Height × Spread
40 to 70 ft. × 40 to 60 ft.

Zones
To Zone 4

Saucer Magnolia
Magnolia × soulangiana

Magnolias are the aristocrats of spring-blooming trees. The large saucer-shaped flowers appear from fuzzy gray buds and seem to float on the upturned branches of the tree like water lilies on the surface of a pond. The large flowers can be five to ten inches wide and appear white suffused with pink or rose colors. The saucer magnolia has a multistemmed habit that forms a broad, rounded tree reaching twenty to thirty feet in height. The smooth gray bark is highly ornamental in the winter months as are the fuzzy buds that terminate the branches. Plant it as a specimen tree or in a mass to create an unrivaled spring-blooming display. Site your magnolia carefully to avoid losing the gorgeous flowers to a late frost.

Bloom Period and Seasonal Color
White to rose-pink in spring.

Mature Height × Spread
20 to 30 ft. × 20 to 30 ft.

Zones
To Zone 4

When, Where, and How to Plant
Plant in the spring; magnolias are among the more difficult trees and shrubs to transplant. Fall planting should be avoided. Plant in full sun to promote strong flowering. Avoid placing the trees in warm southern exposures; plant in a northern exposure to keep the buds tight and protected until the danger of late frost has passed. Magnolia roots will not compete well with those of other plants. Locate your tree where its roots can grow unimpeded. Follow the general instructions for planting trees on page 190.

Growing Tips
Magnolias under the right conditions will thrive with minimal care. Mulch the root zone, and water during prolonged droughts. Consult page 191 for information on tree fertilization.

Care
Prune in early summer after flowering. Do not remove the lower branches of the saucer magnolia if at all possible; its full pleasing habit is better left alone. Remove vigorous branch shoots that grow straight up from older limbs. These will deplete the main branches of energy and threaten the natural form of the plant. The saucer magnolia is sometimes susceptible to attack by magnolia scale. The scale appears on branches and has a waxy covering over a hard shell-like body. Dormant oil sprays applied before growth begins in the spring will suffocate scales. Light infestations can be removed by hand.

Landscape Merit
Magnolias are effective as a single specimen or in group plantings. They are particularly striking when placed against a dark evergreen background such as the Oriental spruce or the Norway spruce. Drifts of the so-called "minor bulbs," like Siberian squill, make a major impact under a magnolia.

We Recommend
Magnolias, for all their beauty, at times have a limited performance in Michigan landscapes. Their early-blooming habit gets them in trouble, as late frosts can wreak havoc on the flowers of exposed specimens. 'Alexandrina' has deep red-purple blossoms that open later in spring, giving them additional protection against late frost.

When, Where, and How to Plant

Plant in spring or fall. Shadblow is adaptable to different light exposures, from full sun to deep shade. Trees planted in full sun will in general have more blooms and a better fall color. Soils should be well-drained, slightly acidic, and not too wet. Follow the general tree planting instructions on page 190.

Growing Tips

Keep newly planted trees moist until established. Mulch after planting with 2 to 3 in. of organic material. Consult page 191 for advice on fertilization.

Care

The shadblow sometimes experiences problems with the bacteria called fireblight; in summer, branches or shoots die back, looking as if they have been scorched by fire. The characteristic "shepherd's crook" or curved terminal stem alerts you to the infection. There is no guaranteed cure for this disease, but you should remove infected branches. Disinfect your pruners after each cut with isopropyl alcohol to prevent spreading the disease. Avoid fertilizing, because excess nitrogen will produce soft new growth, which is more susceptible to the spread of the bacteria. Provide protection from rabbits the first few years after planting. Surround small plants with chicken wire screening supported by bamboo canes.

Landscape Merit

Shadblow is a wonderful small tree for entrance gardens, patio plantings, or shrub borders. The fleeting white delicate flowers of shadblow are enhanced by a backdrop of dark evergreens, which bring the clear white blossoms into focus. A grouping of dark spreading yews is very effective in contrast to the smooth gray bark. In a small garden, underplant with Canadian wild ginger, ferns, and windflower.

We Recommend

Amelanchier arborea is a larger tree-sized serviceberry with the same delightful characteristics, but it generally does not develop the thicket-type growth of *A. canadensis*. It reaches more than 30 ft. in height. The hybrid selection 'Autumn Brilliance' is a wonderful tree form that has brilliant red fall color and beautiful spring blossoms and summer fruits.

Among our native trees, few can match the four-season appeal of the amelanchier, also called shadblow. It often occurs as an understory plant in woodlands, where its delicate white flowers appear on the gray branches well before spring truly kicks into gear. In June the early flowers produce purplish-black fruits that are treasured by birds and humans alike. Shadblow in fall is remarkable for its myriad of leaf colors ranging from yellow to orange-red. The winter months expose the smooth gray reflective bark that is spectacular on specimens with a multistemmed habit. The smaller size of shadblow makes it perfect for small gardens and for use in patio plantings. Group plantings work well in naturalized landscape plantings where the bountiful fruits draw wildlife to the garden.

Other Names

Amelanchier, Serviceberry

Bloom Period and Seasonal Color

White flowers in early spring; yellow to red fall color.

Mature Height × Spread

15 to 20 ft. × 10 to 15 ft.

Sugar Maple

Acer saccharum

Few native Michigan trees can rival sugar maple for its fall color display. Thousands of tourists flock to the northern parts of the state to take in the fiery splashes ranging from orange to red and yellow. While the sugar maple is a major component of the moist woods of Michigan, it has been neglected by homeowners in favor of trees that may have fancier names but not as much beauty. While the fall display is hard to beat, the sugar maple is a four-season tree. Spring brings forth light-yellow flowers that contrast beautifully with the dark bark of older mature specimens. The sugar maple in summer produces a cool leafy canopy, which brings welcome shade to our homes.

Bloom Period and Seasonal Color
Yellow flowers, late April to early May; colorful fall foliage.

Mature Height × Spread
60 to 75 ft. × 40 ft.

When, Where, and How to Plant
Transplant as a balled-and-burlapped or container-ized tree in fall or spring. Choose a site in full sun or partial shade with moist, well-drained soil. Plant this tree where it has room to grow and where it will receive little root disturbance. Follow the general directions for planting trees on page 190. Avoid planting too deeply, or roots may grow horizontally, circling other main roots and causing the tree to decline.

Growing Tips
Water the tree during the first few years of establishment, and mulch around its base to conserve moisture. Mulching also protects the young bark of sugar maples from damage caused by lawn mowers. Wounds to the trunks are entry points for fungi that cause trunk decay and eventual death. Consult page 191 for information on fertilization.

Care
Trees should not be used near sidewalks or driveways where excessive de-icing salts are used. Stressed trees may suffer from *Verticillium* wilt, a fungus that is found in the soil and enters the plant through its roots. It moves into the tissues that conduct water and food, disrupting their function and causing portions of the tree to die as the fungus spreads. Encourage healthy growth by watering during droughts and fertilizing in the late fall.

Landscape Merit
Use sugar maple primarily as a shade and lawn tree. It deserves all the space it needs but can be underplanted as it matures with shade-tolerant perennials. Its widespread surface roots and dense shade prevent turfgrass from establishing underneath its canopy.

We Recommend
One of the toughest urban-tolerant sugar maple cultivars is 'Legacy'. Known for its dark-green leathery foliage, this selection has proven to be a vigorous grower with good yellow to orange fall color. 'Morton' or Crescendo™ is a newer selection that has received good reviews in the Midwest. It exhibits excellent heat and drought tolerance and superb orange-red fall color.

When, Where, and How to Plant

Plant in the spring, as fall planting is generally less successful. Sweetgum prefers full sun and a deep, moist, acidic soil. Plant in an open area because root development will suffer in a confined space. The coarse, thick, fleshy roots of the sweetgum make it a challenge to transplant successfully. Plant smaller trees that have been root-pruned in the nursery or are grown in a container. Follow the general planting instructions on page 190.

Growing Tips

To aid establishment, keep the rootball moist. Mulch after planting with 2 to 3 in. of organic material. If chlorosis or leaf yellowing develops as a result of high soil pH, fertilize using a formulation known to have an acidic reaction, following the manufacturer's instructions. Mulch every year with composted oak leaves and pine needles to lower the soil pH.

Care

Its strong central leader maintains the symmetrical form of this tree. Do not prune or alter the central leader or the pyramidal habit may be lost. The roots of older trees will eventually rise to the surface and should be covered with mulch to protect them from lawn mowers. You may need to rake up the woody seed capsules that can jam or clog lawn mowers. Provide a large mulch ring and let the fruits collect on your wood chips instead of on your lawn. Sweetgum is pest- and disease-free.

Landscape Merit

Sweetgum's primary use is as a lawn or street tree. Avoid planting in confined spaces.

We Recommend

The sweetgum has many cultivated varieties available, but not all are adaptable to Michigan's climate. When choosing a tree at a nursery, be sure to ask about the seed source or region of origin of the tree. 'Moraine' is a northern selection hardy to Zone 5 with an upright oval habit and brilliant red to yellow fall color.

The American sweetgum has many virtues. For foliage quality alone, this large shade tree rates as one of our outstanding North American trees. The glossy leaves are star-shaped and resemble the maple, for which it is often mistaken. The fall color is a blend of yellow to purple to red and can be quite spectacular in open, full-sun plantings. The stems often have corky ridges that aid in their identification and provide winter interest. If it has a fault, it's the fruits—spiky woody seed capsules that hang from the branches like ornaments. After they fall, the fruit can be a prickly nuisance for the barefoot crowd, so site your sweetgum in an open area and provide a large mulch ring.

Bloom Period and Seasonal Color
Lustrous green foliage with beautiful fall color.

Mature Height × Spread
60 to 75 ft. × 40 to 50 ft.

Zones
To Zone 5

Tuliptree

Liriodendron tulipifera

The tuliptree is among the largest of the eastern North American trees and grows naturally in the southern half of the Lower Peninsula. In moist forests, it has an impressive straight trunk with dark-gray deeply furrowed bark. Few have witnessed the unique flowers of the tuliptree because they are simply too high in the canopy for easy viewing. There is a debate over whether the tree gets its common name from the resemblance of the flowers or the foliage to the tulip. The rarely-seen flowers have a tulip shape with six yellow petals flushed bright orange at the base. The foliage, somewhat tulip-shaped in outline, is bright green in the summer with spectacular golden-yellow fall color.

Bloom Period and Seasonal Color
Yellow flowers in late spring.

Mature Height × Spread
70 to 90 ft. × 35 to 50 ft.

Zones
To Zone 4

When, Where, and How to Plant

Plant in the spring, in full-sun locations that have deep, rich, well-drained soil. Place well away from the house because large limbs are susceptible to breakage from storms and the roots are very aggressive. The tuliptree is generally difficult to transplant. Plant smaller trees that have been root-pruned in the nursery or are grown in a container. When planting, retain as much of the root system as possible. Follow the general instructions for planting trees on page 190.

Growing Tips

The tuliptree will suffer in hot, dry periods; water well during establishment, and mulch the root zone. Follow the general instructions for tree fertilization on page 191.

Care

Young plants are particularly susceptible to sunscald, so wrap the trunk during the winter with a paper tree wrap. Start at the bottom, overlapping the paper so that it covers the entire exposed trunk up to the side branches. Trees are susceptible to *Verticillium* wilt, a fungus that is found in the soil and enters the plant through its roots, eventually causing parts of the tree to wilt. Remove all infected branches, and burn them. Promote good health through watering in drought periods and fertilizing in late fall. Aphids are not uncommon on tuliptree foliage. They excrete a substance called honeydew. Honeydew is the growing substrate for sooty mold, a fungus that causes the twigs or leaves to turn black. This isn't life-threatening for the tree, but the honeydew can drip on cars, making a mess. Aphids can be controlled by chemical sprays, but this is not recommended. They have natural predators that should keep their population levels under control.

Landscape Merit

Homeowners can use the tuliptree as a lone specimen in a large open lawn or plant many together to create a tall canopy and a woodland effect. It makes a first-rate shade tree for those who can handle its eventual size of 70 to 90 ft.

We Recommend

Plant the species.

When, Where, and How to Plant

Plant in spring or fall, in full sun. Plant far away from buildings or they may interfere with the spread of this large tree. White ash is adaptable to a wide range of soils but prefers good drainage and may require watering in periods of prolonged drought. Follow the general planting instructions for trees on page 190. Because ash trees in metro Detroit have suffered a decline recently, we recommend you consult your county extension office for the latest information and recommendation before deciding to plant an ash tree in that area.

Growing Tips

Keep newly planted trees well-watered until established. A 3-in. layer of organic mulch will help conserve moisture. Consult page 191 for information on fertilizing trees.

Care

Vigorous white ash trees that are sited correctly are normally not bothered by pests and diseases, but trees under stress are susceptible to attack. The ash-lilac borer can be a serious pest of the white ash, particularly if trees are allowed to come under drought stress. The insect appears in two stages, an adult stage that deposits eggs into the tree and a larval stage, which tunnels through the wood and causes damage. It is important to control both stages of this insect as they appear. Pheromone traps attract and capture the adult moth. Monitoring population levels will alert you to when it is time to take control measures. Consult your local extension service for current control recommendations.

Landscape Merit

The white ash is a large tree more suited for use in open lawns or around homes that have enough space to accommodate its height of 50 to 60 ft. and open, spreading branches.

We Recommend

Some outstanding selections are available for lawn and street tree plantings. 'Autumn Purple' is the most popular selection of the white ash. It has superior, long-lasting fall color that is reddish-purple. The summer foliage is a glossy green produced on a tree that reaches 45 to 60 ft. in height. 'Chicago Regal' is the perfect choice for narrow street tree plantings with its upright narrow growth habit and purple fall color.

In Michigan's magnificent hardwood forests, it's easy to become mesmerized by the incredible size and strength of our native trees. The white ash is easily recognizable among these giants by its straight trunk with conspicuous diamond-shaped furrows and forked ridges. While content to develop into a towering tree in a mixed native canopy, the white ash also has value as a solitary specimen in gardens or in an allee along city streets. Its attractive compound leaves provide valued shade and subtle fall colors of yellow to purple and maroon. The winged seeds of the ash hang in bunches, persisting through the winter season and then tumbling down to the ground, often creating a mess. For the home landscape, look for smaller, seedless cultivars.

Bloom Period and Seasonal Color

Deep-green summer foliage, yellow to purple and maroon fall color.

Mature Height × Spread

50 to 60 ft. × 50 to 60 ft.

White Fir

Abies concolor

Evergreen trees are valuable in the winter landscape, both for the color they offer and for the protection they give from harsh winter winds. An outstanding but under-utilized evergreen tree is the white fir. Often found in arboreta and botanical gardens, it still has limited avail-ability in the nursery trade. It forms a large tree, reaching thirty to fifty feet or more with a narrow, pyramidal habit. The bluish-green needles are very colorful and have a unique way of curving upward off the stem as if reaching for the sky. The waxy needles are extremely tough and rarely experience yellowing or winterburn. The branches of this stately conifer are whorled and cast a dense shade. A large tree is stunning on a winter day.

Other Name
Concolor Fir

Bloom Period and Seasonal Color
Attractive bluish-green evergreen needles.

Mature Height × Spread
30 to 50 ft. × 15 to 30 ft.

When, Where, and How to Plant

Plant in spring. Avoid late-fall planting, which may not leave enough time for root development before winter. Plant in full sun in a rich, moist, well-drained soil. Heavy clay soils with poor drainage and high alkalinity (pH) will not work for this tree. Plant smaller-sized trees to ensure better success. Larger balled-and-burlapped trees are difficult to transplant successfully. Follow the general planting instructions on page 190.

Growing Tips

Although this tree is known for its tolerance of hot, dry conditions, it will need help the first few years of establishment. Water in prolonged periods of drought and in the fall before the soil freezes. Consult page 191 for tree fertilization information.

Care

In windy exposed situations you may want to erect a burlap screen on the windward side of the plant to prevent windburn. This will be needed only the first few years as the tree becomes established. Pruning is generally not required. The main stem or leader of the plant should never be cut or topped, or the pyramidal form of the tree will be lost. Look for plants in the nursery that have a single or main trunk and a low branching habit already well established. White fir is pest- and disease-free.

Landscape Merit

These trees are appropriate for larger landscapes and are effective as screens or privacy plantings. Use them as a backdrop for deciduous hollies or the colorful stems of the redosier or gray dogwood. They also combine well with spring-blooming shrubs such as forsythia and the 'Arnold Promise' witchhazel. White fir can also be used as a tall hedge, but this requires continual pruning.

We Recommend

Abies concolor is considered the best fir for the Midwest. The Nordmann fir, *Abies nordmanniana*, is another exceptional dark-needled fir that has performed well on the campus of Michigan State University. It reaches 40 to 60 ft. with a narrow, pyramidal habit. It is available through mail-order nurseries.

When, Where, and How to Plant

Plant in the spring. White oaks prefer well-drained, slightly acidic soil. Oaks are somewhat difficult to transplant because of their thick, fleshy taproots. Plant trees whose trunks are 3 in. in diameter or smaller to lessen the likelihood of transplant shock. Plant in full sun, and allow enough room for these trees to develop. Follow the general instructions for tree planting on page 190.

Growing Tips

The white oak is somewhat drought-tolerant, but it will need water as it becomes established. Mulch after planting with 2 to 3 in. of organic mulch. Consult page 191 for information on tree fertilization.

Care

Gypsy moths relish oak leaves and therefore represent a threat, sometimes causing repeated defoliation. A certified arborist may be contracted to spray your trees if damage warrants control. Several new biological controls may someday prove effective in curbing the voracious feeding of this imported pest. Oak wilt, a fungus, may be a problem, especially on red oaks. Symptoms include wilting leaves that turn brown. Prune oaks only while dormant because fresh pruning cuts during the growing season attract the bark beetles that spread this disease.

Landscape Merit

This is a specimen shade tree. Plant away from your house or other buildings that would eventually become engulfed by trees planted close by. Oaks placed in open areas will develop into impressive trees that may someday provide shade for family gatherings at picnic tables.

We Recommend

The chinkapin oak, *Quercus muhlenbergii*, is one of the few native oaks that is tolerant of alkaline soils. The leaves have beautiful wavy margins and a lightish underside. Like the white oaks, the chinkapin grows tall and wide. The red oak, *Quercus rubra*, is also a Michigan native but grows at a faster rate and generally occupies moister sites. The large leaves with their distinct pointed lobes turn a beautiful red in fall.

The oaks have been long recognized as symbols of strength and durability. These impressive giants are unparalleled in their architectural beauty. A large oak tree connects us to our past and future, as many trees grow to be more than five hundred years old. The white oak, a native tree common throughout the Lower Peninsula, is particularly notable for its tremendous girth and wide-spreading horizontal branches. The emerging leaves and flowers appear together in soft-pink and pastel colors. The crimson fall color of the leaves ushers in cooler temperatures. Gardeners with a small residential lot may not be able to accommodate an oak, but others who have open land can plant grand, majestic trees—and will be doing future generations a great favor.

Bloom Period and Seasonal Color

Crimson fall color.

Mature Height × Spread

50 to 80 ft. × 50 to 80 ft.

White Pine

Pinus strobus

To catch a glimpse of Michigan's past, travel to Hartwick Pines State Park near Grayling. You'll see amazing stands of the state tree of Michigan, the white pine. Once a dominant tree in northern Michigan, the white pine was the major species of lumber harvested between 1850 and 1900. In northern parts of the state, large white pines are still a common sight. Their distinctive silhouette of graceful horizontal branches is displayed in a layered fashion on tall, majestic trees. The aromatic blue-green needles have a slightly nodding habit, which gives the tree a weeping effect. White pines planted in the landscape grow quickly, displaying a habit and form that make them valuable as a single specimen tree or as an effective windbreak.

Bloom Period and Seasonal Color
Aromatic blue-green needles.

Mature Height × Spread
50 to 80 ft. × 20 to 40 ft.

When, Where, and How to Plant
Transplant in spring or early fall. Choose locations in full sun and in well-drained soil away from exposure to salt. Wind-blown salt in the form of tiny droplets of water blown off the street can stick to needles and cause burning. Plant following the general instructions on page 190.

Growing Tips
Keep newly planted trees moist, especially going into winter. Mulch after planting with 2 to 3 in. of organic material. Consult page 191 for information on fertilizing trees.

Care
Keeping your pine trees healthy will discourage the development of pests and diseases. Some problems to look out for, however, are white pine weevil and blister rust. The larvae (worms) of the white pine weevil attack the terminal branches of white pine. The symptoms are white drops of a sticky resin on the branches. The adult form of the weevil emerges in late summer, but by this time the shoot is dead. Homeowners should prune out the infected branches by midsummer and burn them. White pine blister rust is a serious disease that causes a canker that will kill individual branches or whole trees if the main trunk becomes infected. You should check with local county extension agents to see if white pine blister rust is a common problem in your area.

Landscape Merit
The white pine is a fast-growing, long-lived tree that can be used in landscapes with enough open space so it can develop properly. Plant it as a single specimen or in naturalistic groupings to form a screen. Trees spaced 25 to 30 ft. apart will form a dense privacy barrier when young; later, the wide-spreading branches will meet in the upper canopy.

We Recommend
'Fastigiata' is a unique form of the white pine with limbs that angle upward instead of horizontally. This prevents ice and snow from accumulating and makes this selection less vulnerable to breakage.

Yellowwood
Cladrastis lutea

When, Where, and How to Plant

Plant in spring, as fall planting is generally less successful. Plant in full sun to partial shade in well-drained soil. Trees suffer in poorly drained, wet soils, so avoid low areas or spots where water accumulates for any length of time. Follow the general directions for tree planting on page 190. In heavy or poor soils, plant the top of the root system 3 to 4 in. above the surrounding grade.

Growing Tips

Keep the rootball of newly planted trees moist until establishment. Consult page 191 for information on tree fertilization. Mulch after planting with 2 to 3 in. of organic material. A mulch ring will protect the trunk from lawn mowers, which may damage the bark. Wounds create entry points for fungus, which attacks the wood and causes rot and decay.

Care

Yellowwood is generally pest- and disease-free. Prune in late fall because spring pruning results in excessive sap flow or bleeding. The yellowwood, with its distinctive vase-shaped habit, tends to develop narrow crotches that are susceptible to breakage over time. This occurs when two branches fork off in opposite directions, forming a weak point as they grow into each other at their point of attachment. Eventually a weak crotch develops, and the trunk splits. When the tree is in its formative stages, prevent narrow crotch angles from developing through selective pruning. Remove the weaker or smaller of two branches that are beginning to compete with each other.

Landscape Merit

The American yellowwood makes a fine specimen tree for properties with enough room for it to grow. Place it where you can enjoy its smooth gray bark in the winter months and its fragrant blooms in early summer.

We Recommend

For the plant collector, 'Rosea' is a pink-flowered form that has not been adequately tested for its cold hardiness in Michigan and is difficult to find. It is available from small mail-order nurseries.

The yellowwood is a moderate-sized shade tree, reaching a height of thirty to fifty feet and a spread of forty feet or more. When you come upon the American yellowwood in full bloom or view the smooth gray bark in the depths of winter, you can begin to appreciate its spectacular beauty. In early summer, fragrant white flowers hang gracefully from the branches in long chains. The tree's graceful appearance continues through the summer with compound leaves that arch out and have a weeping effect. The leaves become a radiant yellow in fall and contrast beautifully with the smooth, reflective gray bark that resembles the bark of the native beech. The upright spreading branches of this tree come off a short trunk, creating an impressive winter scene. The botanical name is synonymous with Cladrastis kentukea.

Bloom Period and Seasonal Color
White flowers in early summer followed by yellow fall foliage.

Mature Height × Spread
30 to 50 ft. × 40 to 50 ft.

Zones
To Zone 4

Woodland Flowers and Ferns

In springtime, the woods of Michigan are a spectacle of natural beauty. Although the tall trees are still bare, signs of life begin to appear as strengthening sunlight filters toward the earth, warming the soil. Soon trillium, cranesbill, and bloodroot push up through the thick mat of leaves and open their pristine flowers toward the sun.

We share the responsibility for preserving and protecting Michigan's native plants, so admire the woodland flowers where they grow but never disturb them. When buying plants for a woodland garden, purchase only nursery-propagated plants or plants that have been rescued with the landowner's permission from sites slated for development.

Cultivating a woodland garden encourages flowers and ferns that may once have grown in the region. You will experience pleasure in seeing these plants in your own backyard, a small but satisfying reflection of Michigan's biodiversity. A woodland garden doesn't have to be large. Even a tiny spot under a shade tree can be effective. The goal of a woodland garden is not to pack it with continuous or overwhelming bloom, but to set a stage for a naturalistic drama.

Responsible Buying

A good source for native plants is a responsible wildflower rescue operation, such as the one at Cranbrook House and Gardens Auxiliary in Bloomfield Hills each spring. Wildflower rescues are also now operating elsewhere in the state.

Otherwise, buy only plants that have been propagated in a nursery, and refuse to buy plants that were dug from the wild. Many of the nurseries in the mail-order source list (see page 234) offer nursery-propagated wildflowers and ferns.

Digging plants on public land is illegal, and anyone collecting plants for his or her own use on private land must have the owner's permission. In addition, the large-flowered white trillium, the Michigan lily, native orchids, and some other plants are protected by the state's Christmas Greens Act.

Beginning Your Woodland Garden

A successful woodland garden mimics the conditions the plants prefer in nature, where they grow amid decaying leaves. These plants prefer a rich soil high in organic material such as leaf

mold or well-rotted compost. This soil retains moisture but drains well and allows air and water to penetrate easily. Nutrients are returned to the soil as the organic material breaks down.

After setting plants into the ground, firm the soil and water well. A mulch of pine needles, shredded leaves, or shredded bark will conserve moisture and discourage weeds from growing while the wildflowers and ferns get established. Continue to water during dry periods. In a humus-rich soil, most woodland plants will not require additional fertilizer. They will appreciate an annual mulch of shredded leaves, mimicking conditions where they grow naturally.

We selected plants for this chapter that are easy to grow and generally free of insect pests and disease. As a category, woodland wildflowers tend to be quite carefree, requiring minimal maintenance. If desired, you can usually divide them in the spring to increase your supply, but regular division is not as crucial as with many more demanding perennials.

For more information about native plants, see Gardening with Native Plants, page 250.

Creating a Woodland Garden

Wildflowers and ferns are at home in many sections of the garden, where they make happy companions to bulbs like daffodils, snowdrops, winter aconite, and windflower. The bulbs' colorful flowers precede or complement the delicate pinks, blues, and whites of many native spring blooms. Add further interest to the woodland garden by creating winding paths with natural materials such as pine needles or wood chips. A curving walk draws visitors into the scene and invites them to enjoy a closer look at the flowers, many of which are small.

Most woodland plants are low growing and look most natural under tall trees. You may, however, design an island bed in a shady area or tuck a few plants in the shade near the house, combining them with hostas, astilbes, goat's beard, ferns and other perennials, which will grow and stay attractive after many of the woodland wildflowers are finished for the season.

A spring triumph, the delicate white flowers of bloodroot push up through the brown and desiccated leaves of winter to shine with a radiant beauty. The protective blue-green leaves arise folded, hugging the flowering stem, and expand to form unusual lobed leaves with a wavy margin. The sap prevalent in the root and other parts of the plant is a bright orange-red, hence the common name. Native Americans used bloodroot for fabric dye and face paint. In April and early May, bloodroot is widespread in Michigan, blooming in rich deciduous woods and flood-plain forests. The flowers are short-lived but appear over a two-week period. This native wildflower is an easygoing garden resident, spreading to form colonies in woodland gardens or any shady border.

Bloom Period and Seasonal Color
White flowers in early to mid-spring.

Mature Height × Spread
4 to 6 in. × 8 in.

When, Where, and How to Plant
Plant bloodroot in early spring or September. Choose locations with partial shade, preferably with spring sun and summer shade. Bloodroot prefers moist, humus-rich soil and the spring sun and filtered light found beneath deciduous trees, although it tolerates average garden conditions. Plant at the same level it was growing in the pot. If planting dormant rhizomes, plant so the roots are $1/2$ to 1 inch deep; avoid planting too deeply. It tolerates considerable sun if provided with ample moisture. Space 6 to 10 in. apart.

Growing Tips
Water new plants thoroughly. Mulch such as shredded leaves or finely shredded bark will help the plants stay moist. Extra water during dry spells is beneficial and will help prolong the foliage display. Special fertilization won't be needed in good garden conditions. Mulch yearly with chopped leaves.

Care
Rhizomes can be easily divided for propagation. Do this when the foliage dies back in late summer. Dig and cut the rhizomes into pieces, and plant them $3/4$ to 1 in. deep. Keep the divisions well-watered. Despite standard advice, bloodroot can also be divided in spring after flowering and even when in flower. Wear gloves to protect your hands from the sap. Dig carefully, disturbing the roots as little as possible, cut apart, and replant. It is carefree.

Companion Planting and Design
Plant bloodroot where you will notice its early bloom. Use it in woodland gardens in drifts with ferns and foamflowers, but also consider bloodroot for shaded locations near doorways, combined with spring bulbs. Try a combination of bloodroot and blue-violet windflower with the deep purple-green foliage and dainty flowers of the Labrador violet, *Viola labradorica*.

We Recommend
Purchase only nursery-grown plants, and never collect plants from the wild. A choice form called 'Multiplex' has fully double flowers. What the flowers lack in simplicity they make up for with beauty and staying power, lasting almost twice as long in the garden. The first double-flowered form was discovered in 1907 near Whitmore Lake. The double form will not bloom if planted too deeply.

Christmas Fern

Polystichum acrostichoides

When, Where, and How to Plant

Plant in early spring or from late September into early October. Select a site in dappled shade, as under tall deciduous trees, to full shade. The soil should be moist and enriched if needed with organics such as compost or shredded leaves. Dig a hole as deep as the plant's container and twice as wide. Remove the fern from its container and gently loosen the rootball. Plant so it is growing at the same depth it was in the pot, no deeper.

Growing Tips

Water well and regularly until the fern is established, then water during unusually dry weather. The fronds of Christmas fern will be at their best when plants are growing on moist sites. Beyond an annual mulching with chopped or composted leaves, no fertilizing is necessary.

Care

Ferns have few pest or disease problems. Because it is evergreen, the fronds of Christmas fern should not be removed in late fall. Examine plants in spring, pruning out any fronds that have become unattractive, taking care not to damage the emerging shoots. Christmas fern may be divided carefully to increase your supply. Dig up the slender rhizomes. Each will have multiple growing tips that can be separated into individual plants. During your spring garden cleanup, be careful of the emerging shoots called fiddleheads. Don't clean out beds with a metal rake or you'll risk damage to them.

Companion Planting and Design

Christmas fern fronds are somewhat coarse. They make a dramatic planting around water, be it a pond, lake, or creek. Use as a groundcover for shady areas combined with foamflower. The dark-green leathery fronds contrast nicely with the paler green maple-shaped leaves of the foamflower.

We Recommend

Another native evergreen woodland fern, the marginal shield fern, *Dryopteris marginalis* (18 to 24 in.), is also suited to culture in a woodland garden. It has slow-growing vase-shaped clumps and shiny fronds.

There is a wide range of fern types, and some are better suited to garden culture than others. Christmas fern, a common native woodland fern, adapts easily to cultivation. It is simple to grow in partial shade and moist, well-drained soil. Christmas fern has a stiffer habit—it's not as lacy as some ferns—but in the wooded garden, it makes a wonderful complement to spring wildflowers and bulbs such as snowdrops. It can hold its own with hostas and other residents of the shady garden. A bonus comes in spring, when its crosiers, also called fiddleheads, look silvery against the older, green fronds. Early colonists in New England are said to have used the dark-green fronds of this evergreen fern in holiday decorations.

Bloom Period and Seasonal Color

Grown for dark evergreen foliage.

Mature Height × Spread

12 to 18 in. × 12 to 18 in.

Foamflower

Tiarella cordifolia

Our native foamflower grows so enthusiastically it could be included in the groundcover section. The overlapping bright green, maple-shaped leaves create a patterned carpet throughout the season. Fluffy white flowers appear in mid-spring, obscuring the foliage in a foamy mass. One of the easiest woodland plants to grow, foamflower spreads by runners (stolons), creating drifts. It occurs in the northern and eastern part of Michigan's Lower Peninsula, often forming extensive mats in deciduous and mixed woods and wet forests. The foamflower foliage is as appealing as its frothy flowers. The hairy, coarsely toothed leaves are evergreen and make a perfect foil for trillium, wild blue phlox, bloodroot, and other natives. The persistent leaves add interest to the woodland floor when most of the spring-bloomers have disappeared.

Bloom Period and Seasonal Color
White flowers in mid- to late spring.

Mature Height × Spread
6 to 12 in. × 2 ft.

When, Where, and How to Plant
Plant foamflower in spring, in partial to full shade and cool, moist, humus-rich soil. This is not a plant for dry soils. Too much sun is a detriment, causing the foliage to fade and scorch. Soil should be rich in organic matter for the best results. Plant foamflower in the garden 8 to 12 in. apart or more; plants will spread. Dig a hole and position the plant so that the soil level is the same as it was in the pot. If the plant has runners, cover them lightly with soil.

Growing Tips
Water thoroughly after planting. Apply mulch such as shredded leaves or finely shredded bark to conserve moisture. In woodland conditions, no extra fertilization is necessary. Mulch annually with shredded leaves.

Care
Pests and disease shouldn't be a concern. Divide clumps in spring to propagate or to control spread. Foamflower produces small plantlets on the ends of runners, much like a strawberry. Once these have formed roots, you can easily sever them from the mother plant to transplant in another location.

Companion Planting and Design
Foamflower is unsurpassed among natives for use as a groundcover in shade. Plant it in natural areas under trees and shrubs, and as a carpet for the woodland garden. It has an innate ability to weave together plants in the shade. Try foamflower with the crested woodland iris (*Iris cristata*), fringed bleeding heart (*Dicentra eximia*), and Christmas fern for spring flowers followed by an interesting foliage texture in the summer season.

We Recommend
Some plants have foliage marked or mottled with burgundy, and many new cultivars in the trade offer this feature. Some of these may look unnatural massed in a native woodland garden, but they will bring interest to shade gardens and a mosaic of shade-loving groundcovers. One of the prettiest, 'Eco Running Tapestry' (12 to 15 in.), has prominent wine-red centers and a vigorous spreading habit.

Jack-in-the-Pulpit
Arisaema triphyllum

When, Where, and How to Plant

Purchase Jack-in-the-pulpit only from reputable sources that have propagated and grown it in a nursery. Plant container-grown plants in spring in a well-drained but moist setting that receives sun in early spring before the trees leaf out. Enrich the soil with organic matter such as shredded leaves, which also make a good mulch. Space the plants about 12 in. apart.

Growing Tips

Jack-in-the-pulpit does best in moist locations. Water during drought. Use shredded leaves to mulch, conserve soil moisture, and provide nutrients as they decompose. No other fertilizer should be needed.

Care

To increase your supply, plants may be divided after the foliage begins to turn yellow in the fall. Dig up the plants and look for the small round corms. Replant these 6 in. deep. Or, wearing gloves, remove the berries and crush them gently to locate the seeds. Sow the seeds in fall or refrigerate them to sow in spring. It will take several years for the new plants to flower. A rust disease may infect some Jack-in-the-pulpits. It is reportedly more serious on the Asian species. The brown spores of the rust will become obvious in spring. Remove and destroy infected plants.

Companion Planting and Design

A native spring wildflower garden of Jack-in-the-pulpits, trilliums, mayapples, and Dutchmen's britches is one way to celebrate Michigan's natural heritage. Or introduce Jack to epimedium, pulmonaria, and bleeding heart. Unlike many wildflowers, Jack-in-the-pulpit has a long season of interest with its vivid red berries in the fall.

We Recommend

Watch specialty nurseries and catalogs for the many unusual species, such as the one called gaudy Jack (*Arisaema sikokianum*) with a dark purple spathe, a white knoblike spadix, and mottled foliage. Another unusual Jack-in-the-pulpit is *Arisaema dracontitum*, or green dragon, which has an elongated long spadix. It grows wild in some moist woods in central and southern Michigan.

Anyone who wanders the Michigan woods in late April or May may have met Jack-in-the-pulpit. It is one of the most unusual native wildflowers, and an easy one to teach youngsters to recognize. The arching hood or spathe (the pulpit) is purple, green or white. Inside is a spike-shaped structure called the spadix (Jack), which bears the tiny flowers. In fall, the plant develops shiny red berries. Jack-in-the-pulpit is native to rich, moist woods and is easy to grow in locations that duplicate those conditions. Native Americans used it for medicinal purposes. The plant contains oxalic acid crystals that make it distasteful to some animals. Many other species of Arisaema are available for enthusiasts, who have elevated this plant to cult status.

Bloom Period and Seasonal Color
Late April to May, purple or brown and green.

Mature Height × Spread
1 to 2 ft. × 12 to 18 in.

Lady Fern
Athyrium filix-femina

Ferns bring the cool, lush feeling of Michigan's north woods to your garden. Grown for their delicate texture and verdant splendor, ferns are often overlooked because they lack flowers. For all their delicacy, ferns are easy to grow if given the partial shade and rich, moist soil they require. Lady fern is an excellent example. Its fine texture, upright lacy fronds, bright green color, and adaptability make it a particular favorite. Lady fern is supremely at home in woodland gardens, but you should also consider it for the shady side of your house, for edging a walk, or for waterside plantings. A difficult and shady spot in your garden where little else grows could be the perfect place for this carefree plant.

Bloom Period and Seasonal Color
Grown for its green lacy fronds.

Mature Height × Spread
2 to 3 ft. × 2 ft.

When, Where, and How to Plant
Plant in early spring or late September through early October. Although it will grow in somewhat drier conditions, the best place for native ferns is in moist, humus-rich soil. A good spot is in dappled shade, such as under tall deciduous trees. Dig a hole as deep as the container and twice as wide. Ferns must be planted at the same depth they were growing in their containers. Planting the rhizomes too deeply may cause the plant to die. Space lady ferns 2 ft. apart.

Growing Tips
Water well and regularly until the fern is established. Water during dry weather, although lady fern is more tolerant of drier conditions than many ferns. Grown in organically rich soil and mulched annually with shredded leaves, ferns require no additional fertilizer.

Care
Native ferns are usually free of pests and diseases. Cut or gently pull off old fronds in late fall or during a late-winter garden cleanup. Be careful not to step on the ferns or to injure the emerging fronds. Ferns can be divided in early spring to propagate. To avoid breakage, do this before the fiddleheads begin to unfurl. Sever the rhizome cleanly with a sharp knife, and replant at the same depth. Disturb the roots as little as possible.

Companion Planting and Design
The delicate green fronds of lady fern make a fine groundcover in a naturalized setting. In a mixed planting, they provide the ultimate contrast for bold-leaved hostas and Japanese sedges. Use them in woodland gardens with bloodroot, Virginia bluebells, and other plants that go dormant later in the season. Or underplant with spring bulbs. By the time they finish blooming, the ferns will hide the ripening bulb foliage.

We Recommend
It's hard to improve on the species, but for something completely different, *Athyrium nipponicum* 'Pictum', the Japanese painted fern, has beautiful silvery blue-gray fronds touched with burgundy. It's wonderful with purple-leaved heucheras like 'Palace Purple'.

Large-Flowered White Trillium

Trillium grandiflorum

When, Where, and How to Plant

Plant trilliums in fall, if available, or in spring. The best spot is in the woodland garden, where the trillium will get sun before the trees leaf out. Trillium favors moist, slightly acidic, well-drained soil that is rich in organic material. Enrich the site if necessary with leaf mold, well-rotted compost, or other amendments. Plant trillium so the rhizome is about 4 to 5 in. deep, and space plants 12 to 18 in. apart.

Growing Tips

Water new plants and keep moist. In woodland conditions, trillium won't need fertilizer. Water during periods of dry weather. In spring and fall, mulch with chopped or composted leaves.

Care

Trillium is easy to grow once established. It has no serious diseases or pests other than deer. It often produces self-sown seedlings. Commercial growers have tried to propagate trillium by tissue culture and from seed, but so far it has proved too time-consuming and expensive. To protect trillium, refuse to buy plants collected from the wild. Plants labeled "nursery grown" may have been dug illegally and then potted and held in a nursery for a season or two. Plants may be purchased from responsible wildflower rescue operations, which have the landowner's permission to dig plants at sites slated for development. In the woods, help educate children and others who admire trillium to look, but not to touch.

Companion Planting and Design

Trillium's distinctive flowers add a pure, artistic beauty to a woodland setting. Once established, it is easy to grow and makes a spectacular plant with native ferns, wild geranium, wild ginger, and bloodroot. A natural choice for a woodland garden, trillium will also thrive in a shady corner of a more conventional landscape.

We Recommend

Trillium is difficult to find in the trade, so ask other gardeners to share their seedlings with you. Reputable growers are increasing their stock by propagating by division. Continue to check local sources, or check page 234 for possible mail-order sources.

Trilliums are abundant in woodlands across Michigan in May, when the elegant white flowers open as the sun warms the soil under still-leafless trees. The large-flowered white trillium is native to each of Michigan's eighty-three counties. It is easy to recognize with its three showy white petals, which fade to pale pink as they mature. In the garden, trilliums are easy to grow and long-lived once established. Take care to grow trilliums responsibly (see We Recommend). While trilliums remain common in undisturbed woodlands, they are disappearing in other areas as development erodes their natural habitat. All trilliums are protected in Michigan. It is illegal to dig them from public or private property without the landowner's written permission or a bill of sale.

Bloom Period and Seasonal Color
White flowers, fading to pink, in spring.

Mature Height × Spread
12 to 24 in. × 12 to 18 in.

Maidenhair Fern

Adiantum pedatum

Ferns are notoriously hard to identify for beginning naturalists. When in the Michigan woods, it is a relief and a joy to come upon a clump of maidenhair fern. The distinctive fan-shaped fronds on dark wiry stems are both beautiful and easy to recognize. This is an especially delicate and graceful fern. Maidenhair fern is native to moist, well-drained woods. For all its delicacy, it is easy to grow given enough water, a soil rich in organics, and shade. In the right location, it will slowly spread from a creeping rootstock to form a large, airy clump. Bring one of the most beautiful natives, the unique maidenhair fern, to your own backyard to remind you of the cool Michigan woodlands.

Bloom Period and Seasonal Color
Grown for its delicate foliage.

Mature Height × Spread
12 to 18 in. × 18 in., spreading to several feet.

When, Where, and How to Plant
Plant in early spring or from late September to early October. Select a spot in a woodland-type setting in partial to full shade. The soil should be moist; maidenhair ferns will not survive planting in a spot that dries out. The planting soil should also be rich in organic matter. If necessary, dig in shredded leaves or compost before planting. When planting, dig a hole the same depth and slightly wider than the container. Plant the fern at the same depth it was growing in the pot—planting the rhizome too deeply may kill the plant. Space about 3 ft. apart.

Growing Tips
Water well and regularly until the fern gets established, then water regularly if it is planted on sites where the soil dries out. Mulch ferns annually with shredded leaves to conserve moisture and to provide nutrients as the leaves decompose. No other fertilizer is needed.

Care
Native ferns have few pest or disease problems. Growing maidenhair fern in a moist spot will help it stay healthy. During your spring garden cleanup, be careful of the emerging shoots called fiddleheads. Don't clean out beds with a metal rake or you'll risk damage to them.

Companion Planting and Design
Maidenhair fern is wonderful in woodland gardens and in frontal locations in shady beds. It makes a lovely edging plant along a shady woodland path or drift under trees and shrubs like pagoda dogwood. Contrast its fine texture with woodland perennials and wildflowers.

We Recommend
If you have moist, or even damp, soil and plenty of room, you should try the following native ferns. The ostrich fern, *Matteuccia struthiopteris* (3 to 5 ft.), is native to swampy, wet woods where it creates a bold architectural presence. Cinnamon fern, *Osmunda cinnamomea* (3 to 4 ft.), a vase-shaped beauty, forms slowly spreading clumps and is best for cool, moist garden sites, especially those near streams or ponds.

When, Where, and How to Plant

Plant Solomon's seal in early spring or early fall. Choose partial shade and cool, moist soil rich in organic matter for best results. It will tolerate some sun with adequate moisture and will also perform well in dry shade once established. Plant in the garden 18 to 20 in. apart. Dig a hole and position the plant so that the soil level is the same as it was in the pot.

Growing Tips

Water new plantings during drought. If provided with the humus-rich soil they require, extra fertilization won't be necessary. Apply an organic mulch, preferably shredded or composted leaves, every year.

Care

Solomon's seal has no significant pests or diseases. The fleshy rhizomes are easy to dig and divide. Do this in spring, when the rhizomes are still dormant, for best results. Cut the rhizome into sections with a sharp knife. Each piece should contain at least one bud, or growing point. Plant rhizomes 1 to 2 in. deep with the bud facing upward and in the direction you want the plant to grow. Keep new divisions moist until established.

Companion Planting and Design

Use Solomon's seal in the woodland garden, but also in shady beds, near outdoor seating areas, and under trees and shrubs. As a focal point, its distinctive form and texture are unmistakable. Combine Solomon's seal with Virginia bluebells and bloodroot, flowers that disappear by midsummer, or use it to complement lungwort, hosta, astilbe, fern, and wild oats in a mixed shady garden.

We Recommend

The great Solomon's seal, *Polygonatum commutatum*, sometimes listed as a variety of the above species, is quite impressive, growing to 5 ft. Use it where you have room to let it dominate. Variegated Solomon's seal, *P. odoratum* 'Variegatum' (18 to 24 in.), a selection of a plant native to Europe and Asia, has leaves edged in cream. It gives a lift to shaded areas.

A glade of Solomon's seal is the epitome of refinement. It doesn't need flashy flowers to do what it does best—add a note of woodland grace to the garden. Statuesque stems arch over, each carrying two rows of leaves above dangling pairs of creamy-white flowers. Unlike spring ephemerals, it isn't here today and gone tomorrow. Solomon's seal remains in the garden all season long. Later the flowers give way to blue-black berries, and in autumn the foliage turns to a warm straw-brown. Solomon's seal is native to the southern half of the Lower Peninsula, where it grows in woods and woodland edges. It has adapted itself to moist roadside borders, and you may see occasional stands emerging from the forest along roads in southeastern Michigan.

Bloom Period and Seasonal Color
Creamy-white flowers in mid- to late spring.

Mature Height × Spread
2 to 3 ft. × 18 to 20 in.

Virginia Bluebell
Mertensia virginica

If you've never seen Virginia bluebells before, one glimpse of these native beauties will turn you into a permanent admirer. The leaves of Virginia bluebell spring up suddenly from the forest floor in early spring. In May, their sweet pink buds and porcelain-blue blooms nod on tall stems. The flowers remain attractive for several weeks, taking on a pink blush as they fade. As with many other woodland plants, Virginia bluebell requires a shady site with well-drained but moist and fertile soil—the kind it finds in the Michigan woods, where it grows naturally. With those conditions, Virginia bluebell will spread quickly, frequently self-sowing. It returns for many springs as a testament to your foresight in introducing this beautiful plant into your garden.

Bloom Period and Seasonal Color
Blue flowers in spring.

Mature Height × Spread
12 to 24 in. × 1 ft.

When, Where, and How to Plant
Container-grown plants are best set out in spring, before the Virginia bluebell goes dormant. Planting later will be an act of faith on your part; the foliage and flowers will be gone by early summer. It prefers areas that are moist (especially in spring), but if planted in part to full shade, a well-drained spot is the best choice. The soil should be rich with organic material. If this does not describe your garden, amend the soil with well-rotted compost or leaf mold. Plant Virginia bluebells at the depth they were growing in the containers, and space the plants about 18 in. apart.

Growing Tips
Virginia bluebell needs adequate moisture. Fertilizer should not be necessary as long as the site is rich in organic material. A mulch of shredded leaves or shredded bark will conserve moisture and discourage weeds.

Care
These hardy plants have no serious diseases or pests, although they are a particular favorite of some rabbits. Plantings may be left undisturbed for years. The best time to divide is as the foliage dies back. Virginia bluebell goes dormant after it flowers. The large leaves must stay on the plant after flowering, turning yellow, and then brown. During this period the plant is making nutrients. If you are planting Virginia bluebell where it will be highly visible, such as along a frequently traveled path or in an often-visited perennial bed, place it near hostas and ferns, which grow quickly in mid- to late spring and will disguise the ripening bluebell foliage.

Companion Planting and Design
Woodland gardens, under tall deciduous trees, in shady borders, and along streams are ideal spots for Virginia bluebell. Use it in mass or in combinations with other woodland plants such as bloodroot, large-flowered white trillium, foamflower, and fringed bleeding heart. Or team it with daffodils, whose clear yellow makes a beautiful contrast.

We Recommend
Virginia bluebells are available in the trade. If you cannot source plants easily, be persistent. Check the mail-order sources page in the back, or contact local plant societies.

Wild Blue Phlox
Phlox divaricata

When, Where, and How to Plant

Plant wild blue phlox in spring or in September. It prefers early spring sun followed by partial to full shade in summer. Moist, rich soil high in organic matter is ideal. The plants will tolerate summer sun, but only if moisture is plentiful. Plant in the garden 12 to 14 in. apart. Dig holes and position the plant so that the soil level is the same as it was in the pot.

Growing Tips

Water thoroughly after planting, and water during drought. Apply a mulch, such as shredded leaves or finely shredded bark, to help the plants stay moist. If provided with the humus-rich soil they require, wild blue phlox won't need fertilizing.

Care

There are no serious pest or disease problems. Shear back plants after blooming to encourage new foliage. To propagate wild blue phlox, divide in spring or late summer. Gently pull apart sections and plant at the same level they were growing. Get a significant portion of roots on each division. Firm pieces into the soil, then water and mulch.

Companion Planting and Design

Plant this delicate native in woodland gardens, and in shade plantings with other native woodland wildflowers and ferns. Use it to edge a woodland walk. Its spreading nature makes it suitable for use as a groundcover in the woodland garden or under shrubs. Plant it in drifts combined with the dangling red-orange and yellow flowers of wild columbine.

We Recommend

Although a white-flowered form of wild blue phlox is available, it is scrawny compared to the selection called 'Fuller's White' (8 to 12 in.). This isn't as delicate as the species, but it is showy, staying covered with large white flowers for close to a month. Look for creeping phlox, *Phlox stolonifera* (6 to 8 in.), another ground-covering woodland phlox. Native to the southeastern United States, it is lower-growing and quite shade-tolerant.

Large drifts of wild blue phlox are a remarkable sight in mid-spring. Widespread in the rich deciduous woodlands of the Lower Peninsula, this agreeable native wildflower is easy to grow in a partly sunny or shady garden. Wild blue phlox, sometimes called wild sweet William because of its light fragrance, forms loose clusters of five-petaled, soft-blue flowers on wiry stems. The narrow dark-green leaves on prostrate stems root at the leaf joints to form a spreading clump. It prefers the filtered sun of deciduous woods. Well suited to a native woodland garden, wild blue phlox mingles naturally with trillium, foamflower, and ferns. This adaptable native is equally at home in a shade garden, wooded suburban lot, or partially shaded perennial bed.

Bloom Period and Seasonal Color

Blue or white flowers in mid- to late spring.

Mature Height × Spread

12 to 14 in. × 12 to 14 in.

Wild Columbine
Aquilegia canadensis

Dainty and curious, the spurred flowers of columbine are among the most intriguing of the garden and appear in May and June. Attached to each petal is a long hollow spur of red-orange, sticking out backward and ending in a knob. From the side the flower looks something like a whimsical jester's hat. The long spurs hold its sweet nectar, making wild columbine a hummingbird's delight. Its leaves, which are green with a hint of blue, are rounded, deeply lobed into three leaflets. Slender branching stems hold the flowers aloft. This Michigan native is an easy-to-grow plant for a well-drained spot in sun to partial sun. From leaf to stem to flower, the effect columbine presents is airy and sprightly.

Other Name
Eastern Columbine

Bloom Period and Seasonal Color
Red-orange and yellow flowers in late spring to early summer.

Mature Height × Spread
12 to 24 in. × 1 ft.

When, Where, and How to Plant
Plant container-grown wild columbine in spring or September. Well-drained, light, average to rich soil is best for columbine. It also grows in sandy or gravelly spots. Good drainage is a critical factor in growing columbine successfully. If planted in heavy clay or where the soil stays wet in winter, the plant will suffer. Choose locations in sun to partial sun. Place container-grown columbine at the same depth in the garden as it was growing in its pot. Space 12 in. apart.

Growing Tips
Water after planting and mulch to conserve moisture. Fertilization is unnecessary. Mulch yearly with a 2-in. layer of shredded or composted leaves.

Care
Leafminers and caterpillars are the most serious pests affecting columbines, but wild columbine is less affected than most. If leafminer does appear, cut the foliage down to the base. Individual columbine plants are relatively short-lived. Because wild columbine self-sows so readily, however, it will keep the population increasing with new plants. The small jet-black seeds may be collected and scattered while still fresh. Seed-grown plants usually flower the following year. To prevent self-sowing, deadhead plants before the seed capsules open.

Companion Planting and Design
Wild columbine works well in the sunny edges of woodland gardens and may also be added to a rock garden or perennial bed. Use it in generous drifts and then let it self-sow, finding new spots on its own. Try combining it with wild ginger, Solomon's seal, Virginia bluebells, and woodland phlox.

We Recommend
A selection of wild columbine called 'Corbett' (18 in.) has light-yellow flowers. A wide range of other columbines and hybrids are available to gardeners. They come in different colors—white, blue, pink, red, yellow, purple—and sometimes with double flowers. The 'Song Bird' hybrid columbines are vigorous, and flowers are plentiful; they were good performers at the Michigan State University Horticultural Gardens.

Wild Geranium

Geranium maculatum

When, Where, and How to Plant

Plant container-grown wild geraniums in spring or September. Wild geranium does best in well-drained soil and partial sun to partial shade. Up to a half-day of sun is acceptable and will increase flowering. Flowering is reduced in deep shade. Place wild geraniums 10 to 12 in. apart in the garden, and take care not to plant them too deeply. After planting, apply a mulch of shredded bark or leaf mold to conserve moisture, keep the root zone cool, and discourage weeds from germinating.

Growing Tips

Water new plants and keep them moist until established. To preserve the foliage effect, water during dry spells. Mulch with shredded leaves in spring and fall.

Care

Wild geranium requires no special care and is trouble-free. If it becomes lanky, cut it back to encourage more compact growth. Divide clumps in spring to increase your stock. Wild geranium often self-sows.

Companion Planting and Design

Wild geranium is suited to shady borders and the edges of woodland gardens with rich and somewhat moist soil. Try combining it with other woodland plants and wildflowers such as wild blue phlox, Solomon's seal, Siberian bugloss, and lady or maidenhair ferns. Trillium and bloodroot are other excellent companions. In the right situation, wild geranium functions like a groundcover. Try it in sweeps under deciduous trees, with drifts of Canadian wild ginger.

We Recommend

Though there are few named cultivars of wild geranium existing in the trade, you can find the species. Also, there are countless other hardy geraniums well suited to Michigan gardens. See the entry for bigroot geranium and hardy geranium for more ideas.

Those who take spring walks in Michigan's woods will recognize wild geranium. It grows in moist woods throughout much of the Lower and some of the Upper Peninsula, especially near ponds and swamps and along streams. This is a different plant from the red, salmon, or pink garden pot plants Pelargonium, *which are commonly called geranium. (Sometimes it seems that botanists do these things with plant names to drive the rest of us crazy!) Wild geranium is a hardy geranium. Its leaves are deeply lobed or palmate, like fingers on a hand. The slender stems end in five-petaled rose-purple flowers. The petals often have veins of a darker color. Wild geranium is an easy-to-grow addition to the woodland garden.*

Other Name
Spotted Cranesbill

Bloom Period and Seasonal Color
Rosy-purple, pink, or white flowers in late spring.

Mature Height × Spread
12 in. to 20 in. × 12 in.

Zones
To Zone 5

Plant Sources

Many seeds and plants are available at local nurseries and garden centers. Others may be purchased through the mail from specialty nurseries, some of which appear below. Check with each firm to see whether there is a charge for its catalog. Most are free.

If you have computer Internet access, you can obtain more information about the nurseries below by entering the nursery's name into a search engine like **yahoo.com** or **google.com**. Find the company's Website and scan its catalog listings and information on how to order plants or a catalog.

Browsing through catalogs is an essential winter gardening activity!

Arborvillage Farm Nursery
P.O. Box 227
Holt, MO 64048
Trees, shrubs

Arrowhead Alpines
P.O. Box 857
Fowlerville, MI 48836
Trees, shrubs, perennials

B & D Lilies
P.O. Box 2007
Port Townsend, WA 98368
Lilies

Kurt Bluemel, Inc.
2740 Greene Lane
Baldwin, MD 21013-9523
Ornamental grasses, perennials

Bluestone Perennials, Inc.
7211 Middle Ridge Road
Madison, OH 44057-3096
Perennials, shrubs

Brent and Becky's Bulbs
7463 Heath Trail
Gloucester, VA 23601
Bulbs

Carroll Gardens
444 E. Main Street
Westminster, MD 21157
Perennials, roses, shrubs, trees

Chiltern Seeds
Bortree Stile
Ulverston
Cumbria LA12 7PB, England
Seeds

Crownsville Nursery
P.O. Box 797
Crownsville, MD 21032
Perennials, grasses

Eastern Plant Specialties
P.O. Box 226W
Georgetown, ME 04548
Trees, shrubs, perennials, wildflowers

Ferry-Morse Seeds
P.O. Box 1620
Fulton, KY 42041-0488
Seeds, plants, bulbs

Forestfarm
990 Tetherow Road
Williams, OR 97544-9599
Trees, shrubs, perennials

Heronswood Nursery
7530 NE 288th Street
Kingston, WA 98346
Perennials, trees, shrubs

High Country Gardens
2902 Rufina Street
Santa Fe, NM 87505
Perennials, roses, grasses

Jackson & Perkins
1 Rose Lane
Medford, OR 97501-0702
Roses, perennials, bulbs

Klehm's Song Sparrow Perennial Farm
13101 E. Rye Road
Avalon, WI 53505
Perennials, shrubs, trees, roses

McClure & Zimmerman
108 W. Winnebago Street
P.O. Box 368
Friesland, WI 53935
Bulbs

Oikos Tree Crops
P.O. Box 19425
Kalamazoo, MI 49019-0425
Trees, shrubs

Old House Gardens
536 Third Street
Ann Arbor, MI 48103
Heirloom bulbs

George W. Park Seed Co.
1 Parkton Avenue
Greenwood, SC 29647-0001
Seeds, bulbs, plants

Plant Delights Nursery, Inc.
9241 Sauls Road
Raleigh, NC 27603
Perennials, grasses

Prairie Nursery, Inc.
P.O. Box 306
Westfield, WI 53964
Native wildflowers, native grasses

Roslyn Nursery
211 Burrs Lane
Dix Hills, NY 11746
Trees, shrubs, perennials

John Scheepers, Inc.
23 Tulip Drive
Bantam, CT 06750
Bulbs

Seed Savers Exchange
3076 North Winn Road
Decorah, IA 52101
Vegetable and flower seeds

Seeds of Change
P.O. Box 15700
Santa Fe, NM 87506-5700
Organically grown vegetable and flower seeds

Select Seeds
180 Stickney Road
Union, CT 06076-4617
Heirloom flower seeds, annuals, perennials

Siskiyou Rare Plant Nursery
2825 Cummings Road
Medford, OR 97501
Perennials, trees, shrubs, grasses

Thompson & Morgan Inc.
P.O. Box 1308
Jackson, NJ 08527-0308
Seeds, plants, bulbs

Wavecrest Nursery
2509 Lakeshore Drive
Fennville, MI 49408
Trees, shrubs, perennials

Wayside Gardens
1 Garden Lane
Hodges, SC 29695-0001
Perennials, shrubs, roses, bulbs

We-Du Nurseries
Route 5, Box 724
Marion, NC 28752-9338
Perennials, wildflowers

White Flower Farm
P.O. Box 50
Litchfield, CT 06759-0050
Perennials, shrubs, roses, bulbs

Public Gardens

Michigan has many excellent gardens and arboreta. This list offers a selection of them. Before visiting, call to check the current hours, admission costs, and special displays.

Ann Arbor

The University of Michigan's Matthaei Botanical Gardens covers 350 acres and has an indoor conservatory with more than 1,000 plant varieties. It is a teaching and research facility that is open for public tours. Outdoor attractions include the Gateway Garden of New World plants, walking trails, a woodland wildflower garden and prairie, rose and perennial gardens, an herb knot garden, a shade garden, and a reconstructed wetland. 734-998-7061.

Nichols Arboretum, near the University of Michigan's central campus, was founded in 1907. Landscape architect O. C. Simonds incorporated many native plants in the original design for the rolling terrain along the Huron River. Since then, the Arb, as it is known, has grown to 123 acres. It is a favorite spot for students and area residents as well as a teaching laboratory. The original peony garden and a prairie have been restored. 734-998-9540.

Battle Creek

The Leila Arboretum is a 72-acre park and botanical garden with initial plantings in 1922. It features many mature trees and a large planting of conifers, a new native wildflower garden and labyrinth, and a children's garden to open in 2002 or 2003. The arboretum also maintains the W. K. Kellogg Community Garden in downtown Battle Creek with seasonal displays. 616-969-0270.

Bloomfield Hills

The 40 acres around Cranbrook House include spring bulb displays, perennials, roses, a bog garden, an herb garden, wildflowers, an Oriental garden, statues, and reflecting pools. The home was built in 1908 for George and Ellen Scripps Booth, who founded Cranbrook. The Cranbrook House and Gardens Auxiliary maintains the house and grounds. 248-645-3149.

Burton

The For-Mar Nature Preserve and Arboretum, part of the Genesee County parks system, is located on 380 acres and includes a 120-acre arboretum. A visitors' center, which opened in 1996, is named for Forbes and Martha Merkley, who gave the land for the preserve in 1968. There are collections of conifers and of flowering trees including crabapples, maples, lilacs, viburnums, and North American native species. 810-789-8568.

Dearborn

The 70-acre Henry Ford–Fair Lane estate, built by Henry and Clara Ford, is considered a significant example of Jens Jensen's landscape work in the prairie style. Fair Lane, now part of the University of Michigan-Dearborn campus, includes gardens and renovated vistas, a greenhouse, and Clara Ford's potting shed. 313-593-5590.

Detroit

The Anna Scripps Whitcomb Conservatory and Gardens are operated by the City of Detroit on Belle Isle. The Victorian-style conservatory includes a palm house, orchids, and ferns; there are seasonal displays. The surrounding grounds and gardens are popular sites for weddings. 313-852-4064.

The Detroit Garden Center in the historic Moross House on East Jefferson Avenue features a garden designed by the Garden Club of Michigan. There is a library of gardening and horticulture books as well as class offerings. 313-259-6363.

East Lansing

Michigan State University has several sites of particular interest to gardeners:

- The W. J. Beal Botanical Garden is among the oldest continuously operated botanical gardens in the United States. The Beal Garden, established in 1873, is an outdoor laboratory for the study and appreciation of plants. Collections focus on plant diversity, economic botany, and ecology. There is a special section on Michigan's threatened and endangered plants. 517-355-9582.
- The Horticultural Demonstration Gardens, which opened in 1993, cover $7^1/_2$ acres of perennial gardens, rose beds, and an extensive display of annuals. It is a test site for the All-America Selections of annuals. There is an adjacent indoor butterfly house. 517-355-0348.
- Part of the Horticultural Demonstration Gardens is the Michigan 4-H Children's Garden, designed with suggestions from youngsters around the state. Visitors can touch, pinch, and smell plants as they wish. Features include an Alice in Wonderland maze, an alphabet of plants, and a science discovery garden. 517-355-0348.
- The Clarence E. Lewis Landscape Arboretum is a teaching laboratory and demonstration site for landscape plants, shrubs, groundcovers, and perennials. The arboretum includes a Japanese garden and the Mawby Fruit Collection of fruit plants grown in Michigan. 517-355-0348.
- A display garden of ornamental grasses is in front of the Hancock Turf Center.
- A new garden of perennials and annuals is located outside the Radiology Center on Service Road.

Flint

Guided tours of Applewood, built for Charles Stewart Mott in 1916 as a gentleman's farm, are available to educational groups and garden clubs; tours must be arranged in advance. The landscape of the estate's eighteen acres has been renovated during the last two decades. It features a formal perennial garden and collections of lilacs, rhododendrons, azaleas, daylilies, hostas, wildflowers, roses, and annuals. The apple orchard includes 25 heritage varieties that Mott planted. 810-233-3031.

Grand Rapids

The Frederik Meijer Gardens, which opened in 1995, includes more than 125 acres and a 15,000-square-foot conservatory. James van Sweden designed an area in the front in the style of the New American garden. There are also an English perennial and bulb garden, a collection of more than 100 sculptures, a woodland garden, nature trails, a boardwalk, and a tram. A 25-acre landscaped sculpture park will open in 2002. 616-957-1580.

Grosse Pointe Shores

The Edsel and Eleanor Ford House, completed in 1929, is surrounded by 87 acres, most of which are now open for public viewing. The Fords hired Jens Jensen, the Chicago landscape architect who specialized in naturalistic designs and native plants, to plan the grounds. They include a rose garden and a reflecting pool. The Ford House offers programs related to its grounds, such as spring wildflower tours, and tree and flower walks. 313-884-4222.

Hillsdale

The 40-acre Slayton Arboretum at Hillsdale College has more than 1,100 plant species as well as wildlife, walking paths, and gazebos. 517-437-7341.

Lansing

Frances Park is part of the Lansing parks system, a 58-acre facility with more than 150 varieties of roses and an overlook view of the Grand River, themed displays of annual plants, a woodland garden, rhododendrons, azaleas, and hostas. 517-483-4277.

The City of Lansing has renovated Cooley Gardens in downtown Lansing, a 1.4-acre perennial garden just a few blocks from Michigan's Capitol. 517-483-4277.

Midland

Dow Gardens is the former estate of Herbert H. Dow, who founded Dow Chemical Co. The 100-acre facility includes displays of bulbs, annuals, perennials, wildflowers, roses, and crabapples. A children's garden, collection of woody plants, and a sensory trail are added features. Dow Gardens is a display garden for the All-America Selections. 800-362-4874.

Niles

The conservatory at Fernwood Botanical Garden and Nature Preserve contains more than 100 species of tropical ferns. This is just one feature of these 105 acres. Fernwood also has a nature center, an arboretum, wilderness and hiking trails, and a tall-grass prairie. 616-695-6491.

Rochester

Landscaping on the 25 acres surrounding Meadow Brook Hall, an estate completed in 1929 for Matilda Dodge Wilson and Alfred Wilson, includes a cutting garden, a rose garden, a children's garden, and many ornamental displays. Meadow Brook Hall is on the campus of Oakland University. 248-370-3140.

Royal Oak

In its early days, the 125-acre Detroit Zoological Institute was known for its magnificent landscapes and plantings. Many of the noteworthy vistas have been restored in recent years, and volunteers plant and maintain "adopt-a-gardens" on the property. 248-398-0900.

Saginaw

Roses and perennials are the star attractions at the Lucille E. Andersen Memorial Garden, which is administered by the City of Saginaw's central parks system. A Marshall Fredericks sculpture, "The Flying Geese," is also featured. The garden is adjacent to the Andersen Enrichment Center, a conference and event facility. 989-759-1362.

Tipton

Hidden Lake Gardens, operated by Michigan State University, is a nearly 800-acre preserve with both natural and landscaped areas. It includes the Harper Collection of dwarf and rare conifers as well as a large selection of hostas, wildflowers, ornamental trees and shrubs, an All-America display garden, a conservatory, and six miles of paved drives through the property. 517-431-2060.

Words About Roses

Though lovely and romantic, roses can be needy plants. Certain ones, especially hybrid teas, are like strict drill sergeants, demanding that gardeners adhere to a time-consuming regime of maintenance, disease and pest prevention and winter protection. One misstep, and the hapless gardener will pay.

Dedicated rosarians argue that these are merely gardening tasks and a small sacrifice for roses' beauty, long season of bloom and the satisfaction achieved from cultivating prizeworthy specimens. Other gardeners, though, are reluctant or flat-out unwilling to take on this extra work, particularly those repeated dousings often required to prevent fungal diseases.

When we identified plants for this book, we sought those that are relatively easy to grow and maintain and are relatively free of insects and disease when given the right growing conditions. For this edition, we have included two roses that fit those criteria, both found in the shrub chapter. 'William Baffin' (page 190) is a beautiful climber with deep pink-colored blooms. It is in the Canadian Explorer series, an outstanding hardy group of roses with much to offer Michigan gardeners. The other rose is really a category, the hybrid rugosas, such as 'Frau Dagmar Hastrup' (page 183). Again, these roses provide hardiness and disease- and pest-resistance as well as beauty.

In fact, quite a few roses are rugged enough to make them dependable landscape plants in our climate with modest care. Their flowers are lush and often fragrant. Roses can be used as specimen plants, with annuals and perennials, and planted as hedges or to ramble up a trellis or arbor. Of course roses are also excellent as cut flowers.

Types of Roses

The categories of roses sometimes overlap, but these are of special interest to Michigan gardeners:

Hybrid teas are the most popular roses and often thought of as the classic rose. They have a long season of bloom and are available in nearly every color. Hybrid teas require the regular application of fungicides to control blackspot and powdery mildew. In Michigan, they require winter protection (see Winter Protection below).

Old garden roses and **antique roses** are a diverse group with refined beauty and, in many cases, exquisite fragrance. Most bloom in early summer, but some newer hybrids repeat bloom later in the season and also are more resistant to disease. The full-flowered David Austin or English roses are bred to have the flowers and fragrance of antique roses, with the disease resistance and repeat bloom of modern shrub roses.

Floribunda roses bear clusters of blooms much of the summer. 'Betty Prior' is a single-petaled beauty that, at its peak, is covered in clusters of deep-pink flowers with golden centers; it is much more disease-resistant than most hybrid teas. 'Nearly Wild' has single pink flowers with the look of a wild rose and is hardy through Zone 5. The Michigan Nursery and Landscape Association in 1997 gave 'Nearly Wild' one of its Growers' Choice awards, which are made to plants the trade group says deserve wider use in Michigan.

Polyantha roses are low-growing shrubs bearing clusters of small flowers. One of the most popular is a beautiful and versatile selection called 'The Fairy', which has clusters of light-pink double flowers produced from late spring through frost. 'The Fairy' can be pruned hard each spring to stay relatively short. It makes a spectacular groundcover or low hedge.

The tough **rugosa rose** and its hybrids, sometimes also lumped in with shrub roses, are notable for their ability to survive in many soils and climates. They have attractive blooms, some with fragrance, and orange-red hips. Because some rugosas sucker and expand over a wide area, they may be planted on slopes to control erosion.

Shrub roses generally are vigorous, and many tolerate winters in Michigan. The Canadian Explorer series, which includes many shrubs as well as some climbing or large bush roses like 'William Baffin', is hardy to Zone 3, Michigan's coldest region, without protection. Because they are so hardy and need minimal care, the Explorers are good candidates for hedges and screens. In a six-year evaluation of shrub roses at the Chicago Botanic Garden, top performers included the English roses 'Constance Spry', 'Lucetta', and 'The Reeve' as well as Canadian roses 'Assinboine,' 'Champlain', 'Henry Kelsey', 'Jens Munk', 'John Davis', and 'William Baffin'. 'Carefree Wonder' is another favorite for its abundant bloom over a long season.

Climbing roses include ramblers, everbloomers, large-flowered climbers, and climbing hybrid teas and miniatures, among others. Check hardiness since, with their large aboveground growth, climbers can be tricky to grow and overwinter.

Species roses are the wild roses found in nature. According to the American Rose Society, most species roses are medium to large plants and the flowers, usually with five petals, may not be as numerous as modern rose growers expect. However, species roses offer interest other than their flowers. For example, the purple-gray foliage of *Rosa glauca* makes a more lasting impact in the garden than its lovely but more transitory pink flowers.

Roses in the Landscape

Beds of hybrid tea roses are popular landscape features, but roses also make fine additions to perennial borders and other plantings. Many have sparse foliage low on their stems, so plant companions such as lavender to fill in around a rose's leggy base. Or plant a clematis with a climbing rose in a complementary color. This way, you will get double pleasure from the same planting space and a longer season of bloom.

Roses can also be used with perennials as groundcovers and hedges. Repeat-bloomers are excellent choices for massing, if you have a sunny location with good air circulation and a source of moisture. There is a spectacular massed planting of 'Nearly Wild' roses facing the waterfront in Petoskey overlooking Little Traverse Bay.

Planting Tips

Choose a site that gets at least six hours of sun a day. Morning sun is preferred. Place roses where their roots will not have to compete with those of shrubs and trees.

The soil should be well-drained and of at least average fertility. Contact your county office of the Michigan State University Extension for information on how to get your soil tested. Do this well before planting so you can make any adjustments needed.

Many roses are grafted. Examine the base of the stem; on a grafted rose, you should be able to see a knobby spot. This is the bud union, where the top and the hardy rootstock have been grafted together. A grafted rose should be planted so the bud union is one to two inches below soil level. Own-root roses are planted so they are growing at the same level they were in the container.

How to Plant Bareroot Roses

Bareroot roses are planted in spring. Soak the roots of bareroot roses for a few hours before planting. Meanwhile, dig a hole at least eighteen inches deep and wide. Remove the soil from the planting hole and mix it with a tablespoon of superphosphate and some well-rotted compost. Some rosarians suggest putting part of this mixture at the bottom of the planting hole to make a mound.

Prune away any broken or dead canes on the rose. Cut back long canes to about twelve inches. Make all cuts on a 45-degree angle and slightly above an outward-facing bud. Use scissors or bypass pruners to avoid crushing the stems.

Place the bareroot rose in the planting hole, gently spreading out the roots. Fill in with soil and firm. Water and add more soil as needed. When you have the rose at the correct level and it has been well watered, mound up soil from elsewhere in the garden about twelve inches around the newly planted rose. This helps prevent it from drying out while the roots get established. Hose off the soil after about three weeks, or when you see new growth beginning.

How to Plant Container-Grown Roses

Container-grown roses may be planted in spring or early summer if they receive plenty of water as their roots get established and when the weather is hot and dry.

Container-grown roses do not require soaking and do not have to be planted on a mound. Remove the rose from the container, minimizing disturbance to the roots. The hole should be as deep as the container and twice as wide. Remove the soil from the hole and enrich it as described above. Place the rose in the hole so it is growing at the same level or slightly deeper than it was in the container. Replace the soil, watering several times during the process.

What Next?

Mulch around the base of the plant with shredded bark or other material, leaving several inches free of mulch right around the stem.

Roses need at least one inch of rain or water from the hose each week, although certain roses such as rugosas and shrub roses generally tolerate drier conditions once established. A soaker hose is good for this purpose because it delivers water right at soil level, rather than wetting the foliage, which can promote disease. It is important to keep up with watering all fall, until the soil freezes, if there is scanty rain. Adequate moisture at the end of the growing season will help the plants better survive the winter.

Roses, especially the repeat-bloomers, are heavy feeders. Many fertilizers and fertilizing schedules are available. Some people apply a slow-release pelleted fertilizer at the beginning of the season and supplement it every six weeks with a product such as 12-12-12. Others prefer to use organic fertilizers. Ask for specific recommendations where you buy your rose, or contact your county extension office for suggestions.

Stop feeding roses and stop deadheading the old flowers in August to give them time to harden off before winter.

Minimizing Problems

Roses can be a smorgasbord for disease such as blackspot and powdery mildew and insects such as aphids, Japanese beetles, rose chafers, and midges. Buy healthy plants from reputable sources. Space them properly at planting. If you don't want to get into the cycle of spraying, choose roses that resist pests and disease. Another way to minimize problems is with careful autumn cleanup of old rose foliage, including any leaves that have fallen on the soil around the plants. This will remove spores that could overwinter and carry problems into next season.

Winter Protection

Hybrid teas and floribunda roses require winter protection in Michigan. For all other roses, check with the retailer when you purchase the plants to see whether winter protection is needed. The idea with winter protection is to keep the plants cold so they won't repeatedly freeze and thaw.

Winter protection is applied after the roses go dormant and following several hard freezes, typically sometime in December in southern Michigan. Mound up soil from elsewhere in the garden to a depth of about twelve inches at the base of the plant, or use rose cones to protect them. You can also fold several sheets of newspaper into long strips and staple them together to make a collar or ring around the base of the rose. Fill the collar with soil, pine needles, or oak leaves. Good snow cover provides excellent winter protection. Remove winter protection in early April or when the threat of below-freezing weather is past.

Pruning

Early April is also the time to do major rose pruning on hybrid teas. Remove all dead wood and cut back hybrid teas to live wood, which will be greenish white inside. The overall height after pruning should be ten to twelve inches, cutting just above an outward-facing bud. Remove any canes that rub each other or crowd the inside of the plant to let light and air reach the interior, which can mean less blackspot and mildew.

Dead wood should also be removed from shrub roses and rugosas in the spring and unusually long canes may be shortened as desired. Wait to prune climbers that bloom only in June and floribundas until after they flower. In the fall, cut back only the longest canes on hybrid teas that might whip around in the winter wind.

If you're considering planting roses, check your library for rose reference books written specifically for northern gardeners, such as *Tender Roses for Tough Climates* by Douglas Green (Chapters Publishing). Reputable mail-order or local nurseries that specialize in roses can also offer advice and recommendations, as can regional rose societies. Its members know from experience which roses are the strongest performers in your area and soils.

Integrated Pest Management

Let's face it: Sometimes, plants get in trouble. Maybe mysterious caterpillars are nibbling on plants in the windowbox, or something is chewing holes in the hosta leaves. The phlox and lilac look gray and ghostly, and there are little brown galls hanging on the Colorado spruce.

What's a Gardener to Do?

The first impulse used to be to reach for a chemical—any chemical. In a struggle for control, many gardeners believed they could get the upper hand through relentless application of various products promising to kill all bugs or wipe out every disease.

But indiscriminate use of pesticides harms beneficial insects, birds, helpful microorganisms in the soil, and the water supply. These are important members of the healthy garden community. It's only when populations get out of balance that gardeners need to become concerned. There are many strategies to try before resorting to chemicals, which should be used only as a last resort.

Playing Detective

Gardeners should start by playing detective and identifying the source of the trouble. Some damage is acceptable. If you expect your garden to be flawless, ease up. Certain problems don't require any action except the passage of time. If a pest or disease problem needs action, be creative in finding the least toxic solution possible.

This approach is called Integrated Plant Management, or IPM. It is a strategy to manage plant pests and diseases while doing as little damage as possible to the environment.

Sometimes the solution is to change the way you care for plants, like how they are watered. It may mean moving them to where they get more sun, or improving drainage so they don't stand in water.

Sometimes it requires a change in how much plant damage you are willing to accept. In some cases, it may involve banishing a problem plant entirely and switching to one that is more resilient.

Plant damage can include things like chewed leaf margins, yellowing, and wilting or stunted growth. Culprits may include insects, diseases, insufficient soil nutrients, too much or too little water, or an improper site for that plant.

To help track down the cause, check reference books at the library or at a garden center or nursery. Take along a sample of leaves or stems that show the damage, or a photo. Your county's office of the Michigan State University Extension can also help diagnose the problem and determine solutions. Or for timely information on managing pest and disease problems go to Michigan State University Extension's IPM Website—see page 254 for more details and the Web address.

Keep Your Eyes Open

Problems may be caught while they are still minor if you monitor your plants regularly. If, for instance, there is an outbreak of aphids on your roses, you may be able to keep the population at tolerable levels if you hose off the plants with a strong spray of water each day for a week or two.

Your actions can also depend on knowledge of plant problems, pest life cycles, and the weather. Perhaps your lawn has brown spots in the spring and you suspect grubs. Don't apply any product without verifying that a significant grub population is present. (See page 89 for details on how to do that.) You also have to know when grub control is effective.

Sometimes something as simple as increasing soil moisture can minimize turf damage. For example, irrigated lawns recover from grub damage better than unirrigated ones.

Perhaps your perennial border includes roses, phlox, or beebalm, all of which are likely to get foliar diseases when the leaves stay wet. Using a soaker hose that delivers water at soil level, rather than an overhead sprinkler, can reduce the incidence of powdery mildew.

For plant pests, try handpicking the offenders, trapping them, or excluding them with nets or barriers. Certain biological controls like the bacterium *Bacillus thuringiensis* (*Bt*) can act as insecticides for controlling specific plant pests.

Rethinking Priorities

Gardeners may also need to rethink their priorities and how much plant damage they are willing to tolerate. Perfection is unnatural in the garden. Don't get into a cycle of using chemicals in pursuit of something that is impossible to achieve. Recognize that your garden is part of nature, and try to fit in and appreciate the natural world in your backyard rather than control it. Instead of grabbing for a spray, wait to see what happens next. Weather and insect cycles are beyond your control. Next season will probably be different—maybe better, maybe worse.

If damage on certain plants is inevitable, plant something else. There are so many resistant choices that thrive without needing extra coddling just to survive. If you love roses but hate the blackspot and powdery mildew that can disfigure the leaves of some hybrid teas every summer, try growing 'William Baffin' or another of the tougher cultivars.

Clean up and dispose of old leaves around plants that are especially susceptible to foliage diseases or whose leaves may host overwintering insects. Plants on this list include crabapples, roses, phlox, beebalm, peonies, and iris, among others.

The Last Resort

If you must resort to chemical controls, target your specific pest. Consult your county extension agent for the most up-to-date recommendations. If appropriate for your pest, start with horticultural oils and insecticidal soaps, which break down rapidly so they have less lasting impact on the environment and may not be as damaging to beneficial organisms, animals, and people. Use botanical insecticides cautiously. Though made from plants and considered natural, these can still be toxic to a wide range of insects rather than one specific pest.

An IPM Success

The battle against purple loosestrife in Michigan is an example of how integrated pest management can work. Purple loosestrife is native to Europe. It was brought to this country as an ornamental plant. For generations, it was grown in gardens and prized for its beautiful purple spikes of flowers in the summer.

However, in the U.S., purple loosestrife lacked natural enemies to keep its population in check. It began spreading through wetlands and along waterways, choking out native vegetation and imperiling food and habitat sources for wildlife. Dense stands of loosestrife hinder recreation on the water as well as water flow. They choke out or outcompete native flora for resources.

As the problem became apparent, people tried traditional approaches like burning stands of loosestrife and treating it with herbicides. But these methods were either ineffective or too hard to use on a large scale. The sale or distribution of loosestrife is now illegal in Michigan.

In 1994, several state agencies began a program to release beetles that consume purple loosestrife. The beetles won't completely rid the state of these invasive plants, but they can make its growth less dense so native vegetation has a chance to reestablish. They also are more environmentally friendly than using herbicides.

The Purple Loosestrife Project is a joint effort of Michigan State University, the Michigan Sea Grant Program, and a number of state and federal agencies. It enlists citizens, property owners, teachers and school children to help rear and release the beetles each year. In this way, the program is expanding statewide and many people in Michigan are having the opportunity to take active roles as environmental stewards.

For more about the Purple Loosestrife Project, go to www.miseagrant.org/pp/.

IPM in Your Michigan Garden

Of all the things a gardener can do, choosing the right plants is the best strategy for avoiding problems that return year after year. The plants profiled in this book are selected for their hardiness and tough character, proven over the years right here in Michigan gardens.

Toxic Plants: Caution

Ingesting certain common garden plants can be toxic or cause digestive problems or reactions. This is of special concern to gardeners who have young children and pets.

Teach youngsters never to eat plants or mushrooms they find outdoors. Keep indoor plants where children and pets cannot reach them. Store bulbs in a safe location until they are planted.

Here is a list of plants profiled in this book that may be poisonous, have toxic or irritating parts including leaves, nuts, or berries, or have been reported as causing adverse reactions in humans or animals if ingested. If you have concerns about a plant that has been eaten, don't rely on a list to tell you what's safe. Call your doctor or the Poison Control Center of Children's Hospital of Michigan, 800-764-7661. The center, located in Detroit, can provide help twenty-four hours a day, seven days a week. It is designated a regional poison control center by the American Association of Poison Control Centers.

Trees and Shrubs:

Amur chokecherry (leaves)

Bottlebrush buckeye

Boxwood

Hydrangea

Kentucky coffeetree

Oaks

Rhododendron

Serviceberry (leaves)

Staghorn sumac

Winterberry

Yew

Bulbs, Perennials, and Wildflowers:

Anemone

Autumn crocus

Bleeding heart

Bloodroot

Butterfly weed

Clematis

Cushion spurge

Daffodil

Gloriosa daisy

Goldenrod

Hellebore

Iris

Jack-in-the-pulpit

Lily-of-the-valley

Sneezeweed

Snowdrop

Tulip

These other common garden and indoor plants are considered toxic:

Angel's trumpet	Larkspur
Azalea	Lobelia
Bittersweet	Mayapple
Buttercup	Mistletoe
Caladium	Monkshood
Calla lily	Moonseed
Castor bean	Morning glory
Cherry	Mother-in-law plant
Cotoneaster	Nightshade
Datura	Peace lily
Delphinium	Periwinkle
Dieffenbachia	Pokeweed
Elderberry	Poppy
Elephant ear	Red maple
English ivy	Rhubarb (leaf)
Holly	Sweet pea
Hyacinth	Tomato vine
Ivy	Wisteria

Sources: Children's Hospital of Michigan; *Common Poisonous Plants and Mushrooms of North America* by Nancy J. Turner and Adam F. Szczawinski (Timber Press, 1991).

Gardening with Native Plants

Michigan is renowned for its distinctive natural landscape and abundance of natural areas. Our shorelines, lakes, prairies, forests, and wetlands draw visitors from all over the world. Residents enjoy heading up to the lake or woods to vacation, reinvigorating their senses and souls when the pace of daily life gets overwhelming.

These days, though, what used to be rural and remote in Michigan is rapidly becoming developed. Woodlands and fields are being dug up for housing developments. County roads, once lined with gray dogwood and Michigan holly, are now lined with a numbing number of discount and convenience stores. Population growth and development sprawl mean that Michigan's natural areas are disappearing, and the trend is unlikely to diminish in coming years.

What does that mean to gardeners? For many of us, it means changing the way we think about the spaces we maintain.

Bring the Natural World Closer

Early settlers built gardens to exclude and control the wildness of the natural world. Today, more people are using native plants to bring the natural world closer and to take an active role in preserving biodiversity for future generations. Native plants are those that originated in our region before European settlers arrived and have adapted to continue growing here.

Some people may be intimidated by the prospect of growing native plants. They may be unfamiliar with the plants themselves, compared to mainstream perennials. They may worry that the natives won't be attractive or, if introduced, will do too well, dominating the plantings and the character of their gardens.

The native plants we selected for this book, which are designated with this symbol Ⓝ, can be easily integrated into your existing garden. You can plant just one, or just a few, or design an entire landscape. A good start is to consider a native tree when choosing one for your lawn or street. Or choose a native shrub for use as a privacy screen. In a perennial garden, native and non-native perennials and grasses can flourish when grown side by side. You don't have to switch entirely to natives, although some gardeners may choose to do that. Others will start new beds featuring native plants. Once you introduce more native plants, you'll notice and appreciate nature's seasonal rhythms in your own garden.

Reasons to Go Native

Here are a few more reasons to garden with native plants:

Many natives require **less supplemental water.** Some native plants have deep roots. They have evolved to survive in this region without extra moisture—although, during drought, gardeners may choose to provide water to keep them healthy and attractive.

Natives need **no supplemental chemicals**. Given the right site, soil, and light, native plants will thrive without additional fertilizers or pesticides.

Once established, natives generally require **less routine maintenance**. In most cases, chores like dead-heading and pruning, as well as extensive soil preparation, are unnecessary. Cleanup can be limited to an early-spring gathering of old foliage or errant branches that need cutting back to maintain size or shape.

Natives provide a **habitat for wildlife**. Birds, butterflies, other insects, and mammals that occur naturally in our region will use native plants for food and shelter. Especially in urban and suburban areas, landscapes incorporating native plants create a welcome green oasis for wildlife.

A community or grouping of native plants can **absorb storm water runoff** and even **help filter pollutants from the water and soil**. This can ease the burden on sewer systems and reduce what goes into nearby lakes and rivers.

Natives are usually, although not always, **less invasive**. That means they won't get out of control like exotics such as vinca, Norway maple, or purple loosestrife, which can outcompete and crowd out native plants. Certainly there are exceptions: pokeweed comes to mind, for its ability to spread from seed. However, since the pokeweed's berries are a favorite with migrating birds, it's a valued plant among birding enthusiasts.

It comes down to making choices. By planting natives, you can help preserve Michigan's diverse natural heritage.

Working with Nature

Gardening with natives is sometimes called natural landscaping. Perhaps the most important guideline to making it work is to select plants that fit the site, rather than trying to adapt the site to fit a particular plant's requirements. Work with nature. Don't fight it. Coaxing plants to survive where they would not, except for extraordinary measures, is a waste of time when there are so many plants to choose from. Plants sited incorrectly become stressed and are more prone to disease and insect problems.

After planting, mulch native plants to conserve water in the soil. Woodland plants (see chapter 8, page 220) especially thrive with an annual application of two or more inches of leaf compost. As the leaves decompose, they return nutrients to the soil, which nourishes the plants. Allow leaves that fall in the autumn to remain. It's all part of the natural cycle.

With an eye on design, some prairie or meadow gardens of native plants may look weedy to people accustomed to manicured lawns and gardens. To offset this, many gardeners who use native plants include a strip of grass that can be mowed around the perimeter. They may also incorporate some plants with bright flowers. These elements may reassure worried neighbors that the yard is, in fact, a designed and kept area.

Check local ordinances, too. Some communities take a relaxed approach to the enforcement of weed ordinances that can thwart gardeners who want to turn portions of their yards into havens for native perennial plantings. If that is a concern to you, plant native trees and shrubs, which look no more or less weedy than non-native woody plants.

For inspiration on gardening with native plants, walk through a Michigan woodland in May, when trilliums carpet the forest floor. Admire the tenacity of dune plants that survive the intense heat and light of a July afternoon along Lake Michigan. Look carefully at the places where native plants grow, and observe the related plants that form their communities. These will guide you in selecting native plants for your own garden.

Helpful Resources

Another helpful resource is Edward Voss's three-volume survey, *Michigan Flora*. Published by Cranbrook Institute of Science and the University of Michigan Herbarium in 1972, 1985, and 1996, this set represents an enormous body of knowledge for anyone seriously interested in native plants and forty years of study by Dr. Voss, an outstanding professor at the University of Michigan.

Another valuable book on Michigan native plants is *Michigan Trees*, by Burton Barnes and Warren H. Wagner Jr. This book has wonderful illustrations of our native trees and includes the size and location of Michigan champion trees.

Natives are increasingly showing up in public plantings, and local groups of native plant enthusiasts sponsor walks of members' gardens. This is a great chance to see what people in your own area are already doing with native plants.

Ironically, some native plants like Joe-pye weed and goldenrod became fashionable in European gardens before they did in their home territory. Today, many more North Americans are appreciating these plants and the advantages they offer.

Michigan has many clubs and organizations that promote the use of native plants. Among them are the local chapters of the Wild Ones, the Wildflower Association of Michigan, and the Michigan Botanical Club. For links, see Web Addresses, page 254.

Protecting Native Plants

When purchasing native plants, be sure they have been propagated and grown in nurseries rather than taken from the wild, or that they have been rescued with the owner's permission from land slated for development. This protects the supply of native plants, some of which are on state or federal lists of threatened or endangered species. Patronize nurseries that specialize in native plants. To find them, contact the groups mentioned in the previous paragraph.

Plants Native to Michigan

Among the plants selected for this book are many that are native to Michigan. They include:

Groundcovers

Canadian wild ginger, page 54

Creeping juniper, page 55

Ornamental Grasses

Little bluestem, page 94

Prairie dropseed, page 97

Switch grass, page 98

Tufted hair grass, page 100

Wild oats, page 101

Perennials

Beebalm, page 108

Black snakeroot, page 110

Blazing star, page 111

Butterfly weed, page 117

Culver's root, page 122

Goldenrod, page 127

Heliopsis, page 129

Joe-pye weed, page 133

New England aster, page 138

Purple coneflower, page 141

Rudbeckia, page 142

Sneezeweed, page 148

Turtlehead, page 151

Shrubs

Arborvitae, page 158

Arrowwood viburnum, page 159

Ninebark, page 167

Gray dogwood, page 171

Hazelnut, page 172

Michigan holly, page 179

Redtwig dogwood, page 180

Spicebush, page 182

Staghorn sumac, page 184

Trees

Black gum, page 195

Hop-hornbeam, page 200

Kentucky coffeetree, page 202

Pagoda dogwood, page 205

Pawpaw, page 207

Redbud, page 208

Shadblow, page 211

Sugar maple, page 212

Tuliptree, page 214

White ash, page 215

White oak, page 217

White pine, page 218

Woodland Flowers and Ferns

Bloodroot, page 222

Christmas fern, page 223

Foamflower, page 224

Jack-in-the-pulpit, page 225

Lady fern, page 226

Large-flowered white trillium, page 227

Maidenhair fern, page 228

Solomon's seal, page 229

Virginia bluebell, page 230

Wild blue phlox, page 231

Wild columbine, page 232

Wild geranium, page 233

The inspiration of nature is all around us. Bring to it your own style of gardening. Even in the midst of a city, growing native plants is a way to reintroduce nature.

As people become more accustomed to seeing and appreciating native plants, they will be more inclined to consider the ways that the soil, climate, plants, wildlife, and the gardener's fates are intertwined.

Gardeners on the Web

Becoming an educated gardener and gardening consumer is easier today than it was just a few years ago. Many people now have access to computers, the Internet, and the resources of the World Wide Web, and there's a lot of information out there.

Whether you surf at home or at the local library, you can read the latest university horticulture research and locate nurseries that carry a specialty plant you crave. You can obtain lists of garden tours and classes, ask questions, get answers, and even chat with other gardeners.

All you need is a search engine, such as **yahoo.com** or **google.com**. In the search entry field, type in a few words about what you want to track down. To narrow the responses, use a two- or three-word phrase like "purple coneflower," enclosed with double quotation marks. The more specific you can be, the faster you'll get relevant hits.

Many readers already have their lists of favorite gardening sites. Here are a few of ours:

www.msue.msu.edu is the Michigan State University Extension site, which includes many features that are valuable to gardeners. The Home Horticulture section has entries about how to grow and maintain more than 1,000 plants.

The Web address **www.msue.msu.edu/ipm/landCAT.htm** takes you to the Michigan State University Extension Landscape CAT (Crop Advisory Team) Alert. This publication comes out either each week or every other week all growing season. You can subscribe for a fee to get it by mail, or read it free on the Web. The CAT Alert has timely information about managing pests and disease, updates on current insects, weather news, and searchable archives. There are also links to other Michigan State University CAT Alerts on vegetables, field crops, fruits, and greenhouse plants.

The U.S. Forest Service's Eastern Region, which includes Michigan, has a helpful guide to weeds and invasive plants, including a ranking of how invasive the weeds are. Go to **www.fs.fed.us/r9/weed/**.

If your interest is in a particular plant, use the Web to find out if there's a specialty group with similar interests. Many popular garden plants have organizations for enthusiasts, and most are on the Web. For example, go to the site of the American Hosta Society, **www.hosta.org**, or the site of the American Rose Society, **www.ars.org**. Sometimes Web visitors can even ask questions of experienced members.

Those wanting to learn more about growing native plants should visit the home of the Wild Ones, **www.for-wild.org**. It has a list of Michigan chapters and contact numbers. The Wildflower Association of Michigan, **www.wildflowersmich.org**, is another popular site. See also the U.S. Environmental Protection Agency's "green landscaping" project, **www.epa.gov/greenacres/**.

The Michigan Botanical Club, **www.michbotclub.org**, maintains the official list of Michigan's largest trees. Global ReLeaf of Michigan, **www.globalreleaf.org**, runs the annual Michigan Big Tree Hunt and you can find out more about it on the Web.

Notable out-of-state plant databases with relevance to Michigan gardeners include those run by the Chicago Botanic Garden, **www.chicagobotanic.org**, and Ohio State University's Plant Facts, **plantfacts.ohio-state.edu**.

Glossary

Acid soil: Soil with a pH of less than 7.0.

Alkaline soil: Soil with a pH greater than 7.0. It lacks acidity, often because it has limestone in it. Most plants grow best in soils where the pH is between 6.0 and 7.0.

All-purpose fertilizer: Powdered, liquid, or granular fertilizer with a balanced proportion of the three key nutrients—nitrogen (N), phosphorus (P), and potassium (K). It is suitable for maintenance nutrition for most plants.

Annual: A plant that lives its entire life in one season. It is genetically determined to germinate, grow, flower, set seed, and die the same year.

Balled-and-burlapped: A field-grown tree or shrub that is dug for sale or transplant and the rootball is wrapped in protective burlap and twine.

Bareroot: Plants without soil around their roots. When plants are purchased bareroot by mail, they may be covered with moist peat, shredded paper, or other material and wrapped in plastic to keep them damp until planting. Bareroot plants should be planted as soon as possible so they don't dry out.

Barrier plant: A plant with thorns or spines that is sited purposely to block foot traffic or other access to the home or yard.

Bedding plant: Annuals, generally, that are spaced and planted throughout an area for masses of bloom and color. Michigan is a leader in bedding plant production.

Beneficial insects: Insects or their larvae that prey on pest organisms and their eggs. They may be flying insects, such as ladybugs, parasitic wasps, praying mantids, and soldier bugs, or soil dwellers such as predatory nematodes, spiders, and ants.

Berm: A raised planting bed.

Bract: A modified leaf on a plant stem near its flower that resembles a petal. Often a bract is more colorful and visible than the actual flower, as in dogwood or poinsettia.

Bt: *Bacillus thuringiensis* is a natural soil bacterium that is sometimes used an insecticide.

Bud union: The place where the top of a plant is grafted to the rootstock, as with some roses.

Bulb: An underground storage structure of a plant.

Cankers: Lesions in the bark of woody plants, usually caused by bacteria or fungi.

Canopy: The overhanging branches and leaves of a tree.

Chlorosis: An unnatural condition of the foliage, which instead of being green is yellow or yellowish. Chlorosis is often caused by nutrient deficiencies (usually iron) attributed to high soil pH.

Cold hardiness: The ability of a plant to survive the winter cold. Plants are rated by their cold hardiness to specific areas, depending on the coldest expected winter temperatures. For a map of U.S. Department of Agriculture Hardiness Zones for Michigan, see page 21.

Composite: A flower that is actually composed of many tiny flowers, such as a daisy or sunflower. Composites usually have flat clusters of tiny, tight florets, sometimes surrounded by wider-petaled florets. Composite flowers are highly attractive to bees and beneficial insects.

Compost: Organic matter such as garden or kitchen waste that has decomposed through microbial and macrobial activity until it is reduced to a spongy, fluffy texture. Added to soil of any type, compost improves the soil's ability to hold air and water and to drain well.

Corm: A bulb-like structure, actually an underground stem, under the soil at the base of the stem of plants such as crocus and gladiolus.

Crown: The base of a plant at, or just beneath, the surface of the soil where the roots meet the stems.

Cultivar: A cultivated variety. A cultivar is a naturally occurring form of a plant that has been identified as special or superior and is selected for propagation and production.

Deadhead: A pruning and maintenance chore in which the faded flower heads are cut or snapped off plants to improve their appearance, abort seed production, and stimulate further flowering. Deadheading is especially important to keep annuals such as marigolds flowering throughout the season.

Deciduous plants: Unlike evergreens, these trees and shrubs lose their leaves in the fall.

Desiccation: Drying of foliage tissues, usually due to drought or wind. Winter desiccation is a particular problem with broadleaf evergreens exposed to afternoon sun. Plants continue to lose water through their leaves but, since the soil is frozen, their roots can't absorb water to replenish their supply and the leaves dry out. This is also called winterburn.

Division: The practice of splitting apart perennial plants into several smaller segments. Division can be used to control a plant's size and to increase the supply. Certain plants require regular division to stay healthy and productive.

Dormancy: The period when perennial plants temporarily cease active growth.

Dripline: The area beneath a tree where rain drips from the outer edge of the canopy.

Established: The point at which a newly planted tree, shrub, or flower begins to produce new growth, either foliage or stems. This is an indication that the roots have recovered from transplant shock and have begun to grow and spread.

Evergreen: Perennial or woody plants that do not lose their foliage annually with the onset of winter. Needled or broadleaf foliage will persist and continues to function for several years.

Foliar: Of or about foliage; most often used when talking about treatment, as in foliar sprays.

Floret: A tiny flower, usually one of many forming a cluster, that comprises a single blossom.

Germinate: To begin growing. Germination is a fertile seed's first stage of development.

Graft (union): The point on the stem of a woody plant where a stem from a desirable ornamental plant is inserted into the roots of a hardier one, resulting in a plant with the best characteristics of each one. Roses are commonly grafted.

Groundcover: Plants spaced close together so they cover the bare soil as they grow.

Harden off: To expose a plant gradually to conditions so they become accustomed to it over a period of time. For example, annuals grown in greenhouses should be hardened off for several days before planting outdoors in the spring.

Hardy bulbs: These will survive the winter outdoors in Michigan. Examples are daffodils, tulips, and ornamental onions. Tender bulbs, such as dahlias, must be lifted and stored indoors for the winter, then replanted outside in the late spring.

Heaving: Pushing up and out of the soil during the winter as a result of repeated freezes and thaws. Some plants, such as coralbells, are more likely to suffer heaving damage than others. Perennials planted in the fall should be mulched after the soil freezes the first winter to protect them from heaving.

Herbaceous: Plants having fleshy or soft stems that die back with frost, as opposed to woody plants.

Hybrid: The offspring of genetically different parents, usually of different species and the same genus. Hybrids may be created by intentional or natural cross-pollination between two or more plants.

Integrated Pest Management (IPM): The practice of determining the cause of, and acceptable levels of, plant damage and then methodically setting out to try solutions, starting with the least toxic means possible.

Leader: The primary or terminal shoot of a tree.

Mulch: A layer of material placed over bare soil to protect it from erosion and compaction, to conserve soil moisture, and to discourage weed seeds from germinating. It may be inorganic (gravel, fabric) or organic (wood chips, bark, pine needles, chopped leaves).

Naturalize: (*a*) To plant seeds, bulbs, or plants in a random, informal pattern as they would appear in their natural habitat; (*b*) to adapt to and spread throughout a habitat.

Nectar: The sweet fluid produced by glands on flowers that attract pollinators such as hummingbirds and honeybees, for which it is a source of energy.

Organic fertilizer: A substance made from material that is living, or once was, such as fish emulsion, bone meal, or manure.

Organic material, organic matter: Any material or debris that is derived from plants. It is carbon-based material capable of undergoing decomposition and decay.

Peat moss: Organic matter from peat sedges (United States) or sphagnum mosses (Canada), often used as a soil amendment to improve water-holding capacity and to make the soil more acidic. Peat moss is a non-renewable resource.

Perennial: A flowering plant that lives over two or more seasons. Many die back to the ground with frost, but their roots survive the winter and generate new shoots in the spring. While some people assume perennials live forever, some survive only two to three years. These are often called short-lived perennials.

pH: A measurement of the relative acidity (low pH) or alkalinity (high pH) of soil or water based on a scale of 1 to 14, 7 being neutral. Individual plants require soil within a certain range, usually 6.0 to 7.0, so nutrients can dissolve in moisture and be available to them. Soil tests to determine pH are available through the county offices of the MSU Extension.

Pinch: To remove tender stems and/or leaves by nipping them off with a thumb and finger. This pruning technique encourages branching, compactness, and flowering in plants.

Pollen: The yellow, powdery grains in the center of a flower. A plant's male sex cells, they are transferred to the female plant parts by means of wind, insects, or other animal pollinators.

Raceme: An arrangement of single-stalked flowers along an elongated, unbranched axis.

Rejuvenation pruning: The removal of old woody stem material to promote the development of new healthy vigorous growth.

Rhizome: An underground stem that lies horizontally in the soil, with roots emerging from its lower surface and growth shoots from a growing point at or near its tip, as in bearded iris.

Rootbound (or potbound): The condition of a plant that has been confined to a container too long. Roots wrap around themselves and even swell out of the drainage hole in the bottom of the container. Successful transplanting or repotting requires untangling and trimming away of some of the matted roots.

Root flare: The place at the base of a tree trunk where the bark tissue begins to differentiate and roots begin to form just before entering the soil. This area should not be covered with soil when planting a tree.

Self-seeding: The tendency of some plants to sow their seeds freely, as with Brazilian verbena and wild oats. Self-sowing plants can become weedy. Volunteer plants may need to be pulled the following season.

Semievergreen: Intermediate between being fully evergreen and deciduous. In Michigan, semi-evergreen plants, like leatherleaf viburnum, will lose most of their foliage in a harsh winter; in milder winters, the leaves will persist.

Shearing: The pruning technique of cutting plant stems and branches with long-bladed pruning shears (hedge shears) or powered hedge trimmers. It is used to remove all growth at a uniform level, as in late winter or early spring to prune away old foliage on ornamental grasses.

Sidedress: To apply fertilizer or organic matter near the sides but not right on the base of a plant, or between plants.

Slow-acting fertilizer: Fertilizer that is water insoluble and therefore releases its nutrients gradually depending on soil temperature, moisture, and related microbial activity. Typically granular, it may be organic or synthetic.

Soil test: A measurement of nutrients in and other characteristics of the soil. A soil test is recommended before planting and plant selection to ensure that plant material is suited for the site.

Stoloniferous: Spreading from slender stems just on or under the ground.

Sucker: A new growing shoot. Some underground plant roots, like those of forsythia, produce suckers to form new stems and spread in this way to form large plantings or colonies. Certain plants produce root suckers or branch suckers as a result of pruning or wounding.

Taproot: A type of root, as in a dandelion or carrot, that grows straight down. Tap-rooted trees are often difficult to transplant.

Thatch: Accumulated plant material such as old roots on the soil surface.

Thinning out: The selective removal of old woody stems to promote young vigorous shoots.

Topdress: The application of fertilizer or compost to the soil surface around a plant.

Topping: The removal of the central leader or a large part of the crown of a tree. Topping destroys a tree's natural habit and causes disfigurement.

Tuber: A fleshy underground structure where new growth begins.

Tuberous roots: Clump-forming underground roots, as in dahlias.

Variegated: Having various colors or color patterns. Plant foliage may be streaked, edged, blotched, or mottled with a contrasting color, often green with yellow, cream, or white. Many hostas and pulmonarias show variegation.

Volunteer: (*a*) The unaided establishment of a plant; (*b*) a self-sown plant.

Winter mulch: The application of a non-matting mulch, like evergreen boughs or clean straw, to prevent the alternate freezing and thawing that can cause heaving. Apply a winter mulch after the ground freezes and remove before new growth begins in the spring.

White grubs: Fat, off-white, wormlike larvae of Japanese beetles. They reside in the soil and feed on plant (especially grass) roots until summer, when they emerge as beetles to feed on plant foliage.

Wings: (*a*) Corky tissue that forms edges along the twigs of some woody plants such as winged euonymus; (*b*) the flat, dried extension of tissue on some seeds, such as maple, that catch the wind and help them disseminate.

Woody plants: Those with woody stems or trunks, usually trees and shrubs such as maples and yews, but certain perennials such as lavender may have woody stems as well.

Bibliography

Armitage, Allan M. *Armitage's Garden Perennials.* Timber Press, 2000.

Armitage, Allan. *Herbaceous Perennial Plants.* Varsity Press, 1989.

Art, Henry W. *A Garden of Wildflowers: 101 Native Species and How to Grow Them.* Garden Way Publishing, 1986.

Bailey, Liberty Hyde. *The Standard Cyclopedia of Horticulture* (three volumes). Macmillan Publishing Co., 1963.

Bales, Suzanne Frutig. *Roses. Burpee American Gardening Series.* Prentice-Hall, 1994.

Ball, Jeff and Liz Ball. *Rodale's Flower Garden Problem Solver.* Rodale Press, 1990.

Barnes, Burton and Warren H. Wagner Jr. *Michigan Trees.* University of Michigan Press, 1992.

Bennett, Jennifer and Turid Forsyth. *The Harrowsmith Annual Garden.* Camden House, 1990.

Bird, Richard. *Growing and Propagating Showy Native Woody Plants.* University of North Carolina Press, 1992.

Brennan, Georgeanne and Mimi Luebbermann. *Beautiful Bulbs.* Chronicle Books, 1993.

Brooklyn Botanic Garden handbooks: *Butterfly Gardens,* 1995; *Natural Insect Control: The Ecological Gardener's Guide to Foiling Pests,* 1994; *Perennials,* 1991; *Shrubs: The New Glamour Plants,* 1994; *Trees: A Gardener's Guide,* 1992.

Brown, George E. *The Pruning of Trees, Shrubs and Conifers.* Faber and Faber, Ltd., 1972.

Bryan, John E. *John E. Bryan on Bulbs.* Burpee Expert Gardener Series. Macmillan, Inc., 1994.

Burrell, C. Colston and Elizabeth Stell. *Landscaping with Perennials.* Rodale Press, 1995.

Callaway, Dorothy. *The World of Magnolias.* Timber Press, 1994.

Clausen, Ruth Rodgers and Nicolas Ekstrom. *Perennials for American Gardens.* Random House, 1989.

Coffey, Timothy. *The History and Folklore of North American Wildflowers.* Houghton Mifflin Co., 1993.

Crockett, James Underwood. *Annuals.* Time-Life Books, 1979.

Crockett, James Underwood. *Crockett's Flower Garden.* Little, Brown and Co., 1981.

Crockett, James Underwood. *Crockett's Victory Garden.* Little, Brown and Co., 1977.

Cullina, William. *The New England Wild Flower Society Guide to Growing and Propagating Wildflowers of the United States and Canada.* Houghton Mifflin Co., 2000.

Darke, Rick. *The Color Encyclopedia of Ornamental Grasses: Sedges, Rushes, Restios, Cat-Tails, and Selected Bamboos.* Timber Press, 1999.

Dirr, Michael. *Manual of Woody Landscape Plants.* Stipes Publishing Co., 1990.

DiSabato-Aust, Tracy. *The Well-Tended Perennial Garden.* Timber Press, 1998.

Everett, T.H., editor. *New Illustrated Encyclopedia of Gardening.* Greystone Press, 1960.

Faust, Joan Lee. *The New York Times Book of Annuals and Perennials.* Times Books, 1980.

Ferreniea, Viki. *Gardening with Wildflowers.* Random House, 1993.

Fiala, Fr. John. *The Flowering Crabapples.* Timber Press, 1994.

Frankel, Edward. *Ferns: A Natural History.* The Stephen Greene Press, 1981.

Frederick Jr., William H. *The Exuberant Garden and the Controlling Hand: Plant Combinations for North American Gardens.* Little, Brown and Co., 1992.

Garden Club of America. *Plants that Merit Attention, Volume I—Trees* (1984) and *Volume II—Shrubs* (1996). Timber Press.

Greenlee, John. *The Encyclopedia of Ornamental Grasses.* Michael Friedman Publishing Group, 1992.

Griffiths, Mark. *Index of Garden Plants: The New Royal Horticulture Society Dictionary.* Timber Press, 1994.

Harper, Pamela and Frederick McGourty. *Perennials: How to Select, Grow and Enjoy.* HP Books, 1985.

Harper, Pamela. *Designing with Perennials.* Macmillan Publishing Co., 1991.

Heath, Brent and Becky Heath. *Daffodils for American Gardens.* Elliott and Clark, 1995.

Hensel, Margaret. *English Cottage Gardening for American Gardeners.* W.W. Norton and Co., 1992.

Hill, Lewis and Nancy Hill. *Bulbs: Four Seasons of Beautiful Blooms.* Storey Communications, 1994.

Hillier Manual of Trees and Shrubs, The. David and Charles Publishers, 1993.

Hole, Lois. *Lois Hole's Bedding Plant Favorites.* Lone Pine Publishing, 1994.

Hollingsworth, Buckner. *Her Garden Was Her Delight.* Macmillan Publishing Co., 1962.

Jelitto, Leo and Wilhelm Schacht. *Hardy Herbaceous Perennials.* Timber Press, 1990.

Jimmerman, Douglas, editor. *Better Homes and Gardens Bulbs for All Seasons.* Meredith Corp., 1994.

Knox, Gerald, editor. *Better Homes and Gardens Step-By-Step Successful Gardening.* Meredith Corp., 1987.

Kowalchik, Claire and Willim Hylton, editors. *Rodale's Illustrated Encyclopedia of Herbs.* Rodale Press, 1987.

Lacy, Allen. *Gardening with Groundcovers and Vines.* HarperCollins Publishers Inc., 1993.

Loewer, Peter. *The Annual Garden: Flowers, Foliage, Fruits and Grasses for One Summer Season.* Rodale Press, 1988.

Lyon-Jeness, C. "They hoed the corn." *Michigan History Magazine,* July-August, 1994.

MacKenzie, David. *Perennial Ground Covers.* Timber Press, 1997.

Mathew, Brian and Philip Swindells. *The Complete Book of Bulbs.* Reader's Digest Association, Reed International Books Ltd., 1994.

Mathew, Brian. *The Year-Round Bulb Garden.* Souvenir Press, 1986.

McKeon, Judith C. *The Encyclopedia of Roses: An Organic Guide to Growing & Enjoying America's Favorite Flower.* Rodale Press, Inc, 1995.

Osborne, Robert. *Hardy Roses.* Garden Way Publishing, 1991.

Ottesen, Carole. *The Native Plant Primer.* Harmony Books, 1995.

Ottesen, Carole. *Ornamental Grasses.* McGraw Hill Publishing Co., 1989.

Phillips, Ellen and C. Colston Burrell. *Rodale's Illustrated Encyclopedia of Perennials.* Rodale Press, 1993.

Reilly, Ann. *Parks' Success with Seeds.* Geo. W. Park Seed Co., Inc., 1978.

Roth, Susan. *Better Homes and Gardens Complete Guide to Flower Gardening.* Meredith Books, 1995.

Rutz, Miriam. *Genevieve Gillette: From Thrift Garden to National Parks.* Manuscript.

Rutz, Miriam. *Public Gardens in Michigan.* 1996.

Safe and Easy Lawn Care. Taylor's Weekend Gardening Guides. Houghton Mifflin Co., 1997.

Smith, Helen V. *Michigan Wildflowers.* Cranbrook Institute of Science, 1979.

Sommers, L. K. "Innocent recreations." *Michigan History Magazine,* July-August, 1994.

Sperka, Marie. *Growing Wildflowers.* Scribner's, 1973.

Spongberg, Stephen A. *A Reunion of Trees.* Harvard University Press, 1990.

Springer, Lauren. *The Undaunted Gardener.* Fulcrum Publishing, 1994.

Sternberg, Guy and Jim Wilson. *Landscaping with Native Trees.* Chapters Publishing Ltd., 1995.

Still, Steven. *Manual of Herbaceous Ornamental Plants.* Stipes Publishing Co., 1994.

Stuart, David and James Sutherland. *Plants from the Past.* Penguin Books, 1989.

Sunset Lawns and Ground Covers. Sunset Publishing Co., 1994.

Taylor's Guide to Annuals. Houghton Mifflin Co., 1986.

Taylor's Guide to Perennials. Houghton Mifflin Co., 1986.

Taylor's Guide to Roses. Houghton Mifflin Co., 1995.

Taylor's Guide to Shade Gardening. Houghton Mifflin Co., 1994.

Taylor's Master Guide to Gardening. Houghton Mifflin Co., 1994.

Thomas, Graham Stuart. *Ornamental Shrubs, Climbers and Bamboos.* Timber Press, 1992.

Thomas, Graham Stuart. *Perennial Garden Plants, or, The Modern Florilegium,* third edition. J.M. Dent, Ltd., 1990.

Tripp, Kim and J.C. Raulston. *The Year in Trees.* Timber Press, 1995.

Voss, Edward G. *Botanical Beachcombers and Explorers.* University of Michigan Herbarium, 1978.

Voss, Edward G. *Michigan Flora* (in three parts). Cranbrook Institute of Science and University of Michigan Herbarium; 1972, 1985, 1996.

Watson, Gary, editor. *Selecting and Planting Trees.* The Morton Arboretum, Lisle, Ill.

Wells, James, Frederick W. Case Jr. and T. Lawrence Mellichamp. *Wildflowers of the Western Great Lakes Region.* Cranbrook Institute of Science, 1999.

Wilson, Jim. *Landscaping with Container Plants.* Houghton Mifflin Co., 1990.

Wilson, Jim. *Landscaping with Wildflowers.* Houghton Mifflin Co., 1992.

Winterrowd, Wayne. *Annuals for Connoisseurs.* Prentice-Hall, 1992.

Wister, Gertrude S. *Hardy Garden Bulbs.* E.P. Dutton and Co., Inc., 1964.

Woods, Christopher. *Encyclopedia of Perennials.* Facts on File, 1992.

Wyman, Donald. *Ground Cover Plants.* Macmillan Publishing Co., 1966.

Wyman, Donald. *Wyman's Gardening Encyclopedia.* Macmillan Publishing Co., 1986.

Yeo, Peter. *Hardy Geraniums.* Timber Press, 1985.

Photography Credits

Thomas Eltzroth: pages 23, 26, 28, 29, 30, 31, 32, 33, 35, 36, 37, 38, 41, 42, 43, 44, 45, 47, 48, 49, 50, 51, 53, 55, 57, 61, 62, 63, 64, 65, 67, 69, 73, 75, 77, 79, 80, 81, 83, 85, 86, 88, 91, 92, 93, 100, 102, 103, 104, 105, 107, 109, 110, 111, 120, 125, 127, 129, 130, 131, 132, 135, 136, 140, 142, 143, 148, 149, 151, 152, 154, 155, 158, 164, 165, 173, 184, 185, 187, 190, 196, 197, 201, 203, 204, 207, 213, 214, 216, 218, 220, 221, 228, 230, Back Cover (First and Fourth photos)

Liz Ball and Rick Ray: pages 13, 17, 18, 22, 24, 25, 40, 46, 72, 108, 112, 117, 121, 137, 141, 145, 147, 150, 153, 160, 166, 178, 180, 181, 186, 191, 194, 199, 208, 210, 224, 226, Back cover (Second and Third photos)

Pam Harper: pages 39, 52, 54, 56, 58, 59, 74, 82, 94, 106, 113, 128, 144, 156, 163, 168, 174, 177, 179, 182, 195, 205, 206, 209, 211, 212

Mark Turner: pages 66, 71, 76, 78, 116, 123, 134, 159, 161, 176, 222, 225, 227, 231

Tim Boland and Laura Coit: pages 10, 14, 122, 157, 167, 170, 175, 188, 189, 192, 193, 198, 233

Dency Kane: pages 34, 96, 98, 115, 133, 138, 139, 162, 223

Michael Dirr: pages 171, 172, 183, 215, 219

Jerry Pavia: pages 70, 99, 202, 229

William Adams: pages 101, 217, 232

Dave MacKenzie: pages 97, 114, 118

Charles Mann: pages 60, 95, 124

Cathy Barash: pages 126, 146

Ralph Snodsmith: pages 68, 169

Rob Cardillo: page 200

Lorenzo Gunn: page 27

Robert Lyons: page 119

Plant Index

Abies concolor, 216
Abies nordmanniana, 216
Acer griseum, 206
Acer maximowiczianum, 206
Acer saccharum, 212
Acer triflorum, 206
Achillea 'Coronation Gold', 152
Aconite, Winter, 71, 76, 81, 82, 189
Adiantum pedatum, 228
Aesculus pavia, 161
Aesculus parviflora, 161
Ageratum, 37, 44
    Hardy, 150
Ajuga reptans, 53
Ajuga, 52, 66
Alchemilla alpina, 134
Alchemilla conjuncta, 134
Alchemilla mollis, 134
Alleghany Spurge, 62, 206
Allium aflatunense, 74
Allium christophii, 78
Allium giganteum, 74
Allium karataviense, 78
Allium sphaerocephalum, 74
Allium spp., 74
Allium, Drumstick, 74
Allspice, Carolina, 163, 167
Alternate-leaf Dogwood, 205
Alumroot, 116, 130
    Maple-leaved, 130
    Purple, 183
Amaranth, Globe, 31
Amelanchier arborea, 211
Amelanchier canadensis, 211
Amelanchier, 211
American
    Filbert, 172
    Hop-Hornbeam, 200
    Smoketree, 192
    Sweetgum, 213
    Yellowwood, 219
Amsonia, Arkansas, 114
Amsonia hubrectii, 114
Amsonia tabernaemontana, 114
Amsonia tabernaemontana var.
    montana, 114
Amur Chokecherry, 193, 248
Andropogon scoparium, 94
Anemone, 98, 164, 248
    Hybrid, 99, 113
    Japanese, 132
    Japanese Hybrid, 114
Anemone blanda, 81, 170
Anemone × *hybrida*, 132
Angel's Trumpet, 249
Angelwing Begonia, 47

Anglojap Yew, 157
Annabelle Hydrangea, 156
Annual Pinks, 120
Annuals, 22
Antique Rose, 240
Antirrhinum majus, 45
Aquilegia canadensis, 232
Arborvitae, 158, 160
Arisaema dracontium, 225
Arisaema sikokianum, 225
Arisaema triphyllum, 225
Arkansas Amsonia, 114
Aromatic Aster, 94, 138
Arrowwood Viburnum, 159
Artemisia absinthium, 106
Artemisia ludoviciana, 106
Artemisia versicolor, 106
Artemisia, 28, 74, 106, 144, 150
Aruncus aethusifolius, 126
Aruncus dioicus, 126
Asarum canadense, 54
Asarum europaeum, 54
Asclepias incarnata, 117
Asclepias tuberosa, 117
Ash, White, 215
Asimina triloba, 207
Aster, 81, 95, 114, 115, 122, 127,
    132, 133, 138, 142, 148,
    151, 164
    Aromatic, 94, 138
    Calico, 138
    False, 115
    Heath, 138
    New England, 138
    Smooth, 97, 138
Aster ericoides, 138
Aster laevis, 97, 138
Aster lateriflorus, 138
Aster novae-angliae, 138
Aster oblongifolius, 94, 138
Astilbe, 26, 53, 56, 60, 107, 110,
    134, 140, 146, 229
    Dwarf Chinese, 56, 208
Astilbe × *arendsii*, 107
Astilbe chinensis var. *pumila*, 56
Astilbe simplicifolia, 107
Astilbe chinensis var. *taquetii*, 107
Athyrium filix-femina, 226
Athyrium nipponicum, 226
Autumn Crocus, 66, 248
Azalea, 175, 249
    Hybrid, 175
Baldcypress, 194, 197
Baptisia alba, 113
Baptisia australis, 113
Baptisia australis var. *minor*, 113

Baptisia lactea, 113
Barberry, 177
Barrenwort, 57, 140
    Longspur, 57
    Red, 57
Basil, 43
Bayberry, 160, 172
Bean, Castor, 249
Bean, Hyacinth, 34
Beautyberry, 193
Beebalm, 108
Beech, 219
Begonia, 26, 47
    Angelwing, 47
    Fibrous-rooted, 47
    Wax, 47
Begonia × *semperflorens-cultorum*, 47
Bellflower, 109
    Carpathian, 109
    Peach-leaf, 109
Bergamot, 108
Bethlehem Sage, 79, 116, 140
Betula nigra, 209
Big-leaf Ligularia, 100
Bigroot Geranium, 52, 56, 57, 101,
    112, 208, 233
Birch, River, 81, 179, 180, 209
Bishop's Hat, 57
Bittersweet, 249
Black
    Gum, 195
    Snakeroot, 110
Black-eyed Susan, 32, 94, 97, 111,
    141, 142
Blazing Star, 32, 98, 108, 111,
    129, 164
Bleeding Heart, 112, 225, 248
    Fringed, 112, 137, 146, 224, 230
Bloodroot, 54, 222, 224, 226, 227,
    229, 230, 233, 248
Bloody Cranesbill, 128, 144
Blue
    Aster, 132
    False Indigo, 113, 114, 129, 147
    Fescue, 92
    Flax, 120
    Oat Grass, 92, 98, 120
    Sage, 38
    Spirea, 66, 164
    Spruce, Colorado, 57, 204
    Star, 113, 114, 116, 129
    Windflower, 170
Bluebeard, 115, 164, 177
Bluebell, Virginia, 54, 226, 229,
    230, 232
Bluestar, 112, 167, 181

Bluestem, Little, 94
Boltonia, 24, 95, 115, 118, 127, 133, 141, 181
Boltonia asteroides, 115
Boneset, 133
Borage, 43
Botanical Tulip, 77
Bottlebrush Buckeye, 161, 248
Bowman's Root, 101, 113, 116, 181
Boxwood, 162, 248
    Common, 162
    Korean, 162
Brazilian Verbena, 24, 31, 39, 44, 117
Bridal Veil Spirea, 183
Bronze Fennel, 44, 67
Brunnera macrophylla, 146
Buckeye
    Bottlebrush, 161, 248
    Red, 161
Bugbane, 110
    Japanese, 110
    Kamchatka, 110
Bugleweed, 53
Bugloss, Siberian, 101, 112, 116, 140, 146, 205, 233
Bulbs, Hardy, 63
Burkwood Viburnum, 176
Busy Lizzie, 35
Buttercup, 249
Buttercup Winter Hazel, 170, 175
Butterfly Weed, 32, 39, 97, 117, 136
Buxus 'Green Velvet', 162
Caladium, 249
Calamagrostis × *acutiflora* 'Karl Foerster', 93
Calamagrostis brachytricha, 93
Calamint, 97, 118
Calamintha nepeta ssp. *nepeta*, 118
Calendula officinalis, 43
Calico Aster, 138
Calla Lily, 249
Callicarpa dichotoma, 193
Calycanthus floridus, 163
Campanula carpatica, 109
Campanula persicifolia, 109
Campanula spp., 109
Canadian Wild Ginger, 54, 56, 211, 233
Carex morrowii, 58
Carex muskingumensis, 58
Carolina Allspice, 163, 167
Carpathian Bellflower, 109
Caryopteris, 164
Caryopteris × *clandonensis*, 164

Castor Bean, 249
Catmint, 67, 92, 109, 119, 120, 124, 135, 144
    Faassen's, 119
Cedar, White, 158
Cercidiphyllum japonicum, 201
Cercis canadensis, 208
Chasmanthium latifolium, 101
Cheddar Pinks, 92, 120, 144, 149
Chelone glabra, 151
Chelone obliqua, 151
Cherry, 170, 193, 249
    Ornamental, 193
Cherry-pie, 33
China Pinks, 120
Chinese
    Astilbe, Dwarf, 56, 208
    Juniper, 165
    Witchhazel, 189
Chinkapin Oak, 217
Chionodoxa forbesii, 71
Chionodoxa gigantea, 71
Chionodoxa luciliae, 71
Chionodoxa sardensis, 71
Chive, 74
Chokecherry, Amur, 193, 248
Christmas
    Fern, 172, 223, 224
    Rose, 137
Chrysanthemum, 132
Cilantro, 97
Cimicifuga racemosa, 110
Cimicifuga simplex, 110
Cinnamon Fern, 228
Cladrastis kentukea, 219
Cladrastis lutea, 219
Classic Zinnia, 48
Clematis heracleifolia, 121
Clematis × *jackmanii*, 121
Clematis spp. and cultivars, 121
Clematis terniflora, 121
Clematis, 121, 248
    Jackman's, 188
    Sweet Autumn, 121
    Tube, 121
Cleome, 25
Cleome hassleriana, 25
Clethra alnifolia, 186
Climbing
    Hydrangea, 166
    Rose, 188, 241
        'William Baffin', 188
Coffeetree, Kentucky, 202, 248
Colchicum, 66
Colchicum autumnale, 66
Coleus, 26, 29, 47

Coleus × *hybridus*, 26
Colorado Blue Spruce, 57, 204
Columbine, 130, 182
    Eastern, 232
    Hybrid, 128
    Wild, 231, 232
Common
    Boxwood, 162
    Lilac, 174
    Smoketree, 192
    Snowdrop, 76
    Yarrow, 150
    Zinnia, 48
Concolor Fir, 216
Coneflower
    Orange, 142
    Purple, 32, 94, 98, 111, 122, 125, 129, 141, 143, 164
Convallaria majalis, 60
Convallaria majalis var. *rosea*, 60
Copper Fennel, 44
Coralbells, 58, 130
Coreopsis, 38, 39, 67, 117, 125, 149
    Threadleaf, 124, 144, 150
Coreopsis grandiflora, 150
Coreopsis verticillata, 150
Corneliancherry, 81, 196
Cornus alternifolia, 205
Cornus amomum, 171
Cornus controversa, 205
Cornus florida, 205
Cornus mas, 196
Cornus officinalis, 196
Cornus racemosa, 171
Cornus stolonifera, 171, 180
Corylopsis glabrescens, 170
Corylopsis pauciflora, 170, 175
Corylus americana, 172
Cosmos, 27, 37, 38
Cosmos bipinnatus, 27
Cotinus coggygria, 192
Cotinus obovatus, 192
Cotoneaster, 249
Cottage Tulip, 77
Crabapple, 81, 165, 170, 181
    Flowering, 198
Cranesbill
    Bloody, 128, 144
    Dalmatian, 52
    Spotted, 233
Creeping
    Juniper, 55, 209
    Phlox, 231
    Thyme, 61, 120, 135
Crested Woodland Iris, 224
Crocosmia, 39, 67, 106, 119

Crocosmia × crocosmiiflora
  'Lucifer', 67
Crocus, 66, 68, 70, 82
  Autumn, 66, 248
  Dutch, 55, 68
  Snow, 68, 76
Crocus chrysanthus, 68
Crocus tommasinianus, 68
Crocus vernus hybrids, 68
Culver's Root, 98, 111, 122, 148
Cushion Spurge, 123, 248
Cypress, 194
Daffodil, 41, 52, 59, 60, 62, 68, 69,
  71, 72, 80, 81, 96, 124, 146, 176,
  198, 230, 248
  Trumpet, 69
Daisy, 32, 81, 129, 141, 142
  Gloriosa, 31, 32, 37, 39, 106, 248
  Shasta, 108, 125
Dalmatian Cranesbill, 52
Darwin Tulip, 77
Datura, 249
Dawn Redwood, 197
Daylily, 44, 73, 106, 108, 118, 119,
  122, 124, 125
Dead Nettle, 59
  Spotted, 59
Delphinium, 249
Deschampsia caespitosa, 100
Diabolo® Ninebark, 167
Dianthus chinensis, 120
Dianthus deltoides, 120
Dianthus gratianopolitanus, 120
Dicentra eximia, 112, 224
Dicentra spectabilis, 112
Dieffenbachia, 249
Dill, 24
Dogwood, 196
  Alternate-leaf, 205
  Flowering, 205
  Giant, 205
  Gray, 167, 171, 216
  Japanese Cornel, 196
  Pagoda, 182, 205, 228
  Redosier, 171, 216
  Redtwig, 180, 204
  Red-twigged, 160
  Silky, 171
Dropseed, Prairie, 97
Drumstick Allium, 74
Dryopteris marginalis, 223
Dusty Miller, 28, 31, 38, 47
Dutch Crocus, 55, 68
Dutchmen's Britches, 225
Dwarf
  Bearded Iris, 123

Chinese Astilbe, 56, 208
Fothergilla, 168
Iris, 70
Eastern Columbine, 232
Echinacea purpurea, 141
Elderberry, 249
Elephant Ear, 249
Emperor Tulip, 81
English
  Ivy, 249
  Lavender, 136
Epimedium, 57, 201, 225
Epimedium grandiflorum, 57
Epimedium × rubrum, 57
Epimedium spp., 57
Epimedium × versicolor, 57
Eranthis cilicica, 82
Eranthis hyemalis, 82
Eupatorium coelestinum, 150
Eupatorium maculatum, 133
Euphorbia dulcis, 123
Euphorbia polychroma, 123
European Wild Ginger, 54
Faassen's Catmint, 119
False
  Aster, 115
  Indigo, Blue, 113, 114, 129, 147
    Prairie, 113
    White, 113
Fanflower, 40
Feather Reed Grass, 93, 108,
  115, 133
  Korean, 93
Fennel, 44
  Bronze, 44, 67
  Copper, 44
  Purple, 44, 124, 152
Fern, 53, 54, 60, 79, 112, 140, 146,
  172, 182, 205, 211, 222, 227,
  228, 229, 230, 231
  Christmas, 172, 223, 224
  Cinnamon, 228
  Japanese Painted, 137, 226
  Lady, 226, 233
  Maidenhair, 54, 172, 228, 233
  Marginal Shield, 223
  Ostrich, 228
Fernleaf Peony, 139
Fescue, Blue, 92
Festuca glauca, 92
Fibrous-rooted Begonia, 47
Filbert, American, 172
Fir
  Concolor, 216
  Nordmann, 216
  White, 216

Flame Grass, 24, 95, 115, 181
Flax, Blue, 120
Floribunda Rose, 240
Flowering
  Crabapple, 198
  Dogwood, 205
  Tobacco, 29, 33
Foamflower, 58, 222, 223, 224,
  230, 231
Foeniculum vulgare 'Purpurascens', 44
Forget-me-not, 146
Forsythia, 169, 170, 216
Forsythia × intermedia, 169
Fothergilla, 168
  Dwarf, 168
Fothergilla gardenii, 168
Fountain Grass, 96, 167, 181
  Purple, 96
Fragrant Winter Hazel, 170
Fraxinus americana, 215
French Marigold, 32, 37
Fringed Bleeding Heart, 112, 137,
  146, 224, 230
Galanthus elwesii, 76
Galanthus nivalis, 76
Galium odoratum, 54
Garden
  Phlox, 108, 125
  Snowdrop, 76
Garlic, 74
Gaudy Jack, 225
Gayfeather, 111
Geranium, 28, 30, 38, 52, 233
  Bigroot, 52, 56, 57, 101, 112,
    208, 233
  Hardy, 52, 113, 116, 120, 128,
    130, 134, 147, 149, 233
  Wild, 227, 233
  Zonal, 30
Geranium × cantabrigiense, 52
Geranium macrorrhizum, 52
Geranium maculatum, 233
Geranium sanguineum, 128
Geranium sanguineum var.
  striatum, 128
Giant
  Dogwood, 205
  Onion, 74
  Snowdrop, 76
Gillenia stipulata, 116
Gillenia trifoliata, 116
Ginger
  Canadian Wild, 54, 56, 211
  European Wild, 54
  Wild, 182, 227, 232
Ginkgo, 199

Ginkgo biloba, 199
Globe Amaranth, 31
Gloriosa Daisy, 31, 32, 37, 39,
    106, 248
Glory-of-the-Snow, 71, 175
Goat's Beard, 126
    Korean, 126
Goldenrod, 97, 127, 133, 138,
    148, 248
    Rough-leaved, 110, 112, 116
    Showy, 127
    Stiff, 127
Gomphrena globosa, 31
Grandiflora Petunia, 42
Grape Hyacinth, 72, 185
Grass
    Blue Oat, 78, 92
    Feather Reed, 93, 108, 115, 133
    Flame, 95, 115, 181
    Fountain, 96, 167, 181
    Japanese Silver, 95
    Korean Feather Reed, 93
    Maiden, 95
    Porcupine, 95
    Purple Fountain, 96
    Red Switch, 113, 133
    Silver, 33
    Spangle, 101
    Switch, 32, 94, 98, 132, 142, 151
    Tall Purple Moor, 99
    Tufted Hair, 100, 147
Grasses, Ornamental, 90
Gray Dogwood, 167, 171, 216
Great Solomon's Seal, 229
Green Dragon, 225
Groundcovers, 49
Gum, Black, 195
Gymnocladus dioicus, 202
Hair Grass, Tufted, 100, 147
Hamamelis × *intermedia*
    'Arnold Promise', 189
Hamamelis vernalis, 189
Hamamelis virginiana, 189
Hardy
    Ageratum, 150
    Geranium, 52, 113, 116, 120,
        128, 130, 134, 147, 149, 233
Hardy Bulbs, 63
Hazelnut, 172
Heath Aster, 138
Helenium autumnale, 148
Helen's Flower, 148
Helianthus annuus, 46
Helictotrichon sempervirens, 92
Heliopsis, 117, 125, 129
    Sunflower, 39, 67, 111, 129, 141

Heliopsis helianthoides ssp.
    scabra, 129
Heliotrope, 31, 33
Heliotropium arborescens, 33
Hellebore, 76, 137, 248
Helleborus niger, 137
Helleborus orientalis, 137
Hemoerocallis hybrids, 124
Heuchera, 101, 107, 110, 130, 134
Heuchera spp., hybrids, and
    cultivars, 130
Heuchera villosa, 123, 130, 183
Hickory, 172
Holly, 179, 216, 249
    Michigan, 167, 179, 194, 209
Hop-Hornbeam, 200
    American, 200
Hosta, 26, 53, 56, 58, 59, 60, 107,
    118, 124, 126, 130, 131, 140,
    146, 201, 223, 226, 229, 230
Hosta plantaginea, 131
Hosta spp. and hybrids, 131
Hyacinth, 249
    Bean, 34
    Grape, 72, 185
Hybrid
    Anemone, 99, 113, 132
    Azalea, 175
    Columbine, 128
    Lily, 119
    Rugosa, 181
    Salvia, 144
    Tea, 240
    Yarrow, 152
Hydrangea, 173, 248
    Annabelle, 156
    Climbing, 166
    Oakleaf, 173
    Panicle, 173
    Smooth, 156
Hydrangea arborescens
    'Annabelle', 156
Hydrangea petiolaris, 166
Hydrangea quercifolia, 173
Hydrangea spp., 173
Hydrangea Vine, Japanese, 166
Icy Bluestar, 167
Ilex verticillata, 179
Impatiens, 26, 28, 35, 42
Impatiens walleriana, 35
Indigo
    Blue False, 113, 114, 147
    White False, 113
    Wild Blue, 128
Iris, 70, 119, 129, 147, 248
    Crested Woodland, 224

Dwarf Bearded, 123
Dwarf, 70
Reticulated, 70
Siberian, 92, 113, 128, 130, 134,
    144, 147
Tall Bearded, 147
Yellow Flag, 100
Iris cristata, 224
Iris histrioides, 70
Iris reticulata, 70
Iris sibirica, 147
Ironwood, 200
Ivy, 62
    English, 249
Jack-in-the-Pulpit, 54, 225, 248
Jackman's Clematis, 188
Japanese
    Anemone, 132
    Bugbane, 110
    Cornel Dogwood, 196
    Hybrid Anemone, 114
    Hydrangea Vine, 166
    Painted Fern, 137, 226
    Sedge, 58, 123, 226
    Silver Grass, 95
    Spicebush, 182
    Spurge, 62
    Witchhazel, 189
Jasmine Tobacco, 29
Joe-pye Weed, 98, 99, 122, 133,
    148, 151
Johnny-jump-up, 41
Jonquil, 69
Juniper, 55, 169, 177
    Chinese, 165
    Creeping, 55, 209
    Pfitzer, 165
    Sargent, 165
Juniperus chinensis, 165
Juniperus horizontalis, 55
Juniperus sargentii, 165
Kale, Ornamental, 74
Kamchatka Bugbane, 110
Katsuratree, 201
Kentucky Coffeetree, 202, 248
Korean
    Boxwood, 162
    Feather Reed Grass, 93
    Goat's Beard, 126
    Lilac, 174
    Rhododendron, 71, 170, 175
Koreanspice Viburnum, 176
Lablab purpureus, 34
Labrador Violet, 222
Lady Fern, 226, 233
Lady in the Bathtub, 112

Lady's Mantle, 123, 128, 130, 134, 147, 149
Lamb's Ear, 61, 66, 78, 118, 120, 123, 135, 144, 152
Lamb's Tongue, 135
Lamium, 59
Lamium maculatum, 59
Lantanaphyllum Viburnum, 177
Large-Flowered
  Tickseed, 150
  White Trillium, 227, 230
Larkspur, 249
Lavender, 61, 78, 117, 120, 135, 136, 152
  English, 136
Lavandula angustifolia, 136
Lawns, 83
Leatherleaf Viburnum, 177
Lenten Rose, 137, 180
Leucojum aestivum, 79
Leucojum vernum, 79
Liatris spicata, 111
Ligularia, Big-leaf, 100
Ligularia dentata, 100
Lilac, 178
  Common, 174
  Korean, 174
Lilium hybrids, 73
Lily, 44, 73, 119
  Calla, 249
  Peace, 249
  Plantain, 131
Lily-of-the-Valley, 60, 248
Linden
  Littleleaf, 203
  Silver, 203
Lindera benzoin, 182
Lindera obtusiloba, 182
Liquidambar styraciflua, 213
Liriodendron tulipifera, 214
Little Bluestem, 94
Littleleaf Linden, 203
Lobelia, 249
Long-leaved Lungwort, 140
Longspur Barrenwort, 57
Love-in-a-Mist, 36
Lungwort, 140, 229
Magnolia, 213
  Saucer, 210
  Star, 71, 72, 75, 185
Magnolia × soulangiana, 210
Magnolia stellata, 185
Maiden Grass, 95
Maidenhair Fern, 54, 172, 228, 233
Maiden Pinks, 120
Malus spp., 198

Maple, 62, 199
  Maximowicz, 206
  Paperbark, 206
  Red, 249
  Sugar, 212
  Three-flowered, 206
Maple-leaved Alumroot, 130
Marginal Shield Fern, 223
Marigold, 28, 37, 39
  French, 32, 37
  Pot, 33, 43
  Signet, 32, 37
Matteuccia struthiopteris, 228
Maximowicz Maple, 206
Mayapple, 225, 249
Mealy-cup Sage, 38, 39
Melampodium, 33, 39
Melampodium paludosum, 39
Mertensia virginica, 230
Metasequoia glyptostroboides, 197
Michigan Holly, 167, 179, 194, 209
Milkweed, 117
  Swamp, 117, 151
Miscanthus, 95, 118
Miscanthus sinensis, 33, 95, 115
Mistletoe, 249
Molinia caerulea ssp.
  arundinacea, 99
Monarda didyma, 108
Monkshood, 249
Montbretia, 67
Moonseed, 249
Moor Grass, Tall Purple, 99
Morning Glory, 34, 249
Moss
  Phlox, 123
  Rose, 40
Mother-in-law Plant, 249
Mother-of-Thyme, 61
Multiflora Petunia, 33, 42
Muscari armeniacum, 72
Muscari botryoides, 72
Myrica pensylvanica, 160
Naked Boys, 66
Narcissus, 54, 69
Narcissus spp. and hybrids, 69
Nepeta × faassenii, 119
Nepeta mussinii, 119
Nettle, Spotted Dead, 59
New England Aster, 138
Nicotiana, 29
Nicotiana alata, 29
Nicotiana langsdorffi, 29
Nigella damascena, 36
Nightshade, 249
Ninebark, Diabolo®, 167

Nordmann Fir, 216
Norway Spruce, 169, 204, 210
Nyssa sylvatica, 195
Oak, 172, 199, 217, 248
  Chinkapin, 217
  Red, 217
  White, 217
Oakleaf Hydrangea, 173
Oat Grass, 92
  Blue, 78, 92, 120
Oats, Wild, 57, 101, 116, 229
Obedient Plant, 122
Old Garden Rose, 240
Onion, 74, 78
  Giant, 74
  Ornamental, 68, 74, 78, 92, 123
  Turkistan, 78
Orange Coneflower, 142
Oriental
  Poppy, 114
  Spruce, 204, 210
Ornamental
  Cherry, 193
  Kale, 74
  Onion, 68, 74, 78, 92, 123
Ornamental Grasses, 90
Osmunda cinnamomea, 228
Ostrich Fern, 228
Ostrya virginiana, 200
Oswego Tea, 108
Ox-eye Sunflower, 129
Pachysandra, 62
Pachysandra procumbens, 62, 206
Pachysandra terminalis, 62
Paeonia lactiflora and hybrids, 139
Paeonia tenuifolia, 139
Pagoda Dogwood, 182, 205, 228
Palm Sedge, 58
Panicle Hydrangea, 173
Panicum virgatum, 98
Pansy, 41, 72, 77
Paperbark Maple, 206
Pasqueflower, 77
Pawpaw, 207
Pea, Sweet, 249
Peace Lily, 249
Peach-leaf Bellflower, 109
Pelargonium, 233
Pelargonium × hortorum, 30
Pennisetum, 96
Pennisetum alopecuroides, 96
Pennisetum setaceum, 96
Peony, 113, 114, 116, 139, 144, 147, 167
  Fernleaf, 139
Pepperbush, Sweet, 186

Perennials, 102
Perennial Salvia, 144, 152
Periwinkle, 249
Perovskia atriplicifolia, 143
Petunia, 35, 38, 42, 74, 167
    Grandiflora, 42
    Multiflora, 33, 42
Petunia × *hybrida*, 42
Pfitzer Juniper, 165
Phlox divaricata, 231
Phlox paniculata, 125
Phlox stolonifera, 231
Phlox, 149
    Creeping, 231
    Garden, 108, 125
    Moss, 123
    Wild Blue, 224, 231, 233
    Woodland, 79, 232
Physocarpus opulifolius 'Monlo', 167
Physostegia virginiana, 122
Picea abies, 204
Picea omorika, 204
Picea orientalis, 204
Pinchusion Flower, 117
Pine, White, 218
Pink Turtlehead, 151
Pinks
    Annual, 120
    Cheddar, 92, 120, 144, 149
    China, 120
    Maiden, 120
Pinus strobus, 218
Plantain Lily, 131
Poinsettia, 123
Pokeweed, 249
Polyantha Rose, 241
Polygonatum biflorum, 229
Polygonatum commutatum, 229
Polygonatum odoratum, 229
Polystichum acrostichoides, 223
Poppy, 249
    Oriental, 114
Porcupine Grass, 95
Porteranthus trifoliatus, 116
Portulaca, 40, 48
Portulaca grandiflora, 40
Pot Marigold, 33, 43
Prairie
    Dropseed, 97
    False Indigo, 113
Prunus maackii, 193
Prunus serrula, 193
Pulmonaria, 140, 225
Pulmonaria longifolia, 140
Pulmonaria saccharata, 140
Pulmonaria spp., 140

Purple
    Alumroot, 183
    Coneflower, 32, 94, 98, 111,
        122, 125, 129, 141, 143, 164
    Fennel, 44, 124, 152
    Foutain Grass, 96
Queen Anne's Lace, 44
Quercus alba, 217
Quercus muhlenbergii, 217
Quercus rubra, 217
Red
    Barrenwort, 57
    Buckeye, 161
    Maple, 249
    Oak, 217
    Switch Grass, 98, 113, 133
Redbud, 75, 208
Redosier, 180, 216
    Dogwood, 171, 180
Redtwig Dogwood, 180, 204
Red-twigged Dogwood, 160
Redwood, Dawn, 197
Reed Grass, Feather, 93, 108, 115, 133
Reticulated Iris, 70
Rhododendron, 175, 248
    Korean, 71, 170, 175
Rhododendron mucronulatum
    'Cornell Pink', 175
Rhubarb, 249
Rhus copallina, 184
Rhus typhina, 184
River Birch, 81, 179, 180, 209
Root, Culver's, 98, 111, 122
Rosa glauca, 241
Rosa rugosa, 181
Rosa 'William Baffin', 188
Rose, 33, 36, 71, 109, 119, 121, 181
    Antique, 240
    Christmas, 137
    Climbing, 241
        'William Baffin', 188
    Floribunda, 240
    Hybrid Tea, 240
    Lenten, 137, 180
    Moss, 40
    Old Garden, 240
    Polyantha, 241
    Rugosa, 33, 181
    Shrub, 52, 109, 116, 135, 149,
        181, 241
    Species, 181, 241
Rough-leaved Goldenrod, 127
Rudbeckia, 96, 118, 129, 142
Rudbeckia fulgida ssp.
    sullivantii, 142
Rudbeckia hirta, 32

Rudbeckia triloba, 142
Rugosa Rose, 33, 181, 241
Russian Sage, 32, 33, 118, 124, 133,
    135, 141, 143, 181
Sage
    Bethlehem, 79, 116, 140
    Blue, 38
    Mealy-cup, 38, 39
    Russian, 32, 33, 118, 124, 133,
        135, 141, 143, 181
    Scarlet, 38
    Texas, 38, 44
    Violet, 144
    White, 106
Salvia, 74, 92, 106, 120, 144
    Hybrid, 144
    Perennial, 144, 152
Salvia coccinea, 38
Salvia farinacea, 38
Salvia splendens, 38
Salvia × *superba*, 144
Salvia verticillata, 144
Sanguinaria canadensis, 222
Sargent Juniper, 165
Saucer Magnolia, 210
Scarlet Sage, 38
Schizachyrium scoparium, 94
Schizophragma hydrangeoides, 166
Scilla bifolia, 75
Scilla mischtschenkoana, 75
Scilla siberica, 75
Sea Foam, 106
Sedge, 58
    Japanese, 58, 123, 226
    Palm, 58
Sedum, 32, 61, 70, 74, 77, 78, 96,
    99, 109, 118, 145, 164
Sedum spp., 145
Senecio cineraria, 28
Serbian Spruce, 204
Serviceberry, 71, 211, 248
Shadblow, 208, 211
Shallot, 74
Shasta Daisy, 108, 125
Shining Sumac, 184
Showy Goldenrod, 127
Shrub Rose, 52, 109, 116, 135,
    149, 181
Shrubs, 153
Siberian
    Bugloss, 101, 112, 116, 140, 146,
        205, 233
    Iris, 92, 113, 128, 130, 134,
        144, 147
    Squill, 71, 75, 175, 210
Signet Marigold, 32, 37

Silky Dogwood, 171
Silver
    Grass, 33
    Japanese, 95
    Linden, 203
Smokebush, 156, 192
Smoketree
    American, 192
    Common, 192
Smooth
    Aster, 97, 138
    Hydrangea, 156
Snakeroot, Black, 110
Snapdragon, 45, 151
Sneezeweed, 67, 122, 125, 133, 141, 148, 248
Snow Crocus, 68, 76
Snowdrop, 54, 68, 70, 71, 75, 76, 79, 81, 82, 205, 223, 248
    Common, 76
    Garden, 76
    Giant, 76
Snowflake, 79
    Spring, 79
    Summer, 59, 79
Solidago rigida, 127
Solidago rugosa, 127
Solidago speciosa, 127
Solidago spp. and hybrids, 127
Solomon's Seal, 58, 107, 182, 229, 232, 233
    Great, 229
    Variegated, 229
Spangle Grass, 101
Species
    Rose, 181, 241
    Tulip, 61, 71, 77, 80
Speedwell
    Spiked, 149
    Woolly, 149
Spicebush, 182
    Japanese, 182
Spider Flower, 25, 37, 38
Spiked Speedwell, 149
Spiraea thunbergii, 183
Spiraea × *cinerea* 'Grefsheim', 183
Spirea, 183
    Blue, 66, 164
    Bridal Veil, 183
    Thunberg, 183
    Vanhoutte, 183
Spirea × *vanhouteii*, 183
Sporobolus heterolepsis, 97
Spotted
    Cranesbill, 233
    Dead Nettle, 59

Spring Snowflake, 79
Spruce
    Colorado Blue, 57, 204
    Norway, 169, 204, 210
    Oriental, 204, 210
    Serbian, 204
Spurge
    Alleghany, 62, 206
    Cushion, 123, 248
    Japanese, 62
Squill, 54, 68, 72, 75, 81, 82, 185
    Siberian, 71, 75, 175, 210
    Twinleaf, 75
Stachys byzantina, 135
Staghorn Sumac, 184, 248
Star, Blazing, 32
Star Magnolia, 71, 72, 75, 185
Star-of-Persia, 61, 78, 92, 135
Stiff Goldenrod, 127
Stonecrop, 122, 142, 145
Sugar Maple, 212
Sumac, 184
    Shining, 184
    Staghorn, 184, 248
Summer Snowflake, 59, 79
Summersweet, 186
Sunflower, 46
    Heliopsis, 39, 67, 111, 129, 141
    Ox-eye, 129
    Swamp, 148
Swamp
    Milkweed, 151
    Sunflower, 148
Sweet
    Autumn Clematis, 121
    Pea, 249
    Pepperbush, 186
    Potato Vine, 40
    Shrub, 163
    William, Wild, 231
    Woodruff, 54
Sweetgum, 172, 213
    American, 213
Switch Grass, 32, 94, 98, 132, 142, 151
    Red, 98, 113, 133
Syringa meyeri, 174
Syringa patula
    'Miss Kim', 174
Syringa vulgaris, 178
Tagetes patula, 37
Tagetes tenuifolia, 37
Tall
    Bearded Iris, 147
    Purple Moor Grass, 99
Tanacetum ptarmiciflorum, 28

Taxodium distichum, 194, 197
Taxus × *media*, 157
Tea, Oswego, 108
Texas Sage, 38, 44
Threadleaf Coreopsis, 124, 144, 150
Three-flowered Maple, 206
Thuja occidentalis, 158
Thunberg Spirea, 183
Thyme, 61, 70, 77, 78
    Creeping, 61, 120, 135
    Mother-of-, 61
    Woolly, 77, 78
Thymus praecox ssp. *arcticus*, 61
Thymus serpyllum, 61
Tiarella cordifolia, 224
Tickseed, 150
    Large-flowered, 150
Tilia cordata, 203
Tilia tomentosa, 203
Tobacco, 29
    Flowering, 29, 33
    Jasmine, 29
Tomato Vine, 249
Trees, 190
Trillium, 54, 224, 225, 227, 231, 233
    Large-Flowered White, 227, 230
Trillium grandiflorum, 227
Triumph Tulip, 77
Trumpet Daffodil, 69
Tube Clematis, 121
Tufted Hair Grass, 100, 147
Tulip, 41, 68, 72, 80, 81, 123, 183, 248
    Botanical, 77
    Cottage, 77
    Darwin, 77
    Emperor, 81
    Species, 61, 71, 77
    Triumph, 77
    Waterlily, 77
Tulipa bakeri, 77
Tulipa clusiana, 77
Tulipa hybrids, 80
Tulipa kaufmanniana, 77
Tulipa tarda, 77
Tuliptree, 214
Tupelo, 195
Turkistan Onion, 78
Turtlehead, 117, 132, 151
    Pink, 151
    Rose, 151
    White, 151
Twinleaf Squill, 75
Vanhoutte Spirea, 183
Variegated
    Hosta, 110

Solomon's Seal, 229
Verbena bonariensis, 24
Verbena × hybrida, 24
Verbena, 48
    Brazilian, 24, 31, 39, 44, 117
Verbena tenuisecta, 24
Vernal Witchhazel, 189
Veronica, 78, 109, 149
Veronica incana, 149
Veronica spicata, 149
Veronica virginica, 122
Veronicastrum virginicum, 122
Viburnum, 156, 176
    Arrowwood, 159
    Burkwood, 176
    Koreanspice, 176
    Lantaphyllum, 177
    Leatherleaf, 177
Viburnum × burkwoodii, 176
Viburnum carlesii, 176
Viburnum dentatum, 159
Viburnum rhytidophyllum, 177
Viburnum × rhytidophylloides, 177
Vinca, 62
Viola, 41
Viola labradorica, 222
Viola tricolor, 41
Viola × wittrockiana, 41
Violet Sage, 144
Violet, Labrador, 222
Virginia Bluebell, 54, 226, 229,
    230, 232

Waterlily, 73
    Tulip, 77
Wax Begonia, 47
Weigela, 187
Weigela florida, 187
White
    Ash, 215
    Cedar, 158
    False Indigo, 113
    Fir, 216
    Oak, 217
    Pine, 218
    Sage, 106
    Turtlehead, 151
Wild
    Blue Indigo, 128
    Blue Phlox, 224, 231, 233
    Columbine, 231, 232
    Geranium, 227, 233
    Ginger, 182, 227, 232
        Canadian, 54, 56, 211, 233
        European, 54
    Oats, 57, 101, 116, 229
    Sweet William, 231
'William Baffin' Climbing Rose, 188
Windflower, 81, 211, 222
    Blue, 170
Winter
    Aconite, 71, 76, 81, 82, 189
    Hazel
        Buttercup, 170, 175
        Fragrant, 170

Winterberry, 179, 248
Wisteria, 249
Witchhazel, 76, 189, 204, 216
    Chinese, 189
    Japanese, 189
    Vernal, 189
Wonder Bulb, 66
Woodland Flowers and Ferns, 220
Woodland Phlox, 79, 232
Woolly
    Speedwell, 149
    Thyme, 77, 78
Wormwood, 106
Yarrow, 38, 106, 144, 149, 152
    Common, 150
    Hybrid, 152
Yellow Flag Iris, 100
Yellowwood, 219
    American, 219
Yew, 169, 177, 211, 248
    Anglojap, 157
Zinnia, 24, 28, 32, 37, 39, 44, 48
    Classic, 48
    Common, 48
Zinnia angustifolia, 48
Zinnia elegans, 48
Zinnia spp., 48
Zonal Geranium, 30

Meet the Authors

Tim Boland

Tim Boland is the Curator of Horticulture at the Morton Arboretum. Previously, Boland was the Nursery Manager at Michigan State University. In addition, he is a teacher, garden writer, and photographer. Boland graduated from Michigan State University with a bachelor's degree in ornamental horticulture and a master's degree in botany. Boland has had an extensive career in horticulture including internships at the Scott Aboretum and at the Royal Horticultural Society's Garden, Wisley, England. He also has an interest in plant conservation, ecological restoration and sustainable horticulture. Boland shares a home and garden with his wife and co-author Laura Coit and their two children.

Laura Coit

Laura Coit is a horticulturist, garden writer, teacher, and botanical illustrator. Previously, Coit was Horticulturist at the Horticultural Demonstration Gardens at Michigan State University, where she designed and planted the DeLapa Perennial Garden. She graduated from Cornell University with a bachelor's degree in floriculture and ornamental horticulture and has worked in a variety of public gardens. Coit is married to co-author Tim Boland with whom she has two children—Conor and Clare. The entire family likes to garden together and to go camping in Michigan.

Marty Hair

Marty Hair is the garden writer for the Detroit Free Press, where she had also been a news and feature staff writer and editor since 1978. She graduated from the University of Michigan with a bachelor's degree in English and a master's degree in journalism. She is an advanced Michigan Master Gardener. Among her honors, Hair has received the prestigious Quill and Trowel award for garden writing. Her articles about gardens, nature, and the environment have appeared in newspapers and magazines throughout the country. She and her husband and their daughter live in the metropolitan Detroit area.